BTEC NATIONAL
Book 1
Public Services

Nick Cullingworth

n Thornes

s Kluwer business

Published in 2007 by:
Nelson Thornes Ltd
Delta Place
27 Bath Road
CHELTENHAM
GL53 7TH
United Kingdom

07 08 09 10 11 / 10 9 8 7 6 5 4 3 2 1

A catalogue record for this book is available from the British Library

ISBN 978 0 7487 8190 4

Cover photograph Getty Images
Illustrations by Pantek Arts Ltd
Page make-up by Pantek Arts, Maidstone, Kent

Printed and bound in Slovenia by Korotan

Contents

Introduction

Millions of people work in Britain's public services. They include firefighters, police officers, soldiers, sailors, air crew, prison officers, civil servants, teachers and nurses. Their work is varied, exciting, demanding, responsible – and vitally important. In Britain the importance of the public services is widely recognised and billions of pounds are spent on them. They provide secure, relatively well-paid jobs and excellent careers for the right people. Because of these advantages many people want to work in the public services – and this is where BTEC National Public Services courses come in. These courses tell you what the public services are all about, and prepare you for public service work. They won't ensure that you get into a public service – but they will get you off to a flying start by giving you the knowledge and skills you need, both for public service work and for further studies.

How do you use this book?

Covering all 6 core units of the new 2007 specification and 3 specialist units, this book has everything you need if you are studying BTEC National Certificate or Diploma in Public Services. Simple to use and understand, it is designed to provide you with the skills and knowledge you need to gain your qualification. We guide you step by step toward your qualification, through a range of features that are fully explained over the page.

Which units do you need to complete?

BTEC National Public Services Book 1 provides coverage of 9 units for the BTEC National Diploma in Public Services. To achieve the Diploma, you are required to complete 6 core units plus 12 specialist units that provide for a combined total of 1080 guided learning hours (GLH). BTEC National Public Services Book 1 provides you with the following:

Core Units	Specialist Units
Unit 1 **Government, Policies and the Public Services**	Unit 7 **Physical Preparation and Fitness for the Uniformed Services**
Unit 2 **Team Leadership in the Uniformed Public Services**	Unit 9 **Outdoor and Adventurous Expeditions**
Unit 3 **Citizenship, Contemporary Society and the Public Service**	Unit 22 **Understanding Aspects of the Legal System and Law Making Process**
Unit 4 **Team Development in the Public Services**	
Unit 5 **Understanding Discipline within the Uniformed Public Services**	
Unit 6 **Diversity and the Public Services**	

BTEC National Public Services Book 2 offers coverage of a further 9 specialist units, providing the 1080 Guided Learning Hours required for the Diploma.

Is there anything else you need to do?

1 Do all the work the tutors set you.
2 Never be afraid to ask for help if you need it.
3 Develop your fitness, 'people skills' and sense of responsibility.
4 Get wise to the internet - and use the internet wisely.
5 Visit the public services and meet the people who work in them.

Turn over now for your guide to the features of this book.

We hope you enjoy your BTEC course – Good Luck!

Features of this book

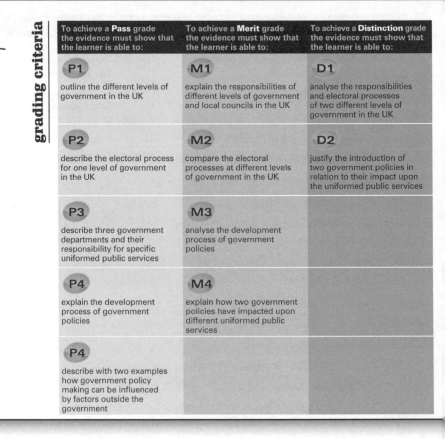

Learning Objectives

At the beginning of each Unit there will be a bulleted list letting you know what material is going to be covered. They specifically relate to the learning objectives within the specification.

Grading Criteria

The table of Grading Criteria at the beginning of each unit identifies achievement levels of pass, merit and distinction, as stated in the specification.

To achieve a **pass**, you must be able to match each of the 'P' criteria in turn.

To achieve **merit** or **distinction**, you must increase the level of evidence that you use in your work, using the 'M' and 'D' columns as reference. For example, to achieve a distinction you must fulfil all the criteria in the pass, merit and distinction columns. Each of the criteria provides a specific page number for easy reference.

UNIT 1

Government, Policies and the Public Services

This unit covers the following objectives:

- The different levels of government in the United Kingdom and the democratic election process at each level
- The responsibilities of government departments and other levels of government for specific public services
- The processes involved in developing government policies and the influences that can affect government policy decisions
- Government policies in the United Kingdom and how they impact upon the uniformed public services.

Unit 1 is about the relationship between the government, the public services and ordinary people. In it you will find out about how British government works, both nationally and locally. You'll discover how the government can influence and even control the public services. And you'll learn how both the government and the public can keep an eye on what the public services are doing, and how they spend our money

The unit also covers law-making, how government policy develops, and the pressures acting on governments to make them change their policies. In addition you'll study how government policy affects the public services and their relationship with all of us.

grading criteria

To achieve a **Pass** grade the evidence must show that the learner is able to:	To achieve a **Merit** grade the evidence must show that the learner is able to:	To achieve a **Distinction** grade the evidence must show that the learner is able to:
P1 outline the different levels of government in the UK	**M1** explain the responsibilities of different levels of government and local councils in the UK	**D1** analyse the responsibilities and electoral processes of two different levels of government in the UK
P2 describe the electoral process for one level of government in the UK	**M2** compare the electoral processes at different levels of government in the UK	**D2** justify the introduction of two government policies in relation to their impact upon the uniformed public services
P3 describe three government departments and their responsibility for specific uniformed public services	**M3** analyse the development process of government policies	
P4 explain the development process of government policies	**M4** explain how two government policies have impacted upon different uniformed public services	
P4 describe with two examples how government policy making can be influenced by factors outside the government		

UNIT 1

activity
INDIVIDUAL WORK

P2

Your friend, or a member of your family, is about to vote for the first time. In a short role play with a partner, tell them how the system works and what they will have to do on polling day.

case study 1.1 — Different kinds of election

May 2007	Northern Ireland Assembly
May 2007	English local council and mayoral
May 2007	Scottish local council
May 2008	GLA and London mayoral
May 2008	English local council and mayoral
May 2008	Wales unitary local authority
June 2009	European Parliamentary
May 2009	Northern Ireland local government
May 2009	UK local and mayoral

http://www.electoralcommission.org.uk

In addition to these, a general election (for the UK Parliament) is called at least every five years – on a date to be fixed by the Prime Minister.

activity
INDIVIDUAL WORK

(a) Research the differences between general elections and European Parliamentary elections.
(b) What factors might determine the date on which a prime minister called a general election? List as many as you can think of.
(c) Why is it important to vote?

Candidates in general elections must be British, Commonwealth or Republic of Ireland citizens, aged 21 or over. The following cannot stand for election: bankrupts; civil servants; police officers; armed forces personnel; government-nominated directors of commercial companies; judges; members of parliament in non-Commonwealth nations; those convicted of electoral malpractice; members of the House of Lords.

> **remember**
> Voting is not the only democratic process. Demonstrating peacefully and collecting petitions are also democratic processes.

i   www.libdems.org.uk   www.labour.org.uk   www.conservatives.com

Link   See Unit 4 page 161 for more information

Progress Check

1. Outline the role of the House of Commons in deciding government policies
2. Why is the House of Commons more powerful than the House of Lords?
3. Give four roles of the Prime Minister
4. Name four government departments which have responsibility for at least one uniformed public service
5. What are the three main kinds of election that take place in England? What extra kind of election do they have in the rest of Britain?
6. Give five campaigning methods used by major political parties before a general election
7. Where do the police get their money from?
8. What are the main roles of (a) ministers and junior ministers and (b) civil servants in a government department?
9. What does accountability mean, and why does it matter?
10. Which uniformed public services have an ombudsman and what is the ombudsman's role?

Activities

are designed to help you understand the topics through answering questions or undertaking research, and are either *Group* or *Individual* work. They are linked to the Grading Criteria by application of the D, P, and M categories.

Case Studies

provide real-life examples that relate to what is being discussed within the text. It provides an opportunity to demonstrate theory in practice.

An Activity that is linked to a Case Study helps you to apply your knowledge of the subject to real life situations.

Keywords

of specific importance are highlighted within the text and then defined in the glossary,

Remember boxes

contain helpful hints, tips or advice.

Information bars

point you towards resources for further reading and research (e.g. websites).

Links

direct you to other parts of the book that relate to the subject currently being covered.

Progress Checks

provide a list of quick questions at the end of each Unit, designed to ensure that you have understood the most important aspects of each subject area.

Acknowledgements

The author and publishers would like to thank the following for permission to reproduce material.

ACAS, Amnesty International, The Audit Commission, BBC News Online, BMJ Journals, The Cabinet Office, *The Daily Telegraph*, Electoral Commission, Friends of the Earth, Greenpeace, Guardian News and Media Ltd, HM Courts Service, HM Prison Service, The Home Office, Kirklees Council, The Law Society, Leeds Metropolitan University, London Borough of Hillingdon, The Metropolitan Police Authority, Qualifications and Curriculum Authority, Reuters, Sandwell Metropolitan Borough Council, The Scotsman Publications Ltd, Surrey Police Association, Times Newspapers, University of Delaware, University of New Mexico, West Midlands Police.

Crown copyright material is reproduced with the permission of The Controller of Her Majesty's Stationery Office © Crown Copyright.

Every effort has been made to contact copyright holders, and we apologise if any have been overlooked.

Picture credits

Alamy: Figs 1.2, 1.3, 1.8, 2.6, 2.7, 3.5, 3.6, 4.3, 4.6, 5.1, 5.8, 6.1, 6.2, 6.3, 7.14, 7.16, 7.17, 9.1, 9.3, 9.5, 9.6, 9.9, 22.4, 22.6, 22.9

Corbis: Fig. 6.6

Getty: Figs 3.2, 3.9, 4.1, 5.9, 7.18

David Hoffman: Figs 3.1, 3.4, 4.7, 4.10, 5.5, 6.9

NT Stockbyte 6: Fig. 1.5

Science Photo Library: Fig. 7.15.

Government, Policies and the Public Services

This unit covers:

■ The different levels of government in the United Kingdom (UK) and the democratic election process at each level

■ The responsibilities government departments and other levels of government have for specific public services

■ The processes involved in developing government policies and the influences that can affect government policy decisions

■ Government policies in the UK and how they impact upon the uniformed public services

Unit 1 is about the relationship between the government, the public services and ordinary people. In it you will find out about how British government works, both nationally and locally. You'll discover how the government can influence and even control the public services, and you'll learn how both the government and the public can keep an eye on what the public services are doing and how they spend our money.

The unit also covers law-making, how government policy develops, and the pressures acting on governments to make them change their policies. In addition you'll study how government policy affects the public services and their relationship with all of us.

grading criteria

To achieve a **Pass** grade the evidence must show that the learner is able to:	To achieve a **Merit** grade the evidence must show that, in addition to the pass criteria, the learner is able to:	To achieve a **Distinction** grade the evidence must show that, in addition to the pass and merit criteria, the learner is able to:
P1 outline the different levels of government in the UK Pg 16	**M1** explain the responsibilities of different levels of government and local councils in the UK Pg 18	**D1** analyse the responsibilities and electoral processes of two different levels of government in the UK Pg 25
P2 describe the electoral process for one level of government in the UK Pg 17	**M2** compare the electoral processes at different levels of government in the UK Pg 17	
P3 describe three government departments and their responsibility for specific uniformed public services Pg 22		

1

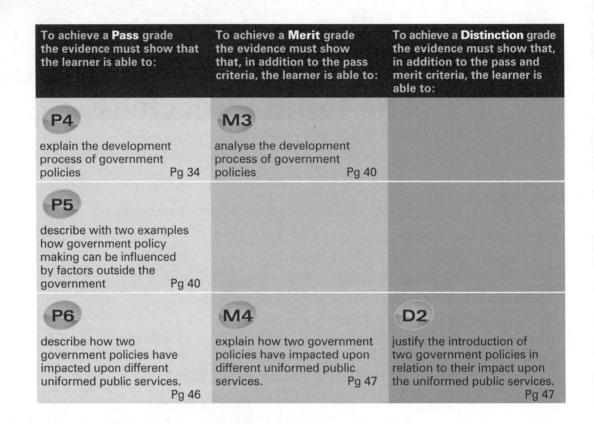

To achieve a **Pass** grade the evidence must show that the learner is able to:	To achieve a **Merit** grade the evidence must show that, in addition to the pass criteria, the learner is able to:	To achieve a **Distinction** grade the evidence must show that, in addition to the pass and merit criteria, the learner is able to:
P4 explain the development process of government policies Pg 34	**M3** analyse the development process of government policies Pg 40	
P5 describe with two examples how government policy making can be influenced by factors outside the government Pg 40		
P6 describe how two government policies have impacted upon different uniformed public services. Pg 46	**M4** explain how two government policies have impacted upon different uniformed public services. Pg 47	**D2** justify the introduction of two government policies in relation to their impact upon the uniformed public services. Pg 47

The different levels of government in the UK and the democratic election process at each level

Levels of government and their responsibilities

The system of government we have in the United Kingdom has two main levels: central government and local government. They are both:

- public services because they are paid for by the taxpayer and exist to make our lives better, more secure and more comfortable
- **democratic**, because the public can choose the people who run central and local government when elections are held.

We will look at them in more detail below.

Central government

Central government for the whole of the UK is based in London – more specifically Westminster, where the Houses of **Parliament** are situated.

The ways in which central government operates in relation to other major organisations and the public are outlined in Fig 1.1.

The heart of central government is Parliament (consisting of the House of Commons and the House of Lords). Central government also includes the Prime Minister, the **Cabinet**, the government **ministers** and their **departments**. All these make the big decisions on what the government does, and how these decisions should be carried out.

Central government has a huge range of responsibilities, which are discussed in more detail below.

 Link

See pages 4–10 for more on central government.

Fig 1.1 The main 'players' in central government

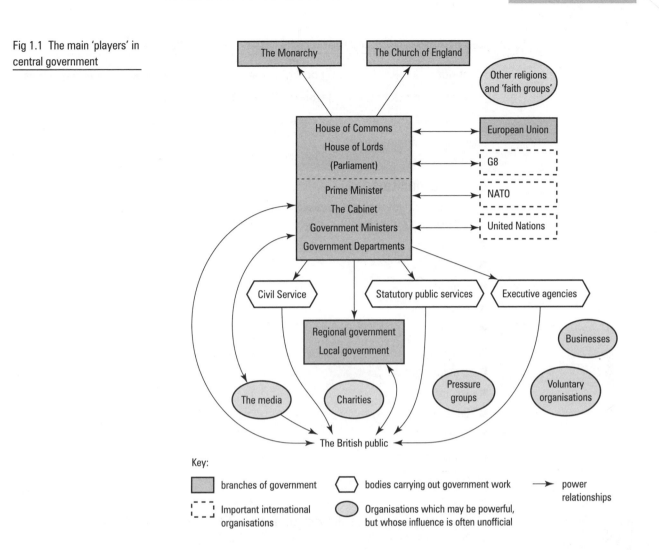

Key:

▨ branches of government

⬡ bodies carrying out government work

→ power relationships

⬚ Important international organisations

⬭ Organisations which may be powerful, but whose influence is often unofficial

Devolved parliaments

Devolved parliaments are the governments (often called 'assemblies') of Scotland, Wales and Northern Ireland. They operate in a similar way to the UK Parliament, but with fewer powers and responsibilities.

Government for England (as opposed to Scotland, Wales and Northern Ireland) is based in London.

Regional governments

In recent years there has been talk of setting up regional assemblies in various parts of England, e.g. the North East. However, a referendum in the area seemed to show that the idea was unpopular, so it has been shelved for the time being. The nearest thing to a regional government in England at present is the Greater London **Authority** (GLA), which has an elected mayor and a special assembly. It has responsibility for police, fire and rescue and ambulance services, transport, development, culture, environment and health, and, in 2002/3, spent nearly £5billion.

There are regional government offices which deliver central government funding, advice, etc. to nine main **regions** in England. The regions are:

East Midlands	North East	South West
East of England	North West	West Midlands
London	South East	Yorkshire and the Humber

Their responsibilities are shown in Table 1.1.

Table 1.1 Regional government responsibilities

Economy	Local government	Preparing for emergencies
Education and skills	**Community** safety	Public health
Environment and rural	People and **sustainable** communities	Transport
European funding	Planning	

Local authorities

These are local government areas such as **county councils**, **city councils** or **metropolitan councils**. They have responsibility for:

- business
- community
- education
- environment
- health
- housing
- employment
- leisure
- culture
- social care
- transport.

Other local authorities

Big local authorities such as county councils are sometimes subdivided into smaller local government areas such as **district councils** and **parish councils**. These bodies are run by elected **councillors**.

District councils typically represent around 100,000 people and have a wide range of responsibilities. These include refuse collection, community affairs, the environment, planning, business and development, housing, policing, social care, health and transport. Parish councils represent around 1000 people and have small local powers to do with the environment, policing, footpaths, land usage, voluntary organisations and local health and safety issues.

Metropolitan councils

These are local authorities, which operate in big cities, towns and urban areas. They operate a wide range of local services.

remember

The jobs of the government are (a) to create an environment in which **wealth** can be made, (b) collect as much of that wealth as they can in taxes, and (c) redistribute money to benefit society and the less well off.

Link

See pages 8 and 10 where local government is discussed in more detail.

Other institutions in the government process

The monarchy

The monarchy used to have an important **role** in government. Now the monarch (the Queen in 2007) carries out **ceremonial** duties only. The main duties are:

- Reading the Queen's speech at the opening of Parliament – this is written for her by the government and sets out the main laws which the government hopes to pass during the next parliamentary session.

- Giving 'royal assent' to Bills which have been passed by Parliament – this changes them into laws which we all have to follow.

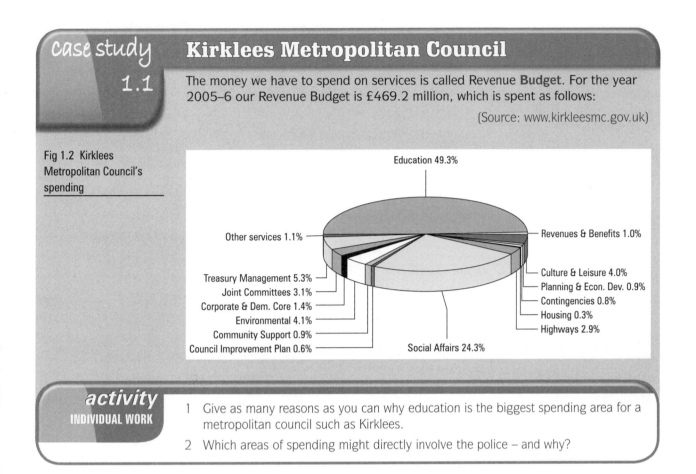

case study 1.1 **Kirklees Metropolitan Council**

The money we have to spend on services is called Revenue **Budget**. For the year 2005–6 our Revenue Budget is £469.2 million, which is spent as follows:

(Source: www.kirkleesmc.gov.uk)

Fig 1.2 Kirklees Metropolitan Council's spending

activity

INDIVIDUAL WORK

1 Give as many reasons as you can why education is the biggest spending area for a metropolitan council such as Kirklees.

2 Which areas of spending might directly involve the police – and why?

The monarch is the official Head of State: Britain does not have a president.

The Church of England is an **established church** (i.e. the traditional 'official' church of England), but it plays no active part in government. However, the monarch is Supreme Governor of the Church of England. A number of bishops sit in the House of Lords, but they do not belong to any political party.

House of Commons
This is, at least in theory, the most powerful and important part of the government. It can, in extreme cases, sack the Prime Minister through a vote of No Confidence in the government – which would force a general election.

The House of Commons contains 646 **representatives**, called **MP**s (Members of Parliament) who are elected by regions called constituencies throughout the UK. Nearly every MP belongs to a political party – usually Labour, Conservative or Liberal Democrat. Table 1.2 shows the composition of the House of Commons in 2006.

The main work done by the House of Commons consists of:

■ Debates – these are **structured** discussions held by MPs. The aim is to find out what action should be taken in a political crisis or to decide whether a proposed new law should be added to the law of the land.

■ Statements and questions – ministers make statements to other MPs about important political issues. There are also times in the week when government ministers, including the Prime Minister, have to answer questions from MPs.

■ Committee work – many MPs belong to committees which investigate and make recommendations on political matters (e.g. transport **policy** and defence issues). They also analyse the work the government does.

case study 1.2

Composition of the House of Commons

Table 1.2 State of the parties at 20 October 2006

Labour	352	
Conservative	196	
Liberal Democrat	63	
Scottish National Party/**Plaid Cymru**	9	(SNP 6/PC 3)
Democratic Unionist	9	
Sinn Fein	5	(Have not taken their seats and cannot vote)
Social Democratic & Labour Party	3	
Independent	2	
Independent Labour	1	
Ulster Unionist	1	
Respect	1	
Speaker and 3 Deputies	4	(Do not normally vote)
Total no. of seats	646	
Current working majority (352 Labour MPs less 285 of all other parties excluding Speaker and Deputies and Sinn Fein	67	

activity

GROUP WORK

1 What are the advantages and disadvantages for a government of having a working majority of 67?

2 Which of the political parties mentioned come from Northern Ireland?

Link   See pages 13–15 for general elections and pages 14–16 for local elections.

House of Lords

The House of Lords is like the House of Commons except that:

■ Its members are not elected.

■ It has less power.

Its job is mainly to scrutinise (examine line by line) proposed new laws (called 'Bills') which are sent to the House of Lords by the House of Commons.

Many members of the House of Lords are very clever and experienced people (e.g. retired judges) who are very skilled at this kind of work.

United Kingdom Parliament
www.parliament.uk
Directgov
www.direct.gov.uk

Fig 1.3 House of Commons
– the heart of government

Branches of government

The British government, and many other Western democratic governments, is divided into three main branches: **executive**, legislative and judicial. Of the three, the **legislature** (legislative branch) is regarded as the most powerful.

Executive
This is the part of government which does the work of putting government policy into practice. It includes government ministries, departments and agencies, and the public services.

Legislative
This is the part of government which makes the law: i.e. Parliament, which consists of the House of Commons and the House of Lords, and a great many parliamentary committees.

Judicial
This is the part of government which interprets and applies the laws; it comprises judges and the courts.

These three branches provide '**separation of powers**', which is a very important element in a democracy. They advise, criticise and influence each other, and they provide some safeguard against extreme or unreasonable government actions.

Main roles at government levels

Prime Minister (PM)
Prime Ministers are chosen either by MPs or the membership of the party to which they belong (the system differs for different parties and changes from time to time). The Prime Minister is the head of the government and the leader of their party. The main roles of the Prime Minister are:

- to choose government ministers
- to run cabinet meetings to discuss major political issues involving the day-to-day running of the country
- to answer questions about overall government performance at Prime Minister's Question Time (i.e. once a week)
- to represent Britain at **summit meetings** with other world leaders
- to declare war
- to call general elections.

The Prime Minister sets the tone of a government, and presents an important image both to the British people and to the rest of the world. The Prime Minister's **personality** and use of communication **skills** are important factors in determining the success of the government.

10 Downing Street
www.number10.gov.uk

Government ministers

Ministers are experienced and able MPs who are put in charge of government departments. Each department specialises in a certain kind of government work.

Government ministers are usually members of the Cabinet, who meet regularly with the Prime Minister to make decisions about the running of the country.

Members of Parliament (MPs)

The 646 MPs who sit in the House of Commons are elected by the people in their constituencies in each general election. They belong to different political groupings, called parties, which have different ideas (policies) on how to run the country. The party which has the most MPs usually forms the government.

The work of an MP is divided between their own **constituency** and Parliament. It can include the following.

Constituency work

MPs hold '**surgeries**' in which they listen to constituents' problems (These problems are often difficult ones which cannot be solved by, say, the police or local councillors.)

They meet local people; encouraging local enterprise, safety or environmental campaigns and other good causes.

Parliamentary work

MPs listen to and take part in debates, sitting on committees (where they question people and discuss major issues) and carrying out work connected with a government department to which they may be attached.

In the debating chamber of the House of Commons, government MPs sit at one side and MPs from other parties sit at the other. The MPs of non-governing parties are called the Opposition, and they have a general duty to question and criticise the government.

Members Series Factsheet M1, *You and Your MP* (Revised October 2005, House of Commons Information Office)

Mayors

Mayors are in effect the 'Prime Minister' of a city or local government area. They are normally chosen by their fellow councillors, and their duties are often ceremonial. However, this is not the case in London, where the mayor is elected by the people of London and has considerable political power.

case study 1.3 — Departments of State and Ministers

Government departments (2007)

- Cabinet Office
- Department for Communities and Local Government
- Department for Culture, **Media** and Sport
- Ministry of Defence
- **Ministry of Justice**
- Department for Children, Schools and Families
- Department for Environment, Food and Rural Affairs
- Foreign and **Commonwealth** Office
- Department of Health
- Home Office
- Department for International Development
- Law Officers' Department
- Leader of the House of Commons
- Northern Ireland Office
- Privy Council Office
- Scotland Office
- Department for Business, Enterprise and Regulatory Reform
- Department for Transport
- HM Treasury
- Wales Office
- Department for Work and Pensions
- HM Household.

activity
GROUP WORK

1 Match the following public services to the government department which oversees their work:

(a) Fire and rescue service

(b) Royal Marines

(c) The Meteorological Office

(d) The prison service

(e) The Border and Immigration **Agency**

(f) MI5

(g) The **NHS**

(h) The Environment Agency

(i) Emergency planning

(j) RSPCA

(k) HM Revenue and Customs

(l) **VOSA** (Vechicle Operators and Services Agency)

(m) The Ambulance Service

(n) Traffic wardens.

activity
GROUP WORK

2 Find out the names of the ministers currently in charge of each of these
government departments.

(a) Home Office
www.homeoffice.gov.uk

(b) Department for Transport
www.dft.gov.uk

(c) HM Treasury
www.hm-treasury.gov.uk

(d) Department of Communities and Local Government
www.communities.gov.uk

(e) Cabinet Office
www.cabinetoffice.gov.uk

(f) Ministry of Defence
www.mod.uk

(g) Department for Business, Enterprise and Regulatory Reform
www.berr.gov

(h) Department for Children, Schools and Families
www.dcsf.gov.uk

(i) Department for Innovation, Universities and Skills
www.dius.gov.uk

London Assembly and the Greater London Authority
www.london.gov.uk

Council members

Council members, or councillors, are elected in local elections. Some belong to political
parties; others are independent. Their job is to represent the views of ordinary local
people, help to solve local problems and – in some cases – act as a link between local
people and public services such as the police, the fire and rescue service, and the NHS.

Suffolk Coastal District Council
www.suffolkcoastal.gov.uk
New Forest District Council
www.newforest.gov.uk
Birmingham City Council
www.birmingham.gov.uk

London Assembly

This is a kind of mini-parliament of 25 elected members; it scrutinises the action of the
Mayor of London, often through committees.

Democratic election processes

A democratic process is any system by which ordinary people can choose their leaders
and influence the actions they take.

In Britain, the main democratic process is voting. A vote in which ordinary members of
the public can choose their leaders is called an election.

case study 1.4

Different kinds of election

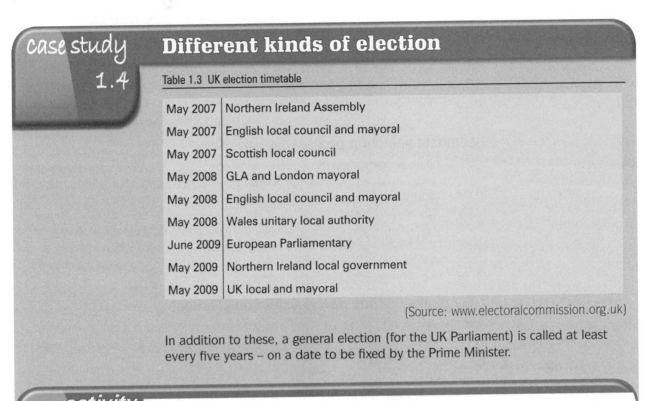

Table 1.3 UK election timetable

May 2007	Northern Ireland Assembly
May 2007	English local council and mayoral
May 2007	Scottish local council
May 2008	GLA and London mayoral
May 2008	English local council and mayoral
May 2008	Wales unitary local authority
June 2009	European Parliamentary
May 2009	Northern Ireland local government
May 2009	UK local and mayoral

(Source: www.electoralcommission.org.uk)

In addition to these, a general election (for the UK Parliament) is called at least every five years – on a date to be fixed by the Prime Minister.

activity
GROUP WORK

1 Research the differences between general elections and European Parliamentary elections.

2 What factors might determine the date on which a prime minister called a general election? List as many as you can think of.

3 Why is it important to vote?

Fig 1.4 Demonstrations are part of the democratic process

remember

Voting is not the only democratic process. Demonstrating peacefully and collecting petitions are also democratic processes.

Who is entitled to stand for election?

Candidates in general elections must be British, Commonwealth or Republic of Ireland **citizens**, aged 21 or over. The following cannot stand for election: bankrupts; **civil** servants; police officers; armed forces **personnel**; government-nominated directors of commercial companies; judges; members of parliament in non-Commonwealth nations; those convicted of electoral malpractice; members of the House of Lords.

Candidate selection processes

Each of the main political parties selects candidates in a different way, and the rules are constantly changing. The basic **procedure** is to apply by filling in a form addressed to the local branch of the party. A shortlist is produced, and those on the shortlist have to give a speech and answer questions at a selection meeting. Sometimes, the head office of a party will impose a candidate on the local party. Problem areas are the shortlisting of ethnic minority and women candidates, and the rejection of local candidates in favour of well-known outsiders. The end result is that each major party chooses one candidate for each constituency.

The influence of the party system on elections

In Britain and in most other Western-style democracies, politicians group themselves into political parties. Political parties are organisations whose members think broadly alike on how a country should be governed.

Political parties are normally classified as left, right or centre; the whole range of parties is sometimes called 'the political spectrum'.

Table 1.4 The political spectrum in Britain

Country/region	Far left	Centre left	Centre	Centre right	Far right
England	SWP	Labour	Lib-Dem	Conservative	BNP
Scotland		Labour SNP	Lib-Dem	Conservative	
Wales		Labour Plaid Cymru	Lib-Dem	Conservative	

Country/region	Left	Centre left	Centre	Centre right	Right
Northern Ireland	Sinn Fein	SDLP	Alliance	Unionists	Democratic Unionists

Table 1.5 Some differences (simplified) between left, centre and right political parties

Left	Centre	Right
Internationalist	Mildly nationalist	Nationalist
High taxation	Medium taxation	Low taxation
Approve of **nationalisation** – e.g. major services being run by the government	Like partial **privatisation**	Approve of privatisation – e.g. public services being run by private companies

The main influences of the party system on elections are:

- Most candidates belong to a political party.
- Voters often vote for the party (policies) rather than for the candidate (personality).

- Many voters always vote for a particular party, so changes of government are brought about by the 30% or so of 'floating voters' who do not always vote for the same party.
- At a general election, big political parties can spend millions of pounds supporting their candidates and paying their expenses.
- Different constituencies vote for different parties, often because of social and economic factors in those constituencies (e.g. affluent rural areas vote Conservative; poor urban areas vote Labour).

Representatives

Representatives for the British Parliament are called MPs. Those for the Scottish Parliament are Members of the Scottish Parliament (MSPs). Then there are Members of the Welsh Assembly and Members of the Northern Ireland Assembly. Scotland, Wales and Northern Ireland therefore have MPs who sit in the British Parliament in Westminster, plus elected members of their own national assemblies who do not sit in Westminster. Like Westminster MPs, these other representatives are all elected by their constituents. There are also Members of the European Parliament (MEPs), who have bigger constituencies and sit in the European Parliament in Brussels.

Period of election

General elections

An MP elected in a general election will normally remain in Parliament until at least the next general election. General elections are typically four years apart and must never be more than five.

MPs are often re-elected, and those in '**safe seats**' can remain as MPs for upwards of 25 years. However, MPs who are elected by a small majority may lose their seats at the next general election.

When MPs resign or die they have to be replaced; this means a by-election which can take place at any time. MPs elected in by-elections may lose their seats at the next general election.

Fig 1.5 MP campaigning before an election

Local elections

See page 16 for information about local elections.

Publicity and electioneering activities undertaken

Electioneering (campaigning before elections) is expensive. The costs of electioneering by the main parties before the 2005 general election are shown below.

Table 1.6 Funds spend on electioneering by main parties for 2005 general election

Labour	£17.94m
Conservatives	£17.85m
Liberal Democrats	£4.32m
Total spending by main parties	£40.11m

(*Source*: www.electoralcommission.org.uk)

Political parties use a wide range of methods to make the public notice them, and vote for them at elections. These include

- canvassing (calling from house to house, or talking to people in the street)
- delivering leaflets etc.
- putting up posters and stickers
- fundraising activities and stunts
- setting up organisations (e.g. women's **forums**)
- getting support from celebrities (e.g. Delia Smith supporting Labour)
- using logos and 'branding' their publicity
- party political broadcasts
- getting interviewed on radio or TV
- meetings, speeches and visits by prominent MPs to **marginal constituencies**
- photo opportunities associating candidates with worthy causes (e.g. children's centres).

Liberal Democrats
www.libdems.org.uk
The Labour Party
www.labour.org.uk
Conservatives
www.conservatives.com

The voting systems

Personal

Voting in British general and local elections is always secret. The traditional method is as follows. In the weeks before the election a poll card is sent to each elector, giving the address of the polling station. On election day, which is always a Thursday in Britain, voters go to a polling station and get their name checked on the electoral register, which is a list of people eligible to vote at that station. They are given a slip of paper with the names of the candidates, in alphabetical order. They go into a polling booth (a small cubicle where no one can see them) and, using the pencil provided, put a cross next to the name of their chosen candidate. The ballot paper is then folded so that the cross is not visible; it is then shown to the officer in the polling station and put into a ballot box.

Voting by post

In England, Scotland and Wales, you can choose to vote by post, if you cannot or do not wish to attend your polling station. You do not have to give any reason for asking for a postal vote.

- Applications can be made for a single election, for a specified period or indefinitely.
- A postal vote can be sent to your home address or any other address specified by you.
- Postal votes are usually despatched about a week before polling day.
- Postal votes can be posted back to the council offices or returned by hand to the council offices or polling station.
- Postal votes have to be received at the council or polling station by the close of poll on polling day.

Voting by proxy

This means appointing someone to vote for you in your polling station.

- You need to tell your proxy which candidate(s) you wish to vote for.
- You have to provide a reason to vote by proxy for a single election. You can only vote by proxy on an indefinite basis for the following reasons: physical incapacity, overseas voter, studying or a journey by sea or air from your home to your polling station, and certain occupations, e.g. armed forces.
- Your local council can supply you with a form to apply to vote by proxy.

Other voting systems

Because there is often a low turnout at British elections, other voting systems are being tried in an effort to make the process simpler and easier, and to encourage more people to vote. These include:

- e-voting – both using the internet and in special kiosks at polling stations or other public places
- telephone voting
- voting by text messaging
- extended voting (voting takes place for more than just one day)
- early voting (it is possible to vote before the allocated polling day)
- all postal elections (all voters have to vote by post and there are no polling stations).

Easy Guide to Voting, Prepared for The Electoral Commission by COI (April 2006), Product code EC4

The Electoral Commission

www.electoralcommission.org.uk

About My Vote – find out more about elections across the UK

www.aboutmyvote.co.uk

activity
GROUP WORK
1.1

P1

Produce a wallchart suitable for a community centre showing the different levels of government in the UK.

Election-day activities for different elections

The general principle is the same for general and local elections: elections are held on Thursdays; schools are given a day off if they are used as polling stations; and candidates and parties are listed on a ballot paper. Preference is shown by putting a cross next to one chosen candidate. If anything is written on the ballot paper, the ballot paper is considered 'spoilt' and is not counted.

In European elections and some Northern Ireland elections, the system is different as it is possible to vote for more than one candidate, marking them in order of preference.

Political canvassing is not allowed on election day, and there must be no attempt to influence voters outside the polling booths.

After a British general or local election the votes are counted and the candidate with the most votes wins the seat. This is called the 'first past the post' system. The European election system mentioned above is called 'proportional representation'.

Local elections, e.g. parish, district, county, metropolitan boroughs elections

The rules for local elections are rather complicated as Table 1.7 shows.

Table 1.7 Rules for local elections

Frequency of elections	Numbers of councillors elected	Types of council
Every four years	All councillors	English county councils, London borough councils, and around two-thirds of non-metropolitan district councils
Each of the three years when county council elections are *not* held	One-third of the total	All other district councils and the metropolitan districts
Every two years	Half the total each time	A few district councils
Every four years	All councillors	Scotland, Wales, Northern Ireland

(*Source*: www.direct.gov.uk)

Responsibilities of elected bodies

Elected bodies have a responsibility to all the voters in an electorate. Representatives have to serve not only the people who voted for them but also those who voted for other, unsuccessful, candidates.

The House of Commons is a national elected **body** and has the following main responsibilities:

- making laws
- checking the government and its work
- defence, foreign affairs, economic and **monetary** policy
- social security, employment, **equal opportunities**, etc.
- meeting European Union (**EU**) obligations.

Local elected bodies have the following responsibilities:

- safeguarding citizens
- protecting individual rights
- liaising with the Department for Communities and Local Government (and other departments of central government where necessary)
- organising local services such as education, firefighting and the police
- protecting the environment.

activity
GROUP WORK 1.2

P2

Your friend, or a member of your family, is about to vote for the first time. In a short role-play with a partner, tell them how the system works and what they will have to do on polling day.

activity
INDIVIDUAL WORK 1.3

M2

Design and write a leaflet for first-time voters explaining general elections, local elections and European elections – and the differences between them.

The responsibilities government departments and other levels of government have for specific public services

The government departments' responsibilities for the public services

The Ministry of Defence

The Ministry of Defence (MoD) is the government department responsible for the army, the Royal Air Force and the Royal Navy. Its overall responsibility as stated in its *Annual Report and Accounts 2005–2006* is to 'Achieve the **objectives** established by Ministers for Operations and Military Tasks in which the United Kingdom's Armed Forces are involved, including those providing support to our civil communities'. The 'Ministers' in this context are mainly the Prime Minister and the **Secretary** of State for Defence, although other ministers, such as the Home Secretary, may be involved if the MoD is 'providing support to our civil communities'.

At present (2007) the MoD has a wide range of responsibilities. These include large-scale operations in Iraq and Afghanistan, and **peacekeeping** in the Balkans, especially Kosovo. These operations are carried out in conjunction with the US-led **coalition** in Iraq, and **NATO** in Afghanistan. The commitment in Iraq and Afghanistan is to stay there 'till the job is done' – which may take some time.

Other responsibilities are:

■ taking part in United Nations-led peacekeeping in Cyprus, the Democratic Republic of Congo, Georgia, Liberia, and Sierra Leone

■ ensuring security of the UK's Overseas Territories, including the Falkland Islands, Gibraltar and the Sovereign Base Areas in Cyprus

■ maintaining 'a minimum nuclear **deterrent** capability' – which includes the nuclear submarines carrying Trident nuclear missiles

■ helping in serious disasters, such as the Pakistan Earthquake of 2005

■ supporting the civil authorities at home, including in Northern Ireland, responding to civil emergencies, provision of search and rescue and fisheries protection services, and the investigation and disposal of suspected explosive devices.

> **remember**
> The armed forces are very mobile and can be sent to other parts of the world at short notice. Published information is often out of date, and sometimes the facts are hard to get at because of security reasons.

Link
See Unit 3, pages 133 and 136–137, for more information on the armed forces' activities in other parts of the world.

The Home Office

> **remember**
> The Criminal Justice and Court Services Act 2000 re-named the probation service as the National Probation Service for England and Wales.

The Home Office, one of the biggest government departments, is responsible for maintaining law and order within Britain. Its objective is 'to protect the public, and build a safe, just and tolerant society'.

The Home Office oversees the work of the police and the Border and Immigration Agency. The National Probation Service and HM Prison Service joined the new Ministry of Justice in 2007.

> **activity**
> **INDIVIDUAL WORK 1.4**
> **M1**
> Give a short presentation suitable for a school **citizenship** class explaining why and how local and national government have different responsibilities.

The police

There are 43 police forces in England and Wales. They are responsible both to the Home Office and to their local communities.

The Home Office's responsibilities to the police are:

■ *To fund them* – the money is collected by the Treasury in the form of taxes and is then allocated to the Home Office. The police also receive money from local council tax through their force's police authority.

■ *To give other kinds of support that will enable them to work more effectively* – the police receive many other kinds of support through the Home Office. Some of this is to do with training them and developing their skills, some is to do with ensuring that they use information effectively, and some is to do with helping the police meet future challenges in a rapidly changing society.

case study 1.5 — Responsibilities of the Home Office

To protect the public, we focus on six key objectives:

1 protecting the UK from terrorist attack

2 cutting crime, especially violent and drug-related crime

3 ensuring people feel safer in their homes and daily lives, particularly through more visible, responsive and **accountable** local policing

4 rebalancing the **criminal justice system** in favour of the law-abiding majority and the victim

5 managing offenders to protect the public and reduce re-offending

6 securing our borders, preventing abuse of our immigration laws and managing migration to benefit the UK.

(Source: www.homeoffice.gov.uk)

activity
GROUP WORK

1 Imagine that you are the Home Secretary, in charge of the Home Office. With your group, agree on six measures that you would put forward to protect the UK from 'terrorist attack'.

2 Note down, in groups, your own views on immigration, immigration laws and migration to the UK. If possible, agree on what you write down.

3 Collect newspaper cuttings dealing with immigration, immigration laws and migration to the UK. In each case, decide whether the views expressed (if any) agree with the ones that you have written down.

4 What problems do you think the uniformed public services face when dealing with (a) **migrants** and (b) **asylum seekers**?

The overall **strategic** responsibilities of the Home Office to the police are:

- to set goals
- to develop policy
- to provide support services.

The Home Office has set up various organisations to help the police in these ways.

Executive agencies
These are bodies funded by the Home Office, such as the Forensic Science Service, the Serious Organised Crime Agency, the National Policing Improvement Agency, and the Criminal Records Bureau.

Other Home Office initiatives which support the police
- Policing Policy and Operations **Directorate** – helps the police service tackle major national operational challenges; has responsibility for the Olympics, animal rights and firearms policy; and oversees agencies
- Centrex and the Police Information Technology Organisation (now the National Policing Improvement Agency) – police training
- Police and Crime Standards Directorate – helps to raise police performance
- The Police Standards Unit – supports police forces, basic command units and **Crime and Disorder Reduction Partnerships** to raise their performance
- Offender-based Interventions Unit – tackles specific types of criminality

- Police Reform Unit – improves police performance and increases time spent on frontline duties
- Police Finance Unit – responsible for police grant funding, police numbers, special constabulary and **civilian** volunteers, income generation by the police and non-Home Office police forces.

Home Office – Police
www.police.homeoffice.gov.uk

Her Majesty's Inspectors of Constabulary
These **teams** of inspectors visit police forces and offer constructive criticism and motivating praise. Their reports inform the Home Office and the public about the performance of the forces they inspect. They make the police more open and accountable and raise standards.

Non-departmental public bodies
The Home Office funds many independent organisations whose work, directly or indirectly, helps the police. Examples of these **non-departmental public bodies** are the Independent Police Complaints **Commission** (IPCC) and the Police Advisory **Board**.

Despite the Home Office funding, organisations such as the IPCC are set up to be independent and unbiased; they are not expected to 'whitewash' complaints against the police.

Independent Police Complaints Commission (IPCC)
www.ipcc.gov.uk

The National Probation Service
The National Probation Service, like the police, comes under the overall control of the Home Office (2007) but it will soon come under the new Ministry of Justice. Its main responsibilities are given in the government's Correctional Policy Framework.

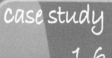

case study 1.6

Home Office aims

Home Office Aim 3

'To ensure the effective delivery of justice, avoiding unnecessary delay, through efficient investigation, detection, prosecution and court procedures. To minimise the threat to and intimidation of witnesses and to engage with and support victims.'

Home Office Aim 4

'To deliver effective custodial and community sentences to reduce reoffending and protect the public, through the prison and probation services in **partnership** with the Youth Justice Board.'

(Source: www.homeoffice.gov.uk)

activity
GROUP WORK

1 Research, using the internet and other sources, recent cases where the National Probation Service has been accused of failing to protect the public adequately.

2 Research actions taken by the government which might reduce the risk of such failures happening again in the future.

The National Probation Service and prison service are both part of the National Offender Management Service (NOMS).

NOMS itself has a chief executive and board which are based in the Home Office. The aims of NOMS are to protect the public and reduce reoffending. It is the responsibility of the Home Office to see that NOMS works, and also to use it as a way of building partnerships with private and voluntary organisations. Responsibility for NOMS will pass to the new Ministry of Justice.

The prison service

The prison service is – like the National Probation Service – part of the National Offender Management Service. Responsibility for the prison service will shortly move from the **Under-Secretary** of State for Criminal Justice in the Home Office to the new Ministry of Justice.

HM Prison Service

www.hmprisonservice.gov.uk

Border and Immigration Agency

This directorate is a part of the Home Office; overall responsibility for it therefore lies with the Home Secretary, who is assisted by a Minister of State for Citizenship, Immigration and Nationality. These two develop and enforce the government's decisions on controlling and managing immigration. They are helped by a permanent secretary who is a top civil servant. Working under the permanent secretary is a senior management team of four people, each in charge of one of its main areas of operation: border control, enforcement, **asylum** and managed migration.

Border and Immigration Agency

www.bia.homeoffice.gov.uk and www.ind.homeoffice.gov.uk

Department of Communities and Local Government

This department, which replaced the Office of the Deputy Prime Minister in 2005, has responsibility for the fire and rescue service. It works in conjunction with the Cabinet Office's Resilience **Secretariat**.

The Department is also responsible for the Ordnance Survey, whose maps (and digital mapping) are used by all the major British public services whether for policing, planning or other purposes.

The structure of the Department of Communities and Local Government resembles that of other government ministries, and will be discussed in greater detail below.

See page 23 for structures and individual responsibilities.

Fire and rescue authority links with local government

Fire and rescue authorities are locally based organisations, one for each local fire and rescue service. They consist mainly of elected councillors and their job is to set the annual budget and determine the fire, rescue and public safety priorities for their fire and rescue service. They are a vital link between local government and the local fire and rescue service.

HM Revenue and Customs

HM Revenue and Customs (HMRC) was formed on 18 April 2005, following the merger of the Inland Revenue and HM Customs and Excise.

> **remember**
> Customs officers work closely with the police, and these links are getting more important as international crime becomes a major political issue. Customs officers have many of the powers of arrest etc. that police have.

The government department responsible for HMRC is the Treasury, which collects money for the government, and controls government spending.

HM Revenue and Customs
www.hmrc.gov.uk

Department of Health

This is a large government department which runs hospitals, doctors' services and the ambulance service.

National Health Service

The National Health Service, which was set up to provide free health care at the point of need, is run by the Department of Health.

The ambulance service is run by the NHS through management organisations called NHS **Trusts**. Ambulance Trusts are run by a board of directors. There are 13 ambulance services in England; these are, in effect, regionally based. They all provide emergency cover; some, but not all, provide patient transport services as well.

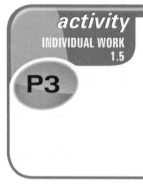

activity
INDIVIDUAL WORK
1.5

P3

Choose any three of the following:

the Home Office, the Ministry of Justice, the Ministry of Defence, the Department for Communities and Local Government, the Department for Health, the Treasury, or a local government council.

Then, for each of the three you choose, produce an organisation chart showing, with brief explanations, how it is responsible for a given uniformed public service. Each organisation chart should be suitable for putting up in the reception area of a public service building.

The roles of individuals and responsibilities to the uniformed public services

In this section, we shall look in more detail at the individual responsibilities that people in government have with regard to the public services.

The Prime Minister (PM)

The Prime Minister is the most important single person in the government and has more power than anyone else. This is because the Prime Minister is the leader of the party which won the last general election – and therefore has more MPs to give support.

The responsibility of the Prime Minister towards the uniformed public services is not a hands-on one, but it is a powerful role all the same. This is especially the case with the armed forces. The Prime Minister can declare war – or enter into agreements with other countries which result in British armed forces going to war. Parliament can only stop this by voting against it and bringing the government down (which in practice is hard to do, especially if a war is looming).

Prime Ministers often have powerful personalities and persuasive skills and, by skilled argument, arm-twisting, media manipulation and other techniques, are likely to get their way on many issues (e.g. security, crime and imprisonment policies).

Deputy Prime Minister

At the time of writing, no one is in this role.

Government ministers

Government ministers are in charge of government departments. Examples of government ministers are the Home Secretary, the Foreign Secretary and the Defence Secretary.

A minister is an MP who, because of experience, ability and interest, has been given (by the Prime Minister) the charge of a government department. The minister usually has several other MPs working under them.

Home Secretary

The Home Secretary is head of the Home Office, which is the ministry in charge of the police, immigration, ID cards and security within the UK. The organisation of the Home Office is shown in Fig 1.6 below.

Fig 1.6 Organisation of the Home Office

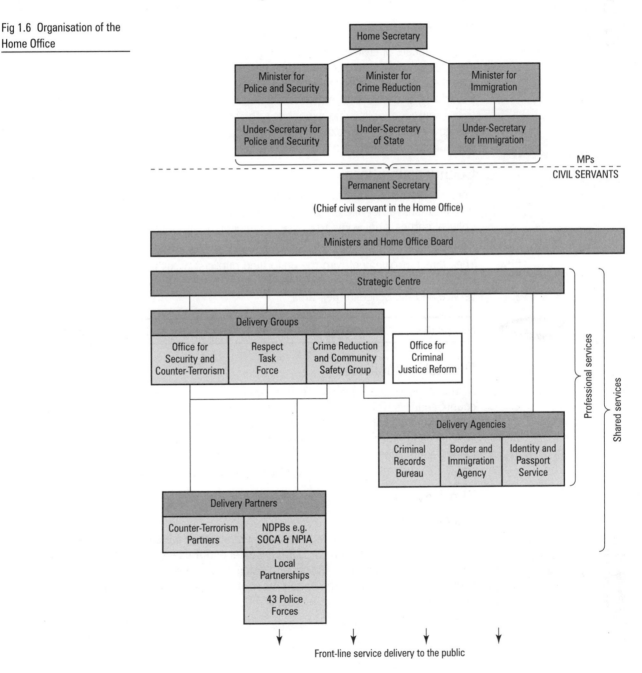

Ministers and under-secretaries are – like the minister – elected MPs. People below the dotted line are all civil servants: they put the minister's wishes into practice and do the skilled, detailed work.

Foreign Secretary

The Foreign Secretary is in charge of the Foreign and Commonwealth Office, a ministry structured like the Home Office but on a smaller scale. It deals with Britain's relationships with other countries and gives advice to British travellers on security risks in other countries.

Ministers

These are MPs who act as assistants or departmental heads within government ministries. They are often called junior ministers to distinguish them from secretaries of state (the heads of government departments) who are also (loosely) called ministers.

Civil servants

Large numbers of civil servants work in government departments, and the ones with the most responsibility are those in the highest grade. Their job is to advise ministers and help them achieve what they set out to do. They must give this help with integrity and impartiality and be apolitical (without political **bias**) in all their judgements. Because of their knowledge, ability and experience, they may be asked to stay in their jobs from one government to the next, so top civil servants may, for example, work for a Labour government and then for a Conservative one.

County councillors

Councillors from counties, cities and metropolitan boroughs are elected in first-past-the-post elections rather like MPs in a general election. Like MPs, many of them belong to political parties – but some too are independent. Their job is to represent local people with regard to local services and other issues.

Their direct involvement with the uniformed public services is by sitting on fire and rescue authorities and police authorities, which oversee the work of the fire and rescue service and the police in their areas.

See page 42 for an account of the West Yorkshire Fire and Rescue Authority.

District councillors

District councillors are people elected to councils which are subdivisions of the big county councils. They can be elected as county councillors as well. They exercise community leadership and develop a working knowledge of the organisations, services, activities and other factors that are important to the community's well-being and identity. In practice, this means that they are likely to liaise with the police, facilitate traffic-calming schemes, encourage Neighbourhood Watch, and so on.

The mayoral role

Local mayors

Many towns and cities have local mayors. Usually they are elected by the council. Their duties are often ceremonial, encouraging local enterprise, opening facilities of various sorts, publicising charitable events and helping to give a sense of pride, community and identity to the local area. They often associate themselves with schemes promoted by the police or the fire and rescue service, in order to highlight the good work that these public services do.

The Mayor of London

The Mayor of London is the Mayor of the Greater London Authority and is more important than other mayors, having a much more far-reaching and political role.

Mayor of London – London issues
www.london.gov.uk

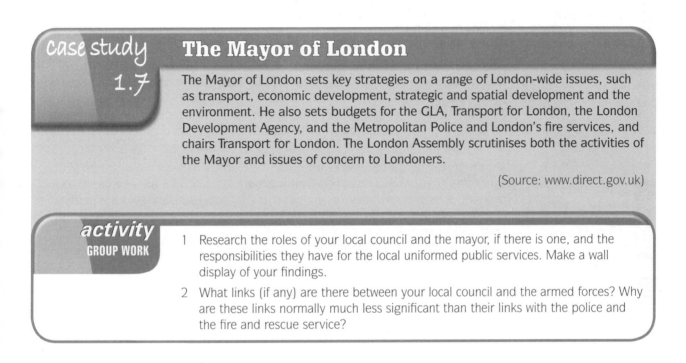

case study

1.7

The Mayor of London

The Mayor of London sets key strategies on a range of London-wide issues, such as transport, economic development, strategic and spatial development and the environment. He also sets budgets for the GLA, Transport for London, the London Development Agency, and the Metropolitan Police and London's fire services, and chairs Transport for London. The London Assembly scrutinises both the activities of the Mayor and issues of concern to Londoners.

(Source: www.direct.gov.uk)

activity

GROUP WORK

1 Research the roles of your local council and the mayor, if there is one, and the responsibilities they have for the local uniformed public services. Make a wall display of your findings.

2 What links (if any) are there between your local council and the armed forces? Why are these links normally much less significant than their links with the police and the fire and rescue service?

activity

INDIVIDUAL WORK
1.6

D1

Write a leaflet for student voters in which you:

1 Explain in some depth what two levels of government (e.g. central and local) do, and why their work is important.

2 Explain why it is important to vote even though there are disadvantages as well as advantages in our voting systems.

Accountability of uniformed public services

The uniformed public services and the government put a lot of work and expense into '**accountability**', i.e. making public the way they do their work and spend our money. This reduces the risk of **corruption**, waste, mismanagement, **discrimination**, **human rights** abuses and other malpractices which can happen when public services are not **monitored**. It makes them more effective, more open and democratic – and also liable to be brought to account if they do things wrongly.

The armed forces do not have inspectorates like those in the civilian uniformed services (see below). Much of the inspection and accountability is **internal**: in other words, the army inspects itself. This protects the secrecy of military operations. However, with internal inspections there is always the risk of a cover-up.

There are a number of ways in which the other uniformed public services are made accountable.

There is a downside to accountability – it can lead to a lot of time-consuming paperwork!

The inspectorates used to monitor public service activities

Civilian uniformed public services have **inspectorates**; these comprise teams of independent inspectors paid by the relevant ministry to visit uniformed public service establishments and report on their findings. The inspectors are often legal experts with an interest in accountability and human rights.

HM inspectorates of constabularies, prisons, probation

There are inspectorates of constabulary, prisons and probation. They carry out two kinds of inspection: announced, where the people being inspected know when the inspection is going to take place; and unannounced, where the inspectors arrive unexpectedly and no preparation has been possible.

Afterwards, the inspectors write reports, which are published on the Home Office or Ministry of Justice websites. These reports make interesting reading. They tell the public what life is really like in prisons etc., and they are usually not afraid to give harsh criticisms which can embarrass both the service being inspected and the government. An example of this was the *Report on an Unannounced Inspection of Harmondsworth Immigration Removal Centre 17–21 July 2006 by HM Chief Inspector of Prisons.*

The prison and probation services are made more accountable by the existence of the independent Prisons and Probation **Ombudsman**. The ombudsman, who has a team of deputies, assistants, investigators and other staff, investigates complaints from prisoners or people who are on probation. Complaints to the Ombudsman are usually serious ones which cannot be dealt with internally.

Furthermore, prisons and other custodial **institutions** have Independent Monitoring Boards (IMBs – they used to be known simply as 'prison visitors'). IMB members are ordinary citizens who, having been made members of an IMB, are allowed unrestricted and private access to prisoners and detainees.

> **remember**
> Some systems may change when the prison and probation services move out of the Home Office and into the new Ministry of Justice.

The Home Office
www.homeoffice.gov.uk
Ministry of Justice
www.justice.gov.uk

> **remember**
> Inspection reports try to tell the truth about the service they are inspecting. They are well worth studying, and what they say is often very different from the government's official line.

Fig 1.7 Prisons are rigorously inspected

case study 1.8

Extract from a prison inspection report

2.23 Staff routinely used surnames alone when they addressed detainees, and we observed staff who entered detainees' rooms without knocking. We were given many examples – by staff as well as detainees – of rude language used to residents, and were told that people who spoke little English were treated particularly badly. Some reported that they were treated 'like animals'. One detainee commented: 'No manners, talk to you like shit. Red badges [senior officers] are okay, everyone else is really bad. Treat you like you are nobody. They have a stinking attitude.'

2.24 Significantly more detainees than the comparator for the IRC estate said that they had experienced victimisation by staff [...], and there was evidence that serious allegations of staff mistreatment were not being followed up. One detainee complained of 'Excessive force used, intimidating behaviour with 3–4 guys marching up the corridors', while another stated that 'The first thing they say to you when you come in here is don't mess about or we'll make life difficult for you here.'

(Source: Owers, A. (2006) *Report on an Unannounced Inspection of Harmondsworth Immigration Removal Centre 17–21 July 2006 by HM Chief Inspector of Prisons*. Her Majesty's Inspectorate of Prisons, London. www.inspectorates.homeoffice.gov.uk

activity
GROUP WORK

Draw up a list of guidelines suitable for workers in an immigration removal centre.

Audit Commission

Financial accountability in all civilian public services is provided by the **Audit Commission**. The Audit Commission is 'an independent public body responsible for ensuring that public money is spent economically, efficiently, and effectively in the areas of local government, housing, health, criminal justice and fire and rescue services'.

The Audit Commission
www.audit-commission.gov.uk

Independent Police Complaints Commission (IPCC)

The IPCC was set up under the Police Reform **Act** in 2002. Its job is to handle serious complaints against the police in a completely independent and unbiased way, uninfluenced by the police or the government.

Independent Police Complaints Commission (IPCC)
www.ipcc.gov.uk

Healthcare Commission

See page 30.

The Defence Vetting Agency

This government organisation is to do with political accountability and security. It carries out national security checks on people, around 140,000 checks and clearances each year. This process is called 'vetting'.

The people in the armed services and the MoD civil service are checked; defence contractors are also vetted. In addition, the agency does paid vetting work for customers in the public and **private sectors**: it checks that people are suitable to hold security clearances for access to government installations, valuable assets, and **sensitive** information.

The Ministry of Defence
www.mod.uk

Local organisations

A number of local organisations help to make the uniformed public services more accountable. Some are outlined below.

Police authorities

Every one of the 43 local police forces in England and Wales has a police authority.

Health authorities

Since 2006 there have been 10 main health authorities in England. They are called Strategic Health Authorities (SHAs) and are responsible for:

- improving health services in their region
- monitoring their quality and efficiency
- increasing the amount of service provided
- ensuring that national schemes for better health are included in regional plans.

They are accountable to local taxpayers and to the government (Department of Health). They run the different kinds of local health trust: Acute Trusts, Ambulance Trusts, Care Trusts, Mental Health Trusts and Primary Care Trusts (PCTs). These specialise in particular kinds of care but are still locally accountable.

Fire and rescue authorities

The principle behind these is exactly the same as that behind the police authorities. There is a committee of councillors and people with expertise and knowledge in matters of firefighting and public safety. This mixture ensures that (a) they are democratically accountable and (b) they know what they are talking about. The authority is a **statutory** body, which means that it must – by law – exist. All fire and rescue services must have a fire and rescue authority so that they can fulfil the roles laid down by central government and at the same time respond effectively to the wishes and needs of local people. Fire and rescue authorities, like police authorities, set a budget and are responsible for supplying their fire and rescue service with the money (and **resources**) it needs.

West Yorkshire Fire and Rescue Service
www.westyorksfire.gov.uk

How public services are accountable

In addition to being inspected and overseen by authorities, public services have systems to demonstrate their commitment to accountability.

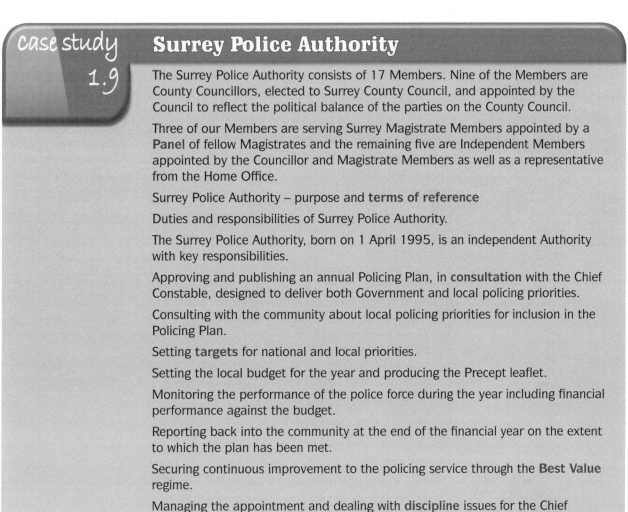

case study
1.9

Surrey Police Authority

The Surrey Police Authority consists of 17 Members. Nine of the Members are County Councillors, elected to Surrey County Council, and appointed by the Council to reflect the political balance of the parties on the County Council.

Three of our Members are serving Surrey Magistrate Members appointed by a **Panel** of fellow Magistrates and the remaining five are Independent Members appointed by the Councillor and Magistrate Members as well as a representative from the Home Office.

Surrey Police Authority – purpose and **terms of reference**

Duties and responsibilities of Surrey Police Authority.

The Surrey Police Authority, born on 1 April 1995, is an independent Authority with key responsibilities.

Approving and publishing an annual Policing Plan, in **consultation** with the Chief Constable, designed to deliver both Government and local policing priorities.

Consulting with the community about local policing priorities for inclusion in the Policing Plan.

Setting **targets** for national and local priorities.

Setting the local budget for the year and producing the Precept leaflet.

Monitoring the performance of the police force during the year including financial performance against the budget.

Reporting back into the community at the end of the financial year on the extent to which the plan has been met.

Securing continuous improvement to the policing service through the **Best Value** regime.

Managing the appointment and dealing with **discipline** issues for the Chief Constable, other Senior Officers and staff of the Authority.

Monitoring complaints against police officers.

(Source: www.surreypa.gov.uk)

activity
INDIVIDUAL WORK

Obtain information about your own local police authority and compare it with the information about the Surrey Police Authority given above. What similarities and differences can you find?

Documents

These systems are made clear and public through the use of official documents which the services produce. Some of them are outlined below.

Annual reports

All uniformed public services produce annual reports, planning outlines, lists of targets and evidence of how well those targets have been met; and they make their accounts public so that everyone knows how much money they have spent, and what they have spent it on.

The uniformed public services have shed much of the culture of secrecy which they used to have in the past. Nevertheless, critics would say that many of these reports contain an element of self-praise, and that they are less reliable than inspection reports and **audits** by independent organisations.

case study 1.10   The armed forces

1 The Armed Forces continued to achieve a high degree of success against the policy and military objectives set for all Operations overseas, including in Iraq, Afghanistan and the Balkans …

The security situation remained fragile, and the number of suicide attacks rose around the turn of the year, but the presence of ISAF and coalition forces continued to prevent Taliban or other armed groups from presenting a credible threat to long-term stability and security in Afghanistan. Recorded opium production fell by 21% in 2005 (compared to 2004), although these levels are unlikely to be maintained into 2006.

(Source: *Ministry of Defence Annual Report and Accounts 2005–2006*, www.mod.uk)

2 In a hard hitting report reflecting fears in the military about an impending crisis, the MPs question Ministry of Defence claims that it is achieving its objectives in Iraq and Afghanistan. The MPs express their concern after the MoD announced yesterday that a Royal Marine from 42 Commando died in an attack by Taliban forces in Helmand province, southern Afghanistan. He is the second Marine killed fighting the Taliban in a week. … "It is just not good enough for the MoD to assure us that it is achieving its objectives in Iraq and Afghanistan without demonstrating how it has reached that conclusion," the report says.

(Source: Richard Norton-Taylor, *The Guardian*, Wednesday 13 December 2006, www.guardian.co.uk)

activity
INDIVIDUAL WORK

1 What differences do you notice in these accounts of the army in Afghanistan, from the Ministry of Defence and from *The Guardian* newspaper?

2 Which would you expect to be more truthful – and why?

Objectives and mission statements

Statutory uniformed public services have mission statements. A mission statement typically consists of aims and objectives. The aims express what the organisation is trying to do; the objectives state what the organisation plans to do in order to achieve its aims. Aims are often expressed in rather high-flown language, perhaps in order to give the reader a good feeling about the organisation. Objectives tell us more, and are more practical in tone.

> **remember**
> Mission statements are often rather like advertising slogans. One of their main aims is to market the organisation to the public.

Here are examples from the Healthcare Commission:

Aims:

'The Healthcare Commission is an independent body, set up to promote and drive improvement in the quality of healthcare and public health.

'We aim to do this by becoming an authoritative and trusted source of information and by ensuring that this information is used to drive improvement.'

Objectives:

'Our main duties in England are to:

> **remember**
> Objectives often say how aims will be achieved.

■ assess the management, provision and quality of NHS healthcare and public health services

■ review the performance of each NHS trust and award an annual performance rating

- regulate the independent healthcare sector through registration, annual inspection, monitoring complaints and enforcement
- publish information about the state of healthcare
- consider complaints about NHS organisations that the organisations themselves have not resolved
- promote the **coordination** of **reviews** and assessments carried out by ourselves and others
- carry out investigations of serious failures in the provision of healthcare.'

(Source: www.healthcarecommission.org.uk)

Internal complaints procedures

Modern uniformed public services have well-organised internal complaints procedures. They can work well – especially for minor matters – since the complaint can be dealt with quickly and effectively. They tend to be confidential and therefore not fully accountable.

Internal complaints systems are used in the prison service. Prisoners, not surprisingly, have many complaints, and it is in everybody's interest for them to be sorted out as quickly and fairly as possible.

case study 1.11 — The prison system for making a complaint

Talking to a member of staff

As a first step, prisoners should talk to a member of staff – preferably their personal officer if they have one. Lots of problems are dealt with very simply and quickly in this way. If the matter cannot be sorted out like this, prisoners can make an application to their landing officer or wing manager.

The landing officer or wing manager will discuss the request or complaint with the prisoner on the same day.

If they cannot help and the prisoner is still unhappy about it, they can make a governor's application. A senior member of the prison's staff will then speak to the prisoner. They may also ask to speak to the medical officer, chaplain or a member of the Board of Visitors. If, after all of this, the outcome is still not satisfactory, prisoners will be advised on how they can take the matter further.

Formal complaints

The next stage will be for the prisoner to make a written complaint. A form for making a complaint tells the prisoner how to complete and return it. Each formal complaint will be returned to them with a reply, which they should receive within seven days. The reply may not be the full answer to their problem, but should at least tell them when they can expect a full reply. If their complaint is rejected, they should be given reasons.

(Source: www.hmprisonservice.gov.uk)

activity
GROUP WORK

1 By studying inspectors' reports of prisons, find out what kinds of things prisoners complain about.

2 Organise a role-play of a prison internal complaint. Afterwards, as a group, review the way in which you dealt with the complaint. Were you successful? What could you have done better? Also discuss what could happen if an internal complaint was not successfully resolved.

HM Prison Service
www.hmprisonservice.gov.uk
The Home Office
www.homeoffice.gov.uk

Management procedures
Management procedures to increase accountability include monitoring, reviewing and **evaluation**.

 Link

See pages 166–173 in Unit 4.

The processes involved in developing government policies and the influences that can affect government policy decisions

Development processes

Government policies originate from various sources outside Parliament. These include:

■ promises made in election manifestos

■ events inside and outside Britain which produce a public awareness of a problem and a need to do something about it

■ policies carried out in other countries such as the USA and EU countries which, directly or indirectly, pressurise the British government to act.

MPs pay close attention to the media, **opinion polls** and public opinion and are keen to respond to problems and issues which may need their attention.

Meetings that will occur to create policies

When it becomes clear that, in the public interest, something should be done about a particular issue, the discussion gets serious and meetings begin to be held. These meetings are the first definite stages in the development of new policies.

Cabinet meetings

The Cabinet consists (2006) of 23 members who are all government ministers. Three other ministers also attend the meetings. Twenty-one members are MPs and two belong to the House of Lords. The Secretary of the Cabinet records its discussions and decisions. Its meetings are chaired by the Prime Minister and concern urgent political issues. The Cabinet cannot make laws itself: its decisions have to be put to Parliament if they are to be made into laws. Cabinet decisions are treated as unanimous: the Cabinet has a tradition of '**collective responsibility**'.

Meetings are not the only activities of the Cabinet. The Cabinet also sets up Cabinet Committees which do a good deal of its work and can also make important decisions.

 remember

Cabinet discussions are secret, and cabinet ministers do not disagree with their colleagues in public.

Parliamentary committees and subcommittees

People often think that most of the work of Parliament is done in debates, but in fact the debates are just the highlights, while the hard graft is done in committees. There are many different kinds of parliamentary committee, and there is only room to mention the main ones here.

Public Bill Committees

Formerly known as Standing Committees, the job of Public Bill Committees is to look at proposed new laws in detail. The committees consist of MPs and are run by the House of Commons. They are set up only to examine one specific Bill (proposed new law).

Select Committees

These look at particular aspects of government work such as education or defence. They are chaired by a senior MP. Their aim is to inform Parliament on major issues which threaten to become political problems in the future – e.g. pension schemes or road congestion. They often take evidence from people outside Parliament – for example business leaders, professors, or the heads of non-departmental public bodies such as the Environment Agency. These committees have a permanent existence.

Joint Committees

These are set up by both the House of Commons and the House of Lords and contain members of each.

Committee of Selection

This committee of MPs chooses the MPs for a Public Bill Committee.

Programming sub-committee

This exists to help organise and facilitate the work of Public Bill Committees.

The use of white papers and green papers in Parliament

Green papers and white papers are documents put out by government departments before a new law is going to be introduced. **Green papers** are consultation papers: the aim is to find out whether people are interested in having a new law on a certain subject, and the papers invite opinions both from experts and members of the public – including email responses over the internet.

White papers are clear proposals for a new law. The general consultation is now over, and it is only a matter of time before a new Bill is put before Parliament for debate and close examination.

Consultation meetings, public meetings or enquiries

Before the appearance of a green paper there is wide consultation (discussion) between MPs and people who are likely to hold views on the appearance of a new law. Such consultation can be either formal or informal; it may take the form of '**focus groups**', surveys or other types of enquiry organised by government departments which want to take soundings on what ordinary people actually think and feel. Professionals are consulted too: for example, before the Education Green Paper in 2001 the government 'consulted thousands of head teachers in the autumn of 2000'. After the publication of the green paper, consultation meetings were arranged with public bodies and professionals who would be concerned with putting the law into practice – in this case more teachers and Ofsted, the body which inspects schools.

Public meetings are meetings to which the public is invited. Local councils and others can arrange them whenever there is a matter of public concern; if the response to such meetings is strong enough they may lead to future legislation or changes in government policy.

Public inquiries are also official investigations of major problems that have become matters of public concern and might lead to changes in the law, or in official procedures. An example was the Shipman Inquiry (2001–2002) investigating murders by Dr Harold Shipman and steps which could be taken to prevent anything similar happening in the future.

Report of the Shipman Inquiry
www.the-shipman-inquiry.org.uk

Representations from outside government

At the early stages of a new law, there is a consultation period or 'a public debate' when anybody is welcome to give their views on the proposals. This is in the government's interest, because, if they find they have got it wrong in the early stages, the idea can be dropped or radically changed without too much loss of face, time or money. During this period, opposition MPs, other public figures and ordinary citizens can all write to the government department sponsoring the proposed new law to say what they think.

From opposition members of parliament (MPs)

Opposition MPs are MPs who do not belong to the governing party, or who are not allied to the governing party. Their job is to criticise what the government does and propose alternative actions. They do this in debates on new laws, by asking awkward questions at Prime Minister's Question Time, by complaining about the government in the media, by making critical speeches and by writing letters to government ministers. They also vote against the government after debates (unless there is some political advantage to be gained by agreeing with the government or by abstaining).

Letters to MPs; MPs' constituency surgeries

MPs may also be able to gain an idea of what ordinary people think about new laws and political issues from their weekly mailbag, or from what people tell them in their constituency 'surgeries' (consultation with the public in the place they represent).

activity

INDIVIDUAL WORK 1.7

P4

You are a member of a **pressure group** which wants to change government policy in a particular area. Write a circular for your group members describing how the government develops a new policy.

The legal processes used to create legislation

A democratic government of the type found in Britain has three sides to it: the legislature, which makes laws, the judiciary, which interprets laws, and the executive, which carries out the laws. We are concerned here with the legislature, which, in effect, is Parliament. (The judiciary is the courts and the executive comprises government departments and – at a lower level – public services.)

The drafting of the statute

A statute is a written law, and the first stage is for a team of lawyers in the Parliamentary Counsel Office (part of the Cabinet Office) to write out the proposed new law. At this stage, it is called a draft Bill. The lawyers follow instructions from the government department that is putting forward the Bill.

Laying before Parliament

This means that the draft bill is shown to MPs so that they can read it and get to know more about it. There are two parts to this process: the first reading, which is a formality; and the second reading, where the bill is properly debated.

Parliamentary readings

See page 37 below.

Voting in the House of Commons and the House of Lords

In the House of Commons voting is announced by the Speaker, who says, 'All those in favour say "Aye!"' and 'All those not in favour say "No!"'. If it is clear from the volume of noise that the House says 'Aye' or 'No', then the vote is recorded accordingly. If it is not clear from the spoken responses whether the house agrees or not, MPs have to get up and walk through two doorways into the 'Aye' lobby or the 'No' lobby, where they are counted by officials (called 'tellers') who give the number of votes for and against to the Speaker, who then announces the result in the House.

Voting in the House of Lords is a simpler affair. Peers are invited to say 'Content' or 'Not content' when it is time to vote in debates or on **amendments**. It is not necessary for the peers to walk through lobbies even if the vote seems close.

Signature by the monarch

The monarch (at present, i.e. 2007, the Queen) signs the bill after it has finally been agreed on by both houses of Parliament. This signing is called giving 'royal assent'. The Queen is not allowed to refuse to sign. Once the Queen has signed, the Bill becomes law. It is then no longer a Bill, but becomes an Act.

Setting dates of implementation

Having produced the Act, Parliament has to decide when and how it is going to be introduced. Some Acts come into force immediately; others, which are more complex, suffer delays. The minister whose department has sponsored the Act in the first place may issue a commencement order. This is a special kind of law, called a **Statutory Instrument**, which does not have to be debated in Parliament; it sets a date for the implementation of the new law.

Issuing guidance and directives to public services to support the implementation and identify their accountability; advertisements in media to publicise the law; financing of charities and organisations to assist in the implementation of policies

Methods of **implementing** new laws vary according to the nature and complexity of the law, and the number of people who will need to know about it before it can be enforced properly.

An example of what has to be done, and the kinds of timetable that have to be followed, is given on page 36, in relation to the Charities Act 2006.

Prince's Trust, NACRO, the crime reduction charity, probation service

Where new laws are being introduced which involve the sentencing of offenders in the community or different approaches to rehabilitation or diversionary measures (to stop at-risk people from offending), organisations such as these are expected by the government to assist in putting the new policies into practice. They are given a timetable for the expected implementation of the new law and are often granted extra money by the government to help them prepare and carry out their new duties.

The numbers in Table 1.8 show the order in which things happen. The whole process can take months.

Prince's Trust

www.princes-trust.org.uk

NACRO

www.nacro.org.uk

case study 1.12 — Charities Act 2006

This document sets out our provisional timetable for implementation of the Charities Act 2006 .... Our aim is to give charities (and others that will be affected by the Act) time to properly prepare for changes that will affect them.

The legislation received Royal Assent on 8th November 2006. .... Parts of the Act will come into force early in 2007, and [other parts] will roll out over the following two to three years.

Implementation will be led by the Office of the Third Sector in the Cabinet Office, working closely with colleagues in the Charity Commission and representatives from the sector itself.

In the first half of 2007, the sector will see:

- A plain English guide to the Charities Act;
- A series of regional events to explain the Act to charities in England and Wales;
- Initial reductions in the regulatory burden on charities, especially smaller charities;
- A modernised framework for the Charity Commission;
- Consultations with the sector begin to ensure clear guidance is available on the public benefit test.

Other key measures in the Act will follow...

(Source: www.cabinetoffice.gov.uk)

activity
INDIVIDUAL WORK

Contact a member of a uniformed public service who has had experience of enforcing, or working with, a new law. Ask them how the new law was implemented, and what help, training or preparation they received to help them adjust to the changes.

Read *Bills and How They Become Law* on www. parliament.uk
See factsheets produced by the House of Commons Information Office
www.parliament.uk
Legislation Series
L1: *Parliamentary Stages of a Government Bill* (Revised January 2007)
L2: *Private Members' Bills Procedure* (Revised November 2004)
L6: *Standing Committees* (Revised February 2006)
L7: *Statutory Instruments* (Revised March 2006)
Members Series
M1, *You and Your MP* (Revised October 2005)
See also www.direct.gov.uk

Table 1.8 Creating legislation

1. *Green paper*
– a consultation document giving general ideas of new laws and asking people what they think
2. *White paper*
– a policy document outlining in some detail the main points, and reasoning behind, a proposed new law

House of Commons	House of Lords
3. *First reading* The title of the Bill is read out by a Clerk The Bill is printed	8. *First reading* A formality. No debate at this stage The Bill is reprinted in the form finally agreed by the Commons
4. *Second reading* Main opportunity to debate the Bill After the second reading, a timetable is set for the committee stages	9. *Second reading* Debate on general principles of the Bill Amendments (changes) may be put forward and can be voted on
5. *Committee stage* Committees debate and vote on the detail of the Bill, clause by clause Possible types of committee: i) *Committee of the Whole House* – for constitutional Bills and parts of the Finance Bill ii) *Public Bill Committee* – usual type; 16–50 Members, in proportion to overall party strengths iii) *Select Committee* (not often used) iv) *Special Standing Committee* (rarely used)	10. *Committee stage* Bills usually go to a Committee of the Whole House or Grand Committee Detailed line-by-line examination. Plenty of debate – all amendments considered
6. *Report stage* Another chance to consider amendments, new clauses and, for MPs not on the committee, to propose changes	11. *Report stage* Further chance to amend the Bill
7. *Third reading* Final chance to debate the Bill The Bill now goes to the Lords	12. *Third reading* Amendments can still be made Passing: the last chance for peers to comment and vote on the Bill

13. *Consideration of amendments*
Depending on which House the Bill started in, each House now considers the other's amendments
If there is serious disagreement, Bills pass back and forth between the Houses until agreement is reached. If no agreement is reached, a Bill is lost
Bills with agreed amendments await royal assent

14. *Royal assent*
Queen's assent formally notified to both Houses

15. *Bill becomes an Act*

Other influences affecting government policy decisions

Laws and policies are closely related. Policy is a general word referring to the intentions of the government, whereas a law is a written definition of acceptable and unacceptable behaviour which carries agreed and formalised punishments.

Many of the things which cause new laws to be passed happen outside the government – in the 'real world'.

What follows are short accounts of a few of the major influences. There are many others, and students are advised to read good newspapers and watch news and **current affairs** programmes on television to achieve a fuller understanding of this complex topic.

National influences

These are influences on the government, and on government law-making, which come from within the country. One of the main ones is the behaviour of the press.

Press reports

Despite the fact that politicians talk a lot and are keen to appear on television, most British people pay more attention to what is written in the newspapers. This means that MPs have to take note of what is written in the press, because, when the newspapers campaign to form public opinion, both newspapers and the public expect MPs to do something about it.

While television is bound by agreements to be politically unbiased, the press can be as biased as it likes. For example *The Guardian* and the *Daily Mirror* are, on the whole, papers which support Labour, while the *Daily Telegraph* and the *Daily Mail* are pro-Conservative. Nevertheless, these newspapers do not support their favourite party all the time, and if a newspaper changes its political stance it can be bad news for politicians. MPs are not young (on the whole) and have long memories. In 1992, *The Sun* (the most widely read newspaper) ruthlessly ridiculed the then Labour leader Neil Kinnock, and the editor later claimed that it was '*The Sun* wot won it' for John Major, a Conservative Prime Minister. Kinnock was expected to win – and he didn't – and *The Sun* felt that its campaign had made all the difference. This gave John Major a confident start, but after a while *The Sun* began to support Labour under Tony Blair. In the 1997 election Blair won against Major by a landslide, and *The Sun* was able to claim some of the credit.

For this reason, if newspapers want to change the law, MPs sit up and take notice. A recent example is the political controversy over 'Megan's law' – a law in the United States which allows the addresses of convicted paedophiles to be published on the internet and elsewhere. Newspapers such as the *News of the World* have been campaigning in favour of having a similar law in Britain, and the government is seriously considering trying it, or, at the very least, running pilot schemes. The idea is probably popular with the majority of British people, but it is less popular with the police, who feel that there is a risk of disturbances, victimisation and vigilante-style action, and of paedophiles going into hiding where they may be even more dangerous to the community.

Demonstrations and strikes

Demonstrations and strikes can have an effect on government policy, but the effect they have is not always the one intended by the demonstrators and strikers.

Back in 1979, the so-called 'Winter of Discontent', Labour was in power, but there were endless strikes, most memorably of council refuse workers who left mounds of rotting rubbish in the street for weeks. Unfortunately for the strikers, what people were aware of, thanks to their noses and the press, was the smell, the rats and the inconvenience, rather than the reasons why the strikers went on strike in the first place. The then Labour government failed to deal firmly with the strikers and was voted out later in 1979 in a general election. The result was a Conservative government which lasted until 1997. The Conservative government under Margaret Thatcher took up 'union-bashing', passing laws such as the 1980 and 1982 Employment Acts which prevented strikes and weakened the **trade unions**. Realising that public sector workers were more likely to strike, the government also started privatising everything it could – council services, railways, steel, gas, and so on. This may have been good for the country as a whole, and for the taxpayer, but it caused large-scale unemployment among low-paid manual workers. Similarly the Thatcher government's reaction to the 1984 Miners' Strike was to close the mines. That government's tough actions were popular except in the poor industrial areas which had suffered under its laws, and the Conservatives continued to have a majority in the opinion polls until after John Major became Prime Minister in 1992.

These examples show that government policy is certainly influenced by national events, but it is even more influenced by knowledge of what policies are popular with the majority of ordinary people. The frequent opinion polls by MORI, NOP, etc. are important in this respect, as they give feedback to the government on what the public thinks of its policies.

Financial constraints

These are factors which affect the amount of money that the government has to spend. A government that has a lot of money to spend has different policies from a government which is trying to save money.

Interest rates

These are the rates of interest at which the Bank of England will lend money to other banks and institutions around the world. In Britain, low interest rates stimulate spending, borrowing, industrial growth and investment. In the short term, they enable more money to be spent on public services, but in the long run they lead to **inflation**. Inflation means higher prices, and if prices rise because of government action the government is likely to become unpopular and be voted out at the next election. High interest rates are good for savers and the stock market but bad for manufacturing industry. They can lead to **recession**, a rise in unemployment and reduced spending on public services.

Wage demands

The government attempts to limit wage rises to the rate of inflation (average price rises), which is usually between 2% and 3% per year. If wage demands (made by trade unions representing large groups of workers) or wage increases exceed the rate of inflation, company profits go down while inflation goes up – a situation that can cause mass unemployment. Public sector (including public service) wage rises are usually lower than those in private industry, but there tends to be greater job security. The overall effects of high wage demands are that the government has less money to spend on public services.

Housing costs

There is a huge need for 'affordable' housing in Britain – which has some of the highest house prices in the world. However, there is also a huge need to conserve the environment, especially the countryside. In addition, building large amounts of cheap housing will have the effect of lowering house prices, which is very unpopular with people who are already house-owners. If it builds a lot of houses, a Labour government risks losing support to the Conservatives, who are considered less likely to follow policies which will reduce house prices. High housing costs cause huge problems to lower-paid public service workers, especially in the London area.

International influences

These have a major effect on government policy, and the size of that effect is growing with increasing **globalisation**.

Immigration/emigration

Although immigration of young workers benefits the country economically, it frightens people who feel that the country is going to be 'swamped' by foreigners. Government policy at present seems to be treading a tightrope, satisfying the country's economic need for good, able workers while at the same time trying to reassure people who feel that Britain's identity and culture are under threat.

Emigration is mainly a political issue when very able young people go to America: then it becomes a 'brain drain'. Most emigrants are older people going to live in sunnier climates.

EU policies

Britain is bound by EU treaties, which means that most European legislation has to be incorporated into British legislation. Britain has therefore to follow policies similar to those of other EU countries except in foreign relations, some aspects of taxation and some aspects of security. This has caused foreign policy problems for the British government, as its position is in some ways closer to that of the USA than to European countries such as France and Germany.

International terrorism

Since the attacks of 11 September 2001 in the USA, the British government has followed the policies of that country's Bush administration and its so-called 'war on **terrorism**'. The armed forces have become involved in unpopular and difficult wars; the police have wanted to be allowed to keep 'terrorist suspects' for 90 days without charge; and 52 people were killed in '**Islamist**' bombings in London in July 2005. International terrorism has therefore greatly affected government policy on security, diversity and law and order issues.

The development of large global companies

Many large global companies (e.g. BP) are partly British-owned. In addition, Britain is dependent on such companies for oil and mineral supplies, for banking services and many other things. The British government cannot therefore have policies which make life difficult for these huge companies – since they in turn can make life difficult for Britain (especially over energy supplies or by relocating overseas, which causes unemployment and political problems here). The overall effect is that globalisation reduces the power of the British government to make policy decisions on its own. It also means that the British armed forces are more involved in overseas activities (which tend to protect these large global companies) than they once were.

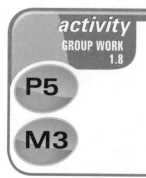

activity

GROUP WORK 1.8

P5

M3

Choose any two government policies which have been introduced in the last 10 years, and produce either a leaflet or a PowerPoint presentation, showing how those two policies came into being. Explain the importance of the different stages of the development of the policy. Your leaflet/presentation should be in a style suitable for schoolchildren visiting a government department.

Fig 1.8 The government has to protect our energy supplies

Government policies in the UK and how they impact upon the uniformed public services

Examples of policies and different uniformed public services

Policies that influence all services

One of the reasons why politics matters to public service workers is the enormous effect that government policies have on the public services. This section contains a brief outline of some of them.

Environmental

All public services now carry out environmental audits to find ways of reducing their carbon emissions and pollution (without undermining their performance). Especially concerned are the armed forces: firing ranges have a damaging impact on the environment; there is environmental damage in exercise areas such as Salisbury Plain, and pollution on land from dependence on motorised vehicles and from low-flying fighter planes, and pollution at sea. Some argue, perhaps correctly, that the armed forces actually care for the environment and that military activities are less damaging than wind turbines, forestry and some kinds of farming.

The British Army

www.army.mod.uk

Civilianisation

Civilianisation is the employing by uniformed public services of people who are not actually members of those services. It takes various forms:

- directly employing civilian (non-uniformed) personnel
- using agencies or private companies to do public service work (these might be specialist organisations, such as the Forensic Science Service, or businesses, such as private waste management companies)
- using volunteers, such as special constables
- blurring the distinction between uniformed and non-uniformed personnel. Community Support Officers, for example, are not police officers, but they do wear uniforms and are therefore not entirely civilian.

Civilianisation is being encouraged for the following reasons:

- It saves public money. People employed by the police to do their paperwork cost less, and may be more efficient, than having the police do all their own paperwork.
- It enables uniformed personnel to focus on the work they do best. Police officers, for example, are expensive to recruit, train and employ. The service gets better value for money if they are allowed to concentrate on policing.
- It makes links with the community. Civilian workers in public services are more likely to be women or from ethnic minority groups; they make uniformed public services more approachable, and, in military establishments, come from the local area and make a valuable link between local people and the uniformed service. Many civilian workers in the police are actually employed to liaise with the local community.
- It enables skilled specialists to be employed, even if they do not fulfil some of the fitness and other requirements for full members of the uniformed public service.

Equal opportunities

Employers have a legal responsibility not to discriminate against employees and not to allow discrimination in the workplace.

See pages 257–265 in Unit 6 for more information on equal opportunities and diversity.

Here is an example of an equal opportunities statement by a uniformed public service.

case study
1.13

Equal opportunities

The West Yorkshire Fire & Rescue Authority are committed to equal opportunity. It is determined to ensure that no job applicant, employee, or service user receives less favourable treatment on the grounds of age, sex, race, colour, ethnic or national origin, nationality, creed, disability, trade union activities, political, or religious beliefs, sexual orientation or marital/parental status, or is disadvantaged by conditions or requirements which cannot be shown to be justified. We seek to ensure that employees are not subjected to harassment of any kind.

activity
INDIVIDUAL WORK

1 Ask an older person who works (or used to work) in a uniformed public service about the changes and progress in equal opportunities which have taken place in their working lifetime.

2 Minority ethnic officers made up 3.5% of all police officers in 2005. The target for 2009 is 7%. The percentage of ethnic minority people in the British **census** of 2001 was close to 9%. What factors are still making it difficult for ethnic minority people to get into (and stay in) some uniformed public services? Discuss the situation, and make a checklist of things that you think could be done to reach the Home Office target.

Human rights

Human rights are of great importance to public services and to governments.

See pages 102–103 in Unit 3 and pages 243–244 in Unit 6 for more information on human rights.

Financial reductions and increases

These are decreases or increases in the money that the uniformed public services receive in their annual budgets. Whether the amount of money goes down or up from one year to the next depends on:

■ the finances of the government

  ▪ the amount of money the government has received through taxation

  ▪ the amount of money the country earns through a favourable balance of payments (i.e. if the country earns more from exports than it spends on imports, or has high earnings through services such as banking and tourism, the government has more money to spend on public services)

- the policies and priorities of the government
  - whether the government wants to spend more money on that service (in recent years a good deal of extra money has gone to the police, because crime and terrorism are major political issues and the government has to be seen to do something about them)
  - whether the government wants to reduce taxation (if it does, there will be less money coming in from the taxpayer to pay for public services)
  - the attitude of the Treasury towards spending, and the arguments put forward by government departments for getting extra government funding
- the workload of the service – for example, money for the fire and rescue service is not rising fast because numbers of serious fires are going down due to improved safety measures and safety awareness
- the level of council tax and how the local authority wishes to spend it – a proportion of police and other local uniformed service money comes from a local tax, council tax. This varies from place to place.

Policies affecting the military services

Declarations of war

Although British forces have (as part of a coalition) invaded southern Iraq and, in a sense, Helmand Province in Afghanistan, there has been no formal declaration of war in either case. When Britain invaded southern Iraq there was a war against the Iraqi government of Saddam Hussein, but in Afghanistan the 'war' is against Taliban **insurgents** who are themselves hostile to the Afghan pro-Western government led by Hamid Karzai. Around 8000 British soldiers are in Iraq, and 6000 in Afghanistan. This is out of a total of about 200,000 regulars in the armed forces.

If these were the only active duties carried out by the British armed forces it would not be a large percentage, but in fact the armed forces are also committed to peacekeeping and other activities in 27 different countries ranging from Gibraltar and Northern Ireland to the Falkland Islands, the Democratic Republic of Congo and Sierra Leone in West Africa.

The immediate concern is that British forces are being overstretched by taking on too many commitments while receiving too little money and resources. There have been serious complaints about the lack of support being received in Afghanistan.

'British troops fighting in Iraq and Afghanistan are too thin on the ground, do not have the equipment they need and there is a significant risk that they will fail in their mission,' a cross-party committee of MPs warns today.'

(Source: Richard Norton-Taylor, *The Guardian*, Wednesday 13 December 2006)

There is another concern about the effect of government policy on the armed forces. The British government regards the war in Afghanistan as important for world security in the future. Tony Blair, Prime Minister in 2006, said that success against the Taliban insurgents in Afghanistan would help establish global security, and he pledged Britain's commitment to the war-torn country 'for as long as it takes'.

> **remember**
>
> Many 'small' wars happen even if they are not openly declared. British armed forces are sometimes involved in advisory, training and other roles which are not well publicised.

However, opponents of government policy question the value – and the morality – of the war in Afghanistan – or Iraq. As neither campaign appears to have the clear approval of the United Nations, these military activities are considered illegal by many people. The British armed forces aim to be a force for good in the world; opponents of these wars therefore feel that a misguided government policy is leading to the abuse of the armed forces and is putting soldiers' lives at risk for no worthwhile reason.

Increased use of reserve forces

If the regular armed forces are overstretched, it can follow that more reserve forces such as the Territorial Army are used. It may be that reserve forces are less effective than the regular ones, and that recruitment to reserve forces will fall below its already relatively low level.

Increased use of technology

Technology is advancing all the time, both in weapons systems and telecommunications. This leads to more accurate targeting and, arguably, to fewer civilian casualties. One political result is that the British government has been able to present its warfare methods as being morally better than those of the enemy, who are usually considered to be 'terrorists' or 'insurgents'.

Links with other international services

Just as globalisation affects what we eat, what we wear, what we think, and where we go for our holidays, it also affects the uniformed public services. The armed forces operate in nearly all parts of the world, and most of what they do is in collaboration with other armed forces or international organisations. In Iraq, they are part of the US-led coalition.

North Atlantic Treaty Organisation (NATO)

NATO was originally set up to protect the West from Communism and the Soviet Union; now it continues to exist to protect the West against other threats. In Afghanistan, the British are part of a NATO force.

See also pages 133 and 136 and Unit 8 in *BTEC National Public Services Book 2* for more information on NATO.

United Nations (UN)

The United Nations is the biggest international peacekeeping organisation. With 147 members in 2005, its aims are to work for international peace and security, develop friendship between nations, and to work together to solve economic, social, cultural and **humanitarian** problems in the world. In Cyprus, the Democratic Republic of Congo, Georgia, Liberia and Sierra Leone, British armed forces are working with UN peacekeeping forces.

Ministry of Defence

www.mod.uk

Combined services activities

The police also have to adjust to globalisation, this time in the form of combating cross-border crime. In Britain, a sign of this is that the government set up the Serious Organised Crime Agency to tackle cross-border and other large-scale crime in 2006.

With government encouragement, links to Interpol and Europol are being strengthened in order to combat the growing threat of organised crime. Table 1.9 shows the major types of international crime that have been identified by Europol.

Europol produces an annual organised crime threat assessment. Here is what Europol has to say about the international help received in making this assessment.

'All EU-Member States and the two Accession States have provided us with their respective contributions. We also received valuable contributions from the institutions at EU-level – Eurojust, Frontex, OLAF, ECB and EMCDDA. Additionally, a number of third parties provided valuable assistance in building up our picture of organised crime as it impacts upon the EU. We are grateful to our law enforcement partners in the US, Canada, Norway and Colombia as well as to Interpol and SECI for their co-operation.'

(Source: introduction to *European Organised Crime Threat Assessment 2006*)

Table 1.9 Major types of international crime

Drugs	Crimes against persons	Financial crime and other crimes against property	Illicit trafficking
Illicit trafficking Cocaine, heroin Synthetic drugs Cannabis Pharmaceuticals classed as drugs Anabolic and doping substances	Illegal immigration Trafficking in human beings Exploitation of children	**Money laundering** Swindling and fraud Counterfeiting and forgery Organised robberies Burglaries and theft Theft of cultural goods	Trafficking in stolen vehicles Tobacco smuggling Illicit firearms trafficking Illegal waste trafficking

Europol – European Law Enforcement Cooperation
www.europol.europa.eu

Policies affecting the emergency services

Government policies affecting the emergency services usually consist of far-reaching Acts of Parliament which in some way change the nature or work of a particular service. An example of such an Act is the Fire and Rescue Services Act 2004. Here is a brief explanation from the *Fire and Rescue Services Act 2004 Factsheet*.

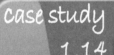

case study 1.14 — The Fire and Rescue Services Act 2004

The Act creates a new package of powers and duties for fire and rescue authorities fit for purpose for the needs of a modern Fire and Rescue Service. This new legislative package covers existing activities such as rescue from road traffic accidents but also allows for roles in other emergencies – such as serious flooding, rescue from other transport accidents and planning and responding to the new terrorist threat – to be recognised. Crucially, the Act provides flexibility to provide for other functions should the role of the Fire and Rescue Service change in the future.

(Source: www.communities.gov.uk)

activity
INDIVIDUAL WORK

1 Research the meaning of the word '**resilience**' in relation to the government and the Fire and Rescue Services Act 2004.

2 In what ways do you think these changes to the fire and rescue service will help the country to deal with major emergencies in the future?

On the face of it, the new Act does not really change what the fire and rescue service does (despite changing its name). However, the emphasis on increased flexibility and its use in civil emergencies, such as disasters and terrorist attacks, opens the way to serious changes in its functions in the future, should the government consider this necessary.

Visit the website of the Department of Communities and Local Government for more on this Act
www.communities.gov.uk

activity
GROUP WORK
1.9

P6

Produce posters suitable for a careers exhibition showing how any two government policies have affected the work of different uniformed public services.

---

remember

MI5 and other secret/security services have many links with organisations (some friendly and some not) throughout the world. The links may be unofficial and questionable, but the intention is to protect British interests.

Link

Fire and rescue station closures

These are likely in some areas because fire deaths and house fires are in steady long-term decline. The fire service is also establishing large regional control centres which will replace the present rather fragmented system.

Police regionalisation

The government has apparently halted plans to merge the present police forces into larger regional forces. However, it has decided to move the prison service and the National Offender Management Service (NOMS) from the Home Office to the Department for Constitutional Affairs – which will become a new Ministry of Justice. The aim of this is to allow the Home Office to concentrate more fully on 'security' matters, such as anti-terrorism and immigration, and bring the prison service into closer contact with the court system.

Target setting standards (attendance times, petrol usage, financial targets)

See page 161 in Unit 4 for more on targets.

Civilian uniformed public services also have environmental audits and set environmental targets with regard to their 'carbon footprints'. Police and fire and rescue authorities, which set budgets, have to try to ensure that the spending of their services is within government-imposed limits.

Social responses to government policies

Many people feel that government policies have little impact on their lives and that there is no point in losing any sleep over them. But then there are other people who, either because a policy affects them directly, or because they think that there is an issue of principle involved, become excited, indignant or angry and want to protest about it.

This is not in itself a bad thing. It is the right of people in a democratic country to protest peacefully about government policies that they disagree with. Problems start to arise when protests interfere with other people's ability to get on with their lives, or if they turn destructive and violent.

The job of the police is to allow protesters to get their protest across without doing anybody any harm.

How their actions affect the public services

It depends what the actions are, what the protests are about and on what scale they are carried out. Large, peaceful, deeply felt protests, on subjects such as human rights, do have an effect, but it might not be immediate. Violent or illegal protests cause work for the public services, and may create more public sympathy for the public services than for the protesters.

Civil disobedience

This is a non-violent protest that breaks the law. For example some pacifists withhold part of their tax because they disapprove of government military spending. They are liable to be taken to court by Her Majesty's Revenue and Customs and could be imprisoned. The police are not usually directly involved.

Demonstrations involving the police and ambulance services

Small, peaceful demonstrations are legal even if they are arranged at short notice, but most police forces expect notification of marches before the event.

See pages 115–116 in Unit 3 for more information on demonstrations.

Terrorism affecting all the services

The work of the police and the armed forces has been strongly affected by the threat of terrorism. This is likely to be a threat for the foreseeable future. There have been changes in the law, notably the Terrorism Act 2000, the Terrorism Act 2006 and the Civil Contingencies Act 2004 – and there may well be more to come. The prison service has been affected because terrorist suspects can be detained for long periods of time or deported under arrangements which are not entirely made public.

Meetings that require police attendance

Meetings which are politically sensitive or which might lead – sooner or later – to violence (e.g. public appearances by well-known politicians, meetings of far-right political parties with a racist agenda, or meetings of Islamist groups) are of interest to the police. Some are actively policed while others are, if possible, kept under surveillance.

Picketing of sites such as military bases and closing companies

The police keep such **pickets** under observation; the size and nature of the police presence depends on whether there is a risk of violence or criminal damage. The main military sites picketed (2007) are Faslane in Scotland and Menwith Hill in Yorkshire.

Sit-ins to prevent road building

The police have to move protesters, using the minimum force necessary, if the protesters are obstructing a highway or preventing people from going about their lawful business (e.g. working).

The Guardian (search the archive for relevant terms)
www.guardian.co.uk

activity
INDIVIDUAL WORK 1.10

M4

D2

You are a local councillor who supports the government. Give a presentation to a group of local people explaining how two government policies have affected the work of the uniformed public services and explaining why this has – on balance – been a good thing.

1. Outline the role of the House of Commons in deciding government policies.
2. Why is the House of Commons more powerful than the House of Lords?
3. Give four roles of the Prime Minister.
4. What are the main roles of (a) ministers and junior ministers and (b) civil servants in a government department?
5. What are the three main kinds of election that take place in England? What extra kind of election do they have in the rest of Britain?
6. Give five campaigning methods used by major political parties before a general election.
7. Name four government departments which have responsibility for at least one uniformed public service.
8. Where do the police get their money from?
9. What does 'accountability' mean, and why does it matter?
10. Which uniformed public services have an ombudsman, and what is the ombudsman's role?
11. Name four duties of a police authority.
12. Outline the main stages that a Bill goes through in Parliament.
13. Name three international influences on British government policy.
14. State three advantages of civilianisation.

Team Leadership in the Uniformed Public Services

This unit covers:

- Styles of leadership and the role of a team leader
- Effective communication to brief and debrief teams
- Using appropriate skills and qualities to lead a team
- What makes an effective team

People who work in the uniformed public services always work in teams of one sort or another; and these teams have leaders. In this unit you will learn about team leadership and how to develop your own leadership qualities and skills.

First you will learn about styles of leadership, and how different styles can suit different situations. You'll look at what team leaders do and how they do it, and you'll find out why teamwork is so necessary in uniformed public service work.

Communication is a vital part of leadership. This unit will show you how to communicate effectively with your team. You will learn about team briefings (before a plan is put into action) and debriefing (how to get useful feedback after the actions have been carried out).

The unit will introduce you to problems that can be faced by team leaders and to ways of overcoming those problems. Finally, you will learn to evaluate your own performance and that of your team.

grading criteria	To achieve a **Pass** grade the evidence must show that the learner is able to:	To achieve a **Merit** grade the evidence must show that, in addition to the pass criteria, the learner is able to:	To achieve a **Distinction** grade the evidence must show that, in addition to the pass and merit criteria, the learner is able to:
	P1 describe leadership styles and their use in the uniformed public services Pg 53	**M1** compare two different leadership styles used in the uniformed public services Pg 56	**D1** evaluate the effectiveness of two different leadership styles in the uniformed public services Pg 56
	P2 describe the role of the team leader and the benefits of teams to the uniformed public services Pg 66		

To achieve a **Pass** grade the evidence must show that the learner is able to:	To achieve a **Merit** grade the evidence must show that, in addition to the pass criteria, the learner is able to:	To achieve a **Distinction** grade the evidence must show that, in addition to the pass and merit criteria, the learner is able to:
P3 describe the required communication skills and the process to brief and debrief a team Pg 74	**M2** demonstrate effective communication skills and the correct process when briefing and debriefing a team Pg 79	
P4 use appropriate skills to lead a team in the practical implementation of a plan Pg 79	**M3** demonstrate effective leadership skills when leading a team in the practical implementation of a plan to achieve a given task. Pg 79	**D2** evaluate own ability to provide effective team leadership, making recommendations for own development and improvement. Pg 88
P5 describe evaluation methods used to assess effective team leadership Pg 88		
P6 describe different types of teams and the stages of team development, including barriers to effective performance. Pg 88		

Styles of leadership and the role of a team leader

Leadership styles

From studying sports team leaders, bosses, teachers and **line managers** at work you will have noticed that they all lead in different ways. Some are strict; some are 'soft'; some seem to get things done; others waste time or wind you up. Of course we don't all like the same kind of leader, and the same kind of leader is not necessarily best for all kinds of teamwork. The leader of an army platoon has a different way of leading from, say, a youth club leader or a person leading a recreational walk for senior citizens. The differences are due to:

■ differences in the team or people being led

■ differences in the leader

■ differences in the task or activity being carried out.

These different ways of leading are called leadership styles. Although people have studied leadership for hundreds, perhaps thousands, of years, modern thinking on the subject began with an American, Kurt Lewin, who, in 1939, identified three main **styles of leadership** which are still recognised today. Lewin called these styles **authoritarian**, **democratic** and **laissez-faire**.

Authoritarian

This style of leadership can be summed up in the words, 'You do as I say!' In its pure form – sometimes called 'autocratic' – the leader has absolute power, is not questioned, and when they say 'Jump!' the team says: 'How high?'

Characteristics of this style are:

- There is a big **power gap** between the leader and the other team members.
- The leader expects immediate and willing obedience.
- Questions and disagreements are strongly discouraged.
- The leader has the power to reward or punish team members.
- The leader, not the team, decides whether the work is being done well or not.
- **Motivation** is often through fear.
- The leader does all the thinking and decision-making and the team simply carries out orders.
- The leader's **authority** comes from their **rank**, physical strength, expertise, seniority or some other **quality** which cannot be questioned.
- Communications are **formal** (e.g. standing and saluting in the leader's presence).
- Team members are expected to behave identically or in predetermined roles.
- Team members are not expected to show their individual personalities.
- Leadership is never delegated to other team members.
- The leadership is always **task-centred**.
- Only the leader really knows what the team is doing.

Democratic

In democratic leadership, the team leader involves the team in decision-making. The position is often that of a chairperson rather than a leader in the traditional authoritarian style. The leader is likely to say things like, 'Well, Victoria, thank you for that contribution. Now let's hear what David has to say.' Consultation and communication between team members is important. The leadership is structured, but team members can make suggestions, question what the leader says, and share their knowledge and experience.

This kind of leadership developed after **humanist psychologists** such as Lewin and Maslow discovered that teams often performed better when they were led democratically rather than in an authoritarian manner. The **management** expert Douglas McGregor (1960) became well known for promoting these ideas.

In democratic leadership:

- The leader prefers to hear what the rest of the team thinks before making decisions or giving orders.
- The leader expects obedience, but not blind, unquestioning obedience.
- The system makes use of team members' experience, knowledge and skills.
- Team members are encouraged to adopt different roles, provided that it benefits the team or its work.
- There is a tendency to hold meetings and have structured discussions before making decisions.
- The team is task-centred but the well-being of the team is also a consideration.
- The power gap between the team leader and members is less than it is with an authoritarian style.

- The leader allows team members to motivate each other and does not normally need to use rewards or punishments.
- Decision-making may take a good deal longer than it does with an authoritarian style.
- Democratic leadership encourages team members to think and to make decisions themselves – although these are then checked by the leader and other team members.
- All the team members know what the team is doing.

ACCEL Team – see website for information about McGregor's ideas on leadership.
www.accel-team.com

Laissez-faire

This style of leadership sometimes seems like a contradiction in terms, since the meaning of 'laissez faire' is (loosely) 'let them do what they like'. If the leader says: 'Yes, Kuldeep, you decide … You don't have to get back to me on this!' a laissez-faire style of leadership is being used.

Characteristics of laissez-faire leadership are:

- Team members are given a free rein to do pretty much what they like.
- The leader makes as few decisions as possible.
- There are few meetings or structured discussions.
- Few orders (if any) are given, and those that are given are not enforced.
- Team members needn't communicate with each other if they don't want to.
- Deadlines are not set; people's work is not checked; and no real effort is made to motivate the team.
- The leader delegates tasks but does not ensure that they are being done.
- Nobody really knows what the team is doing.

> **remember**
> Laissez-faire leadership can work well with people who are self-motivated and like to work on their own. Not everybody likes to obey orders or explain themselves all the time.

Fig 2.1 Many teams are run on democratic lines

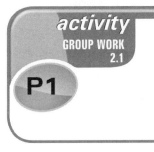

activity
GROUP WORK 2.1

P1

1   Produce a wallchart (suitable for a cadet training establishment) outlining leadership styles.

2   Then contact any three people who work in different uniformed public services and ask them what leadership styles are used in the teams they work with.

3   When you have done 2, include the jobs on your chart, stating briefly in each case what leadership style(s) are used.

Transactional

This is a style of leadership based on the principle that the leader can reward or punish followers. The leader's power comes from being able to give rewards or punishments. In the simplest form, the reward might be a cash bonus and the punishment might be a fine; in practice, however, the rewards or punishments may be suggested rather than real.

The **transactional** style is authoritarian in the sense that there is a power gap and the leader can reward and punish. However, it is also laissez-faire in the sense that the **subordinates** are not monitored during their work but can be rewarded or penalised at the end of it. The weakness of transactional leadership is that it will only motivate people who are motivated by reward and punishment. It is like giving or withholding sweets from young children (which doesn't help the child to learn or develop). It is therefore a negative – even degrading – style of leadership, mainly suitable for subordinates who are low down on Maslow's pyramid of human needs.

See page 66 for more on Maslow's pyramid of human needs.

Transformational

This is a style of leadership based on:

- inspiring other people

- speaking and acting with vision and passion

- appealing to people's enthusiasm and energy.

To some extent, **transformational** leadership resembles the type of religious leadership where leaders inspire their followers and take them towards a 'promised land' of success and self-improvement. Such leaders often 'lead from the front' or lead by example and are admired for their determination and courage (they understand danger, yet act without fear). Some have **charisma**. Head teachers who 'turn around the school' by their energy and inspirational qualities are an example of this style of leader. The strength of transformational leadership is that it really can inspire and change followers – at least for a time. Unfortunately, transformational leaders, although highly effective and motivating, are not always a force for good. If their ideas are bad, their followers will be bad too, as was the case with Hitler. Also, their effects may be temporary, for a personality cult will only work if the personality that inspires it is around. When the leader moves on, the effects can fade quickly.

Bureaucratic

This is a style of leadership based on systems, administration, forms, paperwork, record-keeping, reviewing, monitoring, discipline and businesslike behaviour. It can be either authoritarian or democratic. Although labour-intensive and unproductive it is needed if an organisation is to be consistent, accountable and well organised over a period of time. There is a good deal of **bureaucratic** leadership in British uniformed public services. It makes organisations and **policies** rather difficult to change, but it does have the social advantage of creating employment.

People-oriented

In this kind of leadership the existence and happiness of the team is as important as the work it does. In an amateur cricket team, for example, the captain might think, 'It doesn't matter if we win the match – as long as we all enjoy ourselves.' This **attitude** is characteristic of **people-oriented** leadership.

Table 2.1 shows the relationship between these kinds of leadership and the kinds of team they can be applied to.

Table 2.1 The relationship between task- and people-oriented leadership and kinds of team

		Task-oriented		
		Low	Medium	High
People-oriented	High	Amateur choir		Police CID team
	Medium		The 'average' classroom	
	Low	Any team that lacks interest and **commitment**		**Infantry** unit in combat

Task-oriented

The idea behind **task-oriented leadership** is that 'the job must be done'. The leader believes that the fulfilment of the task is more important than the individual well-being of team members, or the happiness of the team as a whole. This works well in urgent situations, if the team accepts the style of leadership, but it can lead to team members feeling that they are dehumanised or that their individual concerns are being overlooked.

Appropriate style for situation

Many factors need to be considered when choosing an appropriate leadership style for a given situation.

The task

- Is it a routine task or a new task?
- Is it a dangerous task or a safe task?
- How easy or difficult is the task?
- How long is the task likely to take?
- Is the task a one-off or will there be many of them?
- Is the task urgent?
- How important is it to succeed in the task?

The team

- Does the team know what to do?
- Is the team properly equipped?
- Are there a suitable number of people in the team?
- Is the team temporary or permanent?
- Has the team been successful in similar tasks in the past?
- Is the team well motivated?

remember

You can see leadership in action at work, in the classroom, among your friends, and in films and on television. Study the different types of leadership that you come across in everyday life, and decide what style each one is.

- Is team **morale** good?

- Is team health good?

- Is the team physically strong enough (if the tasks are strenuous)?

- What leadership style(s) have worked well with the team in the past?

The relationship between leader and team

- Does the leader know the team well?

- Does the team know the leader well?

- Is the relationship seen as good by the leader?

- Is the relationship seen as good by the rest of the team?

- Does the leader respect the team?

- Does the team respect the leader?

- Can the leader and team communicate well?

- If the team has done previous tasks with this leader, have the tasks been done successfully?

- At what leadership style(s) is the leader best?

The leader

- Does the leader have a history of success?

- Does the leader understand the task?

- Is the leader well aware of any risks/safety considerations?

- Does the leader avoid discrimination, bullying, etc.?

- Does the leader have the support of a wider organisation?

- What responsibilities does the leader have higher up the organisation?

The situation

- Are the leader and team working with people outside the team?

- If so, what are the expectations/needs of those people?

- Are there cultural/gender/age/etc. factors to be taken into account?

- Are there physical and/or psychological dangers in the situation?

- Is the situation life threatening?

- Does the situation demand a task-oriented or people-oriented approach (or both)?

Leadership in practice

In practice, if the team is acting in an emergency, there will be little time to think about all these considerations, but the leader may well be aware of them through experience, training, intuition – or because something seems obvious at the time.

Furthermore, skilled leaders often use a mix of leadership styles. They may be laissez-faire, when working with an experienced person who can be trusted and likes to work independently; democratic with most of the team; and authoritarian when there is simply no time to discuss or 'argue the toss'.

remember

Different styles of leadership come naturally to different people, in different situations, and with different teams.

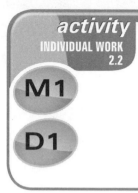

activity

INDIVIDUAL WORK 2.2

M1

D1

You work for a uniformed public service. Research and write a report for your line manager on the **effectiveness** of two different leadership styles as used in at least two different uniformed public services.

Your report should:

1 Describe the styles, giving examples.

2 Explain when and how they are used, and in what kind of circumstances.

3 Give a reasoned opinion on how effective they are in different situations.

4 Give a short list of no more than five recommendations.

Leadership styles used in the uniformed public services

Leadership in the armed forces is relatively authoritarian and aims at being transformational. This is partly because the raw recruit has to be transformed into a soldier, which means bringing about some fairly basic changes in attitude, discipline, strengths and skills. Leadership which inspires admiration and imitation is more motivating for a young soldier than, say, bureaucratic leadership, which belongs more in an office than on the battlefield.

As recruits become more experienced, skilled and **self-disciplined**, their leaders give them more responsibility, including leadership responsibility, by **delegation**. This is not like laissez-faire delegation, because the work of subordinates is monitored and reviewed. Leadership based on delegation motivates subordinates, by giving them the chance to show their initiative, and makes the armed forces much more flexible and quick to respond in combat than the old authoritarian leadership style used to do.

 Link

See Unit 13 in *BTEC National Public Services Book 2* for much more about military leadership.

Fig 2.2 Leadership in the armed forces is often delegated

Military leadership

Military leadership is visionary. It is the projection of personality and character to inspire those they command to do what is required of them. Skill in the techniques of leadership is the foremost quality in the art of command and contributes very largely to operational success. There is no prescription for leadership and no prescribed style of leader. Military leadership is a combination of example, persuasion and compulsion dependent on the situation. It should aim to transform and be underpinned by the **ethos** of Mission Command and a balance of military qualities and skills. Successful military leaders are those who understand themselves, the organisation, the environment in which they operate and the people that they are privileged to lead.

(Source: *Soldier Management: A Guide for Commanders*.
© Ministry of Defence 2004)

activity
INDIVIDUAL WORK

Contact a public service and ask them about the kinds of team leadership they use.

The Ministry of Defence
www.mod.uk

Leadership in the civilian uniformed services is more democratic or **consultative**. There are meetings, and information is exchanged in large quantities. Planning is a democratic process in which different people are expected to give their expertise. There is a good deal of partnership working, which has to be democratic in order to spread ideas and good practice (and to avoid the feeling that one **partner** is trying to dominate the others). In any **diverse** setting, democratic teamwork can make use of the individual differences of team members to produce a more complete and inclusive solution to problems.

In emergencies, however, leadership is always more likely to be authoritarian – especially if a team is well trained. In emergencies there is no time to discuss options: the need is to act correctly – and fast.

Team leader role

Position

By position we mean the rank, office or post held by the leader. Remember that in a large organisation like a uniformed public service, the leader of a team is not the leader of the whole organisation. One team's leader is another team's member.

Every box in the diagram overleaf depicting the Royal Surrey County Hospital NHS Trust organisation chart indicates a team and/or a team leader. The teams work under leaders who are themselves members of management teams.

Team leaders have to balance their responsibilities to their own team with their responsibility to their own leaders and superiors. No team leader has absolute power, and one requirement in any style of leadership, even the most authoritarian, is that team leaders understand the limits of their power.

remember
To find out more about the styles of leadership you should try to visit uniformed public services and see them at work – through visits, work shadowing, or working as a volunteer.

Fig 2.3 Teams within teams

(Source: www.royalsurrey.nhs.uk)

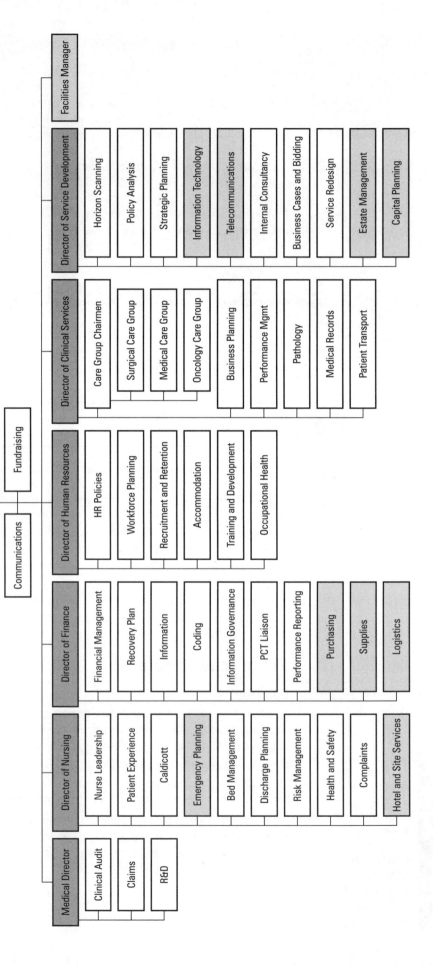

case study 2.2

Senior Project Manager

Salary: £41,424, **incrementally** rising to £48,095, plus £3,053 location allowance

Location: London SE1

This challenging senior role will involve managing a variety of technical systems **projects** for operational users, covering almost the whole range of the electro-magnetic spectrum. You will be working closely with technical specialists and other project managers from across the department, as well as industry partners. You will also be the lead on project management for the department, ensuring that policies, processes and procedures are fit for purpose, that they are in place and are followed. You will mentor other PMs. You will manage the overall programme for Crime and Intelligence Technical Support (CITS), providing the lead on reporting, resourcing and prioritisation, as well as representing the department on key **stakeholder** forums. Key tasks will include planning and implementation, as well as managing third-party delivery.

We need a practical, flexible self-starter with strong people skills and a thorough, can-do approach. Your degree or equivalent will be supported by proven success in managing IT, electronics or related technology projects, and a practical knowledge of project management **methodologies** and techniques. We will also expect highly developed **negotiating**, planning and organizing skills.

(Source: www.metpolicecareers.co.uk)

activity
INDIVIDUAL WORK

1 Identify all the leadership roles in this job advertisement from the Metropolitan Police.

2 Decide which roles will be best served by using authoritarian, democratic or laissez-faire styles of leadership.

remember
Leaders should not be bullying or overly bossy, but they should enjoy taking responsibility and they should not be afraid to tell, or advise, people what to do when the situation demands it.

remember
Training soldiers, aircrew and naval personnel is not cheap, and the money spent and skills gained are wasted if those trained drift off to other careers.

Commanding officer

In civilian public service teams, the leader is often a 'line manager' – the person who is above the rest of the team in rank, pay and in managerial responsibilities.

In the armed forces, leaders are 'commanding officers' and are usually of higher rank than the teams they lead.

Leadership in the armed forces is task oriented in the short term, when the unit has a particular objective to accomplish (e.g. to clear an area of suspected snipers, or to dispose of a bomb). In the long run, however, military leadership is people oriented, because military careers can last over 20 years and commanding officers have to ensure the retention, well-being and development of the individuals in their teams.

Military leadership is traditionally authoritarian, and often still is, especially for new recruits. But increasingly commanders are delegating responsibility and using new leadership techniques. And, as Case Study 2.3. shows, there are times when subordinates need to be treated in a laissez-faire manner.

See Unit 13 in *BTEC National Public Services Book 2*.

case study 2.3 — Advice to commanders

Any barrack regime guards against drugs and alcohol misuse.

Relationships, particularly intimate personal and probably sexual relationships, do not affect the military community.

All personnel demonstrate respect for privacy, decency and the needs and wishes of others.

Vulnerable, young soldiers are protected. Any form of bullying, harassment, intimidation and discrimination is unacceptable.

Unit security and integrity are not compromised.

Communal life in barracks should allow soldiers the maximum degree of privacy. Restrictions and intrusions must be reasonable, appropriate and proportionate for the purpose.

Commanders should establish a clearly understood and properly regulated framework of **rules** and **sanctions** if the rules are disobeyed.

Supervision of soldiers and their accommodation is vital not only for purposes of hygiene but also as a duty of care. It remains the responsibility of the junior commanders, to ensure that the appropriate levels of security, cleanliness, health and safety are maintained and standards of behaviour upheld. Out of hours, 'in-barracks' leadership and management can be the most difficult challenge that the junior commander will face. It is nevertheless vital that the junior commander leads by example and has the **moral courage** to deal swiftly with problems as they occur.

(Source: *Soldier Management: A Guide for Commanders*.
© Ministry of Defence 2004)

activity
GROUP WORK

1   Pick out the laissez-faire aspects of this leadership advice to commanders.

2   Pick out the authoritarian aspects of this advice.

3   Produce a poster giving what you think would be appropriate rules for young soldiers during 'out of hours, in-barracks' time.

4   Contact someone who is in the armed forces and find out what typical rules are in barracks or similar accommodation.

Responsibilities

The responsibilities of commanding officers depend very much on whom they are commanding, the tasks that have to be done, and the situation they are working in.

Their responsibilities include:

- overall organisation
- identifying and setting objectives
- conveying intent (strategies and tactics) and making mission statements
- setting the 'ethos' and 'tone' of the organisation
- encouraging discipline and initiative among subordinates
- monitoring and reviewing performance
- delegating tasks and responsibilities.

Joint Warfare Publication 0–01, *British Defence Doctrine*, 2nd ed. (Ministry of Defence, 2001)

www.mod.uk

Coordinate multi-agencies

With their own well-established team, commanding officers can concentrate on the effective completion of tasks. However, with a new or inexperienced team, they may be more concerned with forming the team than with completing tasks. Increasingly, owing to the changing nature of society, crime and military activity, teams are being set up which combine members of different services or agencies, and these are often called **multi-agency** teams. Here there has to be a special awareness on the part of commanding officers of the different backgrounds and priorities of team members, who have been trained according to the rules and ethos of their own services, and may come from a wide range of cultural or even national backgrounds. Under these circumstances, leadership becomes less authoritarian and more democratic and consultative. Indeed, leading partnerships might better be described as 'management' or '**facilitation**'. This is especially the case in democratic, accountable, **community-based** and information-gathering bodies such as Crime and Disorder Reduction Partnerships.

remember

Peacekeeping and warfare by modern forces are often multi-agency. In the invasion of Iraq, all the armed forces acted together; in Afghanistan, over 30 countries have supplied personnel to work under NATO.

See page 237 in Unit 6 for more on Crime and Disorder Reduction Partnerships.

The Home Office Research and Development

www.homeoffice.gov.uk

Leadership qualities

Leaders differ because their qualities and skills differ. Qualities are inbuilt attributes or abilities (although they can be developed through training, experience, reading, thinking and **self-appraisal**). Skills are abilities which are developed through learning and practice. We will look at qualities first.

remember

Emergency planning, disaster management and relief work are all multi-agency, and multi-agency teams are used to tackle national security issues and international crime.

Decisiveness

Decisiveness is the ability to make a quick, clear, firm and valid decision – and act on it. 'Quick' here means 'as quickly as necessary'. In an emergency it can be vitally important to make a good decision quickly, and decisive people are able to do this. At other times, a decisive person may make the decision to wait before deciding – because all the facts are not yet available and it would be better to wait until they are. Decisiveness is needed in all uniformed public service leadership because:

- Lives and property may be at stake.
- Prompt, effective decisions save time and (public) money.
- Good decision-making is good for team confidence and morale.
- Indecisive leadership causes confusion, stress and low morale.

Adaptability

Adaptability means responding to each challenge in an appropriate way, using initiative and imagination when the team is faced with unfamiliar challenges. However, it should be linked to steadfastness and dependability, otherwise it can come to seem unprincipled, spineless and opportunistic.

In the uniformed public services, adaptability involves:

- working well with people from all social and ethnic backgrounds
- coping with stressful conditions, such as fighting wars or major emergencies
- leading a team whose members are all very different from each other, or whose work is complex and demanding.

case study 2.4   Leading community partnerships

Successful community involvement seemed to be best achieved if:

- **agendas** were not fixed in advance and could therefore be shaped by the partnerships' consultation with a wide spectrum of community views encompassing **excluded groups**;
- visioning techniques were used to enable all relevant stakeholders to construct a shared vision of the future they hoped to achieve. This broad vision could subsequently be translated into workable objectives, through the systematic preparation of an **action plan**;
- meetings of partnerships were run with more flexible agendas, allowed more time for discussion, less rapid decision-making and relied less on jargon in order to facilitate the active and effective involvement of community representatives. Certain individuals in key roles – such as the chair of a local partnership board – can be very influential in determining the style of these meetings;
- the partnership built on existing structures of community organisation and representation in which community groups could easily work and which were therefore more likely to capture the enthusiasm and commitment of local residents;
- partners were encouraged to listen to community representatives even when there were difficulties in reaching agreement on issues of local concern;
- the partnership communicated both project successes and failures to local residents and was open about the limits on change, the comparative costs of different activities and the likely time-scale for seeing meaningful change;
- a patient and collaborative ethos was established among local professionals in which disagreement and conflict was managed effectively and without over-riding the views of the community representatives especially during community forums;
- time was allowed for the skills and attributes of effective partnership working to develop among all members of the partnership;
- community representatives and local professionals recognised that they did not always see the same purposes for community involvement. Local professionals were more likely than community representatives to view the personal development of community representatives as the beneficial outcome of community involvement, whereas community representatives mainly viewed community involvement as an opportunity to achieve policy and service or other tangible gains for their local area;
- the partnership encouraged sharing of resources with other programmes by working in partnership with existing projects operating in the area;
- the initiative was executed with support of enthusiastic local leaders who had a degree of independence from the organising or sponsoring body;
- local businesses were drawn into the partnership.

(Source: Christine Sylvest Larsen (2004) *Facilitating Community Involvement: Practical Guidance for Practitioners and Policy Makers*. Development and Practice Report 27. Home Office)

activity
GROUP WORK

1   Invite a member of a named work-based partnership, or student forum, to talk to you about the work of the partnership, how it is organised, and the best way of getting things done.

2   Draw up a checklist of simple, down-to-earth advice for the leader or organiser of a Crime and Disorder Reduction Partnership, based on the points in the case study and anything that you have learned from your visiting speaker.

Courage

Courage is the ability to control one's fears and act in the way we know to be right. It can be physical courage, which soldiers display when fighting in dangerous places such as Afghanistan, or moral courage, when someone says something which is unpopular but true at a meeting. Courage is not the same as recklessness (which means acting without regard for possible consequences). Courage is needed in the uniformed public services, for example when:

- the police deal with aggressive people who may be armed
- soldiers are fighting or peacekeeping in an unsafe area
- firefighters are making rescues
- any leader has to make a difficult but correct decision.

Compassion

This is the ability to understand, respect and help to lessen the sufferings of others. It is an almost spiritual quality of imagination and empathy – putting oneself 'in the other person's shoes'. Good leaders care for and protect the people they work with, and their overall aim is to try to make the world a better place. In the uniformed public services, compassion can be shown by:

- treating people in custody with dignity and respect
- never **harassing** or abusing team members, clients or members of the public
- treating criminals such as sex offenders professionally and without malice
- being kind and understanding to people who have problems.

Other leadership qualities

Many experts on leadership have identified different qualities with good leadership. Here are some examples.

case study 2.5

Leadership qualities

Table 2.2 Leadership qualities

Honesty	Sense of purpose	Confidence	Image/manner
Skill and knowledge	Respect for others	Responsibility	Loyalty
Age/seniority	Open-minded	Motivational	Sense of justice
Non-discriminatory	Safety-conscious	Good communicator	Energy/endurance
Charisma	Control of emotions	Well-organised	Popularity

activity GROUP WORK

1　Rate the listed qualities in importance for:

(a) teachers

(b) soldiers

(c) prison officers

(d) politicians.

2　Rate yourself or your partner for each of these qualities.

3　Choose any three of these and think of an example which might apply in a uniformed public service.

National School Boards Association – see website for information about leadership qualities
www.nsba.org

Leadership skills

Leadership skills are different from qualities in that they are seen as learned, rather than built into our characters. However, the distinction is not very clear cut: qualities can be improved through training and practice, and skills are much easier for some people to pick up than others.

Communication

Communication has two sides to it: producing and receiving. When A talks to B, A is producing and B is receiving.

Table 2.3 Productive/receptive communication

Producing	Speaking	Writing	NVC: gestures, clothes, expressions, etc.	Drawings, diagrams, maths, etc.
Receiving	Listening	Reading	Observation	Reading/observation

A good team leader is normally a good communicator – able to produce and receive communications in a variety of forms, skilfully and in a manner suited to the situation.

Speaking
Speaking is the most essential productive communication; without it most leadership is impossible. The aims of speech are (a) to convey information and (b) to create the right emotional relationship between the leader and the team.

Good leaders aim to speak in the following ways:

- clearly
- in a way which will motivate or persuade people
- without discriminating against people or hurting their feelings unnecessarily.

Listening
Listening is the skill of hearing and understanding what people say, and picking out and remembering the essential points. When you are studying, listening can be made much more effective by taking notes, but in most uniformed public service work there is no time or opportunity to do this. The best way to get good at listening is to take part in team sports and group or social activities. Part-time jobs working with the public will also be a great help.

Writing
Writing is a skill which becomes increasingly necessary for leaders the higher up the promotional ladder they go. Good writing in a uniformed public service context is:

- clear
- in a style and format fit for purpose.

Reading
There are three kinds of reading, and all are useful for team leaders in the uniformed public services. They are:

- skimming – a quick glance at a document (e.g. a newspaper) just to see what's in it
- scanning – looking for specific information (e.g. a telephone number in a phone book; news items about terrorist alerts in a newspaper)

■ detailed reading – reading every word and making sure that you understand its meaning (e.g. reading a memo from your line manager; reading an assignment **brief**).

Effective reading is vital in managerial leadership posts

Organisation

Good organisation is a mark of a good team leader. Good organisation includes things like planning, punctuality, good time management, orderly paperwork and surroundings, delegating tasks where appropriate and not rushing or skimping tasks.

People who are well organised get more work done, with less stress and effort, than people who are badly organised. They are also better prepared to cope with the unexpected when it turns up because they are in control of their normal workload.

Ways to improve organisation include:

■ Make lists of tasks to be done; don't rely always on memory.

■ Prioritise important or urgent tasks.

■ Don't let other people distract you too much.

■ Review your work from time to time, and ask yourself if you could have done it more efficiently.

Multi-tasking

Skilful leaders have the ability to do several different things at once. This is called multi-tasking. A leader supervising the building of a temporary bridge may (a) help with the building, (b) give advice and ideas, (c) check for safety issues, and (d) notice if people are slacking – all at the same time.

Multi-tasking is a vital leadership skill which can improve **efficiency**, but there is a risk of losing **focus** if too many balls are kept in the air at once!

Planning

Planning comes before organisation. If possible, it should be done systematically, and on paper.

Planning stages

1. Identify the task. Find out what the problem is, and assess the time and resources you have for solving it.

2. **Brainstorm** ideas. This can be done individually, writing down your own ideas as they come to you, or with your team.

3. Sort out which ideas are useful and prioritise them.

4. Write an action plan stating who in the team will do what, and by when.

5. Arrange to monitor the team's progress.

Ways to improve your planning skills

■ Talk to someone whose work involves planning.

■ Get involved in group projects which involve planning, and play an active part in it.

■ Ask someone knowledgeable to check any written plans (especially action plans) that you write.

■ If you do planning as a leader of a team, get feedback from your team members from time to time on how helpful they found the planning and what difficulties they experienced.

Motivating

Motivation means getting people to *want* to work. The psychology of motivation was first outlined by Abraham Maslow in 1943 in his famous 'pyramid of human needs'.

Fig 2.4 Maslow's pyramid
of human needs

(Source: www.age-of-the-sage.org)

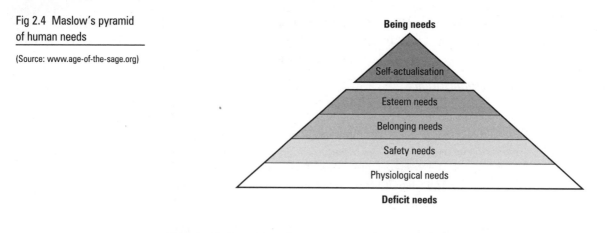

This simple but clever diagram tells us that for people who have nothing (those at the bottom of the pyramid) the first needs are **physiological** ones: drink, food, rest, shelter and sex. These are their strongest motivators.

Once these needs are satisfied the next thing we want, according to Maslow, is safety. People at this level are strongly motivated by offers of money and anything that will bring them security – or at least the feeling of security.

Next come 'belonging needs': community, friendship, etc. People at this level are now really ready for teamwork, because teams provide a sense of belonging.

The term 'esteem needs' refers to the need to be respected and looked up to by others; at this level, people want responsibility and leadership.

According to Maslow, the best motivation for the few people who have all the esteem they can take is 'self-actualisation' – a kind of creative self-fulfilment. This is at the apex (top) of the pyramid, so not many people need this kind of motivation.

> **remember**
> Study what motivates you and other people. Good leaders always understand what motivates the people they lead.

Age of the Sage – see website for information about Maslow

www.age-of-the-sage.org

See page 53 for more on motivation under transactional and transformational leadership.

> **activity**
> **GROUP WORK 2.3**
>
> **P2**
>
> You belong to a unit of **reservists** or volunteers who are holding a seminar on leadership and teamwork. In a group discussion:
>
> 1 Describe a team that you have researched or belong to, and the role of the team leader.
> 2 Explain how the use of teams benefits the uniformed public services.

Benefits of teams to the uniformed public services

There is at present a 'culture of teamwork' in the uniformed public services. The benefits of teamwork are hard to prove 'scientifically', because it is hard to carry out experiments on human beings who are all different and much more complex in their reactions and thought processes than animals. However, there is an almost universal belief in the value and effectiveness of 'good' teamwork and the necessity to organise a service into teams to get the best out of people.

To organisation

Efficiency

If five people together push a car out of a ditch, the job is relatively easy. If the five people push one at a time, the car will still be in the ditch at the end of it all, and everybody will be even more tired than if they had all pushed the car at the same time.

So in jobs requiring manual work, such as unloading lorries (a common job in the army), teams get it done faster, and with less risk of injury, than one person working alone.

With other kinds of teamwork, division of labour can add to the efficiency because each of us is good at different things. If you were to plan a sports competition, one person can take notes (because they are good at it); another person can raise funds (because they're good at that); another person can organise the catering (because they have a catering qualification), and so on. The leader coordinates and monitors the activities to make sure that things get done at the right time.

Positive synergy

'Synergy' means the coming together of energy in such a way that even more energy is generated. Positive synergy is a name given to teamwork when it is going well and the team members are, so to speak, at the top of their game. We see it in sports teams, and it can happen in work teams as well. The team works with flexibility and creativity and is 'more than the sum of its parts'. Reasons for positive synergy are not fully known but could be related to the desire of team members to impress each other and the leader. Zajonc's theory of social facilitation states that groups perform tasks about which they feel confident better when they are being watched (Zajonc, 1965).

To team members, e.g. shared expertise, support

For team members, teamwork is usually more interesting than working alone. If relationships are friendly, there is plenty of supportive feedback and '**social grooming**' which satisfies esteem needs. There is a feeling of security because team members can consult and share their expertise when difficult problems crop up. Many teams offer each other great **moral** and emotional support in times of stress (e.g. after **traumatic** events in the armed forces or in the fire and rescue service).

Fig 2.5 Positive synergy

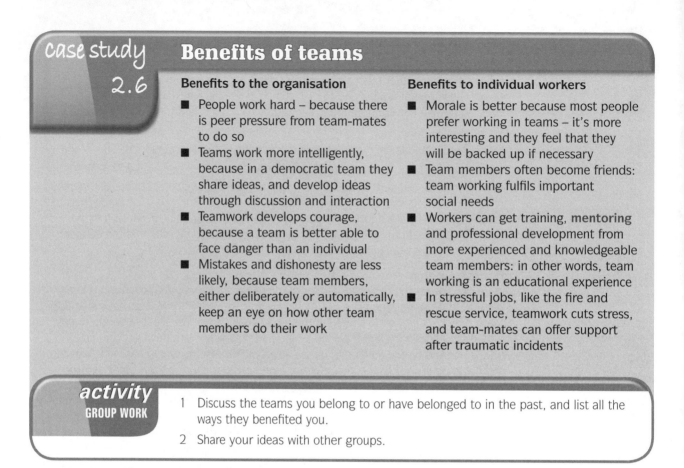

case study **2.6**

Benefits of teams

Benefits to the organisation

- People work hard – because there is peer pressure from team-mates to do so
- Teams work more intelligently, because in a democratic team they share ideas, and develop ideas through discussion and interaction
- Teamwork develops courage, because a team is better able to face danger than an individual
- Mistakes and dishonesty are less likely, because team members, either deliberately or automatically, keep an eye on how other team members do their work

Benefits to individual workers

- Morale is better because most people prefer working in teams – it's more interesting and they feel that they will be backed up if necessary
- Team members often become friends: team working fulfils important social needs
- Workers can get training, **mentoring** and professional development from more experienced and knowledgeable team members: in other words, team working is an educational experience
- In stressful jobs, like the fire and rescue service, teamwork cuts stress, and team-mates can offer support after traumatic incidents

activity
GROUP WORK

1 Discuss the teams you belong to or have belonged to in the past, and list all the ways they benefited you.

2 Share your ideas with other groups.

Effective communication to brief and debrief teams

Effective communication is where the messages sent out by the transmitter (e.g. the speaker) are fully received and understood by the receiver (listener). Briefing is a structured system for telling teams what is going on in their organisation and what their work is going to be in the near future. It allows information to move easily up and down the chains of command and greatly increases the flexibility and responsiveness of an organisation. **Debriefing** is a system of asking team members to review a task they have done, telling the team leader about their successes and their problems in the task, and suggesting improvements for the future.

Briefing in the formal sense takes place at meetings which should not last more than half an hour. In some uniformed public services, briefings are held at the beginning of a shift. In your own course you are likely to have briefings from staff or – in teamwork exercises – from fellow students.

Link

See pages 70–72 for more on briefings.

Communication

Verbal

Briefings, which are essentially the passing of information and instructions to teams by the leader, can be either spoken or written, but the new specifications (BN018453 – Specification – Edexcel Level 3 BTEC Nationals Award/Certificate/Diploma in Uniformed Public Services) concentrate on spoken briefings.

Tone

This is the loudness and pitch of the voice. Skilled speakers vary these to avoid sounding like a speaking clock. On the other hand, don't vary the tone too much, as it can distract your listeners and make you seem anxious and insecure. Your tone in a team briefing should be brisk, businesslike, friendly and down to earth. Humour is not essential – but getting the job done is.

Giving briefings

- Plan what you are going to say, so that you include all the relevant points – and in the right order.

- Speak without notes, but have notes with you to check that you haven't missed anything.

- Keep it brief – don't waffle.

- Make sure that you speak loudly enough for everybody to hear.

- Vary the tone or pitch of your voice as appropriate.

- Stand up straight: do not drape yourself on the furniture.

- Look your listeners in the eye, moving your glance from person to person.

- Don't gesticulate unnecessarily.

- Use words your listeners can relate to, but avoid unprofessional language.

- Answer questions at the end.

- Be calm and polite, avoid sarcasm, and treat your audience (team) with respect.

Listening skills

Listening skills are an important part of a team leader's skill at briefing. This is because communication passes both ways, and a democratically run team will be expected to make comments and ask questions. These must be dealt with attentively and seriously since they may raise important issues of health or safety, and other major points which the team leader may not have covered adequately. Team leaders should make notes of points raised by their teams during briefings – and be willing to act on them. Such willingness is necessary both for the success of the activity being planned, and for the continued good relationship between the leader and the team – for leaders who persistently ignore team feedback can end up being seen as a waste of space.

Non-verbal communication (NVC)

Much of what people know about us comes from the non-verbal signals that we give off, in our clothes, our manner, facial expressions and gestures. The same is true of what we know (or think we know) about other people.

However, these are not the only forms of non-verbal communication. A briefing by a team leader may use other types – especially maps, charts, diagrams, drawings and other visual aids. If you are giving a briefing about, say, an outdoor activity, a sport, the use of a piece of equipment or a problem-solving task, you may well be able to communicate better through diagrams, maps or a practical demonstration than you can through words alone.

Body language

When giving a briefing, you should set out to give a positive impression through your body language. This includes standing or sitting up straight, making eye contact with your team members, and looking and sounding alert and interested.

Team leaders should be aware of the non-verbal communication of their teams. When you are giving a briefing, the reaction of your team, and their level of understanding, may be shown in gestures or postures (and not only obvious ones such as yawning or slumping in their chairs).

See page 209 in Unit 5 for information on discipline.

Briefing teams

When you are briefing teams, you are giving them information which is new to them. To ensure that the information is understood and absorbed, it should be structured and organised in a way which makes it clear and meaningful to your listeners.

Ground orientation

This is the introduction to your briefing. The general topic and purpose of the briefing should be made clear. If the team is one you have never worked with before, you should introduce yourself. You should also clarify how the briefing will be conducted, giving ground-rules for behaviour (if necessary), and say when you will invite comments or answer questions.

Safety points

Safety should be stressed early on in a briefing, and mentioned again in relation to separate pieces of equipment or activities within the main activity. All activities (especially in the uniformed public services) have an element of risk, but this should always be kept to a minimum. Again, if you have never worked with the team you are leading, you may not know how safety conscious they are – so the importance of safety must be stressed.

Summary of situation

Here you outline what you and the team are planning to do, and the time and equipment that will be needed. Your briefing should give just as much information as is necessary – and no more.

Primary aim

This is a clear statement of the main task you expect the team to carry out, and – if necessary – why they are doing it.

Method to achieve aim

This is further information about the primary aim and the equipment, resources, people and time that will be required (or allowed). In most briefings given to skilled and motivated people in the armed forces or emergency services, the choice of method to achieve the aim is not given in detail at the briefing – the people being briefed are expected to use their own initiative wherever possible.

Designated roles

This means telling the team who will do what. After this, each individual team member should know what they are expected to do.

Timings

These are time limits allowed for the activity. If it is a problem-solving exercise, the activity might last 10 minutes; if it is an expedition, it might last several days. (A major activity, of course, is likely to need more than one briefing.)

Equipment

Explaining or facilitating the choice or use of equipment for an activity should be done carefully. Thought should be given to how this phase of the briefing is organised, since

Many people learn best in hands-on situations – and this is particularly true of learning to use equipment.

some people 'turn off' when equipment is being discussed and may not know how to use it when they have to. People may need time to test the equipment for themselves, or even to learn how to use it under supervision.

Team motivation

Good leadership motivates a team, and good briefing is an aspect of good leadership. Team members are often motivated by esteem needs (e.g. getting the good opinion of their team-mates or of the team leader). Team leaders should learn how to express appreciation of their team's efforts, and how to express disappointment without becoming negative. There is no easy formula for motivating teams, but it is essential that the leader should care about the team and its success. The leader's involvement may be shown in a downbeat way, without giving much praise or blame, but the involvement must be there.

Check understanding

This (as any teacher will tell you) is not easy. If you explain something to a group of people and ask them if they understand, they sometimes say they do when they don't. This doesn't mean that they are liars – because it is sometimes hard to know whether we understand something or not until we've tried it, or had time to think it through. Furthermore, we can understand something when it's explained, and then a day later we're no longer sure whether we understand or not.

To check understanding, team leaders can certainly ask their team if they understand, but they should then ask one or two people to explain either to them or to the rest of the group what it is that the team is supposed to be doing, or what it is that you have just explained. (This should, however, be done in a way which will not humiliate them in front of their **peer group**.) If something potentially risky is being done, team leaders should run **simulations**, practice sessions or role-plays, to iron out any difficulties of understanding within the team.

Businessballs.com – this is a useful website, despite the name!
www.businessballs.com
Chartered Management Institute
www.managers.org.uk

Debriefing teams

Debriefing is the process of talking with team members after a task, project or activity has been completed, in order to find out how the task went and what they think of their own, other people's and the organisation's role in carrying out the task. The process of debriefing is sometimes given other names, such as reviewing or self-appraisal: the word 'debrief' is perhaps more associated with the armed forces than with other uniformed services.

Feedback from team to leader

Feedback during the debriefing is from the team to the team leader. This (see below) may need to be acted on. The feedback may be written as well as spoken, and may be done privately or during a team meeting. The quality of feedback is improved if team members know that they can criticise freely. However, if the feedback becomes too destructive, the team leader should make it clear that constructive suggestions are needed if problems are going to be sorted out.

The simplest way to debrief a team is to get the whole team together after the task which forms the subject of the debriefing and ask them how it went. The questions are along the lines of:

case study 2.7 — Specimen briefing

Table 2.4 Specimen briefing

Stage of briefing	What the team leader says	Visual aids, NVC, etc.	Possible questions (at end)
Ground orientation	Right then, team. I've called this briefing to explain what we're going to do, and then you can ask questions and we'll discuss anything that needs discussing	Leader looks cheerful – not sadistic	■ What if we can't walk that far? Twenty-five miles is about twenty miles further than I've ever walked in my life!
Safety points	We're going to do a 25-mile walk, up three big hills, so I want to check your equipment and clothing, and I also want to be sure you're all in good health. During the walk, I want us to keep together – no rushing off in front or lagging back.		■ What if we want to go to the toilet? ■ If we're setting off at seven, what time will we be getting up?
Summary of situation	We'll be setting off at seven in the morning and we probably won't get back until about six at night. The weather forecast is good and we'll be following tracks, so we should be able to do it.		■ I can't see the map properly from here. Martin's big head's in the way.
Primary aim	So our primary aim is to start off at Ribblehead, climb Whernside, Pen-y-ghent and Ingleborough in that order, and get back here at Ribblehead.	Map	■ Can't we drink from streams? It's easier than carrying bottled water all that way.
Method to achieve aim	We'll be walking all the way – not only up and down the hills but between then as well. We'll carry packed lunches and bottled water, and we'll stop for a rest at least every two hours.		■ Neither Stacey nor I know how to read a map. ■ What happens if we go slower than we expect? The train back to Leeds goes at nine.
Designated roles	Chioma and Jason, I want you to do the map-reading on Whernside; Abdulhamid and Aysha, you do the map-reading on the second leg up Pen-y-ghent, and Martin and Stacey – you'll navigate on Ingleborough.		■ What's in the packed lunches? You know I don't eat meat.
Timings	We should aim to complete the first leg by 11 a.m., the second leg by 3 p.m. and the third leg by 6 p.m.		■ (Grumbles) It sounds like a lot of hard work!
Equipment	I've arranged day-sacks, packed lunches – and first aid. I need to check your waterproofs and footwear. Maps and compasses are in the minibus.	Examples of day-sacks	
Team motivation	Are we all up for it?		
Check understanding	Now – has anybody got any questions on any of the things I've said?		

activity
GROUP WORK

1 If you were the team leader, what answers or responses would you give to each of the questions or comments? (Give exact wording.)

2 As a group, comment on the answers and responses that you have each suggested.

3 Write out a short specimen briefing, like the one above, on a group task of your choice.

- What did we do?
- What did we do well?
- What didn't we do well?
- What did we learn about the task?
- What did we learn about ourselves and our skills?
- What would we do differently next time?
- How well did the team leader carry out their role?
- Was the activity worthwhile as a whole?
- Were the equipment and resources adequate?
- Were there any unforeseen consequences?
- Were preparation and follow-up adequate?
- Were there any risks or dangers?

However, people in groups respond differently from individuals on their own, and sometimes what people say in a group is not the same as what they think privately. Many organisations carry on a debriefing in stages so that people can give both their individual and group responses.

Multi-stage debriefing

Possible stages of a multi-phase debriefing are:

1. A survey distributed a day or two after the end of the task – this takes the form of a questionnaire to be answered individually and confidentially and returned to the team leader.

2. Examination of the written feedback – the main points and themes are identified and incorporated into the agenda for a debriefing meeting which includes all team members who participated in the task. The agenda is distributed to team members before the meeting so they know what the meeting is going to be about and can collect their thoughts.

3. The meeting is held; everybody has their say, and notes are taken. Actions which the team think should be carried out are carefully recorded. If individuals have points that they wish to make on their own with the team leader, appointments are made for them to talk with the team leader after the meeting (or in the next few days). Any serious points raised at this stage should be added to the list of points for action made at the group meeting.

4. The points for action (e.g. discussing something that went wrong with a superior officer; sorting out problems with resources, etc.) must now be acted on by the team leader. When something has been done about them, there should be a report back to the rest of the team; this will show the team that debriefing was not just a pointless exercise, and, as well as correcting problems, it will improve the relationship between the team leader and the team.

> **remember**
>
> Don't rush a debriefing and consider seeing people individually if you think they don't feel like speaking in front of a group.

Feedback from leader to team

During or after a debriefing there also needs to be feedback from the leader to the team. The headings below indicate what forms this feedback should take.

Acknowledge success

There should be a clear recognition of success: if the team has done well, the leader should say so. Praise should be given in a way that raises team morale: in other words, it should be honest, and praising A should not be used as a backhanded way of getting at B. Praising the whole team when, in fact, they have not done well is a mistake: team leaders should avoid 'currying favour' with their teams as it undermines their **status** and casts doubt on their judgement.

Identify strengths and weaknesses

Strengths – activities which the team did well – should be mentioned in the debriefing, since developing team strengths is just as important as eliminating team weaknesses. The strengths are probably a reflection of team members' particular talents and interests – and these have to be encouraged if a team is to become outstandingly good at its work. Recognition of strengths makes team members feel valued and is, indeed, a form of praise.

When identifying weaknesses it is best to focus on the weakness itself, rather than on the individual(s) who may be the cause of that weakness. A 'culture of blame' reflects worse on the team leader than on anyone else. Except where weaknesses are clearly due to negligence or misconduct, they should not be considered a disciplinary matter; and personal criticism should be avoided if at all possible.

Development/action points for the future

No team is perfect, and, if team skills are not sharpened and developed, a mood of stagnation, of 'we're going nowhere fast', can sap team morale. Development means learning and practising new skills; **action points** are things that can be done to improve team performance and eliminate weaknesses. The purpose of a debriefing is to make a springboard for the team's improvement, and a successful debriefing is one which results in actions from which the team and its work will benefit.

Development ideas and action points suggested during the debriefing process should be noted down by the team leader and followed up. Perhaps not all the ideas can be acted on, for reasons of cost or practicality, but a team's greatest assets are the skills and commitment of its members; and both these are built up by new training to increase strengths and lessen weaknesses.

activity
INDIVIDUAL WORK 2.4

P3

Write a training leaflet suitable for young expedition leaders, explaining how to brief and debrief a team and the communication skills needed.

Using appropriate skills and qualities to lead a team

Skills and qualities

'Appropriate' skills are learned abilities (e.g. good communication) which suit the situation and the people involved. 'Qualities' are aspects of a person's character which – in this case – help team leaders to relate to and manage their team.

Using appropriate skills is easier if:

- you have the skills
- your team has similar skills
- you communicate well with your team (perhaps because you know them well, have worked with them for some time, or have interests in common).

Time management

Time management simply means making the best use of the time available. The aim of good time management is to do the maximum amount of work in the minimum amount of time. It doesn't mean working harder; it means working smarter.

Smart time management

Good time management can include any of the following:

- making a 'to do' list at the beginning of each day – and following it
- arranging your work area so that everything can be easily found, and there is space to work without having to shift things out of the way first
- being punctual so that you do not waste other people's time
- keeping appointments
- telling the person in advance if you cannot keep the appointment
- checking travel arrangements if you (and the team) have to go somewhere
- avoiding unnecessary conversations
- not allowing yourself to be distracted by others (either in idle chat, or by doing things for other people when you should be doing your own work)
- making timetables and action plans – and setting challenging but achievable targets, for yourself and others
- meeting your own targets and ensuring that the team meets theirs
- delegating work to responsible team members when necessary
- not promising to do things that you can't do
- controlling your emotions
- keeping time free for your own personal/social life and relaxation (a good '**work–life balance**').

Critical path analysis

Critical path analysis is the name for a way of managing time which could be used by team leaders wishing to save time in certain situations. If you were on an expedition and you and your team wanted to pitch a tent, have a meal and go to bed in the shortest possible time, critical path analysis would help you to do this. If pitching the tent and preparing the meal each took half an hour, it would make sense for some team members to pitch the tent while others prepared the meal. Both tasks together would only take half an hour (the 'critical path'). If you pitched the tent before preparing the meal, the whole process would take a full hour – which would be poor time management.

Commitment

For a team leader, commitment is belief in your task and your team (not always in that order). This is a valuable quality in the uniformed public services, especially when doing exhausting and dangerous tasks, such as putting out major fires. Commitment is also shown by teams doing difficult social or probation work (e.g. with sex offenders or other people who may be very hard to work with). It is a complex quality linked to enthusiasm for a job, a desire to help others, courage, persistence, determination and unselfishness. The best ways to develop commitment are to find a job which really interests you and to work with people you respect.

Motivational skills

Leaders can motivate their followers by understanding what they really want and by showing, or suggesting, that they want the same thing too. They should be able to see the purposes of the team from the team members' viewpoint, while at the same time offering an implied promise that they (the leader) can take them further in the direction they want to go. For example, an infantry platoon leader has to be able to suggest that his men (who want to fight successfully) will fight better and be more successful thanks to his leadership. In addition, leaders should know where their followers stand in the **hierarchy** of human needs: what do they really want? If members of the team

Fig 2.6 Commitment

are motivated by esteem needs, leaders must give them that esteem either themselves or by proxy, by making other people esteem the team. Motivational skills come fairly naturally to people who have the skills of a transformational leader, but they can be developed by thinking about motivation and studying it. Finally, leaders should, in some deep way, be motivated themselves: a person who doesn't care won't be able to make other people care.

See page 53 for transformational leadership.

Delegation skills

Delegation means giving jobs and responsibilities to other team members. Some team leaders find it hard to delegate, either because they feel that they have to justify their role as leader by doing all the work themselves, or because they do not trust the rest of their team to do a good job. Other team leaders (although this is rarer) off-load as much work as they can on their team and then go off to the golf course!

Skilled delegation is delegation which:

- is good for team performance as a whole
- is part of a time-management **strategy**, enabling the maximum amount of work to be done, to the best possible standard, in the shortest possible time, and at the lowest possible cost
- uses and develops the skills and abilities of individual team members
- enables the team's work to be more varied and satisfying
- keeps an eye on the delegated work to make sure that it is done on time and is up to standard.

Study guides and strategies – see website for help with developing a schedule
www.studygs.net

Implementing a plan

This means putting a plan into action.

Planning is the thinking that an individual or a team has to do before starting on a task. In some cases the planning continues even after the task has begun – especially if the task is not routine, or has to be done in several stages.

Although, in real life, most planning is done in the head, without writing anything down, some is done in writing (e.g. shopping lists). Written plans are needed for many complex tasks, or for tasks which are being inspected or need to be understood by a number of people. Examples of written plans are circuit diagrams, route cards and flow charts.

Planning is often done in stages. An example is given below.

case study 2.8

Bridging the River Wetfoot

Stage 1. Identify primary aim

The aim is to make a bridge across the River Wetfoot (about 30 feet) wide using ropes – and then to cross the bridge without falling into the river.

Stage 2. Consider factors

Factors are things which will affect the way the task is done, and how likely it is to succeed.

Stage 3. Consider available resources

Resources are the people, materials and time which have to be considered when making a plan.

Stage 4. Consider team member capabilities

What skills and strengths do the team members have? What are their weaknesses? Are they up to the job?

Stage 5. Select course of action

The team and/or the leader decide how to go about the task of bridging the river using the materials provided – and then cross their bridge.

activity
GROUP WORK

1　In the imaginary scenario above, list all the factors that you think would have to be considered by a team leader when planning the building of a rope bridge across the river.

2　What would you want to know about the people, materials and time available? Make a list of points that the leader would want to find out.

3　What style of leadership would you use, if you were the team leader in this exercise? Give reasons for your choice of style.

4　What are the arguments for and against making a written plan in this case? Discuss this question and try to reach agreement on it.

5　Should all the planning be done at the beginning of the task? Give reasons for your opinion.

Leading the team

One of the things you will be expected to do in this unit is to plan and lead a team activity. You will be assessed on how well you plan and lead the activity, and on the debriefing that follows.

Brief team

The purposes of a team briefing are:

■ to give information to the team

■ to motivate the team

■ to get feedback.

The form the briefing takes will depend on your style of leadership. An authoritarian briefing consists of giving the team information and motivating them by telling them what they have to do. There will be no more feedback than is strictly necessary. Decisions are made by the leader and the team is expected to follow them after a minimum of discussion. In a democratic briefing, the leader puts forward ideas – and so does the team – and after discussion the proposals which have been agreed on by the team are carried forward. In a laissez-faire briefing, the leader delegates authority and allows the briefing to run its course without much direction or interference.

Check understanding including overall aim

As already stated, the team leader should try to ensure that the team knows and understands its tasks before the activity begins. This can normally be done through question and answer, with further explanation by the leader if necessary. In authoritarian teams, activities are sometimes run on a 'need to know' basis, with team members being expected to understand only their own roles, rather than the whole task or activity that the team is carrying out. This minimises explanation, but it also reduces team involvement in the decision-making process. This kind of leadership has become associated with the secret services (and with criminal activities). It may be good for team security, but it is poor for accountability!

See page 71 for checking understanding prior to the activity.

Individual roles

Team leaders should, where possible, give team members roles that they are good at or want to do (as long as this does not mean that the less assertive team members end up doing all the hardest and most unpleasant tasks).

Execute plan

The work which the team has been planning should now be carried out to the best of the team's ability. During this stage, the leader still has a key role.

Ongoing quality control

A team is not a clock, which you wind up and then let do its work without further involvement. The leader should be actively involved in checking that the work or other activity is progressing well. This is especially true, of course, in team sporting activities where the leader has a key role to play at all times – both as captain – encouraging and guiding others, and as a skilled and respected participant. If things are going wrong, the leader should make suggestions and give help and guidance when and where it is needed, rather like a football manager giving a 'pep talk' at half time.

See page 159 in Unit 4 for more on quality control.

Safety

Team leaders should either be aware of health and safety issues, or should delegate the role to someone who is. Risk assessments of activities and venues should be carried out, and the health and fitness of team members should be monitored (or observed) if necessary. This can be particularly important with inexperienced teams or with teams doing a difficult and dangerous job (e.g. firefighters attending a major incident, where exhaustion, dehydration, chemical contamination, respiratory damage and burns are special risks).

Performance

There are various ways of monitoring, evaluating and reviewing performance.

See pages 169–173 in Unit 4 for more on ways of monitoring, evaluating and reviewing performance.

Achieve aim

Achievement should be verified by the leader, and appreciation should be expressed to the team. Wherever possible, credit should be given to the team members when the achievement is reported to higher management. Team leaders should not try to unjustly claim personal credit for the insights or achievements of their subordinates.

Debrief team

As stated above, this review of the team's successes and failures is done when the activity is over. Debriefing should not be done immediately after the end of an activity: it is better to wait for team members to collect their thoughts – do it when they have rested and had time to think. On the other hand, debriefing should not be left too long after the activity, or team members will start to feel that the debriefing isn't important and may start to forget how the activity went.

Review and evaluation

The aim of debriefing is to evaluate and learn from the experience of the team activity, so that the team can do better next time. Team leaders should note all comments and – where necessary – act on them. They should also give praise where it is due and show that the team's efforts have been appreciated. Even if the team has not done well, some positive features should be commented on, in order to prevent team morale from sinking too far.

See page 86 below and page 167 in Unit 4 for more on review and evaluation.

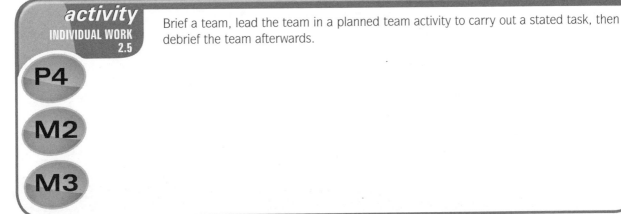

activity
INDIVIDUAL WORK 2.5

P4

M2

M3

Brief a team, lead the team in a planned team activity to carry out a stated task, then debrief the team afterwards.

What makes an effective team?

In order to assess their work, improve their performance and develop their team members, leaders have to have some idea of what an effective team is – and how to build on that effectiveness. Effectiveness is not a target which is reached and where all development stops: development and striving for greater effectiveness are ongoing processes.

Developing the team

Types of teams

The number of different types of team in the uniformed public services is vast. Teams vary in size, name, function, leadership style, permanence, formality and where they fit into the overall management structure.

Work teams

These are teams, departments, groups, **sections**, working parties, etc. which exist in almost any public service workplace. Members may spend most of the day in contact with team colleagues, or in work which is linked to the team.

Project teams

These are temporary teams set up for the duration of a special piece of work or a project that may last weeks, months or years but is not expected to last for ever. The word 'project' sometimes appears in the team's name, and many such teams are linked to local government and can be researched on local government websites.

Cross-functional teams

These are teams whose members are drawn from different departments or teams in a workplace. Members bring different areas of expertise and are useful in developing new services or working with shared issues such as health and safety or diversity.

Inter-service teams

These are teams such as Crime and Disorder Reduction Partnerships where the police, fire and rescue service, and other services and/or organisations work together. Inter-service teams are used in the armed forces (e.g. when marines and soldiers work together) and when the emergency services combine to tackle major incidents.

See pages 151–154 in Unit 4 for more information about types of teams.

Team development

In order to improve, team leaders must:

- be appraised by others
- appraise themselves.

An **appraisal** is a kind of yearly briefing and debriefing and usually focuses on ways of making the individual more effective and on their future career. Appraisal is therefore a review and analysis of a person's performance; it is an important and regular part of **staff development** in the uniformed public services. In a public service organisation, appraisal is usually, although not always, carried out by the leader's line manager (who is likely to be a team leader). In turn, the leader will appraise members of the team.

Self-appraisal is something team leaders should do frequently: that is, look at their own performance and see how they can improve it.

Stages in team development

A model of team development devised in 1965 by Bruce Tuckman, an American management expert, identified the following stages in team development: forming, storming, norming, performing and transforming.

See page 158 in Unit 4 for an explanation of Tuckman's stages in team development.

Barriers to effective performance

This outcome is about team performance as much as it is about the performance of team leaders. This is because there are many possible reasons why teams can fail, either in their work or in sport – and failure cannot always be blamed on the leader. The example opposite applies to sport, but similar things can happen in public service teams.

Lack of commitment

Lack of commitment can mean lack of interest, lack of effort or lack of determination in relation to any form of teamwork. This is perhaps the most common barrier to effective leadership. It can apply to team leaders and to their team members, and the possible signs and causes are many and various:

Leader

- There is poor leadership, which fails to motivate the team.
- Briefs are confusing.
- There is poor communication between leader and team members.
- The style of leadership is wrong for the team members.
- There are changes of leadership.
- The leader doesn't like one or more team members.

Situational causes

- The team is overworked or underworked.
- The team is not valued by its employers.

> **remember**
>
> Sports teams are not the same as work teams, but they have plenty in common. If you study one type of team, you will learn a good deal about the other.

case study 2.9

The sacking of Andy Robinson – England rugby coach

England poised to part with Robinson

Tue Nov 28, 2006 5:00 AM GMT

LONDON (Reuters) – If the media are to be believed, Andy Robinson has coached England for the last time and if he does not resign, he will be paid off and asked to leave …

Universally liked and respected throughout the rugby world, Robinson nevertheless has come under fire from just about every angle.

Former England lock Paul Ackford, now a journalist, wrote in the *Sunday Telegraph*: "Robinson may have the confidence of his squad but he has lost the confidence of almost everyone else.

"England lack shape, they lack direction and, critically, they are losing the respect of the rugby world."

…

Corry [the England rugby team captain] said the constant speculation about his and Robinson's future had been unsettling and made it "impossible to focus purely on our rugby."

He added that the squad, frustrated and angry at their own performances, had gone out and "drowned their sorrows" in a pub on Saturday night.

(Source: Mitch Phillips (2006) www.today.reuters.co.uk)

activity
GROUP WORK

Andy Robinson was 'universally liked and respected throughout the rugby world'. He had also been a trainer to a World Cup-winning team. Discuss possible reasons why (in 2006) such a man nevertheless failed to get good results as a team leader.

- The team is poorly paid.
- The team is not given enough resources, equipment, etc.
- The team is understaffed.
- The workplace is unsuitable or unhealthy.
- The team is made up of temporary workers, trainees, etc.
- The team is from different agencies and hasn't found a way of working together.

Team member

- Team members have not 'bonded' with each other.
- There is conflict between two or more team members.
- There is discrimination or bullying in the team.
- Team members have problems in their private lives.
- Team members are not interested in the work they are doing.
- Team members are not suited to their work (e.g. they lack ability or have too much ability).
- Team members are not motivated by the rewards they are being offered.
- One or more team members is ill or in poor health.
- There are young team members who are inexperienced and/or poorly trained.
- There are 'stick-in-the-mud' old team members who are thinking of retirement.
- One or more team members are not natural 'team players'.
- Team members are suffering from stress.
- The team members are naturally lazy people.
- Team members keep being shifted to or from other teams.
- There are too many observers, people on secondment and other temporary people.

The work/tasks/activities

- The work is too difficult for the team members.
- The work is too easy.
- The work is boring and is (or seems) pointless.

Poor communication

Uniformed public service teams can underperform because of poor communication between the team members, between the leader and the team members or between the organisation the team works for and the team leader.

Possible reasons for poor communication include:

- lack of training in the communication skills required for a given team
- excessive use of jargon and technical language in some aspects of public service work
- loud noises and distractions in the work environment (e.g. when firefighting)
- the use of communication methods which are inappropriate for the circumstances
- wide social and educational differences between team members
- cultural differences and prejudice
- sexism
- a personal dislike of team members which shows itself in persistent misunderstandings
- stress undermining people's listening skills

- problems affecting inter-agency teams whose members have difficulty communicating with team members from other services
- poor **administrative** structures in the public service of which the team is a part
- poor organisation and leadership.

Lack of appropriate skills

It could be said that a team is only as good as the people in it. The success of a team such as a bomb disposal squad is clearly dependent on the technical know-how and expertise of its members, when it comes to the job of making bombs and other hazards safe. A team which consists of novices or, for that matter, older people who have failed to update their skills may well underperform.

If a team is failing because its members lack appropriate skills, the solutions could be to:

- train the team members properly
- remove the present team members and bring in new ones who do have the necessary skills
- move the team onto a different type of work, for which its members are better skilled.

Resource issues – e.g. financial, physical, staff

The public services never have as much money as they would like. This is because governments like to keep taxes down but are also under pressure to provide the best possible public services. The result is that public services have to do as much work as possible, while spending as little money as possible. This means that uniformed public service teams are always at risk of being underfunded.

For the uniformed public services, the biggest cost, by far, is employees' salaries. So a team can save money by having fewer people do more work, but, obviously, this puts a strain on the team because each individual has to work harder. Also, there is a limit to the amount of work that even the most dedicated individuals can do.

The main effects of under-resourcing are:

- low staffing levels
- lack of equipment
- old or unsuitable equipment
- poor work environment
- lack of staff training
- low team morale due to the feeling that they are being undervalued.

If a team is simply too expensive for a public service to run, the work it does can be put out to tender to the private sector (in other words, the work can be done by a private company). The team is laid off, employed in other ways, or paid by a private company instead of by the public service to which it belonged originally (privatisation of prisons and of parts of the NHS are examples of this).

Personal factors

Public service teams often have to work closely together, under stressful conditions. If the right people are in the team, the team is well led, and the work is valued, the chances are that teamworking will be a rewarding experience for the members, with a high level of job satisfaction. However, if the wrong people are in the team and if there is jealousy, mistrust, antagonism, discrimination, etc. among team members or between the leader and the team, things can go rapidly downhill.

See pages 82 and 154 for personal qualities of team members.

case study 2.10

Harmondsworth Immigration Removal Centre

Although **casework** had become more complex, the on-site immigration team had been reformed and now comprised mainly administrative workers with a loss of the expertise of experienced immigration officers. In one case a detainee's grant of bail had been held up by delays in conveying the decision by Immigration and Nationality Directorate (IND) caseworkers and a lack of understanding by the on-site team. The contract monitor and her team spent much time chasing responsible caseworkers from external immigration teams, and many detainees complained of ignorance and confusion about the reasons for their detention and the progress of their case. This caused substantial distress. The IND documentation we examined indicated poor monitoring and explanation of case progress.

(Source: Owers, A. (2006) *Report on an Unannounced Inspection of Harmondsworth Immigration Removal Centre 17–21 July 2006 by HM Chief Inspector of Prisons*. Her Majesty's Inspectorate of Prisons, London. www.inspectorates.homeoffice.gov.uk)

activity

INDIVIDUAL WORK

1   Identify the examples of poor teamwork in this extract from a government report.

2   What barriers to effective performance do you think could have applied in each case? Explain your reasoning.

The Home Office – see website for prison inspection reports; full of useful information

www.homeoffice.gov.uk

Challenges to authority

A challenge to authority means that a team member says or does something which is unacceptable to the team leader or to the organisation to which the team belongs. Such a challenge can take many forms, for example:

- deliberately breaking discipline or safety rules
- undermining or 'bad-mouthing' the team leader behind their back or to their face
- disrupting meetings
- failing, or refusing, to carry out orders
- failing to carry out agreed courses of action
- organising opposition to the team leader among other team members
- attempting to take over the leadership of the team by unauthorised means
- **whistleblowing**.

Some of these things may not be done deliberately or may not be done with the intention of undermining the team leader. Before acting, the team leader should find out if possible:

- whether a deliberate challenge to authority has taken place
- whether that challenge might in some way be justified (e.g. if the team leader has done something wrong – such as issuing unreasonable or dangerous orders)
- who in the team is challenging authority.

Fig 2.7 Inside an
Immigration Removal Centre.
Good teamwork is needed in
places like this

Possible responses to a challenge against authority are:

■ a private talk with the challenger, if there might have been a misunderstanding, or if the issue is a minor one and could be resolved in this way

■ a more far-reaching inquiry into what is going on – interviewing team members individually and then deciding what to do next

■ talking to the team as a whole in an effort to resolve the issue

■ referring the problem to the team leader's line manager and then taking appropriate action

■ using the organisation's **disciplinary system** (e.g. verbal warning, written warning, final warning, and dismissal).

The option(s) chosen depend on the seriousness and nature of the challenge, the personalities and circumstances involved, and the overall situation (e.g. are people's lives or safety being put at risk?)

It should be remembered that what seems like a challenge to authority may be a legitimate (if difficult) question. In extreme cases, the team may be breaking the law; and the challenge is that a whistleblower reports the fact to the authorities. The challenger is not always wrong. Team leaders must therefore be honest with themselves and try to be objective when dealing with this sort of situation. They should not be afraid to call in help if a situation seems to be getting out of hand.

Conflict between team members

This is a serious matter, and team leaders have to sort it out. If such conflict is unchecked it can, in severe cases, lead to bullying, harassment, and even suicide. In any case, it undermines the morale of the team and changes what should be the pleasure of teamwork into a situation which is stressful and annoying.

Team leaders should find out the cause of the conflict and talk confidentially with the individuals involved. The ideal solution is that, after a period of discussion in which the problems are brought to light, goodwill can be restored and the people in conflict can agree to draw a line under the affair and then work together once more in a friendly and constructive manner.

remember
Observant team leaders can sometimes detect conflict before it has caused much damage, and deal with it in a tactful and effective way – if they have taken the trouble to understand their team properly beforehand.

If the conflict involves the work of the team, it may also be that the nature of the teamwork can be changed so that the conflict can be resolved.

If, however, there is no solution to the conflict, it may be necessary to transfer one or more team members to another part of the organisation, and to repair the damage by bringing new people into the team.

Evaluation methods

One of the main jobs of team leaders is to evaluate the work of their teams – and their own work. Without this kind of **evaluation**, team leaders cannot improve the quantity or quality of work that their teams do – nor can they ever know if they themselves are getting better at their jobs.

Evaluation of team leadership and team performance can come from many sources:

(a) external

   (i) by line managers (through appraisal, debriefing, measuring performance against targets, etc.)

   (ii) by inspectors from outside the organisation (inspections can be announced or unannounced, and are usually followed up by spoken comments and a written report)

(b) evaluation of team performance by team leader (this may be ongoing but the main evaluation follows the debriefing)

(c) evaluation of leader by team (this happens in the debriefing, although it can also be done using written evaluation forms that team members fill in individually)

(d) peer evaluation by team members of other team members

(e) evaluation of the team by clients (the people the team work with in society – e.g. young offenders)

(f) evaluation of the team by other teams which liaise with it (this is usually informal, unless there have been obvious problems for one team liaising with another – e.g. when there have been difficulties between police and social work teams in child protection cases, as in the Cleveland abuse scandal in 1988)

(g) self-appraisal by team leaders and team members.

In the above list, items (a), (b), (c), (d) and (g) are all types of evaluation that you are likely to come across in your course.

Goals achieved

Whatever the source of the evaluation, the achievement of goals is the key test of a team's performance. Did the team do what it set out to do?

Goals may take the form of targets set by the government or the public service itself or may be the successful completion of specific tasks. Obviously, if the goals set are too difficult, then the people setting the goals are at fault, rather than the team that fails to achieve them. Goal setting or **target setting** is a skilled business: goals should be challenging but feasible.

See page 161 in Unit 4 for more on targets.

Goals come in two types: quantitative, which relates to the amount of work done; and qualitative, which relates to the standard of work done.

To know whether goals have been achieved and targets met, uniformed public services have to rely on **statistics** provided by the teams themselves. There are risks in this method: teams may vary in their ability to provide consistent statistics or even in their understanding of words: for example, how does one define a 'racially motivated attack'? Furthermore, there is a temptation to 'massage' the statistics, so that it looks as though a goal has been achieved when in fact it hasn't.

Assessment of own team's performance

It is important for team leaders in the uniformed public services to aim for a clear and objective view of how well their team is performing. To some extent this is not their own responsibility: it will be based partly on assessments carried out by their line managers and others in the organisation. Many teams (e.g. watches in the fire and rescue service) can easily be compared because the work they do is similar to work done by other teams, and, as there is a shift system, it will be possible to build up a very clear comparison – over time – of how well each team works.

The team leader's own assessment must be carried out using debriefing techniques.

 Link   See pages 71–74 for more on debriefing.

Debriefing should be carried out either after major team projects or from time to time (e.g. four times a year), and the team leader should keep records of these debriefings. The leader should also have access to the CVs or past histories of team members and have kept a record of their activities since they joined the team. By keeping records over a period of a time, a team leader should be able to build up a picture of the team's performance not only in a given activity but also over a series of activities, so that the development and progress of team members can be tracked.

Assessing the team's performance by this method means comparing the team with itself, by assessing its progress in relation to its own performance in the past. This may, however, be of limited usefulness in the uniformed public services, where teams have to perform against targets, which have been set by the government, the service itself, or by a civilian committee such as a police authority.

remember

You can usually find good examples of targets in your **local policing plan**.

Identification of skills gap

The skills gap is the difference in level between what a team can do and what a team should be able to do. In practice, this is the gap between what the team is doing and what the targets set for it say that the team should be doing.

Recommendations for the future

If there is a skills gap, the team leader has to decide whether it is the skills of certain individuals which are lacking, or whether the whole team is short of skills. The leader then has to do something about it, because a uniformed public services team should not be satisfied with second best; it should work to the top of its ability, and doing nothing is not a serious option. The main choices are:

- **counselling** and/or training the team
- redeploying the poorer team members to other work
- changing the work that the team does.

Reflect on own practice

Teamwork is a learning activity as well as a work activity, and team leaders should always try to learn from their experiences and get better at leadership. This is why it is very important that team leaders should reflect on (think about) their own practice. They should think about their work and the work of their team and ask themselves:

- What do I do best?
- What am I fairly good at?
- What areas do I need to improve in?
- What can or should I do to get better?

case study 2.11 — Examples of police targets

Table 2.5 Police targets

	Measure	Performance 2004–5	Target 2005–06	Performance 2005–6		Target 2006–07
SPI 6a	Number of offences brought to justice	64623	57817	71770	▲	64903
SPI 6b	Percentage of offences brought to justice	24.5%	–	27.7%	▲	M

(Source: www.wypa.org)

activity — INDIVIDUAL WORK

1 Research and make notes on how police targets are set.

2 Do you think the evidence in the case study is a good indication of how well the police are doing in bringing offenders to justice?

3 List all the advantages and disadvantages of setting targets that you can think of.

4 If you were a team leader in the uniformed public service of your choice, would you want to set targets for your team? Give reasons for your answer.

activity — INDIVIDUAL WORK 2.6

P5

Write a guidance leaflet suitable for a cadet group, describing the different ways of assessing and evaluating team leadership.

activity — INDIVIDUAL WORK 2.7

D2

1 As if you were a trainee in a uniformed public service, write a detailed self-appraisal of your own ability to lead a team. Base it on real team-leading experience.

2 Set out reasoned recommendations for the improvement and development of your leadership skills.

activity — GROUP WORK 2.8

P6

Give a presentation using visual aids and/or role-play where appropriate, suitable for school leavers, describing different types of teams and the stages of team development, including barriers to effective performance.

Teamwork involves a learning process, which is cyclical in nature, as the diagram below shows.

The diagram can be applied to any activity in which learning takes place, and learning can start and finish at any of the stages (in rectangles). The learning which takes place in teamwork follows this cycle just as much as any other kind of learning does.

Imagine that a police team receives information that drug-dealing is going on at a particular night club. Evidence comes in and, after a period of abstraction and generalisation (thinking about the evidence), the team leader concludes that drugs are being bought and sold at that club. The leader then tests the **hypothesis** (theory that drugs are being sold) by sending in a plain clothes officer to do a 'sting', posing as a drug-buyer and buying a quantity of a drug from a dealer at the club. Assuming that the sting is successful and someone is selling drugs, the concrete part of the cycle – in this case a drugs raid – takes place. After the drugs raid, there is a period of reflection and observation in which the team is debriefed and the team leader reflects on how the raid went, whether it was successful in catching all the dealers, whether sufficient evidence for a prosecution was obtained, and how well the team carried out the raid. At the same time, the team leader reflects on how well or badly they planned and directed the operation and what they personally should learn from it, in order to be a better leader in the future.

Businessballs.com – see website for more information on Kolb's learning styles
www.businessballs.com

Fig 2.8 The learning cycle (based on Kolb, 1984)

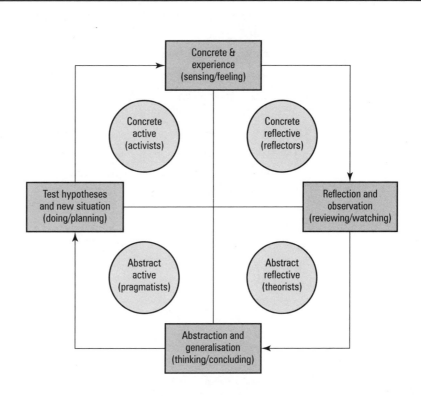

Progress Check

1. Explain briefly three leadership styles.

2. What are the advantages and drawbacks of (a) authoritarian leadership and (b) democratic leadership?

3. What are the advantages and drawbacks of (a) task-oriented leadership and (b) people-oriented leadership?

4. List all the people to whom a team leader has a responsibility.

5. Why is nearly all uniformed public service work done in teams?

6. What is a multi-agency team?

7. What are the particular difficulties or challenges of leading a multi-agency team?

8. Name 10 leadership qualities.

9. Name the three kinds of reading and explain what they are.

10. Give four features of good organisation.

11. What is the difference between organisation and planning?

12. Name the five levels in Maslow's 'pyramid of human needs' and give an example of how each need might be used to motivate a team in the uniformed public services.

13. Name three ways in which teamwork benefits an individual team member and three ways in which it benefits the organisation.

14. How do you check whether somebody understands what you have said to them?

15. What is a debriefing and what can a team leader get out of it?

16. What is appraisal and how is it used in the uniformed public services?

17. What are the three main kinds of feedback that a team leader should give to a team during a team briefing?

18. Give 10 rules of good time management.

19. State four ways in which a team leader can respond to a challenge to authority.

20. What are the advantages and drawbacks of target setting?

UNIT 3

Citizenship, Contemporary Society and the Public Services

This unit covers:

- How different views of citizenship have developed in contemporary society
- The legal and humanitarian rights that 'citizenship' provides for an individual in the United Kingdom (UK) and its impact upon the public services
- How the qualities of a 'good citizen' may be demonstrated in contemporary society and the benefits of these qualities to society and the uniformed public services
- How national and international current affairs are highlighted by the media and influence the public services

Citizenship is an important word for the uniformed public services. It means different things to different people, and the first part of this unit is concerned with sorting out its meanings and why it matters so much. The unit then looks in depth at British citizenship, exploring the human rights and legal protection that British citizens have in Britain and the rights and freedoms that they enjoy.

The third part of the unit examines good citizenship: what it means, how good citizens try to help other people, and the relationship between good citizenship and the uniformed public services. Finally, the unit looks at how international events and the way they are dealt with in the media affect the British public services and their work.

grading criteria

To achieve a **Pass** grade the evidence must show that the learner is able to:	To achieve a **Merit** grade the evidence must show that, in addition to the pass criteria, the learner is able to:	To achieve a **Distinction** grade the evidence must show that, in addition to the pass and merit criteria, the learner is able to:
P1 describe different views of citizenship in contemporary society Pg 100	**M1** analyse different views of citizenship in contemporary society Pg 100	**D1** evaluate different views of citizenship in contemporary society, identifying how they affect the public services Pg 102
P2 describe two legal and two humanitarian rights of citizens in the UK, identifying how they affect the public services Pg 116	**M2** explain the legal and humanitarian rights of citizens in the UK, identifying how they affect the public services Pg 117	

▶

91

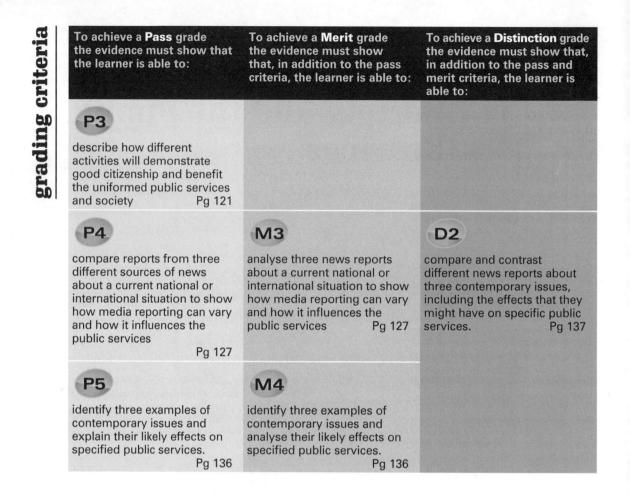

grading criteria	To achieve a **Pass** grade the evidence must show that the learner is able to:	To achieve a **Merit** grade the evidence must show that, in addition to the pass criteria, the learner is able to:	To achieve a **Distinction** grade the evidence must show that, in addition to the pass and merit criteria, the learner is able to:
	P3 describe how different activities will demonstrate good citizenship and benefit the uniformed public services and society Pg 121		
	P4 compare reports from three different sources of news about a current national or international situation to show how media reporting can vary and how it influences the public services Pg 127	**M3** analyse three news reports about a current national or international situation to show how media reporting can vary and how it influences the public services Pg 127	**D2** compare and contrast different news reports about three contemporary issues, including the effects that they might have on specific public services. Pg 137
	P5 identify three examples of contemporary issues and explain their likely effects on specified public services. Pg 136	**M4** identify three examples of contemporary issues and analyse their likely effects on specified public services. Pg 136	

How different views of citizenship have developed in contemporary society

Citizenship is a complex issue, which is why a whole unit of your BTEC syllabus is given over to it, but the basic meaning is fairly clear.

case study 3.1 — Citizenship

In its simplest meaning, 'citizenship' is used to refer to the status of being a citizen – that is, to being a member of a particular political community or state. Citizenship in this sense brings with it certain rights and responsibilities that are defined in law, such as the right to vote, the responsibility to pay tax and so on. It is sometimes referred to as nationality, and is what is meant when someone talks about 'applying for', 'getting', or being 'refused' citizenship.

(Source: *CPD Handbook on Citizenship*, © Citizenship Foundation 2006)

activity
GROUP WORK

1   Why is it a good thing to be a citizen of a country?
2   Do you think that people working in a British uniformed public service should always be British citizens? Explain your view.

Different views of citizenship

Citizenship is:

- having a nationality which is legally valid and enables you to have a passport
- having certain legal rights and responsibilities which are denied to people who are not nationals of that country
- a series of moral and social qualities which include helping other people and the community, and avoiding antisocial behaviour.

Legal view, e.g. a person with rights of residence

The basic Home Office view of citizenship is as follows:

'People who are closely connected with the United Kingdom (including the Channel Islands and the Isle of Man) and, in most cases, the British overseas territories […] are British citizens. British citizens have the right to live here permanently and are free to leave and re-enter the United Kingdom at any time.'

(Source: www.ind.homeoffice.gov.uk)

The rules regarding citizenship are laid down in the British Nationality Act 1981, which came into force in 1983. According to this Act, people are British either by birth or by **naturalisation**.

Birth

People born in the UK before 1983 are automatically British citizens by birth (except for children whose parents were working here as **diplomats** at the time they were born).

Anybody born in Britain after 1 January 1983 is British if at the time of their birth their parents were married and

- one of their parents was a British citizen or
- one of their parents was allowed to stay in Britain permanently.

If their parents were not married, British nationality could only come through the mother. This may change, because the Nationality Immigration and Asylum Act 2002 allows nationality to be inherited from the father, but so far (2006) this has not happened.

Naturalisation

This means obtaining British citizenship legally later on in life. The laws are complex, and may change from time to time, but the situation in 2006 was as follows.

Applicants must:

- have lived legally in the United Kingdom for five years
- be 18 or over
- not be of unsound mind
- be of good character
- know sufficient English, Welsh or Scottish Gaelic
- stay closely connected with the United Kingdom.

Similar rules exist for wives/husbands.

From April 2007 it is also compulsory for people who want to remain indefinitely in the UK to take a citizenship test. This involves showing a basic knowledge of British history, laws and society, and includes demonstrating a reasonable level of English (ESOL3). There are also 'citizenship ceremonies' for people who have passed the test and achieved British citizenship.

Department of Work and Pensions – see website for information on National Insurance

www.dwp.gov.uk

Identity and Passport Service

www.identitycards.gov.uk

UKvisas – see website for information about visas and work permits

www.ukvisas.gov.uk

National Foundation for Educational Research – see website for citizenship education

www.nfer.ac.uk

What Is Citizenship? © Citizenship Foundation 2006 (citizenship education and the theory behind it)

Home Office: British Citizenship – see website for good stuff on citizenship tests

www.lifeintheuktest.gov.uk

Home Office: Border and Immigration Agency

www.workingintheuk.gov.uk

Views of citizenship by different organisations in society

Nearly everybody has opinions of some sort on the meaning of citizenship – and the same is true of organisations. Broadly speaking the uniformed public services, working as they do for the government, are in full agreement with the government (Home Office) view of citizenship. They also have to follow the government's laws about whom they may or may not employ.

Specific public services

Employers, including the public services, have to take citizenship into account when people apply for work. A person with full British citizenship satisfies the nationality requirements for all the uniformed public services. Different uniformed public services have different nationality requirements for applicants, as the next case study shows.

Religious groups

Religious groups, including the main world religions, especially Christianity and Islam, are essentially international in nature. Most religions, even small ones, do not have any form of citizenship requirement for members. However, there are subtle differences. Some are mentioned below.

Established churches

The Church of England (Anglican Church) is traditionally an arm ('estate') of the British government. Since King Henry VIII broke with the Catholic Church in the sixteenth century, the head of the English church has been the Archbishop of Canterbury, and the church has, in a sense, been the national church of England.

The Church of England

www.cofe.anglican.org

Under UK **blasphemy** laws, which have never been used since 1977 and may be repealed (got rid of) before long, the Church of England is protected from offensive or abusive insults which might lead to a breach of the peace. Other churches and religions do not have this legal protection.

case study 3.2 — Nationality requirements for uniformed public services

Table 3.1 Nationality requirements for uniformed public services

Service	Nationality (citizenship) requirement
Police	You must be a British citizen, an **EC/EEA** national or a Commonwealth citizen or foreign national with no restrictions on your stay in the United Kingdom. Foreign nationals and UK citizens who have lived abroad may have to wait some time for security and vetting clearance. All applicants have to be vetted to the same standard before appointment. (www.policecouldyou.co.uk)
Maritime and Coastguard Agency	International applicants can apply, but must first satisfy Home Office entry, permit and **visa** requirements. (www.mcga.gov.uk)
Army	You can join the British Army from the UK or overseas providing you meet the required nationality criteria. Joining from the UK You must be a resident of the United Kingdom or the Irish Republic, and preferably have lived there for a minimum of five years immediately prior to making your application to join the army. Nationality You must also be one of the following: a British citizen a citizen of the British dependent territories a British overseas citizen a British subject under the British Nationality Act 1981 a citizen of an independent Commonwealth country a British Protected Person a citizen of the Irish Republic. Joining from overseas In addition to fulfilling one of the nationality criteria listed above, you must be eligible to hold a full British or Irish passport. If you are from another country, you must hold a full passport from that country. Your passport must show that you have an **immigrant status** in the UK that is valid for a minimum of four years. All applicants must have the right of entry into the UK. You will normally be eligible if you hold UK, Commonwealth or Irish citizenship, and you have a passport permitting you rights of residence within the UK until the start of your **commissioning course**. You must show that you have assimilated into the UK. This normally includes a requirement to undertake a period of **residency**.
London Ambulance Service	No nationality criteria – **Home Office rules** apply.

activity — INDIVIDUAL WORK

1 Why are nationality requirements stricter for the police and the army than they are for the coastguards and for the ambulance service?

2 Using the internet or other sources, find out the nationality requirements for other public services which interest you.

case study 3.3   Her Majesty the Queen

Her Majesty the Queen is the Supreme Governor of the Church of England, and she also has a unique and special relationship with the Church of Scotland, which is a Free Church. In the Church of England, she appoints archbishops, bishops and deans of cathedrals on the advice of the Prime Minister. The two archbishops and 24 senior bishops sit in the House of Lords, making a major contribution to Parliament's work.

activity GROUP WORK

Do you approve, disapprove, or feel completely indifferent to these links between the Church of England and the government? Discuss this within your group and give your reasons.

Sikhs and Jews
Sikhs and Jews and their religions are protected under the Race Relations Act 1976. Their religions are protected by the Act because it is considered that only people who are ethnically Indian are Sikhs, and only people who are ethnically Jewish follow Judaism. Muslims do not have this protection because they originate from many different countries and cannot be considered to be a 'race'.

Religious groups with links to political or nationalist movements
Many religious groups have in the past become linked with political or nationalist movements, and this tends to build a link (often unofficial) between religion and citizenship. In Northern Ireland the Protestants are traditionally in favour of political union with Britain, while the Catholics are traditionally in favour of a political union with Ireland – a traditionally Catholic country. The situation in Iraq is being made more unstable by the opposition of **Shia** and **Sunni Muslims**, who are ethnically different from each other (the Shia have links with Iran, while the Sunni are either Kurds – a separate ethnic group – or Arabs, ethnically closer to the people of Jordan and Kuwait).

Pressure groups

Pressure groups are formed by people who are concerned about some form of injustice or a lack of public awareness about certain important issues. Very often they are unhappy about some aspect of government policy. Their aims are to raise public awareness of problems, help people who suffer from the problems they have highlighted, and – above all – to use the media to put pressure on Parliament to change the laws.

Liberty
The motto of Liberty is 'Protecting **civil liberties** promoting human rights'. This London-based organisation is one of the main groups protesting against new government laws intended to make it more difficult for people to settle in Britain, especially if they are asylum seekers or come from outside Europe.

See page 122 for more on Liberty.

Liberty – a useful and interesting website
www.liberty-human-rights.org.uk
MigrationWatch – website contains immigration information and statistics, but the tone is biased
www.migrationwatchuk.org

Amnesty International
Amnesty International (AI) is a worldwide movement of people who campaign for internationally recognised human rights. It has branches in many countries.

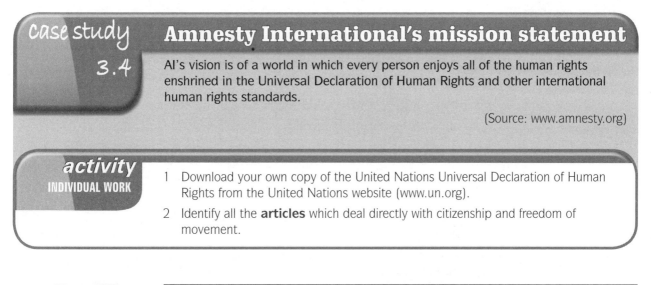

case study

3.4

Amnesty International's mission statement

AI's vision is of a world in which every person enjoys all of the human rights enshrined in the Universal Declaration of Human Rights and other international human rights standards.

(Source: www.amnesty.org)

activity
INDIVIDUAL WORK

1   Download your own copy of the United Nations Universal Declaration of Human Rights from the United Nations website (www.un.org).

2   Identify all the **articles** which deal directly with citizenship and freedom of movement.

Link

See page 103 for more on the United Nations Universal Declaration of Human Rights.

Amnesty International campaigns against cases where citizens are abused or deprived of their **freedoms** in their own or other countries. It supports individuals against the governments who abuse them (and there are human rights abuses in every country in the world). It is independent of any national government, operates all over the world and focuses on the rights of citizens which are often ignored or trampled on by their own or other governments.

A similar organisation, also well worth studying, is Human Rights Watch.

Amnesty International
www.amnesty.org
Human Rights Watch
www.hrw.org

Friends of the Earth
Unlike Liberty and Amnesty International, Friends of the Earth is primarily an environmental protest group.

Friends of the Earth see us as citizens of the world, rather than of nations. This is because environmental threats such as global warming, pollution and the holes in the ozone layer are caused by all countries and affect all countries. They see citizenship as an international duty of care for other people, and the organisation is an international one with branches in many countries. Their idea of citizenship is law abiding: they make it clear that they want to work within the law, not break it.

Friends of the Earth
www.foe.co.uk

Greenpeace
Greenpeace is an international organisation with aims that are broadly similar to those of Friends of the Earth. Part of its mission statement is shown on page 99.

case study 3.5   Values and beliefs

Friends of the Earth want a world where protection of the environment and meeting everyone's needs go hand-in-hand.

Three beliefs underpin our work:

■ **We must look after our planet**

Live within the limits of the natural world. This means polluting and using less.

■ **Everyone has a right to a fair share**

Meet our needs – and keep the environment safe – now and in the future. This is environmental justice.

■ **Realistic alternatives are possible**

Only grow the economy in ways that focus on quality of life and protection of the planet.

The means to these ends is just as important. **We won't compromise** our principles:

■ Work within the law – campaign to change it.

■ Independence from political parties.

■ Don't take money from big companies.

(Source: www.foe.co.uk)

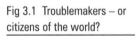

activity
INDIVIDUAL WORK

1 List the advantages and disadvantages of being an apolitical organisation (independent from political parties).

2 List the advantages and disadvantages of not taking money from big companies.

Fig 3.1 Troublemakers – or citizens of the world?

case study
3.6

Greenpeace

Greenpeace's goal is to ensure the ability of the earth to nurture life in all its diversity. Greenpeace organises public campaigns:

- for the protection of oceans and ancient forests
- for the phasing-out of fossil fuels and the promotion of renewable energies in order to stop **climate change**
- for the elimination of toxic chemicals
- against the release of genetically modified organisms into nature
- for nuclear disarmament and an end to nuclear contamination.

Greenpeace does not solicit or accept funding from governments, corporations or political parties. Greenpeace neither seeks nor accepts donations which could compromise its independence, aims, objectives or integrity. Greenpeace relies on the voluntary donations of individual supporters, and on grant-support from foundations.

Greenpeace is committed to the principles of non-violence, political independence and internationalism. In exposing threats to the environment and in working to find solutions, Greenpeace has no permanent allies or enemies.

(Source: www.greenpeace.org.uk)

activity
GROUP WORK

1 Identify and discuss the main differences between this statement and the one from Friends of the Earth.

2 What risks are there that environmental protest groups might become violent in the future?

Greenpeace
www.greenpeace.org.uk

Government initiatives to identify citizenship

Since the late 1990s the British government has tried to encourage the development of an idea of citizenship, especially among young people. Reasons for this include:

- the need to **integrate** a society which is increasingly made up of separate groups of people – especially people from ethnic, cultural and religious **minorities**
- a feeling among ordinary people that crime levels are always going up (even though this is not true according to official crime statistics)
- an ongoing decline in the numbers of people who vote in elections.

Some strategies designed to increase a sense of citizenship are given below:

National Curriculum

The National Curriculum is a set of subjects which must be taught to specific levels in primary and secondary schools. It was introduced in 1988 with the Education Reform Act. At that time citizenship was not a compulsory subject, and the main motive for introducing the National Curriculum was to correct an apparent decline in literacy and numeracy standards.

Citizenship was introduced as a compulsory subject in 2002. The Qualifications and Curriculum Authority (QCA) has this to say about it.

case study
3.7

Citizenship education

Citizenship education equips children and young people with the knowledge, understanding and skills to play an active part in society as informed and critical citizens who are socially and morally responsible. It aims to give them the confidence and conviction that they can act with others, have influence and make a difference in their communities.

(Source: www.qca.org.uk)

activity
GROUP WORK

Discuss your own experience of citizenship education. In your view, has citizenship education so far had the effects that the QCA outlines above?

activity
GROUP WORK
3.1

P1

M1

Produce a leaflet for a diversity awareness course for public service trainees, including views of citizenship from government departments, public service recruitment material, other concerned groups, and citizenship education used in school (include a description of 'good citizenship'). Your leaflet should include a brief analysis of each view, explaining what it means and why it is used in each case.

Citizenship training

After November 2005, people wishing to obtain British citizenship had to take a test on 'Life in the UK'.

Adult classes

The level of English expected to be reached by new British citizens is called ESOL Entry 3; it covers the basic language requirements for living and working here. (ESOL stands for English for Speakers of Other Languages.)

Further education colleges and other centres run classes in ESOL and in citizenship to prepare people for taking the 'Life in the UK' test. You will be able to find out more about these by contacting the person who runs them in your college, or by picking up leaflets at the local Citizens Advice.

Community projects

There are many **community projects** in Britain whose work is connected directly or indirectly with citizenship. Those which are directly connected work with ethnic minority groups, migrants, immigrants and asylum seekers.

Community projects are sometimes set up by central government, sometimes by local government, and sometimes by local people. Some of them are self-help groups set up by minorities who feel that they need an organisation to help them socially and in other ways. To search for funding and to extend their work, groups enter into partnerships with local government, the public services, educational institutions or anyone else they feel may be of help. What they lose in independence they gain in financial support.

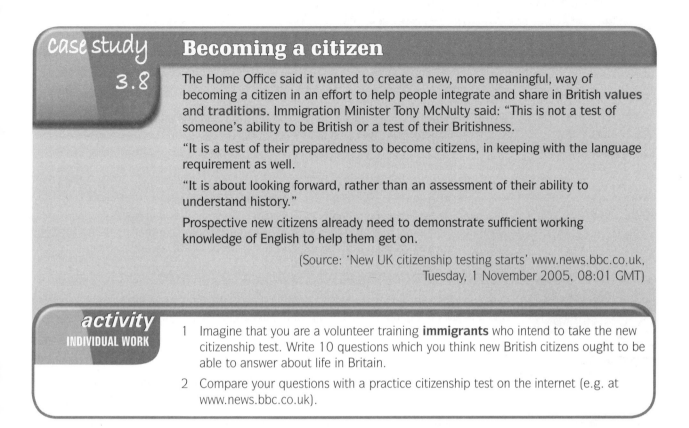

case study 3.8 — Becoming a citizen

The Home Office said it wanted to create a new, more meaningful, way of becoming a citizen in an effort to help people integrate and share in British **values** and **traditions**. Immigration Minister Tony McNulty said: "This is not a test of someone's ability to be British or a test of their Britishness.

"It is a test of their preparedness to become citizens, in keeping with the language requirement as well.

"It is about looking forward, rather than an assessment of their ability to understand history."

Prospective new citizens already need to demonstrate sufficient working knowledge of English to help them get on.

(Source: 'New UK citizenship testing starts' www.news.bbc.co.uk, Tuesday, 1 November 2005, 08:01 GMT)

activity — INDIVIDUAL WORK

1 Imagine that you are a volunteer training **immigrants** who intend to take the new citizenship test. Write 10 questions which you think new British citizens ought to be able to answer about life in Britain.

2 Compare your questions with a practice citizenship test on the internet (e.g. at www.news.bbc.co.uk).

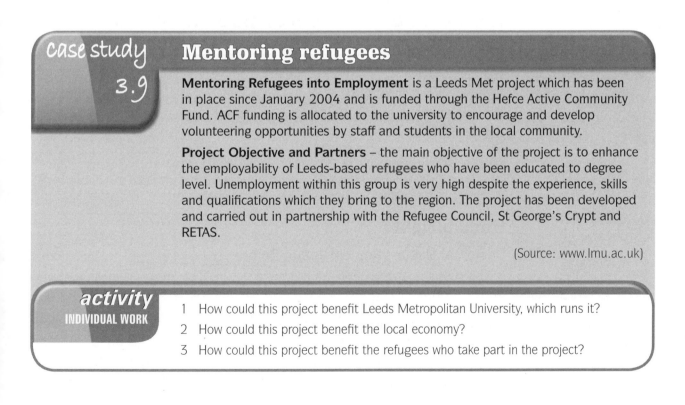

case study 3.9 — Mentoring refugees

Mentoring Refugees into Employment is a Leeds Met project which has been in place since January 2004 and is funded through the Hefce Active Community Fund. ACF funding is allocated to the university to encourage and develop volunteering opportunities by staff and students in the local community.

Project Objective and Partners – the main objective of the project is to enhance the employability of Leeds-based **refugees** who have been educated to degree level. Unemployment within this group is very high despite the experience, skills and qualifications which they bring to the region. The project has been developed and carried out in partnership with the Refugee Council, St George's Crypt and RETAS.

(Source: www.lmu.ac.uk)

activity — INDIVIDUAL WORK

1 How could this project benefit Leeds Metropolitan University, which runs it?

2 How could this project benefit the local economy?

3 How could this project benefit the refugees who take part in the project?

Current concepts of the citizen as a national or global citizen

Globalisation is the idea that human activities influence and are influenced by the whole world, and not just the local area where we live. Much of our food comes from Europe and beyond; much of our culture comes from America; clothes come from China; energy comes from France and Russia; multinational companies operate in many parts of the world; and most of us are travelling far more than our parents and grandparents ever did. Politically, many of our laws come from Europe. We are at war in Iraq and Afghanistan because of alliances with the USA and NATO, and our armed forces are working in several countries to support the United Nations. Because Britain had an empire in the nineteenth century, because it has a relatively high standard of living, and because English is widely spoken in other parts of the world, many people come to England to work, to get education, or to escape persecution in less stable countries. Last but not least, there are environmental issues such as global warming. All these factors are making British people see themselves as citizens of the world as well as citizens of the UK and of Europe.

activity
INDIVIDUAL WORK
3.2

D1

Write an article for a human rights magazine, assessing different ideas of citizenship and how they affect the work, outlook and perceptions of the public services.

The legal and humanitarian rights that 'citizenship' provides for an individual in the UK and its impact upon the public services

Legal rights are rights that we have under the law. They include things like the right to work, the right to claim benefits, the right to open a bank account, and so on. Humanitarian rights – more often called 'human rights' – are rights which refer to having decent and fair treatment from the government, our employers, our teachers, and other people in general. Citizenship, as far as this outcome is concerned, means being a British citizen – having the right to stay in Britain permanently and to have a British passport. The impact on the public services comes from the fact that (a) citizens have legal, human and **democratic rights** which public services must uphold and (b) non-citizens have fewer legal rights but still have human rights.

Human rights

Universal Declaration of Human Rights

The Universal Declaration of Human Rights is a statement of human rights which was agreed by the United Nations in 1948. It was drawn up following the terrible human rights abuses of the Second World War, and in particular the **genocide** of the **Holocaust** – the ultimate human rights crime – when six million Jews were put to death by the Nazis.

The Universal Declaration of Human Rights is the basis of all the human rights documents that have followed it, including the rights listed under the Human Rights Act 1998. Since 1948, our view of human rights has changed slightly: the Universal Declaration has nothing to say about gay and lesbian people, nor about ageism – yet these too are human rights issues. It is well worth downloading your own copy of the Universal Declaration of Human Rights: it is clear, down to earth and not very long.

Universal Declaration of Human Rights
www.un.org

The Universal Declaration of Human Rights has 30 paragraphs, called articles, each stating a human right. The most general and basic ones come at the beginning; the later ones are more specialised but still important.

Here is a brief summary:

1. All people are free and equal
2. The Declaration applies to everybody whatever their race, sex, religion, politics, etc.
3. It applies in all countries
4. Everybody has a right to life, liberty and security
5. Slavery must be banned
6. There should be no torture or cruel punishment
7. No one is above or outside the law
8. Victims should be able to get justice through the law
9. Arrest, detention or exile must be for a valid reason
10. Everyone accused of crime has the right to a fair, public trial
11. All accused persons are innocent until proved guilty and cannot be convicted retrospectively
12. The right to privacy
13. The right to freedom of movement
14. The right to seek asylum
15. The right to have a nationality
16. The right to marriage, families and family protection from the government
17. The right to own property
18. The right to freedom of thought, belief and worship
19. The right to freedom of speech and expression
20. The right to meet peacefully and form organisations – but not to be forced to join any organisation
21. The right to vote, to be served and protected by public services – and to work in them – and the right to a secret vote in free elections
22. The right to social security, cultural freedoms and personal development
23. The right to work, to equal pay for equal work, to fair pay and to join trade unions
24. The right to rest, leisure and holidays
25. The right to special care and protection for mothers and children
26. The right to a free education which encourages tolerance and world peace
27. The right to culture, science and the arts
28. The right to international peace and stability
29. Laws should support the community, uphold the principles of the United Nations, and should only be used to stop people from making others suffer
30. No person or government should undermine the above human rights.

Fig 3.2 Why human rights matter

United Nations

The United Nations (UN) is an international body with 192 member countries. Its headquarters is in New York, but it aims at political neutrality. The UN was set up in 1945, after the Second World War, as a peacekeeping organisation. The **constitution** (main laws) is set out in the United Nations Charter. This begins with four major aims:

- 'to save succeeding generations from the scourge of war, which twice in our lifetime has brought untold sorrow to mankind, and
- 'to reaffirm faith in fundamental human rights, in the dignity and worth of the human person, in the equal rights of men and women and of nations large and small, and
- 'to establish conditions under which justice and respect for the obligations arising from treaties and other sources of international law can be maintained, and
- 'to promote social progress and better standards of life in larger freedom.'

(Source: www.un.org)

The top official of the UN is the Secretary-General, Ban Ki-moon, a Korean.

The main body in the UN is the General Assembly. The issues that it debates and makes decisions on include:

- peace and security
- economic growth and sustainable development
- development of Africa
- human rights
- humanitarian assistance
- justice and international law
- disarmament
- drugs, crime, international terrorism
- organisational and administrative matters.

However, the most powerful body in the UN is probably the Security Council. It has five permanent members – China, France, Russia, Britain and the USA – and 10 non-permanent members.

The Security Council makes resolutions to act in possible or actual conflicts. Resolution 1441, passed in 2002, is the most famous recent one; it contains the words: 'Recognizing the threat Iraq's non-compliance with Council resolutions and proliferation of weapons of mass destruction and long-range missiles poses to international peace and security' and concludes by saying 'that the Council has repeatedly warned Iraq that it will face serious consequences as a result of its continued **violations** of its obligations'. UN resolutions are often ignored, but these words were used to justify the US and British invasion and occupation of Iraq in 2003.

Individual and group beliefs/values

Individual values are the beliefs that each one of us has about what is right or wrong. Group values are the moral beliefs and principles which we share with other people in our group. ('Group' here can be any number of people with whom we are connected – e.g. our families, our **social class**, our ethnic group, our fellow workers or students, believers in the same religion, etc.) Both individual and group values are essential to our happiness: they make us what we are; they bind society together; and they give our lives meaning.

As citizens, we should be able to express our individual and group values. We have a right and a duty to fulfil ourselves as individuals; and it is to the benefit of the group that we do so, because we can then use our abilities and understanding to help the group. Our individual values mean that each of us is different from the other; in other words, every person is unique and has something unique to offer the rest of society. However, our group values mean that we can work with others and cooperate in tasks and organisations which achieve infinitely more than an unaided individual ever could.

Although individual values are usually helpful to society, they can cause problems – serious ones sometimes – by threatening the well-being or even the survival of the group. This matters in the uniformed public services, where loyalty is essential and group members have to work closely together. The next case study is an example of a dangerous conflict between individual and group values.

case study 3.10   **British soldier accused of spying**

Thursday, 21 December 2006, 18:06 GMT

A British soldier has been charged with passing on secret information "to the enemy", believed to be Iran.

Daniel James, 44, confirmed only his name, before the rest of Wednesday's hearing at Westminster Magistrates' Court, in London, was held in secret.

He was later revealed to be a corporal who acted as an interpreter for the Nato commander in Afghanistan.

He has been charged under the Official Secrets Act. The MoD and the Crown prosecutors refused to comment.

BBC security correspondent Frank Gardner said Corporal Daniel James was "incredibly well placed" as interpreter for General David Richards and privy to every conversation the commander had had with Afghans speaking Dari.

"So if the charges do stick, if they are accurate, then this would be potentially a disaster for Nato because their operation in Afghanistan is potentially compromised," he said.

(Source: www.news.bbc.co.uk)

activity
GROUP WORK

1 If the accusation is correct, how do Daniel James's values differ from those of his army colleagues?

2 What motives might he have had for his actions?

3 Are there any imaginable circumstances in which his actions could be morally right?

The social structure

In the last 20 years views of Britain's social structure have changed considerably, and the old Registrar General's scale describing social class is not used. The present system, which originated in 2001 and was used in the 2001 census, is shown in the table.

Table 3.2 Socioeconomic classification

The National Statistics Socioeconomic Classification Analytic Classes	
1	Higher managerial and professional occupations
	1.1 Large employers and higher managerial occupations
	1.2 Higher professional occupations
2	Lower managerial and professional occupations
3	Intermediate occupations
4	Small employers and own account workers
5	Lower supervisory and technical occupations
6	Semi-routine occupations
7	Routine occupations
8	Never worked and long-term unemployed

For complete coverage, the three categories 'Students', 'Occupations not stated or inadequately described', and 'Not classifiable for other reasons' are added as 'Not classified'.

(Source: www.statistics.gov.uk)

Most people in Britain are within sections 3–7 of this classification.

Social structure is usually described in **socioeconomic** terms – in other words, by the occupation type of the main wage-earner in the household. The police, army officers and teachers would be in sections 2 and 3; firefighters would be section 3; and infantry soldiers would be in 6 or 7. In many surveys people make their own choice, so this is a rough guide giving an overall picture, rather than a clear-cut system.

Society is structured along other lines as well – sex, **ethnicity**, religion, age, etc., but although these are important they are less significant for the uniformed public services than the socioeconomic classification. Citizenship is not in itself a socioeconomic factor, but most migrant workers and many new immigrants are in groups 6, 7 or 'Not classified'.

remember
Many people now think of themselves as classless – in order to get away from the class-based discrimination of the past.

National Statistics Online – full of government facts and statistics; also information on social class, i.e. socioeconomic classification
www.statistics.gov.uk

Directgov – for general, down-to-earth government information
www.direct.gov.uk

Social groups

Social groups are any large collections or classes of people who have beliefs or behaviour (values and **norms**) or some other important feature in common. They include:

- economic and occupational groups
- women
- men
- young people
- old people
- ethnic minority groups
- gays and lesbians
- disabled people
- religious or faith groups
- migrants
- asylum seekers.

Many of these groups have suffered discrimination – and some still do. Discrimination limits full citizenship and undermines the sufferer's human rights. In Britain, a number of important anti-discrimination laws have been passed since 1970. Here are the main ones:

- Equal Pay Act 1970
- Sex Discrimination Act 1975
- Race Relations Act 1976
- Disability Discrimination Act 1995
- Protection from Harassment Act 1997
- Human Rights Act 1998
- National Minimum Wage Act 1998
- Disability Rights Commission Act 1999
- Sex Discrimination (**Gender Reassignment**) **Regulations** 1999
- Special Educational Needs and Disability Act 2001
- Employment Act 2002
- Race Relations Amendment Act 2003
- Employment Equality (Sexual Orientation) Regulations 2003
- Employment Equality (Religion or Belief) Regulations 2003
- Employment Equality (Sex Discrimination) Regulations 2005
- Disability Discrimination Act 2005
- The Employment Equality (Age) Regulations 2006
- Equality Act 2006.

Asylum seekers

Asylum seekers are people who flee their country because they are being persecuted and try to settle in another country. Under the **Geneva Convention** and other international laws they are allowed to do this, and many countries, including Britain, have signed up to the Conventions and are legally bound to take people who demand and deserve asylum. Until asylum seekers have established (with the Immigration and Nationality Directorate, formerly called the Immigration Service) that they have a right to stay in Britain, they are kept in holding centres. These are rather like prisons, and the asylum seekers' human and individual rights are limited. If their claim for asylum is

remember
The Immigration and Nationality Directorate (IND) changed its name to the Border and Immigration Agency in 2007.

judged to be false, they are liable to **deportation**. Britain has a so-called 'white list' of countries to which, the government believes, unsuccessful asylum seekers can be deported without putting them at undue risk.

Foreign nationals

Foreign nationals are people who are citizens of countries other than Britain. Their citizenship rights depend on where they are coming from, why, and for how long. If they come from outside Europe, they normally need visas or work permits. There is some official distinction between Commonwealth and non-Commonwealth citizens, and indeed between citizens from different Commonwealth countries. People who enter Britain looking for work are often called migrants. As Britain has a need for skilled, hard-working and well-trained workers, some of them are made welcome. Those who are unskilled, or are in Britain illegally (without travel documents etc.) are liable to deportation and do not have citizens' rights in the country.

Home Office: Border and Immigration Agency

www.bia.homeoffice.gov.uk

www.workingintheuk.gov.uk

www.ukvisas.gov.uk

Legal rights

Both the general public and the uniformed public services have legal rights. The rights are entitlements (things that a person can claim). However, with these rights go obligations or duties: i.e. things that must be done; documents that must be provided, etc.

Relevant to the whole question of citizenship are the Immigration Acts: a series of laws designed to manage immigration into the UK. The aim has been to balance the needs of the country with those of would-be immigrants and asylum seekers.

There are people who say, 'Why should immigrants and asylum seekers come into the country at all?' The simple answer is that the country has, from time to time, a need for immigrants in order to build up the workforce, especially now that so many people are reaching retirement age. As for asylum, Britain is bound by an international agreement (the Geneva Conventions) to take people who have fled a country where they are at risk (e.g. Somalia) and are looking for refuge.

To find out more about the Geneva Conventions, the 1951 UN Refugee Convention and the 1967 Protocol, visit the UNHCR website.

www.unhcr.org.uk

Relevant Immigration Acts

Since the 1950s, a large number of laws have been passed to limit immigration. The main ones are:

- **Immigration Act 1971** – the basic immigration Act, laying down the main principles, defining British citizenship and right of abode
- **Immigration Act 1988**
- **Asylum and Immigration Appeals Act 1993** – fingerprinting; housing of asylum seekers and dependants
- **Asylum and Immigration Act 1996** – forced employers to check papers of foreign employees to make sure that they were entitled to stay in the UK
- **Special Immigration Appeals Commission Act 1997** – set up an appeals commission to deal with appeals on immigration issues

- **Human Rights Act 1998** – incorporated the 1950 European Convention on Human Rights into British law; ensures that asylum seekers and immigrants have human rights protections

- **Immigration and Asylum Act 1999** – imposes fines on carriers who bring passengers without the required documents into the UK; established the National Asylum Support Service (NASS), a branch of the Home Office responsible for housing and looking after asylum seekers in the UK (later scrapped)

- **Nationality, Immigration and Asylum Act 2002** – naturalisation – knowledge of language and society; citizenship; citizenship ceremonies; accommodation centres; detention and removal

- **Asylum and Immigration (Treatment of Claimants, etc.) Act 2004** – deals with assisting unlawful immigration, people-trafficking, failed asylum seekers, marriage, removal, detention, deportation, lists of safe countries, etc.

- **European Union (Accessions) Act 2006** – deals with the rights of Bulgarian and Romanian nationals who wish to work in the UK

- **Immigration, Asylum and Nationality Act 2006** – deals with appeals, employment, information, claimants and applicants; reduces the rights of appeal for people who have been refused permission to stay in the country and for people who are being deported – but Britain remains a signatory to the Refugee Convention.

Over the years, the general effect of these Acts has been to make it more difficult for immigrants and would-be asylum seekers to come and live in Britain.

The Acts are supported by Immigration Rules, which are much more precise and explain to immigration officers how the law is to be interpreted and carried out.

Human Rights Act 1998

Fig 3.3 Human Rights Act 1998 – key provisions

(Source: www.dca.gov.uk)

The purpose of the Human Rights Act is to protect British citizens from abuse by the government and other powerful bodies (called **public authorities**) such as the police.

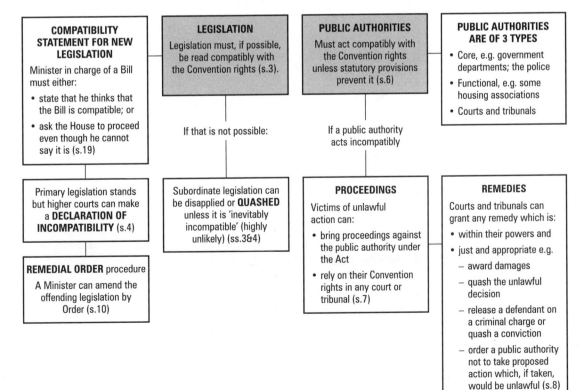

The main points of the Human Rights Act are listed below, under 'articles' and 'protocols'. The articles are:

- right to life
- prohibition of torture
- prohibition of slavery and forced labour
- right to liberty and security
- right to a fair trial
- no punishment without law
- respect for private and family life
- freedom of thought, conscience and religion
- freedom of expression
- freedom of assembly and association
- right to marry
- prohibition of discrimination
- restrictions on the political activity of aliens
- prohibition of abuse of rights
- limitation of use of restrictions on rights.

The protocols are:

- protection of property
- right to education
- right to free elections
- abolition of the death penalty.

The Police and Criminal Evidence Act 1984 and subsequent amendments of legislation

The Police and Criminal Evidence Act 1984, widely known as **PACE**, was brought in to standardise police powers and the ways in which they were allowed to gather evidence. It increased protection for suspects, by laying down rules on how they should be treated, and increased protection for the police, by making them use better documented and more accountable systems for searching, arresting and identifying suspects. The aims were to prevent events like the Brixton Riots (1981), which were the result of heavy-handed and unfair police tactics, and to increase the success rate of police prosecutions, some of which were failing as a result of accusations of dodgy evidence.

The main provisions of PACE giving legal rights to suspects are:

- Suspects must be told the purpose and grounds for the search.
- There are strict rules about **intimate searches** and suspects taking off clothes.
- There must be a reason for searching premises, and a warrant is usually needed.
- The search must be for relevant evidence only.
- Arrested people must be told why they are being arrested, and only necessary force may be used.
- There are strict rules about how long suspects can be kept in police detention before being charged.
- Suspects can see their full official custody record.
- Suspects must have decent treatment while in police custody.
- There is a right to medical treatment, contact with friend or family, and private legal help.

Fig 3.4 The police have to follow the PACE codes of practice

However, there is no true right to silence, and fingerprints can be taken without consent.

Police use the PACE Act in the form of **codes of practice**, which tell them what they can and cannot do at each stage of the search–arrest–charge procedure. These codes of practice are frequently updated and are now available on the Home Office website. They are over 70,000 words long in all. These days, suspects have fewer rights than in 1984, reflecting tougher public attitudes towards criminals.

See Unit 17 in *BTEC National Public Services Book 2* for much more on PACE.

BBC Action Network – campaigning in your local area
www.bbc.co.uk
Home Office: Police
www.police.homeoffice.gov.uk

Documentary records

Citizenship and citizens' rights are a complex matter. Globalisation, the constant flow of people from one country to another, the development of international crime, especially people-trafficking, international inequalities which mean that people from poor countries are desperate to get work in rich countries: all these are serious challenges for the British government. Keeping track of millions of people is a bureaucratic nightmare, especially in these days when modern methods of printing and sophisticated computers make it relatively easy to forge documents and construct false identities.

Without documentary records none of us would be able to prove who we are. These documentary records are sometimes in the form of paper documents, such as passports, and sometimes in the form of documentation kept on computer databases for a host of reasons (e.g. banking, benefits, driving, on-line trading, etc.). An understanding of relevant documentation is vital in many aspects of public service work.

Passports
These are the basic documents required as a proof of citizenship for international travel. Standard passports are issued by the Identity and Passport Service, which is an **executive agency** of the Home Office.

Home Office: Identity and Passport Service

www.passport.gov.uk

Identity cards

Following the passing of the Identity Cards Act in 2006, the government will introduce – over the next few years – identity cards for all British citizens. This is in line with most continental European countries which already have identity cards.

Arguments in favour of national ID cards are that the National Identity Scheme will:

■ help protect cardholders against identity theft and fraud

■ provide a reliable way of checking the identity of people in positions of trust

■ make travelling in Europe easier

■ provide a secure way of applying for financial products and making financial transactions, including those made over the internet

■ offer a secure and convenient way of proving your age

■ help to confirm your eligibility for public services and benefits – and reduce fraud relating to these services and benefits

■ help in the prevention of organised crime and terrorism

■ help combat illegal working and reduce illegal immigration to the UK

■ allow the police more quickly to identify suspects and people they arrest (www. identitycards.gov.uk).

Opponents of the scheme believe that:

■ It is a waste of money.

■ It goes against civil liberties because it increases the power of the state over the individual.

■ The cards will easily be forged, which will lead to even more identity fraud than there is at present.

Birth certificates

A birth certificate is a document recording the birth of a baby. It gives details of when and where the baby was born, who the parent(s) are, and the baby's name. The baby has to be registered within 42 days of birth. Registration can be done by the mother at the hospital, or at a register office. The hospital will also inform the register office when babies are born. Birth certificates are needed at various times in life: when the child starts school, when a passport is required, to obtain a driving licence, when getting married, and sometimes when applying to work in the uniformed public services.

General Register Office – see website for official information on births, marriages and deaths

www.gro.gov.uk

National Insurance

National Insurance is a compulsory government scheme in which people put money towards benefits or their retirement by paying regular contributions during their working life. Payments start at age 16 and go on to retirement age (65 for men, 60 for women – although this will change). When joining the scheme you have to prove your identity, and you get a personal number which stays with you throughout life. National Insurance is for British citizens and anybody with right of residence in Britain.

Visas and work permits

Visas give a right to visit the UK; work permits give the right to work here. Visas (officially called 'entry clearance') are required for citizens of countries other than those in the European Economic Area (EEA), the USA, Canada, Australia, New Zealand, and some other industrialised nations such as Japan and South Korea. Citizens of nearly all the other countries, from Afghanistan to Zimbabwe, require visas.

The arrangements for these are complex. Rights depend on where applicants come from, what their purpose is in coming to Britain and whether they have dependants. People from the EEA, which includes most EU countries and some non-EU European countries, such as Norway and Switzerland, have unrestricted rights of access to Britain. People from Poland, Lithuania, Estonia, Latvia, Slovenia, Slovakia, Hungary and the Czech Republic have to follow procedures for the Workers Registration Scheme if they get a job in the UK. Romania and Bulgaria have, for the time being (2007), special arrangements which make it more difficult for their nationals to work in the UK.

www.workingintheuk.gov.uk

Home Office: Immigration and Nationality Directorate – see website for immigration rules

www.ind.homeoffice.gov.uk

Data protection

We have already said that modern citizenship is bureaucratic in that it involves using documents and storing information about people. As this information is written down or kept in computer databases, it can be stolen or misused. To reduce this risk, to protect our privacy, which is a human right, and to build public confidence about government agencies and businesses that want to collect information about us, two laws called **Data Protection** Acts have been introduced: one in 1984 and one in 1998, which replaced the earlier Act.

Ministry of Justice – see website for full summary of data protection law

www.justice.gov.uk

Residency and citizenship

People who are citizens of Britain by birth (due to their parentage) have a right of residency in the UK.

However, foreign nationals living in Britain have to go through a process called naturalisation to become British citizens. This is dependent upon living legally in Britain for five years, of which the last of those years allows the person indefinite leave to remain in Britain. It is also dependent on being over 18 and 'of **good character**'. Obtaining citizenship is easier if the applicant is married to a British citizen, but it is necessary to be of good character, to be settled in Britain, and to have lived in Britain legally for three years. To become naturalised the person has to fill in forms, pass a citizenship exam and take a citizenship **pledge** at an official ceremony.

Impact on public services

The fact that citizens have rights has a major effect on public service work. The uniformed public services have a lot of power, and there is always the risk that they will abuse it – especially under a bad government. In the past, there have been horrifying examples of what can happen when citizens have no rights and the public services can do what they like. The worst case of all was in the Second World War when six million Jews were killed by the public servants of Nazi Germany – who, at their trials after the war, said that they did it because they were 'following orders'. Now, 60 years later, governments understand the importance of caring for their citizens. There are laws to protect them; and, under a democratic system with '**checks and balances**' and proper accountability, the uniformed public services work to uphold people's rights and freedoms rather than abuse them.

Civil rights

This means 'citizens' rights'. In practice, civil rights are much the same thing as human rights. '**Civil rights**' is a phrase that was used in the USA in the 1950s, 60s and 70s, when black Americans were struggling for equality with white Americans. It means fair treatment, without discrimination. In Britain, there has been a similar if less violent struggle against racism, sexism, and other kinds of discrimination – and in favour of **social justice**.

A raft of major anti-discrimination laws has changed the nature of public service work and the public services' relationship with the people whom they serve. Through police, fire and rescue and health authorities, the services cooperate with local people and work hard to satisfy their needs. Within their own organisations, the uniformed public services promote equal opportunities, in order to reflect the diversity of the society in which they work – and in the process do their jobs more effectively.

> **remember**
> British anti-discrimination laws are still widely criticised by minorities for being muddled and ineffective.

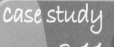 **Link**

See page 107 for the major anti-discrimination laws and pages 243–247 in Unit 6.

Freedom of speech

This is a basic human right. Written US and European constitutions have for many years stressed the importance of this right. Britain does not have a written constitution, but free speech is, in principle, one of our traditions and rights.

In its wider sense, freedom of speech means 'freedom of expression': not just of speech but in TV programmes, films, songs, books, poems, works of art, etc.

In fact, in the eyes of the law, none of us has total freedom of speech, except in our own homes. The true situation is given in the Human Rights Act 1998.

---

case study 3.11   Freedom of expression

Article 10 of the Human Rights Act 1998

Freedom of expression

1. Everyone has the right to freedom of expression. This right shall include freedom to hold opinions and to receive and impart information and ideas without interference by public authority and regardless of frontiers. This Article shall not prevent States from requiring the licensing of broadcasting, television or cinema enterprises.

2. The exercise of these freedoms, since it carries with it duties and responsibilities, may be subject to such formalities, conditions, restrictions or penalties as are prescribed by law and are necessary in a democratic society, in the interests of national security, territorial integrity or public safety, for the prevention of disorder or crime, for the protection of health or morals, for the protection of the reputation or rights of others, for preventing the disclosure of information received in confidence, or for maintaining the authority and impartiality of the judiciary.

(Source: www.opsi.gov.uk)

activity
GROUP WORK

Discuss and try to agree on situations in which (in your view) free speech should not be allowed.

Uniformed public services' role

In the implementation/enforcement/monitoring of legal and humanitarian rights

The police implement legal and humanitarian rights in much of what they do. In preventing violence, they protect people's right to go about their lawful business without unlawful interference; in preventing theft, they protect the right of people to own property. They enforce the legal ban on slavery in the UK by cracking down on people-trafficking and associated activities. Even in taking action against antisocial behaviour they are protecting the right to security and privacy of the communities whose quality of life is being degraded by rowdiness, vandalism and petty crime on the street.

Fig 3.5 Enforcing human rights. British armed forces have a duty to implement, enforce and monitor human rights overseas wherever they are carrying out peacekeeping activities

In relation to demonstrations

Under the Public Order Act 1986, it is legal to hold peaceful meetings, **vigils** and public demonstrations, and it is not necessary to inform the police or local council (although of course they prefer advance notification).

Marches are slightly different because these move about and might stop traffic. For a march, unless it is 'spontaneous', the police require six days' notice, especially if it is a protest or a commemoration. The police need to know:

- the date of the march
- the time and place it will start
- the route
- the name and address of the organiser.

Police advice is slightly different from this.

case study 3.12

Police advice

If you intend to hold a street event or a demonstration within Leeds, which is likely to cause disruption to road traffic, or to attract large numbers of people, you must contact West Yorkshire Police.

You will need to inform the Police of your intentions and seek their permission to proceed with the event.

West Yorkshire Police will be able to provide advice on making sure the event takes place as safely as possible.

(Source: www.westyorkshire.police.uk)

activity
INDIVIDUAL WORK

1 What dangers will these instructions help to avoid?

2 What human rights problems could be caused by these instructions?

---

remember

Holding peaceful demonstrations is a democratic right.

Recently, controls on public protest marches and demonstrations have become stricter following the passing of the Serious Organised Crime and Police Act 2005. There are designated areas, such as the area round Parliament, where marches are not allowed.

Under the Police and Criminal Justice Act 1994 and the Terrorism Act 2000, police can search for weapons before a demonstration. This has sometimes prevented innocent people from getting to the demonstration, as happened in 2003 when people were going to Fairford US Airforce base to demonstrate against the Iraq war: coaches were searched then forced back to London under a heavy police escort.

In a peaceful march or demonstration, the role of the police is to minimise disruption, ensure safety and prevent violence. If violence does break out, the police may stop it, by using warnings and arrests. In the past, especially in Northern Ireland, CS gas, rubber bullets, charges with batons and shields, and water cannon have been used. Such action has been rare in recent years and is linked to rioting rather than to organised demonstrations.

---

remember

Human rights organisations such as Liberty see immigration control and 'the war against terrorism' as separate issues. Politicians often see them as different sides of the same issue.

Role of the Border and Immigration Agency

The Border and Immigration Agency (formerly the Immigration and Nationality Directorate) is a branch of the Home Office; its main aim is to manage immigration so as to protect the country's security and promote economic development. The IND checks that people are not entering the country illegally, deals with asylum applications, arranges deportation for foreign criminals, keeps track of foreigners who are in the country on visas, and arranges for people who may benefit the British economy to be able to arrive and work in the country easily.

activity
GROUP WORK
3.3

P2

Produce a wallchart for a citizens' advice office, outlining:

1 the legal and human rights of people living in Britain

2 how these affect the public services.

activity
GROUP WORK
3.4

M2

Give a presentation suitable for trainee community support officers, explaining the legal and human rights of British citizens living in Britain and what these mean for the public services.

How the qualities of a 'good citizen' may be demonstrated in contemporary society and the benefits of these qualities to society and the uniformed public services

Everybody knows what good citizenship is when they see it, but it is not so easy to define. A possible definition might be: 'behaviour which is of benefit to other people and society'. Benefit, of course, is not the same as giving people pleasure: someone who sells alcohol to underage drinkers may provide pleasure, but it is certainly not to their benefit.

Recognised qualities

Responsibility

This is an awareness of one's duties towards other people and to the wider society. Occasionally there can be a conflict of responsibilities. If you know your friend is stealing cars, you have a responsibility to protect your friend – and you may feel that you should keep quiet about the car-stealing. However, there is a wider responsibility to stop the behaviour even if it means telling the police, especially as your friend too should benefit in the long run.

In uniformed public service work, a sense of responsibility amounts to the same thing: putting the wider needs of society first. If firefighters spend a night out in a forest damping down a fire they do it for the benefit of society, even though they would rather be safe at home, and their families would rather they were at home as well. Their responsibility to society and their service has sometimes to override the demands of their personal life.

Dedication

This is another valuable quality for uniformed public service work. It means 'giving yourself' to the work: getting interested and involved, sticking at it, and always trying to get better at the job. When five young women were murdered in Ipswich in the space of a few weeks towards the end of 2006, around 500 police officers worked on the case, following up leads and phone calls from the public, watching endless footage from CCTV cameras and managing scenes of crime in unpleasant weather so that the forensic teams could get on with their own painstaking work. The work cannot have been enjoyable, but the dedication of the police led eventually to an arrest which, at the time of writing, seems to have solved the case.

Attitudes to other people, e.g. helpful, considerate, non-judgemental; participates in community activities

The good citizenship that many people show in their ordinary lives is good for the people around them. People who are helpful, considerate, non-judgemental, keen on participating in community activities and aware of other people make the lives of all of

> **remember**
> 'Non-judgemental' means tolerant – i.e. accepting that people have a right to be different; not criticising other people all the time.

remember

> Even when dealing with simple inquiries from the public or other routine matters, people in the uniformed services should aim to be polite and helpful – word of mouth is the best advertisement for a service and its work, and it is the most effective form of PR.

us better. These qualities which are so much appreciated in our friends and families are also much needed among people who work in the uniformed public services. Partly this is because the work is teamwork, and teams are usually more effective if team members like and respect each other. Most of us don't like working with people who are grouchy, lazy or backbiting, or who think only of themselves. This matters in uniformed public service work, which can be stressful, with targets to be met, traumatic incidents and long shifts.

Then there are relations with the public. In the case of the police and the prison and probation services, much of the work involves dealing with people who are hostile, difficult to get on with, drunk, mentally ill or who have emotional problems and are themselves under stress. Being helpful and considerate (as far as the situation allows) will sometimes bring results where a more hard-nosed and confrontational attitude would fail.

Awareness of the needs of others

Sensitivity and an interest in other people are valuable qualities in most uniformed public service work. Even the armed forces need these attributes when on peacekeeping duties or working with civilians in potentially hostile environments such as southern Iraq. As shown below, different groups of people have different needs; public service workers should develop an awareness of these needs.

Ethnic minority groups

When working with ethnic minority groups, the following are important:

- avoiding all discrimination and unfairness
- understanding and respecting their culture
- making a reasonable effort to learn the basics of their language – if necessary
- showing a friendly face so that they do not feel that Britain has to be a hostile place
- taking care not to cause unnecessary offence.

Children

When working with children, the following are important:

- treating them with friendliness and respect
- being prepared to listen
- being observant (e.g. of possible signs of abuse)
- liaising with other agencies wherever necessary.

Teenagers

When working with teenagers, the following are important:

- being able to listen and take a genuine interest
- providing or facilitating worthwhile activities
- not being too judgemental
- respecting their point of view
- avoiding **stereotyping** and discrimination.

Elderly people

When working with elderly people, the following are important:

- being aware of their physical and social needs
- listening and taking their concerns seriously
- respecting their independence and dignity.

People with specific learning or physical needs

When working with people with specific learning or physical needs, the following are important:

- giving them as much independence and freedom as possible
- helping them when they need help
- ensuring that they are respected and not discriminated against
- doing whatever is possible to improve their quality of life.

Activities of a 'good citizen'

There is no single blueprint or formula for being a **good citizen** – everybody should try to be a good citizen in their own way.

The volunteer working in public services and in the community

Having said this, there are ways of demonstrating good citizenship which are personally satisfying and which will also be helpful to people who might want a career in a uniformed public service. These involve working for a public service but without getting paid for it. Some of them are outlined in the following case study, which also describes opportunities for volunteering in the community.

<table>
<tr><td>remember</td><td>There are many advantages for public service students in doing voluntary work. There will be plenty of stuff about community volunteers on your local authority website.</td></tr>
</table>

---

case study 3.13

Some opportunities for volunteering

1 Volunteers in public services

Special constables

The Special Constabulary is a force of trained volunteers who work with and support their local police force.

'Specials', as the Special Constables are known, come from all walks of life … and they all volunteer a minimum of four hours a week to their local police forces, forming a vital link between the regular (full-time) police and the local community.

At first, they are asked to spend some weekends training. Later they will take part in regular evening and update sessions working through the national training curricula. They … are trained in police service, self defence, powers of arrest, common crimes, and preparing evidence for court.

Once they have completed their training, they have the same powers as a regular officer and wear a similar uniform.

(Source: www.specials.homeoffice.gov.uk)

St John Ambulance personnel

Our volunteers are expertly trained in first aid to treat injuries … they then use these skills to provide first aid treatment at a wide variety of public events. Volunteers often arrange further medical assistance and transport for patients, or provide comfort and rest to people in need of more prolonged care.

What does it involve?

Commitment – You can give as little or as much time as you wish, give a few spare hours here or there, or commit to a couple of hours each week.

Role – If you wish to learn first aid skills and help others you could develop these skills to treat injuries, care for others and even crew an accident and emergency ambulance.

Training – You don't need any previous first aid experience, as our training will equip you with all the skills you need for the role.

Costs – There are minimal costs involved in becoming a first aid volunteer.

(Source: www.sja.org.uk)

Retained firefighters

To be a retained firefighter you need to be at least 18 years old, physically fit and live and/or work close to the fire station. Just as important are qualities like common sense, commitment and enthusiasm…

Retained firefighters receive:

The rewards
- a basic annual payment (a **retainer**) and fees for emergency response
- fees for training sessions and for duties like equipment maintenance
- a long service bonus

Many retained firefighters are in full-time employment with agreement from their employers to leave work to attend an emergency call. Others commit time after work and at weekends or can offer time between caring commitments for example, when the children are at school.

People who are unemployed are also attracted to this worthwhile commitment.

(Source: www.communities.gov.uk)

Territorial Army

The TA is a reserve force of civilians who fulfil soldier training and operational support on a part-time basis. … It is made up of volunteers who commit large parts of their spare time to training as soldiers and working with the Regular Army. TA soldiers serving in Independent Units complete a minimum of 27 days training a year, comprising some midweek evenings, some weekends and an annual two-week camp.

(Source: www.armyjobs.mod.uk)

2 Volunteers in the community

Youth work, reclamation activities, charity work, and sponsored activities all show good citizenship. In a large metropolitan borough there may be over 100,000 volunteers of this type.

Millennium volunteers

This scheme links volunteer work with career development, and is open to people between 16 and 25. As it says on its website, 'Being a MV is all about getting involved in local issues you care about. So you can make a real difference to others, whilst at the same time gaining experience, confidence and skills. Through volunteering you can make a positive difference to your own life and your community.'

Partner organisations include Citizens Advice, which gives free advice to the public on their legal and other rights. Millennium volunteers work with Citizens Advice in, for example, 'advising, admin and office support, interpreting, IT support, press, PR, publicity work, reception, research, social policy, volunteer recruitment and website design'.

(Source: www.vinspired.com; www.citizensadvice.org.uk)

Duke of Edinburgh's Award Scheme

This is a major and well-known scheme to enable young people to develop their talents, abilities and personal qualities. It encourages initiative, courage and creativity, and supports out of school/college activities.

D of E licenses organisations to run the scheme through Award Groups linked to youth clubs, voluntary organisations, Open Award Centres, schools, colleges, young offender institutes and businesses.

Award Groups are run by adults, and volunteers are heavily involved.

(Source: www.theaward.org)

activity
INDIVIDUAL WORK

Read each of the short extracts about volunteer activities, and put them in order of suitability for someone who would like to join the uniformed public service of your choice.

Link   See pages 123 and 124 for more on volunteering.

activity
GROUP WORK
3.5

P3

Produce a small guidebook for school leavers with the title: 'Why Everybody Likes a Good Citizen'.

1   The first section should contain suggestions on how to be a good citizen, and an outline of suitable voluntary activities.

2   The second section should explain why good citizenship is good news for the uniformed public services and for the rest of society.

Benefits of a 'good citizen' to society

The meaning of the word 'society' varies according to the context. It can mean 'the average person', 'people in general', 'the public', 'the community', 'people and their relationships with others', 'the nation as a whole' and even, at times, 'the world and everybody in it'.

A good citizen could be defined as 'a person whose activities are good for other people'.

Adds value to society

Good citizens add value to society in the sense that they improve the quality of life for other people. They do this by:

- avoiding bad citizenship, such as antisocial behaviour, which reduces people's quality of life

- living lives which set a good example, in the sense that, if everybody did as they do, the world would be a better place

- actively working for others, for example by helping people who need help or by campaigning for justice and freedom.

Supports society to protect the environment

Good citizenship can help the environment in a number of ways, by:

- avoiding criminal activities (e.g. dropping litter, fly tipping, and setting fire to cars)

- sorting household waste for recycling

- each person reducing their 'carbon footprint' by minimising unnecessary air or car travel, driving more economical vehicles, insulating their houses and buying local produce

- each company, organisation, public service, etc. carrying out an environmental audit to see how much waste, pollution and greenhouse gas emission can be avoided.

- actively working to do something that will improve the environment (e.g. planting trees, joining an environmental group, such as Greenpeace or Friends of the Earth, and either campaigning or carrying out voluntary environmental work).

remember

Injustice is unfair, unequal or cruel treatment of others; it includes any infringement of human rights.

Challenges injustice

Good citizens take an interest in what is going on in the world around them and try to challenge (stop) injustice. If they come across an injustice in their everyday life (e.g. a case of bullying) they will confront it and try to stop it from happening.

Some good citizens like to take it further by challenging injustice on a regular basis. They might do this by volunteering. People who join the special constabulary, for example, want to do something about the injustice caused by antisocial behaviour and other types of crime.

A third way to challenge injustice is to campaign against it by forming or joining an organisation to combat injustice.

case study 3.14

Liberty

It is easy to feel frustrated and angry when democratic rights such as free speech and protest are under threat; easy to feel useless when governments try to side-step international standards like the ban on torture.

It would be easy to feel powerless to change anything but, together, we can make a difference.

Stand up for your beliefs today – join Liberty. Together we are stronger to resist attacks on our fundamental rights and freedoms.

As a member, you will get regular newsletters and emails updating you on our campaigns.

Most importantly, you'll play your part in defending our basic rights and freedoms.

(Source:www.liberty-human-rights.org.uk)

activity
INDIVIDUAL WORK

List as many methods as you can think of for volunteers in an organisation such as Liberty to make their protest in a legal yet effective way.

remember

Happiness is not quite the same thing as pleasure. Binge drinking, for example, may bring pleasure in the short run but will not bring happiness in the long run.

Makes a positive difference

This means to change some aspect of society, people's lives or the environment for the better.

Confronts and challenges the origin of injustice

To confront and challenge injustice is to stand up and say that an action is wrong or unfair and – perhaps – to do something about it.

It may mean:

- tackling any situation where someone is doing something wrong
- addressing a problem at college or work where people are being treated unfairly
- campaigning against some social or political wrongdoing.

The origin (cause) of injustice is hard to define: it depends on the injustice and on the way we see it. Some blame human nature; some blame a political or economic system; some blame cultural beliefs and attitudes; and some blame a particular 'unjust' or 'evil' individual. Challenging the origin of the injustice may be even more difficult than challenging the injustice itself.

Sometimes, as in, say, the case of the Iraq war, good citizens can find themselves on opposite sides of the argument. Someone who confronts and challenges the origins of injustice risks making enemies of other good citizens. This is why it is better to confront and challenge the origins of injustice peacefully, using reason and persuasion rather than violence. The peaceful method saves lives, and in the long run is more likely to find a lasting solution to a difficult problem.

Effects fairness

This means treating other people in a well-meaning and equal way. People who do this benefit society because they create a sense of trust and respect which enables people to work and play together without prejudice or hassle.

Improves society through volunteer work

Volunteer work is unpaid work which provides a service to others. It can be informal. If someone sweeps snow off their neighbour's path it is an action done in a volunteer spirit and shows good citizenship. Regular volunteer work, perhaps for a charity or for some other organisation, benefits more people, improving society as a whole.

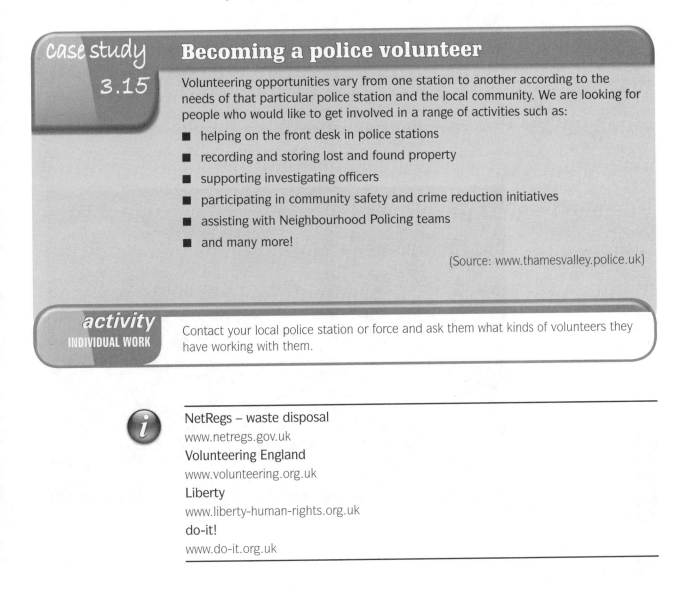

case study

3.15

Becoming a police volunteer

Volunteering opportunities vary from one station to another according to the needs of that particular police station and the local community. We are looking for people who would like to get involved in a range of activities such as:

- helping on the front desk in police stations
- recording and storing lost and found property
- supporting investigating officers
- participating in community safety and crime reduction initiatives
- assisting with Neighbourhood Policing teams
- and many more!

(Source: www.thamesvalley.police.uk)

activity
INDIVIDUAL WORK

Contact your local police station or force and ask them what kinds of volunteers they have working with them.

i

NetRegs – waste disposal
www.netregs.gov.uk
Volunteering England
www.volunteering.org.uk
Liberty
www.liberty-human-rights.org.uk
do-it!
www.do-it.org.uk

Relevance to public services

Good citizenship, as we have seen, is relevant to the public services because the qualities of good citizenship are embodied in the kind of care and protection which public services aim to give. Qualities such as responsibility, dedication, helpfulness, consideration and a non-judgemental absence of bias and discrimination, which we welcome and respect in ordinary people, are (ideally) expressed at a professional level in the statutory public services.

Importance of the volunteer concept

Equally relevant to the public services is the 'volunteer concept', which is seen as a good thing, morally, for society as a whole, expressing as it does a wider and more positive idea of citizenship than simply obeying the law and going to vote every four years. Volunteering is about doing the work for its own sake, because it needs to be done. In a materialistic, consumer-orientated society, it reminds us of the values of selflessness and the fact that life is about more than getting and spending money.

Additional support for specific services

In the public services, 12,000 special constables work for the police, and there are 14,000 retained firefighters who work in other jobs but are available to work as firefighters in emergencies. Then there is the Territorial Army (32,000) and the reservists in the RAF and Royal Navy. There are also volunteers who help out in schemes to rehabilitate offenders, or in mountain rescue etc. These are actively supported by the government – partly because the volunteers are doing useful public service work on the cheap. The volunteer concept is important in the idea of 'resilience' – being prepared for major emergencies. It also gives the uniformed services valuable and supportive links with local communities.

Fig 3.6 Volunteering to save lives

remember

Search your local government website for examples of volunteer work and projects. A typical metropolitan council can have over 100,000 volunteers working in it, in a vast range of activities.

Fig 3.7 Benefits of voluntary
work

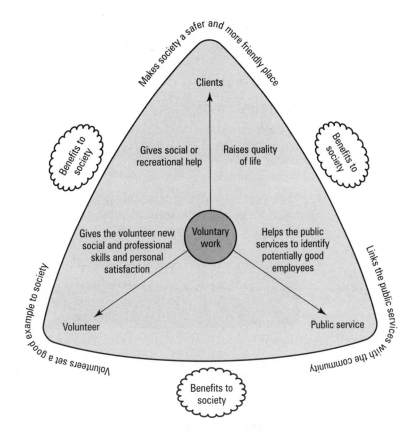

Reduction of crime, fires, injury

There are volunteer organisations which work to reduce crime, fires and injury. Some, such as Neighbourhood Watch, are started by local citizens, assisted by the police where necessary. Societies such as the Royal Society for the Prevention of Accidents (RoSPA) encourage fire and other kinds of safety awareness. Volunteer organisations such as the St John Ambulance Brigade and the Red Cross do valuable volunteer work stewarding at major events, and teaching the general public how to do first aid.

How national and international current affairs are highlighted by the media and influence the public services

National current affairs are events happening in the country which become news or which affect our lives. International current affairs are important things happening in other countries. Contemporary issues are problems and changes affecting society now. They are very often things that people don't agree about (e.g. asylum policy, ways of dealing with the threat of terrorism and global warming). The issues affect the public services by changing the services' work and priorities.

> **remember**
>
> The best way to understand all these major issues is to follow news and current affairs on the television, in the newspapers, on the radio and on the internet.

Media representations of uniformed public services

Unless we work in the uniformed public services (or have close friends and family who do) or unless we are convicted criminals, enemy combatants, or Iraqi and Afghan civilians, most of what we know about the uniformed public services comes through the media.

The media, of course, include newspapers, magazines, television, radio and the internet – all of which deal with news and current affairs. They represent the uniformed public services in the sense that they give a picture or image of what they do. This representation changes all the time depending on:

- the events and situations being described
- the intended audience (readers, viewers, listeners)
- the political or other bias of the newspaper, TV channel, individual journalist or commentator.

Different newspapers, magazines, television, radio, internet

To cover this part of the unit, you should look at as many newspapers and magazines and watch as many TV news programmes as possible. You should also collect articles etc. about the uniformed public services and ask yourself a simple question: Is the writer praising or criticising the uniformed services?

In Britain, all viewpoints about the public services are available, but the majority opinions are the ones which the media usually contain. Some media, such as the BBC, try to give a 'balanced' view, so they both praise and criticise the uniformed public services.

Table 3.3 Rough outline of media viewpoint in the representation of uniformed public services

Views of the uniformed public services			
Medium	Left-wing	Centrist	Right-wing
Newspapers		*The Guardian* *Daily Mirror* *The Independent* *Financial Times* *The Observer*	*The Sun* *The Times* *Daily Telegraph* *Daily Mail* *Daily Express* *Sunday Times*
Magazines	*New Internationalist*	*The Economist* *New Statesman*	*The Spectator*
Television	*Hard Talk* (sometimes)	*Newsnight* *Hard Talk* Euronews CBN Most of BBC News 24	Sky News Fox News
Radio		*Today*	
Internet	www.indymedia.org.uk	Yahoo! news	

Some of the media are obviously biased. Recruitment literature and CDs, etc. put out by the armed forces aim to attract people to join, and these therefore pick out the exciting and enjoyable aspects. **Right-wing** media tend to stress the courage and professionalism of the armed forces. Centrist media give a mixed picture: they praise the armed forces, but they also publicise their mistakes or suspected crimes (e.g. human rights abuses). This group also attacks the government for underfunding the uniformed public services. **Left-wing** and '**radical**' media concentrate on human rights abuses, American influence, and so on. ('Radical' means 'uprooting' and changing the institutions of society; the radical press is against the uniformed public services.)

> **remember**
>
> Many newspapers and other media give a variety of opinions in the same issue or programme, so that readers and viewers can decide for themselves.

Fictional ideas

Many people read crime novels, novels about war, or watch disaster movies or television dramas about the police. These stories are made up, and people watch them for entertainment. However, the writers often put hidden 'messages' in them, suggesting either support for or criticism of the uniformed services. Usually, the hidden message is one of admiration. For example, in the TV series *Dalziel and Pascoe*, the police characters, while not very attractive, nevertheless work hard to make the world a better place and are basically honest. The same is true of *London's Burning*, which puts forward a positive image of firefighters. Representations in fiction are important because they help to form our attitudes to the public services involved, and in most cases make us support the services without our knowing it. It is rare to find fictional portrayals of the uniformed public services which are hostile: one example is the novel: *How Late It Was, How Late*, by James Kelman.

Non-fiction books and articles

In these media, the treatment of the public services depends on the views of the readers who buy the books and magazines, the political leanings (if any) of the publishers, and (in the case of articles) any pressure which might be put on the magazine editors by people who advertise in the magazines (and who are probably their main source of income). Non-fiction books about the public services often take a critical or provocative line, perhaps because many people find attacks more interesting to read than praise.

Radical media reports, service magazines

Radical media reports usually give viewpoints opposed to the policies of the British and US governments. They attack capitalism and big business and support socialism, and they tend to regard the uniformed public services as oppressive organisations designed to support the rich, or carry out US policy. The radical media are sometimes pacifist, but sometimes they support armed struggle by oppressed minorities and may use arguments which support or excuse terrorism.

Indymedia UK – see website for examples

www.indymedia.org.uk

Service magazines are the opposite: these are produced by the publicity departments of the uniformed public services and highlight the good work that the services do. Service magazines tell stories of bravery and endurance, keeping away from controversial issues (such as 'Why are British forces in Iraq?') except to give the same answers as the government.

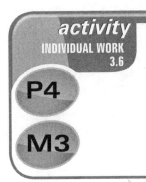

remember

The truth is rarely simple; although both radical and service media should be read, it is not necessary to believe everything you read in them.

activity

INDIVIDUAL WORK 3.6

P4

M3

You work for a community radio station. Research and report on three different examples of radio, TV, internet or newspaper coverage of a particular national or international situation, picking out and explaining the differences.

National issues affecting public services

National issues are problems or situations within Britain which influence the work of the public services.

Illegal immigration

In 2006, it was estimated that there could be between 310,000 and 570,000 illegal immigrants in Britain (as many come in secretly, the number can never be known). The problem is serious because:

- They work in the unofficial economy, and the UK could be losing £6billion in tax revenue because of this.

- Some have been brought here by people-traffickers and are themselves victims of serious organised crime.

- They are widely exploited in Britain by unscrupulous employers.

- They are here illegally, and the government cannot turn a blind eye.

- Many British people feel threatened by this uncontrolled, unknown number of immigrants.

- The media have highlighted the problem, and it has become a serious political issue.

Among the uniformed public services, illegal immigration particularly affects the police, the prison service and the Immigration and Nationality Directorate. As it is an international problem, it affects the whole of Europe and is a major concern of the Organisation for Security and Cooperation in Europe (**OSCE**), as well as of Interpol and Europol.

Government plans are shown in the next case study.

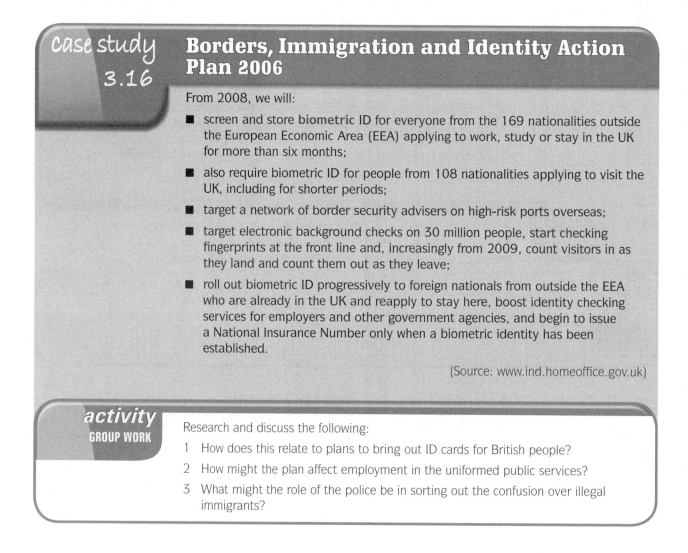

case study 3.16   Borders, Immigration and Identity Action Plan 2006

From 2008, we will:

- screen and store **biometric** ID for everyone from the 169 nationalities outside the European Economic Area (EEA) applying to work, study or stay in the UK for more than six months;

- also require biometric ID for people from 108 nationalities applying to visit the UK, including for shorter periods;

- target a network of border security advisers on high-risk ports overseas;

- target electronic background checks on 30 million people, start checking fingerprints at the front line and, increasingly from 2009, count visitors in as they land and count them out as they leave;

- roll out biometric ID progressively to foreign nationals from outside the EEA who are already in the UK and reapply to stay here, boost identity checking services for employers and other government agencies, and begin to issue a National Insurance Number only when a biometric identity has been established.

(Source: www.ind.homeoffice.gov.uk)

activity
GROUP WORK

Research and discuss the following:

1 How does this relate to plans to bring out ID cards for British people?

2 How might the plan affect employment in the uniformed public services?

3 What might the role of the police be in sorting out the confusion over illegal immigrants?

Borders, Immigration and Identity Action Plan – Using the National Identity Scheme to Strengthen our Borders and Enforce Compliance within the UK (Home Office, December 2006)
www.ind.homeoffice.gov.uk
Central Government Arrangements for Responding to an Emergency: Concept of Operations (Cabinet Office, 31 March 2005)
www.ukresilience.info
South Yorkshire Strategic Framework for Emergency Management (14 December 2006)
www.southyorkshireemergencies.gov
Foreign and Commonwealth Office
www.fco.gov.uk
The Times
www.timesonline.co.uk
The Independent
www.independent.co.uk
The Guardian
www.guardian.co.uk

Increase in gun crime

Although the figures fluctuate from year to year, there has been an overall increase in gun crime in Britain in recent years. This has put the public and the police at risk, with a number of high-profile cases such as the murder of PC Sharon Beshenivsky in 2005.

The Home Office introduced new ways of tackling gun crime after 2005, which was a particularly bad year. These included:

- introducing a minimum five-year sentence for people convicted of possessing an illegal firearm

- making it an offence to possess an air weapon or imitation firearm in public without legal authority or reasonable excuse

- targeting imitation firearms, by making it illegal to manufacture or sell imitation firearms that could be mistaken for real firearms

- tightening security on import routes and international mail, and monitoring online firearm suppliers.

- establishing the Connected programme to support local community groups in their fight against gun crime

- having a successful gun amnesty in 2003 which resulted in the handing in of 43,908 guns and 1,039,358 rounds of ammunition.

The Association of Chief Police Officers (ACPO) has introduced another measure: a new national database on guns used in crimes – the National Ballistics Intelligence Programme – which will be run in London, Birmingham and Manchester. Guns, shells or bullets will be sent to the units, which will then use forensic techniques to match them to earlier crimes.

It is likely that increased gun crime will lead to police having more firearms training and more armed response units.

Housing

Poor housing affects:

■ the police because it is linked to higher crime levels

■ the fire and rescue service because fire-safety standards are likely to be lower

■ teachers because it is linked to educational underachievement

■ the NHS because it is linked to poor health and a shorter life expectancy

■ social workers because disadvantaged people with social and personal problems tend to live in poor housing.

In some modern house-building projects, efforts have been made to 'design out crime' by arranging the buildings so that there are fewer 'hidden' areas where drugs can be dealt, muggers can hide, and so on.

Demographic changes

These are population changes; they can occur nationally and/or locally.

National **demographic changes** include:

■ the rise of the overall population of Britain to over 60 million

■ the arrival of large numbers of economic migrants from the accession countries of the EU in eastern Europe

■ a (broadly) falling birth rate.

Local demographic changes occur in towns, cities and their surrounding districts. They can be changes in overall population density or changes in the age profile or the ethnicity of an area. Examples of local demographic changes (often repeated in different parts of the country) are 'white flight' from inner city districts, the increasing student population near new or expanding universities; and the 'gentrification' of villages, leading to house price rises which mean that local people have no hope of ever affording a house in their own village.

Demographic changes affect police work, because the police have to adapt their methods and priorities to the people who live in an area; therefore, if the area changes, so does their work. Demographic changes also affect police staffing, since government policy is to match the proportion of ethnic minority staff in each police force (e.g. West Midlands) with the proportion of ethnic minority people in the area served. Other public services have similar targets to meet, based on the demography (population mix) of their area.

Ageing population, reduced birth rate

The average age of the British population is increasing. This is mainly as a result of the so-called 'baby boom' at the end of the Second World War and in the 1960s and the decrease in birth rate. Fig 3.8 shows the age profile of the British population.

Many babies were born soon after the Second World War because soldiers came home to their wives and girlfriends, and there was a prospect of peace. The second, wider, baby boom around 20 years ago was when the so-called 'baby-boomers' in turn had their children. Since then the birth rate has been low for a variety of reasons, ranging from low sperm counts to problems with housing and employment, and the expense of bringing up children.

There are now more people older than 65 than ever before, while the relative number of younger people is decreasing. This means that:

Fig 3.8 The ageing
population 2005

(Source: www.statistics.gov.uk)

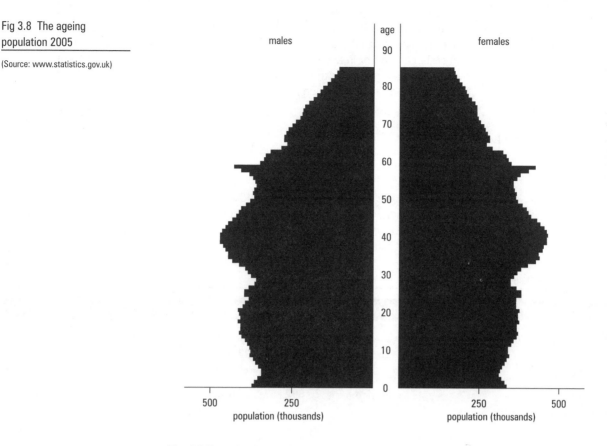

- The NHS and other caring public services have more old people to look after.

- The rate of serious illnesses is higher because old people are more likely to have serious illnesses.

- The cost to the nation of pensions is increasing, while the number of productive workers is decreasing.

- Tax revenue to the government is going down, while the number of people eligible for benefits is going up.

The changes basically mean that the public services have more work to do and less money – and sometimes fewer people – to do it with.

Immigrant groups

See page 226 in Unit 6 for information on immigrant groups.

Government actions

Two kind of government action affect the public services:

- the money that it provides

- the policies that it lays down.

Financial policies

British governments either try to lower tax and squeeze the public services, or raise tax and then spend the extra money on the public services. In practice, governments have little room to manoeuvre, because people need public services and nobody likes paying tax.

remember

In a democratic society, the government has a duty to spend money, as far as possible, on projects and services that the public want it to be spent on.

The amount of money available for government spending is dependent on a figure called the **Gross Domestic Product** (**GDP**). This is the total value of all goods and services produced in a country in a given year; it is equal to total consumer, investment and government spending, plus the value of exports, minus the value of imports. Britain's GDP is around one trillion pounds (one thousand billion) – i.e. £1,000,000,000,000.

As the table shows, only about 6% of this (£61,253,000,000) is spent on the uniformed public services.

Table 3.4 shows that between 2000 and 2006 spending on public order and safety increased faster than public spending on defence. This is because government policy has been to concentrate on law and order – an area which ordinary voters feel strongly about. Despite our involvement in Iraq and Afghanistan there has been a slower rise in defence spending. Defence spending is – under normal circumstances – less popular with the public than spending on civilian uniformed public services, because there is less obvious benefit in our daily lives and therefore fewer votes to be gained.

Table 3.4 Government spending figures (£millions)

	2000–01	2001–02	2002–03	2003–04	2004–05	2005–06
Defence						
National defence	25,632	23,390	27,034	28,730	29,806	31,070
Civil defence	6	3	4	86	35	41
Total defence	25,638	25,392	27,039	28,816	29,840	31,112
Public order and safety						
Police	9,675	11,216	12,065	13,460	14,561	15,489
Fire	1,953	2,084	2,283	2,389	2,541	2,753
Administration of justice	3,576	4,478	4,928	5,372	6,072	5,783
Immigration and citizenship	1,398	1,729	1,797	1,942	1,704	1,547
Prisons and offender programmes	2,942	2,591	2,888	2,983	3,241	3,613
Other public order and safety	645	780	780	847	894	956
Total public order and safety	20,189	22,878	24,740	26,992	29,013	30,141

(Source: PESA (2006) www.hm-treasury.gov.uk)

Reduction of regiments in the army

There have been difficulties in recruiting soldiers and other defence personnel in recent years, and there has been public concern about the apparently small benefit that a heavy defence commitment brings. For both these reasons, the government has felt under pressure to monitor closely and reduce defence expenditure. One result has been the recent merging of army **regiments** – an emotive issue when the regiments have existed for hundreds of years and have done heroic service in two world wars. Regimental traditions are often so strong that there is almost a family feeling within regiments, and reduction of regiments is keenly felt among soldiers past and present, their families, and the communities traditionally linked to the regiments which are being abolished.

remember

A traditional regiment contains roughly 650 people; the new, merged regiments are often bigger than this.

Increased use of civilian roles in the police

Civilian police roles are jobs which are done for the police by people who are not police officers. Some, such as community support officers and traffic wardens do jobs which previously were done by police officers themselves. Some skilled jobs that used to be done by the police are now hived off to specialist services: for example, forensic work such as fingerprinting, which was at one time done by the police themselves, is now done by the Forensic Science Service (FSS). The FSS, formed in 1991, works mainly for the 43 police forces in England and Wales, the Crown Prosecution Service, HM Revenue and Customs, HM Coroners, the Ministry of Defence Police and the British Transport Police.

Development of rapid reaction groups in the armed services

NATO developed the NATO Response Force in 2002. It has about 20,000 troops, is capable of 'rapid deployment' and is designed for 'high-intensity operations'. It is seen as a mainly European force (including British) backed by American 'enablers'.

The European Union has also developed a rapid reaction force which Britain has joined. In 2004 it was agreed that Britain, France and Germany would create **battle groups** of well-trained troops ready to be deployed at a moment's notice to prevent fighting or restore peace around the world. The battle groups will each contain 1500 troops, which could stay at a location for up to 220 days. They are expected to be ready for operation in 2007, but it is likely that they will only be used where the USA is not closely involved.

Impact of placing illegal immigrants in prisons – prison overcrowding

In early 2007 Britain's prisons were full to overflowing, with 80,000 people in custody. The main impacts of this are:

- to overwork the prison service and reduce the time and money for rehabilitation work in prisons
- the proposed building of new prisons
- privatisation of prisons so as to reduce the burden on the taxpayer
- increased sentencing in the community and a changing role for the probation service.

The illegal immigrants, kept in prisons or in detention centres, are deprived of human rights and are being deported, sometimes to countries where they may be tortured, which is in contravention of international agreements. The government says that it is obtaining assurances from these countries that deportees will not be tortured; people opposed to the system say that such assurances are not worth the paper that they are written on.

Fig 3.9 Civilians, doing police work

International events affecting public services

See Unit 8 of *BTEC National Public Services Book 2* for much more information on international events and the public services.

Terrorist activities

Terrorism is politically motivated activity, involving loss of life, the threat of it, or large-scale destruction, which is designed to terrify civilians and publicise a cause. At present, it normally involves bombing, including suicide bombing, but there are other possible forms of terrorism, such as mass kidnapping and hostage-taking, hijacking, biological or chemical attacks, or the dispersal of dangerous radioactive agents. The biggest and most widely publicised terrorist attack in recent times was the destruction of the World Trade Center in New York in September 2001, which killed nearly 3000 people.

In the normal usage of the word, terrorists are civilians (or at least not part of an organised army) and they usually act in small groups. Mass killings on a bigger scale, such as the killing of 800,000 people in Rwanda in 1994, are more usually described as 'killings' or – if it is an attempt to wipe out an entire race or ethnic group – 'genocide'.

At present, much terrorism outside Iraq and Afghanistan is directed at Western countries or their allies. In the last few years, there have been serious terrorist attacks in Indonesia (the Bali bombings), Turkey, India, Pakistan, Egypt, Israel and Spain as well as in Britain and the USA.

President George W. Bush of the USA famously called the attack on the World Trade Center 'an act of war', and this is how Western countries, including Britain, have viewed terrorism. Terrorists also, in their so-called 'martyrdom tapes' in which they attempt to explain their actions, sometimes refer to themselves as 'soldiers'. Certainly, the response to terrorism from the West has been partly a military one – and it is often called 'the war on terror', or 'war on terrorism'.

War on terrorism

This usually refers to a 'war' against 'Islamic', 'Islamist' or 'Jihadist' terrorists – or a shadowy and obscure organisation: Al-Qaida. It is misleading to associate the problem too closely with the Muslim religion, and the word 'Islamic' is unhelpful when dealing with the problem, as it creates feelings of religious persecution – when the problem is really a political one. In addition, the war is not a war against any particular country but more against an idea. Also, much of the 'warfare' is not military but takes the form of intelligence gathering, criminal investigation, propaganda and changes to the law.

Elements of the 'war on terrorism' affecting the public services include:

- intelligence gathering by MI5 and MI6
- telephone monitoring (all calls whether from fixed or mobile phones) by Britain and the USA, including satellite monitoring
- military activities in Afghanistan and Iraq (127 British deaths in Iraq; 22 in Afghanistan at the beginning of 2007)
- investigation of suspected terrorist cells and plots by British police
- the passing of laws such as the Racial and Religious Hatred Act 2005 and the Terrorism Act 2006
- attempts by the government to build bridges between themselves and the British Muslim community
- the '**Islamophobia**' of sections of the British press and public, which leads to problems of harassment and public order.

Northern Ireland

Until the Good Friday Agreement of 1998, the Northern Ireland situation was the main cause of terrorist attacks and fear of terrorism in the UK. The Northern Ireland 'Troubles' were the result of **sectarianism** (divisions, in this case between Protestants who wanted political union with the rest of the UK and Catholics who wanted political union with the Irish republic) and long years of questionable policies by the British and Irish governments. Within Northern Ireland, Protestants and Catholics led rather separate lives, and one aspect of this was that the police force of Northern Ireland, known as the Royal Ulster Constabulary, was predominantly made up of Protestants and appeared to favour Protestants in its law-enforcement activities. Stimulated by this inequality the Irish Republican Army (**IRA**), and the **Provisional IRA**, carried out **paramilitary** and terrorist attacks both in Ireland and, from time to time, on the British mainland. The Troubles lasted from around 1968 to the mid-1990s and claimed around 3000 lives. Effects on the public services were many and various: the army was there in force for many years, and the police service in Northern Ireland has since been renamed and reorganised.

British Broadcasting Corporation (BBC)

www.bbc.co.uk

Bali bombings

Carried out in Bali in 2002 by an Islamist group allegedly linked to Al-Qaida, these resembled bombings in Egypt and Turkey which attacked the West by attacking Western tourists. The main effect on British public services was to heighten Foreign Office travel warnings, and increase collaboration between British, Australian and Indonesian police forces.

Major disasters, e.g. tsunamis, earthquakes, hurricanes

See Unit 14 in *BTEC National Public Services Book 2* for more about these.

Major natural disasters such as earthquakes, hurricanes and **tsunamis** are rare in the UK but they happen in other parts of the world – especially in less developed countries where people live in relative poverty and there is a lack of warning and of expert public service help nearby.

Disasters are often made worse if they are in politically unstable areas, or are linked to wars, '**ethnic cleansing**' and other human-caused events. Droughts that can kill millions are linked to global warming, as are hurricanes and typhoons which may kill thousands. The death toll from earthquakes is affected not only by the violence of the 'quake itself, but the population density, building methods and terrain of the affected area, and the nature of the relief effort.

British uniformed public services, especially the army, the RAF and the fire and rescue service, sometimes send teams overseas to help with natural and other disasters. They often do civil engineering work, such as building temporary bridges, and deliver tents, bedding, food rations, etc. This happened in the Pakistan earthquake of 2005.

The Ministry of Defence – see website for details of some of its activities

www.mod.uk

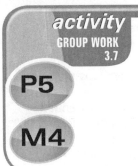

activity
GROUP WORK
3.7

P5

M4

Research and give a joint briefing on three issues recently in the news which could affect particular public services. Your briefing should be a verbal presentation with visual aids, or a PowerPoint presentation. Outline the main features of each issue and go into as much detail as you can about the probable effects on public services.

Activities by international organisations

NATO (North Atlantic Treaty Organisation)

NATO is a political and military alliance; originally against communism, it is now heavily involved in the 'war on terrorism'. Its main activities are fighting and peacekeeping in Afghanistan, where it is supporting the pro-Western government of Hamid Karzai against Taliban 'insurgents'.

NATO

www.nato.int

United Nations (UN)

The organisation runs peacekeeping operations – in places such as the Democratic Republic of Congo – to which Britain contributes military personnel.

United Nations

www.un.org

Occupation of Iraq and Afghanistan

British troop numbers are changing rapidly in these conflicts.

The occupation of Iraq is by a coalition run by the USA which has around 170,000 troops there. Britain, the main partner, has around 5000 troops in southern Iraq and is busy training the police and the new Iraqi army. The occupation of Afghanistan is run by NATO, with some 30 countries contributing. Britain is (2007) fighting the Taliban in the south; US forces are active along the eastern border with Pakistan.

The support needs required by international organisations

Organisations such as the UN and NATO require finance from member countries. In the case of the UN, which has 192 members, not all member countries pay their subscriptions and the organisation sometimes has funding problems which can prevent it from peacekeeping in some international disputes, or in **civil wars**. NATO is better off financially; the UK, for example, pays £110m per year to the NATO regular budget and £58m per year to the UN regular budget.

As well as supplying money, countries such as Britain have to provide armed forces to carry out UN and NATO work, since they do not have their own armed forces. Britain is also likely to provide support and forces for a planned EU rapid reaction force which may intervene in conflicts where NATO or the UN is unable or unwilling to be involved.

Initial action by armed services

The armed services acting under the umbrella of organisations such as NATO often have to defeat an enemy before reconstruction work can take place. It is necessary to have a certain level of peace and stability, together with support from a local population, before the institutions of a country ravaged by civil war (e.g. the police, health services, education, transport **infrastructure**, services such as water and electricity, and an economic base of viable industry) can be built up.

Support actions by other services

Until shortly after the attacks on the USA on 11 September 2001 ('9/11'), US and British policy was to work for stability in the Middle East and in other **volatile** areas. This has now changed, and the two countries wish to work for Western-style democracy. To do this they need the willing support of other nations – notably the EU – and support too from Russia and China, not least because they are permanent members of the UN Security Council.

Training police offers, army personnel

Having intervened in a country such as Iraq or Afghanistan, Western countries draft in police and other public services to give training to the local police, prison service, and so on; this is so that these services can be run in ways that will support the new democracies. Police training is not only given to new police forces in the Middle East, but also in countries, such as Albania, which were previously under communist dictatorship. Meanwhile, the security industry gives private training to security workers in industry and at big installations.

Enabling democratic elections

Elections are an essential aspect of Western-style democracy. However, disputed elections – as have happened in Ukraine, the Democratic Republic of Congo, and Palestine – give rise to political instability and even the risk of civil war. So elections in newly democratic countries need to be observed by the UN and others to make sure that they are run in a reasonably free and fair manner.

activity
GROUP WORK
3.8

D2

You work in the public relations office of a public service. Write a report to your supervisory officer explaining in detail the similarities and differences in the news reporting on three issues happening at the present time. Include an in-depth analysis of the various effects that each issue could have on particular public services.

Progress Check

1. Explain the difference between 'citizenship' and 'good citizenship'.
2. Give six requirements for foreigners who wish to obtain British citizenship.
3. Name three conflicts in different parts of the world which have a religious basis.
4. Choose three protest groups and say what their main aims are.
5. Give three reasons why young people in Britain are taught citizenship.
6. Give four effects of globalisation.
7. What is the Universal Declaration of Human Rights, and why is it important?
8. What is morality, and why does it matter to the public services?

9. Outline the socioeconomic classification of British society.

10. Explain what a social group is and give five examples.

11. Name five laws that aim to prevent discrimination in Britain.

12. What are the main measures in the Nationality, Immigration and Asylum Act 2002?

13. Name five freedoms or rights protected by the Human Rights Act 1998.

14. What is the importance of the Data Protection Act?

15. What kinds of voluntary work can be done in the uniformed public services?

16. Why do most newspapers support the uniformed public services?

17. What are the problems caused by illegal immigration?

18. Explain two major demographic changes which have taken place since 1945.

19. What is the purpose of the 'war on terrorism'? What forms does this 'war' take?

UNIT 4

Team Development in Public Services

This unit covers:

- The use of teams and teamwork activities within the uniformed public services
- Team development
- How teamwork supports performance
- Working as a team member

Nearly everybody who works in a public service works in a team. Being a 'team player' is one of the main qualities that public services look for when they are recruiting. So it makes sense for you to study teams and get better at teamwork. This unit will help you to do both and details a number of techniques for measuring and improving team performance.

First the unit explores the teams which are used in the uniformed public services and how they benefit both the uniformed service and the team members themselves. Then it surveys the many and various activities which teams carry out: some physically active, some to do with thinking and solving problems, and many a mixture of the two.

Next, the unit analyses the roles of individuals in teams and outlines some famous theories about team behaviour. Team building, team performance and team cohesion, and how these are developed in the uniformed public services, are examined as well.

The last section of the unit is about ways of improving your own personal effectiveness as a team member, particularly by working on your communication and organisation.

<table>
<tr><td rowspan="2" style="writing-mode: vertical-lr">grading criteria</td><td>To achieve a **Pass** grade the evidence must show that the learner is able to:</td><td>To achieve a **Merit** grade the evidence must show that, in addition to the pass criteria, the learner is able to:</td><td>To achieve a **Distinction** grade the evidence must show that, in addition to the pass and merit criteria, the learner is able to:</td></tr>
<tr><td>**P1**

describe the types of teams that operate within a named uniformed public services and their associated benefits
Pg 153</td><td></td><td></td></tr>
<tr><td></td><td>**P2**

describe the different types of teamwork activities   Pg 154</td><td></td><td></td></tr>
</table>

grading criteria

To achieve a **Pass** grade the evidence must show that the learner is able to:	To achieve a **Merit** grade the evidence must show that, in addition to the pass criteria, the learner is able to:	To achieve a **Distinction** grade the evidence must show that, in addition to the pass and merit criteria, the learner is able to:
P3 describe ways of developing cohesive teams in the uniformed public services with reference to relevant theorists Pg 165	**M1** analyse the importance of team cohesion in effective team performance, with examples from two named uniformed public services, with reference to relevant theorists Pg 165	**D1** evaluate how team performance is monitored and team cohesion is encouraged within a named uniformed public service, with reference to relevant theories Pg 165
P4 identify the communication skills and personal organisation required when working in a team Pg 181		
P5 describe how targets are set and team performance is monitored Pg 174	**M2** assess the value of different methods of monitoring the performance of a team Pg 174	
P6 take part in five team activities, with support. Pg 174	**M3** take part in five team building activities confidently. Pg 174	**D2** evaluate own performance in team activities, recommending personal development for future teamwork activities. Pg 181

The use of teams and teamwork activities within the uniformed public services

Look at a uniformed public service and you are looking at people who belong to teams. At every level, and in every service, the work is, first and foremost, teamwork. It is as simple as that.

Types of team

A straightforward definition of 'team' is 'a group organised to work together'. This definition suits this unit, because it doesn't say anything about the size of the group, the nature of the organisation, or the kind of work. In the uniformed public services, teams vary enormously in size, in the type of organisation they have, and in the kinds of work that they do.

A relatively recent definition which says more about how teams work is the following, from an American textbook:

'A team is a small number of people with complementary skills who are committed to a common purpose, performance goals, and approach for which they hold themselves mutually accountable.'

(Katzenbach, J. R., and Smith, D. K. (1993) *The Wisdom of Teams: Creating the High-Performance Organization*. Harvard Business School, Boston, page 45)

Formal, informal

A formal team is a team that follows a lot of rules, wears a uniform, and has a traditional role or purpose. An informal team is just the opposite. Details are given in the table below.

Table 4.1 Formality checklist

Aspect of team identity	Formal	Informal
Rules	Plenty of rules, usually written down; team members are expected to obey them	As few rules as possible, not written down, and taken for granted
Roles	Team members have clearly defined roles, or jobs, and are expected to keep to them	Team members may have roles but they can change or swap them at short notice
Name	Formal groups have names, which tend to sound impressive or serious	The group has a name linked to its purpose, but it may rarely be used
Special titles	The different officials in the group all have titles	First names, or even nicknames, are used
Ranks	There is a clearly defined rank order; each rank has a name; higher ranks clearly have higher powers and status	No clearly defined rank order; everybody treats each other as equals
Uniform	A smart uniform is worn – and inspected from time to time	No uniform, unless it is needed for health and safety reasons
Ceremonies	The group has certain ceremonies (e.g. annual dinner or general meeting; passing-out ceremonies etc.)	No formal ceremonies – but they might go out for a drink together from time to time
Customs	Some customary behaviour (e.g. saluting; standing to attention)	No formal customs – only group norms, which are followed unconsciously and rarely defined
Language	Formal or old-fashioned language (e.g. 'My noble lord …', 'Sir!' etc.)	Colloquial and natural – perhaps with some slang
Permanent or temporary	Permanent	Semi-permanent or temporary
Paperwork	Plenty of it, set out and written according to strict rules of layout, grammar, word usage, etc.	No more paperwork than is necessary to do the job – otherwise, the less the better
Meeting times	Fixed, planned well into the future, all written down	Depends on the requirements of the job; usually frequent or daily, but not always written down
Aims and duties	Defined in a legal or semi-legal document, series of documents or constitution	These are probably listed on a **job description** if the team is a work-based one
Duties and routines	These are complex and may take some time to learn	Duties and routines are limited to the work or core activity of the team
Leadership	There is a wide 'power-gap' between leaders and lower officials; there are often a number of leadership or administrative roles (e.g. vice-president, **treasurer**); tends to have authoritarian style of leadership	Narrow power gap between leader(s) and the rest; leadership style is democratic or laissez-faire
Discipline	There is a written code of conduct or system of discipline, with clearly defined procedures for dealing with people who break discipline codes; special permission is needed to do things which are not routine	Discipline is kept to a minimum and tends to be achieved by group consensus or peer pressure rather than by a rule book
Tradition or history	A tradition respected by team members, which has lasted a long time – in some cases hundreds of years	Not much tradition or history – perhaps none at all.
Examples	House of Lords; Crown Court; Army regiments	Recreational teams; teams formed for a specific task, temporary teams; teams which spend a lot of time together; volunteer teams such as mountain rescue

Fig 4.1 How formal is this team?

Size

We think of teams as being organised groups of between, say, five and 15 people, but, from the point of view of this unit, a team can be far bigger than that. **Team spirit**, the sense of belonging to a team and wanting the team to be the best, can (at least in theory) exist throughout large organisations such as a regiment or even a police force.

What happens in practice is that small teams have leaders, and those leaders are themselves members of a team of team leaders, who are themselves led by a leader of team leaders who in turn belongs to a team of leaders of team leaders, and so on. In an organisation where the majority of members are in the lower ranks (such as any uniformed service), this system of teams within teams within teams develops naturally and has many advantages. Fig 4.2 illustrates this principle as it applies to the army.

Fig 4.2 Teams within teams – the army

Infantry	Cavalry
Battalion (Lieutenant-Colonel)	**Regiment (Lieutenant-Colonel)**
650	500 (but can be 650 or more)
Company (Major)	**Squadron (Major)**
100	100
Platoon (Subaltern)	**Troop (Subaltern)**
30	16
Section (Corporal)	
6–10	

NB   A Subaltern is a Lieutenant or 2nd Lieutenant
Numbers given are average for each group/team

⋏ = 10 soldiers

Royal Gloucestershire Regiments
www.glosters.org.uk

Small, large

It is a matter of opinion whether a team is a small one or a large one – and it depends what the average size of a team in a given organisation is. In any organisation a bigger-than-average team would be considered a big one. It might be fair to say that a team with more than 20 people in it is a large one. This is supported by the fact that a team such as a platoon in the army, which consists of 30 soldiers, is itself broken up into smaller units called sections, which have 6–10 soldiers in them – a practical number of people for a small, mobile team working under difficult conditions.

Small teams are likely to be:

- freshly established or temporary
- involved in specialist rather than general work
- less formal than large teams
- relatively close-knit.

Large teams are likely to be:

- permanent, or dealing with a large-scale emergency
- involved in general work
- split into subgroups or teams within teams
- less close-knit.

Temporary project/task teams

The unpredictable nature of some public service work means that teams may be formed and dissolved in a relatively short period of time. When hundreds or even thousands of police are drafted in at short notice to deal with major incidents such as the murders of five women in Ipswich at the end of 2006 or the London bombings of July 2005 (in which over 10,000 police were involved), teams are set up on a temporary basis. Because the work is urgent, the fulfilling of tasks (e.g. searching areas where bodies have been found or going through CCTV footage) is more important than the building of relationships or team spirit within the team. Clearly, temporary teams benefit from having good morale, but building morale is not the major aim that it might be in a permanent team such as a platoon in the army.

Increasingly, temporary project and task teams are multi-service teams or partnerships. In these circumstances, team members have to adapt to (or at least understand) the team behaviour of people from different organisations and even different nations and cultures. This is noticed when, for example, multinational peacekeepers work together. Teamwork norms are slightly different, and this can lead to exasperation with other people in the team.

Permanent groupings

In the uniformed public services, most teams are permanent. Members see each other on a daily basis and relationships are close: team members are perceived as colleagues and even friends. However, even if the team is permanent its work is likely to evolve over time, and members will come and go for various reasons. This means that even permanent teams are constantly evolving and renewing themselves; their character and the character of the people in them changes over time.

In permanent teams, there is likely to be a double agenda that members have to follow: (a) maintaining and building efficiency and success at the tasks for which the team was set up and (b) maintaining the human relationships and job satisfaction which the team provides for its members. Although to the public services and the public the achieving

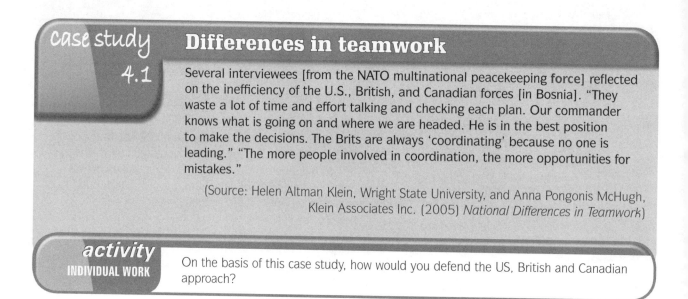

case study
4.1

Differences in teamwork

Several interviewees [from the NATO multinational peacekeeping force] reflected on the inefficiency of the U.S., British, and Canadian forces [in Bosnia]. "They waste a lot of time and effort talking and checking each plan. Our commander knows what is going on and where we are headed. He is in the best position to make the decisions. The Brits are always 'coordinating' because no one is leading." "The more people involved in coordination, the more opportunities for mistakes."

(Source: Helen Altman Klein, Wright State University, and Anna Pongonis McHugh, Klein Associates Inc. (2005) *National Differences in Teamwork*)

activity
INDIVIDUAL WORK

On the basis of this case study, how would you defend the US, British and Canadian approach?

of tasks is the main consideration, to team members the working relationships and job satisfaction may be more important on a day-to-day basis.

Benefits of teams

It is widely agreed that organisations benefit from the teamwork of their employees. However, there is a problem in proving the benefits of teams: there is a lack of evidence as to what happens if people work individualistically, with no teamwork at all. It may, in fact, not be humanly possible for people to work in organisations without also working in teams.

Contribution to organisational productivity and effectiveness

The biggest single difference between a uniformed public service and a company is that the public service does not need to make a profit to go on existing. Nevertheless, just like a company, it has to be productive and effective.

Productivity can be defined (for a public service) as doing as much quality work as possible using the least possible time, staffing and resources. Effectiveness means carrying out work that – in quantity and quality – achieves the aims or targets of the service.

Teamwork of the right type is believed to improve the productivity and effectiveness of an organisation, although this improvement is hard to measure. There are plenty of news items that attribute the successes of the uniformed services to good teamwork, but these do not prove that teamwork improves productivity.

Reduction of alienation

Alienation is a feeling of 'not belonging'. Teamwork involves interacting with other people, often quite intensively and for long periods of time. In a diverse society, teamwork is an effective way of involving people from various backgrounds in a shared task. Shared tasks bond people together (e.g. when parents bring up children) and they have this effect in the work situation. Experience shows that people from a wide range of different backgrounds can work very well together in teams and gain plenty of job satisfaction from the experience. This is particularly the case in services that have a diverse membership (e.g. the ambulance service).

Fostering innovation

Teamwork fosters (encourages) innovation (the use of new solutions to old problems), provided that it is the right kind of teamwork. Figs 4.4 and 4.5 on page 146 show two kinds of team (L represents the leader).

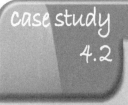

case study 4.2

Successful teamwork

World-Police teamwork puts paid to Cup security fears

BERLIN, July 7 (Reuters) – International police cooperation on a scale not seen before will be the most important security legacy of a World Cup finals that exceeded even the most optimistic hopes of the German organisers.

Before the tournament, authorities had rehearsed for every possible scenario from terrorist bombs to hooligan clashes, and media reports fuelled fears of neo-Nazi provocations, attacks on dark-skinned foreigners and crushes at public viewing areas.

In fact, with just two games left, the World Cup has gone off with barely a hitch, in a carnival atmosphere that surprised and delighted not just foreign visitors but also many Germans. More than 400 fans were arrested in Dortmund when Germany played Poland there, and more than 500 England fans were detained when they played Ecuador in Stuttgart, but police largely attributed the excesses to too much beer and sun.

.....

Behind the scenes, foreign officers worked alongside German colleagues at the federal police headquarters and a special anti-hooligan unit, while Interpol and Europol sent experts to a round-the-clock intelligence centre at the interior ministry.

But the real innovation was the deployment of some 320 uniformed police from 13 European countries to keep an eye on their own travelling fans, mainly at airports.

(Source: Mark Trevelyan, Security Correspondent, 12:28, Fri 7 July 2006, www.worldcup.reuters.co.uk)

activity
INDIVIDUAL WORK

1 Go through this passage and identify all the points where teamwork appears to have been successful.

2 Give reasons why this might have been.

Fig 4.3 Reducing alienation

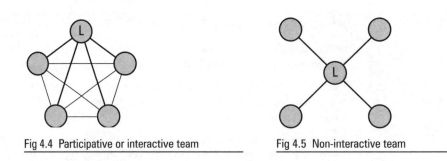

Fig 4.4 Participative or interactive team   Fig 4.5 Non-interactive team

Assuming that it is true that 'two heads are better than one' and that talking to other people is a good way of creating ideas and solving problems, the style of team shown in Fig 4.4 will be much more productive than the one shown in Fig 4.5. This is because the first style encourages interaction and there are 10 possible lines of communication. The second style, by contrast, has only four lines of interaction, and the structure of the team makes it impossible for members to generate ideas except with the leader.

Fig 4.4 shows a democratic, or at least consultative, team structure, which allows ideas to be pooled and problems to be solved collectively as well as individually. The structure depicted in Fig 4.5 is an authoritarian one and has few of the benefits of a more fully developed team, when it comes to fostering innovation. Most people, especially if they are of a sociable disposition (as many public service workers are), are far more creative in a democratic or consultative team.

See pages 50–57 in Unit 2 for more on styles of leadership.

Sharing expertise

It is of course impossible for a person who works totally alone to share expertise with anyone, but teamwork, especially if it is democratically organised, can be a learning experience for the whole team. In an authoritarian team, only the leader can share expertise with the team, but learning works best – for most people – if it is a two-way street. Many of us learn more effectively if we learn actively, by talking to people and doing things, than if we are simply forced to sit and listen all the time.

Implementing change

Teams are an effective way of implementing change within an organisation because of the way in which they interlink.

Changes in organisations start either at the top or the bottom. If they start at the top, briefings can be passed from management to team leaders who in turn brief their teams. If communication is good, and backed up by **in-service training**, change can quickly be achieved by this method. Likewise, if the people at the bottom of an organisation (the 'grass roots') have a concern, team structures allow the message to pass up the **chain of command** so that leaders and managers can do something about the problem. In the army, this process helps to keep ordinary soldiers well aware of the plans of their officers, and they in turn can make the officers, and even the government, aware of problems in, for example, supplies and equipment, such as those which have happened from time to time in Afghanistan.

Teams can also help to implement much needed change outside an organisation, as the next case study shows.

Identification and development of talent

Working in teams is a very good way of getting to know other people. In particular, you discover how people work and what their strengths and weaknesses are. At the same

case study 4.3

Implementing external change

Police team-ups beat Nigeria's scammers

Cooperation between Scotland Yard and Nigeria has improved.

As part of BBC World Service's series on Intercontinental Cops, Jenny Chryss explores how investigators from London and Lagos have linked up to combat corruption and fraud in Nigeria.

Globally, Nigeria has become associated with what is known as "advance fee" or 419 fraud.

Virtually anyone with an email account will be familiar with this crime, which involves sending emails or faxes to potential victims around the world, sucking them into a highly attractive but utterly false financial deal.

Back in Nigeria, the rewards are potentially highly lucrative – but now, owing to a crackdown and much-improved co-operation between police forces globally, it has become more risky for the perpetrators.

"Historically we've always had a problem getting evidence from Nigeria, but that's changing," says Detective Sergeant Mark Radford, head of the Africa desk at New Scotland Yard.

"They're keen to co-operate and bring a lot of the criminals in Nigeria to justice."

(Source: www.news.bbc.co.uk – Sunday 6 August 2006, 23:50 GMT 00:50 UK)

activity
INDIVIDUAL WORK

1 Think of various ways in which police forces from different countries can cooperate.

2 What are the main difficulties that have to be overcome with this sort of international teamwork?

time, other team members are discovering the same things about you. In this way, talent (the potential ability to do a job well) is identified informally and, because teams gossip, news about it is likely to get around.

In fact, team structures can be used more formally by management to learn about the special talents and abilities of their employees. Methods include:

- the monitoring of the team's day-to-day work by team leaders (this can be done by observing and recording the preferred roles of team members – in other words, the things they are best at and the ways in which they prefer to work)

- target setting and the role of different team members in achieving those targets

- systems of staff appraisal (typically, these are annual interviews between the team member and the team leader, assessing the strengths, weaknesses and aspirations/ career plans of the team member)

- teamwork and leadership exercises and training

- in-service training and staff development, where it contains an element of assessment

- **peer assessment** and self-assessment by team members.

Steps should be taken by team leaders who are identifying and developing talent in their teams to use objective methods of assessment, and to avoid favouritism.

Belbin

Meredith Belbin, a British expert on management and **team roles**, showed how the different talents and abilities of people in a team can benefit the team as a whole. One of the lessons of his work is that people are different, and that within a team these differences can – if properly used and understood – add greatly to the effectiveness of the team.

Belbin, M. (1981) *Management Teams: Why They Succeed or Fail*. Butterworth Heinemann

See page 155 for more on Belbin and his influential ideas.

Types of teamwork activities

Teamwork activities are tasks, exercises or actions where people work together with an agreed purpose. They can be divided into:

- task-centred activities, where the aim is to plan or carry out a particular job in the most effective way possible

- **team-centred** activities, where the aim is to 'bond' the team and learn about teamwork as a series of linked skills.

In addition, teamwork activities can be split into:

- **paper-based** exercises, where people get together and plan something which will be practised or carried out at a later date (e.g. planning an expedition)

- activity-based exercises, where groups carry out physical tasks or actively solve problems in ways that show the value of cooperation and teamwork (e.g. collectively building a raft using only a few items)

- work activities, which are carried out collectively or by coordinated team activity (e.g. firefighters putting out a fire).

> **remember**
>
> The word 'exercise' does not relate simply to practice. It can be used even in real planning for real activities.

Paper-based exercises

Paper-based exercises are sometimes used when planning an event, programme, process or activity. They might be on a small scale, where two or three people get together and write a shopping list for a camping trip, or on a very big scale where hundreds of people work on a project (e.g. space exploration, the planning of the Olympic games, a plan of what the country should do if there is an epidemic of bird flu, or designing a new aircraft carrier). Paper-based exercises are used to break down an activity so that:

- the size and scope of a project can be foreseen

- costs and resources can be estimated

- possible problems can be identified and solutions considered

- separate teams can work on different parts of the plan in more detail.

Tabletop Exercise Number 1: Avian Influenza (Prepared by Harvard School of Public Health Center for Public Health Preparedness, Version 1.2.3 (03.24.06). © HSPH-CPHP 2006 www.hsph.harvard.edu

Paper-based exercises can also be used as learning activities in teamwork. The principle is that a problem is set: for example, you are lost in a snowstorm and your car has got stuck; there are a number of items in the car which might help you, and the group has to list them in order of importance. The way the group manages the task, negotiating disagreements and coming up with agreed answers within a certain period of time is a learning experience in teamwork skills.

Disaster

A disaster is a (probably unforeseen) major event involving loss of life and/or property. Disasters are rare and dangerous, so team training cannot be done in real disasters. For this reason, paper-based exercises are very useful for planning the response and assessing the resources needed for different scenarios (possible disasters).

Logistics

Logistics refers to transport and supply – essential in warfare and in large-scale emergency response. To save money and mistakes, logistics should be planned on paper – after which the buying of resources and practical training of personnel can begin.

Activity-based exercises

These are exercises such as physical training, active problem-solving and 'realistic' simulations which build teamwork and professional skills – the kind of skills which the uniformed public services then have to use 'for real' in their work.

Physical training activities

These are exercises involving active teamwork. They often require a degree of strength and coordination. They are intended to develop:

- trust
- cooperation
- teamwork and communication skills
- leadership qualities
- **esprit de corps** in the group.

Often they take the form of getting a team across an imaginary swamp using a few materials – or similar scenarios.

Military/emergency exercises

These can be done as paper or '**table-top**' **exercises**. However, once the basic ideas have been worked out, it is possible to continue the planning process by running large-scale simulations which may take a whole day or (exceptionally) even longer. The government and the public services are increasingly using this method of planning as a way of preparing for major emergencies – both on a local and a national scale. The emergency services are involved, and they often require the help of members of the public prepared to act the part of casualties etc.

> **remember**
>
> It is possible for students to get actively involved in emergency planning. Contact your local authority emergency planning department for more details.

HM Government: Preparing for Emergencies

www.pfe.gov.uk

Cabinet Office

www.cabinetoffice.gov.uk

Civil Contingencies Act 2004. HMSO, London

The LESLP Major Incident Procedure Manual (latest edition). LESLP, London

Work-related team activity

This is the kind of teamwork which is found throughout the public services. Departments, sections, projects, partnerships, squads, crews, units, and watches: there are many names for teams (which in itself is a sign of how important they are).

There can be many different structures. Sometimes the members have interchangeable roles, as with community support officers or a watch in a fire and rescue service. Others, such as a surgeon's team in a hospital or aircrew in the RAF, have highly specialised roles. Teams can be big or small, permanent or temporary, **operative** or management. The best way to research these is to contact your local public services.

case study 4.4

Types of exercises

There are three main types of exercise:

■ discussion-based

■ table-top

■ live.

(A fourth category combines elements of the other three.)

The choice of which one to adopt depends on what the purpose of the exercise is. It is also a question of lead-in time and available resources.

Discussion-based exercises are cheapest to run and easiest to prepare. They can be used at the policy formulation stage as a 'talk-through' of how to finalise the plan. More often, they are based on a completed plan and are used to develop awareness about the plan through discussion. In this respect, they are often used for training purposes.

Table-top exercises are based on simulation, not necessarily literally around a table top. Usually, they involve a realistic scenario and a time line, which may be real time or may speed time up. Usually table tops are run in a single room, or in a series of linked rooms which simulate the divisions between responders who need to communicate and be co-ordinated. The players are expected to know the plan and they are invited to test how the plan works as the scenario unfolds. This type of exercise is particularly useful for validation purposes, particularly for exploring weaknesses in procedures. Table-top exercises are relatively cheap to run, except in the use of staff time. They demand careful preparation.

Live exercises are a live rehearsal for implementing a plan. Such exercises are particularly useful for testing logistics, communications and physical capabilities. They also make excellent training events from the point of view of experiential learning, helping participants develop confidence in their skills and providing experience of what it would be like to use the plan's procedures in a real event. Where the latter purposes are, in fact, the main objective of the exercise, then it is essentially a training exercise or practice drill. Live exercises are expensive to set up on the day and demand the most extensive preparation.

(Source: www.ukresilience.info)

activity
GROUP WORK

1   As a group, design a table-top planning exercise to deal with a possible emergency in your local area.

2   Run this activity within your group.

Achieving work objectives

Objectives are measurable activities and targets used in teamwork. Objectives are descriptions of the kinds of work the team has to do, such as 'Prepare and implement an action plan to reduce community tension' (one of the **National Occupational Standards** for the police). Targets describe when, and how well, a job has to be done. Objectives and targets, set by the government or by some other overseeing body, are worded and defined in such a way that they can only be achieved through skilled and effective teamwork.

Skills for Justice – see website for National Occupational Standards for police
www.skillsforjustice.com

Planning and achieving a project

When a new project is planned, it is usual to recruit and if necessary train a new team to carry it out. The team has to work together to plan and implement the project, and then, when the project is complete, to review it, assess its success and learn the necessary lessons. The whole process is a complicated one, and you should consult the public services about the details.

Types of teams in the public services

Public service teams come in all shapes, sizes, roles, and degrees of **specialisation**. From the highest ranks to the lowest, people work in teams.

Teams can be classified according to:

- the service they work for
- their positions within the organisation
- the links they have with other organisations
- the number of people working in them
- their role
- the links they have with other teams.

Some of them are described briefly below.

Divisional

A divisional team is a team which either heads, or works in, a **division**. Divisions are the largest units in the British army apart from the army itself. There are five divisions in the army, but only two of them are fighting divisions: the others are concerned with administration. The word 'division' is also used in the fire and rescue service in relation to posts and teams which coordinate different fire stations within the area.

Departmental

Many public services have departments of one sort or another, and these are likely to specialise in particular types of work. HM Revenue and Customs, for example, has departments specialising in benefits and credits, organisational development, corporation tax and VAT, detection, intelligence, criminal investigation, etc. A departmental team can be a team composed of the heads of all the departments in an organisation (to ensure that they liaise with each other effectively), and it can also be one of a number of more or less specialist teams within a department. The word 'department' has civilian overtones and is used less in the armed forces than in other uniformed and non-uniformed services. High-level management teams within departments and some civilian services may be called 'boards' or 'committees', suggesting that their roles are to do with planning, thinking and discussion rather than direct action.

Sectional

A section is a small part of an organisation, not usually visible to the public. The word implies that, at some time in the past, the section has been cut off from a bigger department. The work is specialised. An example is the Ministry of Defence's Compassionate Section, which authorises compassionate leave at public expense for soldiers in difficult personal circumstances. A sectional team is a team that works in a section, or a team of section heads (coordinating the work of different sections in an organisation).

The word 'section' is also used in the infantry (army) for a group of about 12 soldiers led by a corporal – a classic example of a close-knit team.

Geographical

This could describe any team whose work is limited to a particular geographical area, whether large or small. Some teams in NATO, for example, will be involved in NATO activities in any countries which are members or where NATO troops are operating. A Neighbourhood Watch scheme is a geographical team operating over a few streets. As the fire and rescue service, the police, the NHS and other services are locally or regionally organised, it follows that most teams in these services are limited by geographical area.

Multi-disciplinary

These are teams involving experts in different fields. A forensic science team going to the scene of a murder would be an example. Some would be experts in DNA sampling, some in fingerprinting, some in forensic psychology, and so on.

Regiment, brigade

Regiments are army groups of around 650 soldiers. Many have been in existence for hundreds of years, and they are proud of their history and traditions. Regiments provide a sense of belonging and an emotional focus which few organisations can match. Although they are perhaps too big to be considered as 'teams', regiments are collections of teams which have been effective over the years and have been much admired. The merging and disbanding of regiments resulting from army funding cuts in recent years has given rise to sadness and bitterness among people who are connected with them.

A **brigade** is a large battle group consisting of several regiments or **battalions** – and containing around 5000 soldiers in all. (A battalion is a body of infantry and the same size as a regiment.)

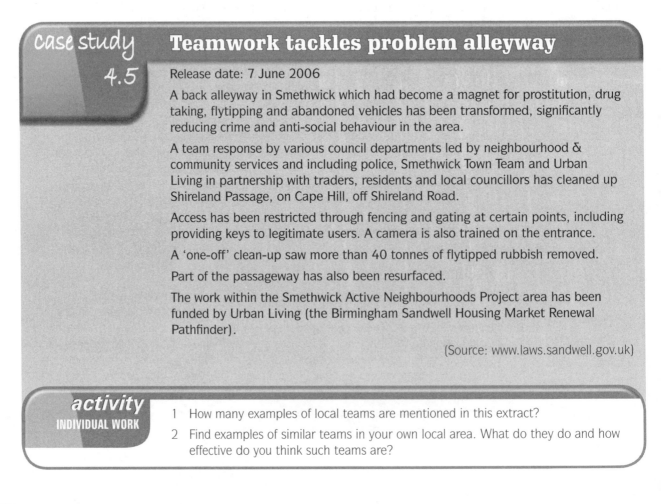

case study 4.5   Teamwork tackles problem alleyway

Release date: 7 June 2006

A back alleyway in Smethwick which had become a magnet for prostitution, drug taking, flytipping and abandoned vehicles has been transformed, significantly reducing crime and anti-social behaviour in the area.

A team response by various council departments led by neighbourhood & community services and including police, Smethwick Town Team and Urban Living in partnership with traders, residents and local councillors has cleaned up Shireland Passage, on Cape Hill, off Shireland Road.

Access has been restricted through fencing and gating at certain points, including providing keys to legitimate users. A camera is also trained on the entrance.

A 'one-off' clean-up saw more than 40 tonnes of flytipped rubbish removed.

Part of the passageway has also been resurfaced.

The work within the Smethwick Active Neighbourhoods Project area has been funded by Urban Living (the Birmingham Sandwell Housing Market Renewal Pathfinder).

(Source: www.laws.sandwell.gov.uk)

activity
INDIVIDUAL WORK

1   How many examples of local teams are mentioned in this extract?
2   Find examples of similar teams in your own local area. What do they do and how effective do you think such teams are?

See Unit 13, *BTEC National Public Services Book 2*, for more on the above.

Force

This term used to be used for the police but the word 'service' is now preferred. As a group, it is usually too big to be considered a team in the normal sense. In military terms, a force is a temporary battle group of an undefined size, probably consisting of the army and the Royal Marines, backed up by sea and air power.

activity
GROUP WORK 4.1
P1

Produce a wallchart on the teams that operate in one uniformed public service, stating what they do and how they benefit both the service and the team members. Your chart should be suitable for a careers exhibition for young people.

Multi-agency/services teams

These are becoming increasingly important (a) because of the risk of large-scale threats to the UK and the growth of resilience and emergency planning and (b) because of the idea of '**joined-up government**' and the belief that social problems are best dealt with by a number of agencies working together in teams. For example, the Safer Bristol Partnership formed the following team to deal with drugs problems in the city:

- Bristol Crime and Drugs Strategy
- Executive Partners
- Safer Bristol Executive Membership
- Avon & Somerset Constabulary
- Avon & Somerset Probation Services
- Avon & Somerset Police Authority
- Avon Fire and Rescue Service
- Bristol City Council
- Crown Prosecution Service
- Government Office for the South West
- HM Prison-Bristol
- The Primary Care Trusts
- Drug Service Providers Forum
- **Voscur** (Bristol City Council, March 2005).

In partnerships of this sort the teams consist of representatives from each of the organisations involved. They meet, make decisions, and then – guided by this planning – the organisations work in their own areas of expertise to carry out the strategy that has been decided.

Specialist teams

These are skilled teams doing a specific type of work.

Search and rescue teams

These are usually run by the Royal Navy, which uses helicopters, or by voluntary groups such as the Royal National Lifeboat Institution (RNLI) or Mountain Rescue.

Project teams

These are set up by a public service for a special purpose. If the project is a pilot scheme or of limited duration, the team may well be disbanded once its work is done.

Emergency services

These are teams which are trained to work together with other teams from other emergency services, especially in the case of major incidents. For major incidents, there is a system for coordinating teams called Gold, Silver or Bronze command, depending on the scale of the incident and the strategic, tactical or operational level. For examples of how they work or what they do, contact your local emergency planning department, or download emergency plans from the internet.

Major Incident Procedure Manual (London Emergency Services Liaison Panel, 2004)

Metropolitan Police – see website for information about specialist teams
www.met.police.uk

remember

Information on projects and project teams is to be found on local authority websites.

activity
INDIVIDUAL WORK 4.2

P2

Produce a leaflet for people intending to apply to a public service, describing the different types of teamwork that they are likely to come across in that service and the ways in which those types of teamwork are used.

Team development

Teams work best if they are the right size for the job. Not only does the number of people have to be right but also they need to have the right skills and the right personalities. Choosing a team and building it up is a skilled job.

Roles in teams

The simplest form of teamwork is based on the fact that several people are stronger than one. If a car gets stuck in a snowdrift, it is easier to get it out if several people are pushing. In this scenario, most of the team roles are the same: push like mad!

Public service teams are usually more complex than this, and they benefit from the fact that each member is different. If everyone can do what they are best at, the team comes out with good work. This means that teams work best if their members do different things, behave in different ways and don't try to be clones of each other. This is especially the case under democratic leadership where the team members are expected to share ideas and pool their knowledge and abilities. These different behaviours of team members are called team roles.

Leader

The leader is the person in a team who allocates work or roles to other team members and is accountable if the team fails in its work. Leaders may be formal or (less often) informal, and may be chosen by people outside the team or (less often) by the team itself. The leadership style of the leader is likely to have a big effect on the way that the team works.

Expert

The expert is the team member who knows more about a specialised or technical topic than other team members and is consulted by them because of this. Experts are chosen (or select themselves) because of their knowledge, not their leadership skills. Experts have status in teams because their information or advice is useful, but they only lead certain types of team (e.g. a surgeon's team).

Team player

A team player is a member who is regarded as cooperative and supportive of the team effort. Team players are loyal, enjoy working with others and will back up the leader.

Theories of team roles

The roles of individual team members vary according to their knowledge, their experience, their abilities, their skills and their personalities. The roles have been classified by experts in team building, and a number of theories of team roles have been devised: two of the more popular ones are those of Belbin and Honey.

Belbin

A classification which most people understand and accept is that devised by Meredith Belbin – a British management consultant and researcher. He defines a team role as: 'Our tendency to behave, contribute and interrelate with others in a particular way.' (See case study on page 156.)

Honey

In 1982, Honey and Mumford advanced some theories about **learning styles** which relate to the roles people adopt in teamwork. They identified four learning styles:

- Activists – they like interactive problem-solving activities and thrive on challenges. They don't like reading or listening or being told in too much detail what to do.

- Pragmatists – they are practical people who learn by doing. They don't like theoretical work, or ideas which bring no obvious benefit.

- Reflectors – they like to think and observe before they speak or act. They don't like being rushed or having to 'perform' in front of others.

- Theorists – they are logical, detached, rational, inquisitive, and like ideas. They don't like working with emotional and intuitive people (www.peterhoney.com).

remember

A team role is not the role of the whole team, but the role of each individual in the team.

Belbin Team Roles

www.belbin.com

Federal Aviation Administration: Human Factors Research and Engineering Group – see website for information on team theory

www.hf.faa.gov

Campaign for Learning – see website for information about Honey's theory

www.campaign-for-learning.org.uk

Team building

In many situations, it is necessary to build a new team from scratch or to revitalise a team which is growing stale and is not meeting its targets. Successful managers are often skilled at this complex process.

Recruitment

This is the process of finding new people for the team. They may be advertised for on the open job market, in appropriate journals and websites, or selected from internal applicants. Alternatively, they can be chosen from the present workforce. Choosing the right personnel for a team depends on, among other things:

- the purpose and ethos of the team
- having appropriate job descriptions
- finding people who can complement the skills and characters of the people already in the team
- being able to offer adequate pay and working conditions to attract suitable applicants
- avoiding unfair discrimination.

Induction

This is a brief period of familiarisation with the workplace, the rest of the team, and the aims and ethos of the team.

case study 4.6   Team roles

Table 4.2 Belbin's team role descriptions

Team role	Contribution	Allowable weakness
Plant (Cerebral role)	Creative, imaginative, unorthodox; solves difficult problems	Ignores incidentals; too preoccupied to communicate effectively
Resource Investigator (People-oriented role)	Extrovert, enthusiastic, communicative; explores opportunities; develops contacts	Over-optimistic; loses interest once initial enthusiasm has passed
Coordinator (People-oriented role)	Mature, confident, a good chairperson; clarifies goals, promotes decision-making, delegates well	Can be seen as manipulative; offloads personal work
Shaper (Action-oriented role)	Challenging, dynamic, thrives on pressure; has the drive and courage to overcome obstacles	Prone to provocation; offends people's feelings
Monitor Evaluator (Cerebral role)	Sober, strategic and discerning; sees all options; judges accurately	Lacks drive and ability to inspire others
Teamworker (People-oriented role)	Cooperative, mild, perceptive and diplomatic; listens, builds, averts friction	Indecisive in crunch situations
Implementer (Action-oriented role)	Disciplined, reliable, conservative and efficient; turns ideas into practical actions	Somewhat inflexible; slow to respond to new possibilities
Completer Finisher (Action-oriented role)	Painstaking, conscientious, anxious; searches out errors and omissions; delivers on time	Inclined to worry unduly; reluctant to delegate
Specialist (Cerebral role)	Single-minded, self-starting, dedicated; provides knowledge and skills in rare supply	Contributes on only a narrow front; dwells on technicalities

(Source: adapted from www.belbin.com)

activity
GROUP WORK

1   Hold or observe a meeting, and identify as many of the team roles as you can.

2   Hold a group meeting on a topic that you all know something about. Assign the above roles to each individual. Participate in the meeting, trying to behave and speak 'in role' as much as possible. Then assess each other's performance.

Fig 4.6 Team building at the rock face

Motivation

Motivation has a lot to do with the nature of the work, the nature of the team, the aspirations and needs of the new team worker, establishing appropriate team roles, and pay and working conditions.

See pages 53 and 65 for more information on motivation.

Training

New team members should get the training they require. However, it weakens teams if they are used as training grounds for new workers who 'sit in' or 'shadow' without getting properly involved with the team. There should be in-service training and staff development for all team members from time to time.

Coaching

This is more linked to sports teams than to work teams; it could be seen as part of training.

Mentoring

This is the use of an experienced member of staff to guide and help new recruits to a team. It is widely used in services such as the police and is of great value, if the mentor and recruit are compatible.

Team knowledge

This develops with time; the most important thing for a new team member is not to rush to judgement about the rest of the team. Equally, it is vital for leaders to understand their teams.

Awareness of team members' strengths

Everybody has strengths and weaknesses, and leaders should allocate tasks to people who are strong at each kind of task, and try to avoid giving team members tasks of a type they are not so good at. Team members should tactfully support other members in areas where they may be weak without, of course, neglecting their own work. Appraisal will help to increase people's awareness of their own strengths and weaknesses.

remember

You should ask people who work in the public services about their experience of mentoring, to acquire an in-depth understanding of the issues involved, and of its value.

Appraisal should be linked to training and staff development to increase team members' strengths and reduce weaknesses.

Team development

Tuckman

In 1965 Bruce Tuckman, an American management expert, produced a model of team development called 'Forming–Storming–Norming–Performing' which has become generally accepted as a description of how teams develop. A summary is given in the table below.

Table 4.3 Tuckman's stages of team development

Stage	Behaviour
Forming	Team members feel dependent on the team leader for direction. Team members 'test the waters' to get to know one another. Some anxiety and uncertainty will occur about how the team will work together and how the team should approach the problem.
Storming	Healthy group conflict and debate should occur during this stage. Team members struggle with the team task as well as the roles each member will play on the team. Openness and willingness to share ideas and hear from all team members is important. Some teams get stuck in this stage and it destroys the team.
Norming	Team members should feel secure about their roles, and during this stage the team focuses on distributing the workload. Team norms (rules) develop and communication continues to be important.
Performing	The team is task focused. The leader often coordinates the team's activities. It is important that team members communicate their progress on the task to other team members. Sharing of resources and knowledge helps the team.

(Source: www.hf.faa.gov – based on Tuckman, B. W. and Jensen, M. C. (1977) Stages of small-group development revisited. *Group and Organizational Studies*, 12, 419–27)

Like any other human relationship, teams evolve. In later theories, Tuckman also studied the way that teams lose their effectiveness after a period of success.

Transforming

This is a stage that Tuckman added to his original four. Transforming is the period when the team has, for whatever reason, ceased to perform effectively. It has to change its identity, its members, its role or its tasks and become, in effect, a new team before it can go through the cycle again and once more reach the performing stage.

Businessballs – see website for information about Tuckman's work

www.businessballs.com

Weaknesses

The idea that 'a chain is only as strong as its weakest link' is sometimes true of teams, as not all members can be equally good at their work. Where it seems that a team member's performance is weak the choices are:

- to ignore the fact
- to change the weak member's role
- to retrain or counsel the weaker member
- to dismiss the weaker member from the team.

The option chosen depends on the circumstances and on the characters of the people concerned.

Sensitivities

In a hard-working and effective team, people take a pride in their work and are deeply involved. This deep involvement means that their emotions are involved as well, and if they feel undervalued or overlooked their feelings may be hurt. Furthermore, because teams work closely together, chance remarks or differences in belief about things unconnected with the team may cause ill feeling. Sensitivity is not a bad quality, but team members should respect other team members and try to avoid actions or words which give needless offence.

Supporting all team members

Teams must be **inclusive**, and everybody must be treated fairly and equally, to avoid favouritism and discrimination. Good work must be recognised not only by the team leader but by team members too, if possible. In the public services, teams give plenty of support to other members outside the immediate work context, just as friends do. They also (e.g. in the fire and rescue service) give valuable mutual support after traumatic or distressing incidents (e.g. when a family is found dead after an arson attack).

How team building is conducted in the uniformed public services

This is a large topic, and the first point to make is that team building is a natural process, thanks to the tendency of individuals to conform or obey when they are in a group. The psychological and social behaviour described by Asch and Milgram applies in uniformed public service teams and helps new members to fit quickly into an established team.

See pages 201–204 in Unit 5 for more on conformity and obedience.

In the uniformed public services, team building is both taught formally and developed informally through:

- initial training, and periods of later training
- the ethos and values of the service, which reinforce the training
- the team-based routines and patterns of everyday work
- the delegation of responsibilities to subordinates
- the use of simulations, 'live' military exercises and problem-solving tasks.

---

case study 4.7 — **Police initial training**

Phase 1: Induction. Critical areas of knowledge essential to any new employee, such as terms & conditions of service, **professional standards**, equality of opportunity, race & diversity, values of the service, role & responsibility, introductions to policing & the organisation, officer safety, first aid and health & safety, society & community.

Phase 2: Community Safety and Partnership. This is the wider context of policing and introduces the understanding that officers will need to properly work with & within their local areas in an increasingly complex society. Learning should help student officers develop their understanding of:

- The needs of the diverse society in which they work
- Their role & the relationship with the wider police and criminal justice system in providing a policing service
- Crime reduction & community safety strategies
- The importance of cooperation with multi-agency & community groups

- Critical thinking, problem solving & independent judgement
- The areas they will police, local issues & policing requirements, and the community with whom they will work
- Building working relationships with partner agencies, criminal justice bodies and the local community.

Phase 3: Supervised Patrol. As officers acquire knowledge of legislation, powers, procedures, inter-personal & technical skills that they will use on a daily basis, they undergo practical and simulated learning activities to assist them in translating learning into **vocational** action. This phase allows them to experience the work of policing their local area within a Professional Development Unit, supported by a tutor constable and operational supervisors.

Phase 4: Independent Patrol. Officers continue their learning within the operational workplace and will work independently with colleagues, other practitioners, groups and organisations to find lasting solutions to policing problems. They will continue to receive coaching and mentoring support from the PDU [Professional Development Unit] whilst working on operational patrol groups. This phase should include a minimum of 30 days protected learning.

The high degree of engagement with the local community is designed to give student police officers the most realistic training possible, enabling them to develop relationships with the local community at the earliest stages of an officer's career. Community engagement is one of the key principles behind IPLDP [Initial Police Learning & Development Programme]. Student officers must be able to understand the needs, expectations and dynamics of their local community, in addition to current relationships between the community and the police service, which is why Phase 2 of the curriculum focuses on community engagement.

(Source: email from Justin Rosa, Home Office)

activity
INDIVIDUAL WORK

Identify all the elements described above which relate directly or indirectly to teamwork.

Team performance

Teamwork and the development of teamwork are big subjects, and they take different forms in different uniformed services. You should contact local services to find out more.

A modern, accountable uniformed public service knows that managers, the government, and indeed the public want to know how well the service is doing. As most services do a vast range of different jobs, the most accurate way of monitoring service performance is to monitor the performance of all the teams within the service. In this way, the strengths and weaknesses become known, and those teams which are underperforming can have the resources, encouragement and training that they need to improve.

Performance indicators

Performance indicators are usually set by central government to provide a measure of how well a public service is doing. The statutory performance indicators for the police are laid down as Statutory Instruments under Section 4 of the Local Government Act 1999. They appear in the National Policing Plan 2006–2009. Performance indicators for the police are classified according to the 'domain' – area of policing (or public perception of the police) that they refer to. These include 'citizen focus', 'reducing crime', 'investigating crime', 'promoting safety' and 'local policing'. There are also differences in the frequency with which performance indicators have to be reported back to the Home Office. (The rules are complex, and there is no room to go into them in detail here.)

There are 29 statutory performance indicators. The table shows two of them.

Table 4.4 Two statutory performance indicators for policing

Statutory Performance Indicator (SPI Number)	Long title	Short title
SPI 5b	Violent crime per 1000 population	Violent crime rate
SPI 5e	Life threatening crime and gun crime per 1000 population	Life threatening and gun crime rate

(Source: Home Office. *Guidance on Statutory Performance Indicators for Policing, 2006/07*)

Target setting

Target setting is used to motivate teams and to monitor performance. Target setting (at least in the police) is itself a team activity as the following case study shows.

case study 4.8 — Target setting

The process of target setting for the Local Policing Plan 2007/08 commenced in early November 2006 with joint Force and Police Authority workshops. The publication of the National Community Safety Plan 2006–2009 coincided with a series of consultation forums hosted by the Police Authority with stakeholder groups and members of the Five Counties Trade Association. Each of these events provided a valuable insight into the expectations of our communities and stakeholders and the key national priorities that will shape policing over the next three years.

(Source: www.gwentpa.police.uk)

activity
INDIVIDUAL WORK

1 How many different kinds of team have had to work together to produce the Gwent local policing targets?
2 What are the arguments for and against setting targets in this way?

Public service targets are figures which, if reached, would show a realistic, achievable yet challenging improvement in the service given within a specific period of time. Targets can apply to success at fighting crime, as in the example above, but they can also be set for more intangible things such as measures of public satisfaction with the service given.

 See pages 166 and 167 for more on targets.

Monitoring

Monitoring team performance is the process of checking or measuring how well the team is doing at fairly frequent intervals. It is useful because it detects problems early on, and, if the team is doing well, it allows its performance to be recognised. Monitoring can be done by the team itself, by the team leader, or by supervisors outside the team. If done insensitively or too often, monitoring can demotivate the team by making members feel that people are breathing down their necks.

case study 4.9

Extract from London policing targets

Table 4.5 Targets for reducing the level of gun-enabled crime

Objective 2: To reduce the level of gun-enabled crime				
	Measures	2004/2005 performance year	2005/06 target	2005/06 Performance year to date (April–Dec 05)
SPI 5e	Life threatening and gun crime per 1000 population	0.92		0.81
PP	Reduce level of gun-enabled crime	–7.9%	4% reduction	+7.6%
PP	Improve detection rate for gun-enabled crime	18.5%	Sanction detection rate 20%	18.9%

(Source: Metropolitan Police Authority. *Policing London: Strategy 2006–09, Plan 2006/07*)

activity
GROUP WORK

What are the difficulties in setting targets for something like crime?

Reviewing performance and performance against targets

The team's performance as a whole can be reviewed at regular meetings, or when its performance is checked against its targets, or when debriefing after a particular task is completed. For a review to be effective, all team members should be in possession of the facts about the team's performance during the period under review – and have had time to look at the figures and assimilate them before the review meeting. A review should be done honestly, but not destructively, and sarcasm should be avoided.

See pages 71–74 in Unit 2 for more on debriefing.

Support and development of team members

Support and development are ongoing processes in many teams, and much of it is done informally through discussion, friendly advice, and so on. Because relationships can be close in an effective team, with a good deal of mutual respect, teams can give support even with members' personal difficulties – up to a point, and depending on the circumstances.

The development of team members is usually reviewed in individual appraisal meetings, which take place once a year, or more often. The team member (appraisee) meets the team leader (appraiser) in a place where the phone isn't ringing all the time. During the meeting, the appraisee's strengths and weaknesses and their aspirations for the future are discussed, and, if necessary, they should be able to request in-service training and other career development help. Good appraisal builds confidence and motivation, and it can boost team performance.

How team performance is evaluated in the uniformed public services

The evaluation of team performance is taken seriously in the uniformed public services, as the following job specification for an assistant manager in the NHS demonstrates.

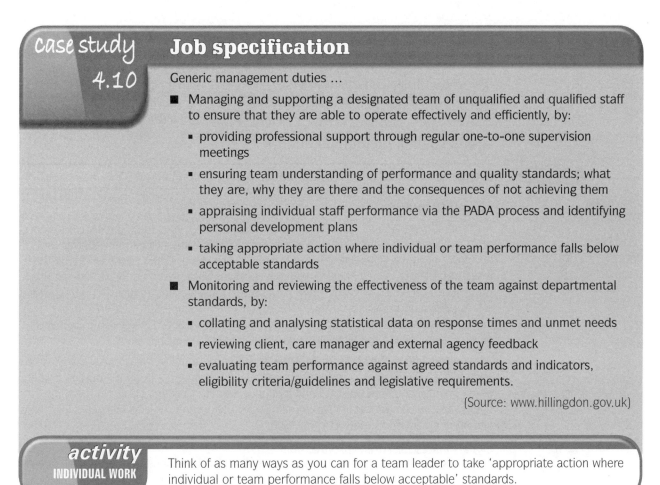

case study 4.10

Job specification

Generic management duties ...

■ Managing and supporting a designated team of unqualified and qualified staff to ensure that they are able to operate effectively and efficiently, by:

- providing professional support through regular one-to-one supervision meetings

- ensuring team understanding of performance and quality standards; what they are, why they are there and the consequences of not achieving them

- appraising individual staff performance via the PADA process and identifying personal development plans

- taking appropriate action where individual or team performance falls below acceptable standards

■ Monitoring and reviewing the effectiveness of the team against departmental standards, by:

- collating and analysing statistical data on response times and unmet needs

- reviewing client, care manager and external agency feedback

- evaluating team performance against agreed standards and indicators, eligibility criteria/guidelines and legislative requirements.

(Source: www.hillingdon.gov.uk)

activity
INDIVIDUAL WORK

Think of as many ways as you can for a team leader to take 'appropriate action where individual or team performance falls below acceptable' standards.

Fig 4.7 It all has to be monitored and evaluated

Team cohesion

Teams which are not unified, which can't work well together, or which break up into small cliques, lack **cohesion** and are no longer likely to be effective teams. Poor cohesion leads to poor motivation, lack of control by the team leader and grumbling and backbiting among ordinary members.

Definition of team goals

These should be set out clearly in the job descriptions of people joining the team and reinforced for new team members during the induction period. A system of mentoring over time will help new team members to 'internalise' both the goals and the ethos of the team (which can be interlinked). The natural tendency for new team members to obey and conform will also help them to identify with team goals.

Group conflict (actual, potential)

See pages 84–86 in Unit 2 for information on group conflict.

Group turnover

Although it depends on circumstances, it is common for teams to be undermined by a rapid turnover of members or, conversely, by people staying in the team too long and becoming negative, stale and backward-looking as a result. Rapid turnover can be the result of poor pay, poor working conditions, or work which is too boring or difficult. It has a knock-on effect by giving team members the feeling that there is something wrong with the team and that maybe they too ought to be thinking of moving on. What's more, it means that many people in the team are inexperienced, so that the old hands have to keep helping them out and consequently become overworked.

At the other end of the scale, the so-called 'canteen culture' in the police ('Things were a lot better 10 years ago – these newcomers know nothing!') can be the outcome when bored and disappointed officers, who feel undervalued, remain too long in the same team. Most people probably give of their best if they spend three to five years in a team and are then either promoted or move on.

Opportunities for career progression

Teamwork should be a learning curve, and should give people the opportunity to gain new skills and enlarge their repertoire or expertise in various team roles. This is not only to improve job satisfaction but also to enable members to progress in their careers, either by promotion or specialisation. Team leaders should try to ensure that team members can, from time to time, do something that will 'look good on their CV'.

See page 154 for a reminder about team roles.

Recognition of contributions

This can take the form of thanks from team leaders or, better still, managers outside the team who have benefited from the team's good work, and praise from the public should find its way back to the team members, when appropriate. Team members should be encouraged to build on their strengths, rather than merely reduce their weaknesses. Not only is this better for their morale and **self-esteem** than merely dwelling on negative features of their work but it also brings about faster overall improvement.

Team leadership

Good leadership can help to make a team cohesive – in other words, bond it so that everybody works well and willingly together. This can be done by setting aims and targets which are worthwhile, developing team skills, delegating responsibility to motivate suitable team members and spread the workload fairly, and by carrying out group activities which develop team spirit and raise morale.

Strong and weak leadership styles

Most teams like to feel that they have 'strong' leadership – leaders they can trust to make good decisions and to back the team up if anything goes wrong. In many cases, weak leaders are those who are perceived as being lazy, selfish or cowardly.

Leadership style often has a big part to play in the effectiveness of teams. For most public service teams a democratic or consultative leadership style works best – except in an emergency (e.g. in warfare) when a more military-style approach coupled with delegation down the chain of command is needed because it allows decisions and actions to be taken at speed. Despite the delegation this is not the same as laissez-faire leadership, because it requires rigorous training in leadership for subordinates, considerable self-discipline and careful monitoring. This method motivates teams effectively in wartime, uses people's energy and originality, and can bring swift, dramatic results.

With this approach, there is strong leadership but authority is delegated to subordinates. This 'manoeuvrist' leadership style requires a good deal of training but it has great advantages:

- It allows decisions to be made by people who are close to the action.

- It enables rapid and flexible response because orders and feedback do not have to pass down or up long chains of command.

- It motivates subordinates by giving them responsibility and allowing them to use more creativity in tackling challenges.

The main principles of this approach, now widely used in the armed forces, are:

- Leaders make sure their teams understand the intentions and tactics of their mission.

- Teams are told what to achieve and why it is necessary.

- Teams are given the resources to do their job.

- The leader uses minimum control so as not to limit the team's freedom of action.

- The teams (subordinates) decide how to achieve their aims.

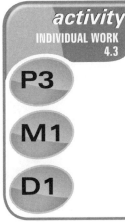

remember

Authoritarian leadership means 'You do as you're told'. Democratic leadership means discussing and reaching agreed decisions. Laissez-faire leadership means letting the team do what they want.

Link

See pages 50–57 in Unit 2 for plenty more on leadership styles. Look also at Unit 13 in *BTEC National Public Services Book 2*.

activity

INDIVIDUAL WORK 4.3

P3

M1

D1

Write a manual for team leaders:

1　Explain how they build cohesive teams in the uniformed public services.

2　Explain why and how much team cohesion matters (with examples from two uniformed public services).

3　Explain the various ways of encouraging and monitoring team performance and cohesion in a particular uniformed public service. You must include the ideas of named theorists in team building.

How teamwork supports performance

Target setting

See page 161 above and page 211 in Unit 5.

Identifying objectives

One of the difficulties of target setting is that people cannot always agree on what the targets (objectives) should be. For many years, the National Health Service has been set targets for cutting waiting lists and waiting times, but health professionals have complained that other health needs (e.g. cancer or obesity screening and the provision of new or expensive drugs) have been neglected because there has been too much emphasis on the target of cutting waiting lists.

Police targets are set by the Home Office and by local police authorities in conjunction with the police themselves. The accurate collection of crime data under the **National Crime Recording Standard** rules is important in this context. The British Crime Survey, which gives crime statistics from public surveys rather than from police figures, is also taken into account.

Fig 4.8 Issues and stages in setting and reaching targets

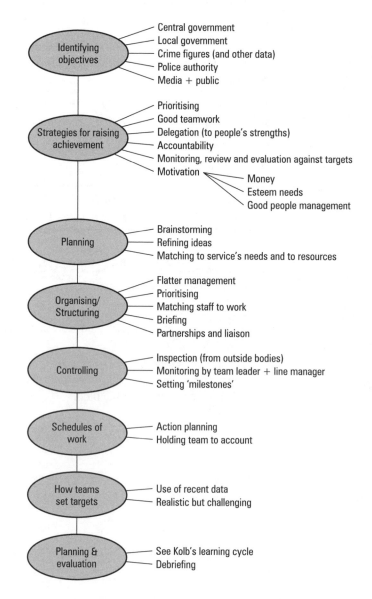

Strategies for raising achievement

These are listed in Fig 4.8 above. There are two main kinds of strategy for raising achievement:

- Strategies outside the team (e.g. government or senior management strategies): these should aim to create conditions in which teams can do their best work. They involve funding, human and other resources, and giving teams sufficient authority (including legal powers) to do their job. They also include 'negative' strategies such as discipline. To raise achievement there has to be a way of measuring achievement and of setting **benchmarks**, **milestones** and targets. This means a system of accountability is needed: people need to know what the team is doing now in order to raise achievement in the future.

- Strategies within the team: good leadership, teamwork, communication and motivation should all be encouraged. The team's work has to be shared out so that people are doing what they are best at. Work should be organised and prioritised so that time and effort are not wasted on irrelevancies. Administration and **bureaucracy**, although necessary, need to be kept under control.

Review and evaluation of outcomes against targets

Outcomes are the achievements of the team; a target is what the team ought to have achieved in a given year or by a given date. Reviewing and evaluating involve deciding how successful work has been over a period of time. This means that there has to be a record of what is being done and a target for what ought to be done. Accurate and accessible record-keeping is essential.

Planning

This should be written down and based on principles, such as those outlined in Kolb's learning cycle, which can be summarised as: experiencing – reflecting – concluding – planning. What this means is that planning should be realistic, and based on situations and problems which are known about. (This is one reason why 'intelligence' is so important in the armed forces and the police.)

Planning should be both:

- creative – generating ideas as in 'brainstorming', producing them uncritically in the first stage
- analytical – refining and clarifying the ideas and linking them to real needs and practical considerations.

See page 89 in Unit 2 for Kolb's learning cycle.

Organising/structuring

This stage develops some previous processes. It involves staffing the team, ensuring that they are matched to their roles, obtaining equipment, researching and clarifying the nature of team tasks, and establishing partnership or **liaison** with other groups where needed.

Prioritising

There are two sides to this:

- identifying what is most important
- identifying what has to be done first.

Both kinds of prioritising should be done for the team as a whole by external management, by the team leader, or by consultation within the team. Then each individual team member should prioritise their own work.

remember

It is best to keep the creative and analytical planning stages separate, since the mental processes needed for each are very different and can interfere with each other if you try to create and analyse at the same time.

 Link

Prioritising is often needed in public service work, where there tends to be too much work to do – and not enough time and resources.

Controlling

A team's work is controlled and coordinated – both from outside and inside the team. Many teams work best with a minimum of control; however, there has to be some control otherwise a team is no longer a team, merely a group of unconnected individuals.

The amount and type of control needed depends on the nature and experience of the team, and the types of task which are being done. Experienced teams normally need less external control because they are better able to control their own activities.

Control is achieved by methods such as:

- external or independent inspection
- inspection from within the organisation
- checks (monitoring) by the team leader.

Scheduling of work

This means setting out timetables for the team's future work.

Stage 1

This is an overall plan agreed (or accepted) by the team. It may stretch ahead for many months.

Stage 2

This is achieved by individual or group action planning. An action plan is a document saying that X will achieve an agreed task Y by a fixed date Z. (The agreed dates should fit in with any dates given on the overall Stage 1 plan.) The team leader or line manager signs when the task is done.

How teams set targets

Targets are set by central and local government, by liaison bodies such as police authorities, and by the public service itself. Targets are often based on statistics and set in terms of percentages.

Teams within a service are sometimes required to set their own targets; these can be set by the team leader or by team members, or agreed by the team as a whole, depending on the leadership style of the team.

Targets should be meaningful and should provide real motivation to perform better. This means that (e.g. in the case of crime reduction targets) they should be based on current trends and be realistic and achievable – yet challenging. A target which is too easy to reach encourages complacency; if it is too difficult to reach, it encourages cheating.

See Fig 4.8 on page 166, where the process is outlined, and page 162 for examples of real targets.

Targets are best set for quantifiable objectives which lend themselves to reliable statistical analysis. It would be sensible for the police to set a target for 'successfully prosecuting sex offenders', but not for 'reducing number of terrorist plots', since that would be largely outside police control, and it is inappropriate to set targets where numbers are small or statistics are unreliable.

How planning and evaluation is conducted in the uniformed public services

The systems used follow the principles outlined above, but each individual service has different procedures, which keep changing all the time as management methods evolve. You are strongly recommended to contact particular public services to obtain the most detailed and up-to-date information.

See page 86 in Unit 2 for more on evaluation.

Monitoring

Monitoring is 'the regular observation and recording of activities taking place in a project or programme'. It can be done by team members or the team leader, by someone specially appointed to monitor progress (from either inside or outside the team) or by managers outside the team. The purpose of monitoring is to check the progress of the team against its targets and to let stakeholders (anybody outside the team who is involved in the team's work) know what is going on. Monitoring can also be used to keep the team well informed about the progress of its work.

Seattle Community Network

www.scn.org

Milestones

Targets sometimes have 'milestones' – intermediate targets set as stages towards reaching the main target. These allow teams to judge whether they are likely to meet their targets in the end.

Responsibilities

The team leader is usually responsible for monitoring a team from within. However, if the team leader is already busy, this might not be the best way of doing it. Furthermore, if the team leader is too authoritarian or is out of touch with the team, the monitoring may be patchy as there may not be complete cooperation from team members. Alternatives are to delegate team monitoring to a dependable team member who is not the leader, or to have systems in place based on self- or peer appraisal so that each team member is involved in the monitoring process. However, if this method is used, it is still necessary to collect together the information from the monitoring, so that stakeholders know where to go for the information they want, and so that action can be taken by the team leader or the team itself if things are not going well.

Accountability

In teamwork, accountability can mean two things:

- transparency and keeping an accessible record of all the team's activities and expenditure
- holding people accountable (responsible) for the work they do and 'calling them to account'.

Transparency and keeping accessible records

In principle, it is highly desirable to do this so that:

- stakeholders know how their money is being spent
- people know what the team is doing and why
- if there is a change of personnel in the team, the new people can pick up the threads without wasting too much time trying to find out what their predecessors were doing.

In practice, however, there are two main difficulties:

- the need to protect confidentiality and comply with the Data Protection Act 1998
- the weight of bureaucracy (unproductive paperwork) needed to monitor and record all the team's activities. The aim should be to be as accountable as possible, especially over matters such as finance, without wasting too much time and money in office work.

Holding people accountable for the work they do and 'calling them to account'

Monitoring involves an element of discipline: making sure that the team does the right things at the right time; that people don't break the law or play the system, are not being incompetent or dishonest, follow the codes of practice and conduct, and so on. Teams may be legally accountable for what they do – meaning that they or their leaders or the public service for which they work could be prosecuted under either civil or criminal law. It is normally the job of team leaders to ensure this kind of accountability. Failing that, there should be monitoring from outside the team; this will pick up any serious cases of incompetence or malpractice.

Driving the Successful Delivery of Major Defence Projects: Effective Project Control is a Key Factor in Successful Projects. Report by the Comptroller and Auditor General, HC 30 Session 2005–2006, 20 May 2005, Ministry of Defence
USDA Forest Service – see website for information on achieving quality through teamwork
www.na.fs.fed.us
Audit Commission – this website is very useful
www.audit-commission.gov.uk

Renegotiation/rescheduling of objectives/targets

Renegotiating and/or **rescheduling** happen when a team has objectives or targets which, for one reason or another, cannot be met. It may be the fault of the team, the fault of the targets, or circumstances may have changed. The easiest thing, of course, is to change the target, and this is often done because any other solution to the problem costs more money. However, governments are reluctant to change their targets because that suggests to the public that they have themselves been incompetent in setting an unreachable target. Changing the target may not cost money, but it could well cost votes. Furthermore, if teams in general have met a government target, but a particular team hasn't, it may mean that that team is not working well and that its way of working, its management or its members should be changed, rather than change the government target. Finally, especially in policing, targets might be reachable in some parts of the country but not in others because of the different socioeconomic characteristics of the areas being policed.

Renegotiating targets is not normally a good thing in that it undermines public confidence by 'moving the goalposts'. It is more honest to miss the target and then ask sensible questions about why the target was missed, possibly renegotiating future targets at an early date.

Fig 4.9 When to renegotiate targets

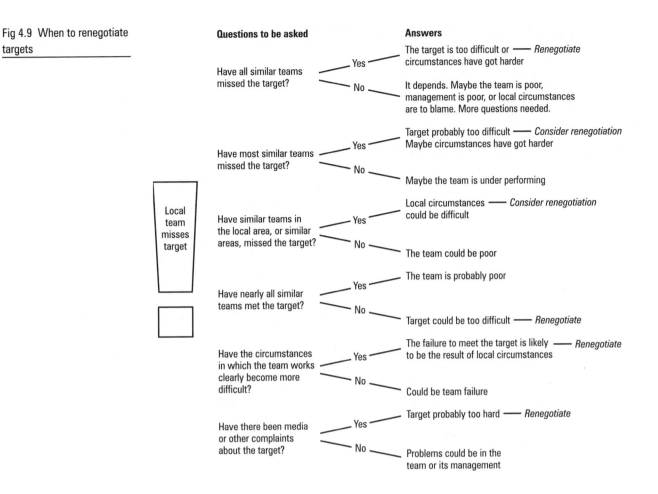

Questions to be asked

Answers

Have all similar teams missed the target?
- Yes — The target is too difficult or — *Renegotiate* circumstances have got harder
- No — It depends. Maybe the team is poor, management is poor, or local circumstances are to blame. More questions needed.

Have most similar teams missed the target?
- Yes — Target probably too difficult — *Consider renegotiation* Maybe circumstances have got harder
- No — Maybe the team is under performing

Local team misses target

Have similar teams in the local area, or similar areas, missed the target?
- Yes — Local circumstances — *Consider renegotiation* could be difficult
- No — The team could be poor

Have nearly all similar teams met the target?
- Yes — The team is probably poor
- No — Target could be too difficult — *Renegotiate*

Have the circumstances in which the team works clearly become more difficult?
- Yes — The failure to meet the target is likely — *Renegotiate* to be the result of local circumstances
- No — Could be team failure

Have there been media or other complaints about the target?
- Yes — Target probably too hard — *Renegotiate*
- No — Problems could be in the team or its management

Maintaining team focus

This is the team leader's responsibility and involves the skilful use of an appropriate leadership style. The extract from a job description for a hospital assistant manager on page 172 shows the qualities needed in a civilian uniformed public service.

Review and evaluation of team working

Review means looking over what has already been done and drawing conclusions about it. Evaluation is more to do with assessing the cost of the work in relation to the benefits that it is bringing. In public service teamwork, this is important because it is an aspect of accountability, and the service is spending the taxpayer's money. Evaluating the costs and benefits of a project is often difficult because there are many hidden costs (e.g. problems for team members' families in the armed forces; depreciation and damage of machinery, etc.) and the benefits may only be obvious in the long term (as is promised by the government in the case of Iraq and Afghanistan). However, difficult as it may be, evaluation must be done, based on reviews and on the targets and milestones that may – or may not – be reached.

See also pages 86–87 in Unit 2.

How teamwork is monitored in the uniformed public services

Teamwork is monitored at a number of levels. The following information relates to the Audit Commission's recommendations for good practice for Crime and Disorder Reduction Partnerships (CDRPs) working in areas with high levels of antisocial behaviour.

case study 4.11 — Hospital assistant manager

Personal Attributes/**Competencies**

1. Accountability and Personal Organisation – ability to be 'results focused', taking responsibility for own actions, being proactive, organised and timely

2. Customer Focus – ability to understand the needs of customers, respond appropriately at all times and seek opportunities to exceed customer expectations

3. Creativity and Innovation – ability to challenge the established way of working, identifying and making the most of new opportunities aimed at enhancing services

4. Personal Development – ability to be proactive and committed to developing personal skills, knowledge and behaviour and supporting others through sharing skills, knowledge and best practice

5. Networking – ability to develop and maintain a network of contacts throughout [the London Borough of Hillingdon] and beyond for sharing information, expertise and ideas

6. Living the Values – ability to be visible, approachable, earn respect and respect the human needs of others, inspire integrity and loyalty, encourage accountability and maintain high morale

7. Team-working – the ability to work with colleagues within own and across other teams, to deliver the overall aims, objectives and values of the department

8. Motivating Others – ability to empower individuals by increasing delegation and demonstrating belief and trust in them, influencing through challenge, negotiation and coaching as appropriate

9. Managing Performance – ability to effectively manage performance at a team and individual level; having the confidence to address poor performance at the right time, in the right way

10. Decision Making – ability to take a broad approach to problem solving which leads to practical decision-making for the benefit of customers and the Council

11. Analytical Ability – ability to recognise the value of information and make [it available as appropriate to teams and decision makers].

(Source: www.hillingdon.gov.uk)

activity — GROUP WORK

1 In pairs, rate yourself and your partner on these qualities.
2 Take your *strengths* and discuss how you can build on them.

The main themes are:

- getting information about the problems
- communicating effectively with the **client group** (communities suffering from antisocial behaviour)
- good communication between partners in the CDRPs
- keeping track of money spent and results achieved
- evaluating what happens to ensure that the scheme is really working.

Each partner has its responsibilities.

CDRPs

- Use the police national intelligence model (NIM) to collect community intelligence.
- Deploy resources cost-effectively.
- Evaluate neighbourhood interventions regularly.

Local government

- Ensure that the council's data are reliable, up to date, accessible to other partners, and conform to the National Standard for Incident Recording (NSIR).
- Use frontline workers (e.g. community support officers) to gather information.
- Use frontline workers to tell residents what the council is doing.
- Support improved performance in CDRPs.

Central government

- Ensure that the police provide neighbourhood solutions.
- Review the performance framework for policing and community safety, shifting the focus to neighbourhood level.
- Ensure that CDRP partners are working together effectively to deliver shared outcomes.

Revision of individual responsibilities

This means that when team performance is monitored, it should if necessary be possible to change people's roles and duties, so that people are working more to their strengths and the team benefits. Revision of individual responsibilities is needed in any case from time to time to allow people to develop their careers and to avoid the staleness and disillusionment which result from doing the same work for too long.

Fig 4.10 There are partnerships to tackle antisocial behaviour

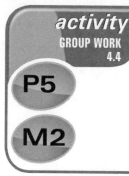

activity
GROUP WORK
4.4

P5

M2

Give a presentation suitable for trainee managers explaining how team targets are set, describing and assessing the usefulness of different methods of monitoring team performance.

Working as a team member

Team working uses a range of skills: skills that we have had from childhood but which can be developed to suit the needs of uniformed public service work. These skills fall into two main categories: communication and personal organisation.

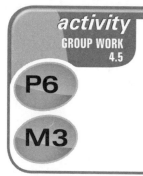

activity
GROUP WORK
4.5

P6

M3

Take part in five team activities – showing as much confidence as you can!

Communication

Communication is either verbal or non-verbal. Verbal communication includes listening, speaking, reading and writing. Non-verbal communication includes gestures, expressions and the way we dress and present ourselves. Other more specialised forms of communication which don't fit easily into either category are mathematics, graphical representation/drawing and music.

Articulation of ideas

In this context, the word 'articulation' usually refers to speech: how clearly we speak and whether we use a wide variety of words, well suited to the meanings, emotions and intentions that we want to put across. As far as teamwork is concerned, the following points can be noted.

Speech

- Team members usually speak to each other in the same '**register**' – using informal but professional language. The similarities in the way that they speak to each other indicate willingness (conscious or unconscious) to suppress individual differences and emphasise the team identity.

- The aim is to speak in ways that people find clear and easy to understand.

- Language that is sexist, racist, or might offend other team members or the people with whom they work is avoided.

- The language competence is good enough for the job.

- Jargon (specialised or technical language) is sometimes used by work teams.

- Interactions often take the form of requests, instructions, commands, advice, questions, descriptions and explanations.

Listening

- Listening and remembering what people say are important in teamwork.

- Note taking is often used to back up listening and to ensure that important points are not forgotten or overlooked.

- Good listening skills build confidence in the people who are talking to you.

Reading

- Effective reading can take any of three forms: skimming (a quick look at a document to see what it is about); scanning (looking for specific information – e.g. a number in the phone book); and detailed reading (close reading – e.g. of the instructions to assemble a piece of furniture).

- Being good at all three types of reading saves time and effort, and is useful in teamwork.

Writing

- The writing done by team members follows certain formats (e.g. filling in forms, text message, email, letter, memo, report, checklist, agenda, **minutes**).

- Training is likely to be given in some of these, so that forms, reports, etc. follow the format which is normal in the team or in the public service to which the team belongs.

- The basic requirement of a piece of writing is that it should be clear and understandable to the reader.

- Typing and word-processing skills are often used in some teams.

- Good spelling, punctuation, word usage and sentence structure are sometimes necessary. (It depends on the team and the work it does, and on who is going to read the piece of writing.)

> **remember**
> Register is the 'level' of language we use (i.e. 'posh' or 'not posh' or 'in between')

Self-presentation

The uniformed public services have rules about self presentation. Case study 4.12 is an example from the army:

Civilian organisations, such as the ambulance service, may be slightly more liberal in their rules about personal appearance, but they prefer their employees to be clean, smart and well groomed.

Another aspect of good personal presentation is 'deportment': standing straight with shoulders back and sitting up properly in a chair and so on. If the job involves a lot of walking, the feet should not be splayed or pigeon toed.

Overall, people in the uniformed public services should behave in a dignified and responsible way in public, so as to give their service a good image.

Building morale/confidence

Building morale and confidence is a complex process and can take time. The main elements are shown in Fig 4.11.

Morale matters. As the army says:

'Success on operations depends above all else on good morale, which is the spirit and ethos that enables soldiers to triumph over adversity. In turn morale is linked to, and reinforced by, discipline.'

(Source: *Soldier Management: A Guide for Commanders*. © Ministry of Defence 2004)

Morale is both an individual quality and a team quality. It is related to respect, self-respect and self-esteem. If the morale of a team is high, the morale of the individuals within it will probably be high too. Team members can themselves do much to raise morale by being positive and supportive towards each other, by helping each other out, by being friendly and by having a sense of humour. Team leaders should avoid discrimination and favouritism, and they should be able to listen to and deal with the

case study
4.12

Some army rules

(a) Hair

1 Males. The hair of the head is to be kept well cut and trimmed, except where authority has been granted otherwise on religious grounds; style and colour (if not natural) is not to be of an exaggerated nature. If a moustache is worn, it is to be trimmed and not below the line of the lower lip. Beards and whiskers are only to be worn with authority, which will usually be granted only on medical or religious grounds, or where tradition permits. The appearance of the beard and whiskers is to be neat and tidy.

2 Females. The hair is to be neat and worn above the collar. Combs, grips, etc., if worn, are to be plain and similar in colour to the hair. Style and colour (if not natural) is not to be of an exaggerated nature.

(b) Make up

1 Males. Make up is not to be worn.

2 Females. Make up (if worn) is to be inconspicuous. Brightly coloured nail varnish is not to be worn.

(c) Jewellery

On formal parades, watches and jewellery (except wedding rings) are not to be worn. At other times only wedding, and/or engagement rings, and one signet ring may be worn on the hands with uniform. Women may wear a single small sleeper or stud earring in the centre of the lobe of each ear. Rings, studs etc. are not to be worn through any other part of the body in uniform, or at any time during operational tours. Watches may be worn in uniform (on either wrist) provided they and their straps are of a sober style and colour. Additional religious accoutrements may be worn where this is mandatory and authority has been granted.

(Source: *The Queen's Regulations for the Army*, Section 5.366. Crown copyright © 1996)

activity
GROUP WORK

Some of these rules are on health and safety grounds; others are to do with the public image of the army.

1 Distinguish between rules related to health and safety and those related to public image.

2 Decide how justified you think these rules are in both cases.

Fig 4.11 Twelve causes of good morale

concerns of the team. Supervisors outside the team should monitor them with sensitivity, show respect, give praise where it is due and avoid thoughtless criticism.

Questioning

There is a fine line between team members' team and personal lives, and this should not be crossed without mutual consent. Friendly interest in a colleague is not the same thing as being downright nosey. People often regard their religious, political or moral views as private, and they should not be questioned on these unless they have indicated a willingness to talk about them, or unless there is some very definite reason linked to the work of the team.

The teamwork itself is a different matter, and people should feel free to ask questions of colleagues and to expect the information and help that they need to be given willingly.

Defusing and resolving conflict

Teams often work at high pressure, and people can become stressed. When ambitious people, or perfectionists, work closely they may feel that they are treading on each others' toes. Teams which are poorly led can become places where bullying, friction, harassment and backbiting occur, and there may be unhealthy competition among team members (perhaps to get into the leader's 'good books'). Conflict within teams is demotivating and can lead to poor work.

Ways of defusing and resolving conflict include:

- not letting it start in the first place, by keeping an eye on what is done and said by other team members and dealing with possible problems before they arise

- working in ways that reduce stress and having a good work–life balance

- telling other people if you feel unhappy

- getting a manager outside the team to resolve differences in a fair and balanced way

- training and workshops in good teamwork and team leadership

- applying discipline systems and anti-harassment policies if things seem to be getting out of hand

- as a last resort, getting justice at an **employment tribunal**.

Tact

This means being aware of and respecting other people's feelings.

Sincerity

This means honesty: doing what you say you will do, and feeling sympathy and respect for other people.

Effective listening

This has two sides to it: (a) looking and acting as if you are listening and (b) listening. Useful tips include:

- making eye contact for about 30% of the time when people are talking to you

- suitable body language (e.g. not folding your arms, fidgeting, picking at your ears or face, etc.) while people are talking to you (you can show sympathy and rapport by subtly mimicking the other person's posture)

- making notes (if there is a serious problem) to show that you really are listening and will do something about the person's concerns

- not breaking off to answer the telephone if someone is saying something important to you.

remember

There are plenty of good books, videos, etc. on body language and communication techniques. Check them out.

Effective listening should result in feedback to the person who has been talking. If you say that you are going to do something as a result of listening to someone's concern, you should do it, or, later, explain why you haven't been able to do it. Teams (and the public services to which those teams belong) should 'close feedback loops' so that clients and stakeholders and the public receive answers to their questions.

See pages 64 and 69 in Unit 2 for more on listening skills.

Concern for team members

Team members should be mainly focused on their own work, but this should be linked to a concern for their team-mates and a willingness to help them out within reason. (The right balance depends on circumstances.)

The importance of communication in teamwork within the uniformed public services

Nothing in teamwork in the uniformed public services is more important than communication. It is through communication that teams are recruited, trained, led and carry out their work. Without communication, a team is not a team but a series of disconnected individuals, like people waiting at a bus stop.

This does not mean that team members are chattering and communicating with each other continuously during working hours. Individuals could be delegated to do work alone and report back later. However, that is still communication in the sense that it is work preparing for a communication (the reporting back).

In the armed forces, teams communicate with their commanders, or with the teams they command, or – most of all – with the other members of the same team. In the police and other civilian uniformed services, there is a huge amount of communication with the public, not all of which will lead to the cracking of major cases; but all of it is needed in the big dialogue which exists, day and night, between the public services and the diverse people whom they serve.

Personal organisation

This involves planning, arranging and carrying out your work in an accurate, orderly, effective and timely manner. Good personal organisation requires imagination – selecting future tasks and visualising how these should be done. It also requires self-discipline and logical thinking to prepare each task in detail and carry it out.

Preparation (organising information/equipment, diary/calendaring events)

Plans should be written down so that you can study them and make alterations if necessary, and so that you can explain to other people what they are.

A plan should follow a planning cycle such as the one shown in Fig 4.12.

Notice that planning goes in stages. The original idea is followed by a **feasibility** study to see if it is possible. If it is, the real planning starts at the 'System design' stage. Once that is done, you (or the team) have to organise and do the work. First, you obtain what you need; then you go ahead and put your plan into action. Once the plan or project is up and running and can look after itself, or if it is winding down again, you can start thinking about the next project.

Action planning will help you and your team to keep to schedule.

Fig 4.12 Planning cycle

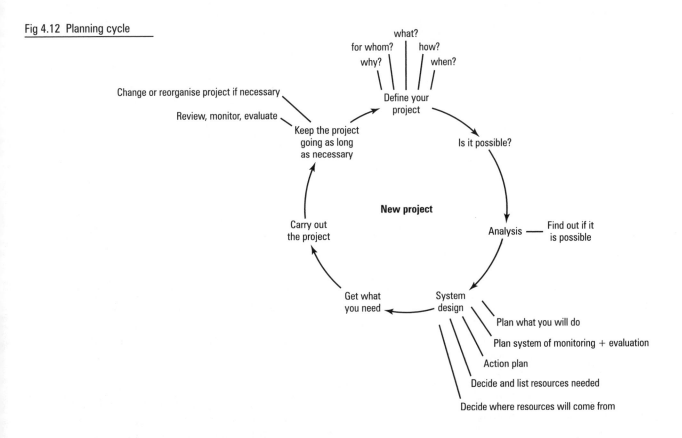

 Institute of Museum and Library Services – for information on National Leadership Grants; project planning: a tutorial
www.imls.gov

Identification of issues

This is the feasibility study part of a project, where you identify strengths, weaknesses, opportunities and threats. The process is called a SWOT analysis. Such an analysis should help you to decide whether the benefits of the idea outweigh the cost and effort of putting it into practice. If they do, then you go ahead.

SWOT and cost:benefit analyses should be discussed at planning meetings.

NB The dates of planning meetings should be agreed and marked on the calendar at the 'Define your project' stage of the process shown in Fig 4.12 above.

Scheduling activities

Further planning meetings will be needed for the 'System design' stage. They will be used for timetabling the planning process, deciding how long everything should take, and writing action plans for each team member. Decisions about action plans may be made democratically, in which case they have to be agreed by the people involved.

Responsibility

In team planning and implementation of a plan, each team member should have clearly defined responsibilities (perhaps written down as they are in a job specification). The leader has responsibilities too: one of the main ones being to ensure that the rest of the team are carrying out their duties. If team members are failing to fulfil their responsibilities, the team leader has to find out why and take action to sort out the problem.

Accountability

This means monitoring and evaluating the project as it develops and allowing stakeholders (people outside the team who are footing the bill or who hope to benefit from the team's work) to know what is happening. There is a risk, however, of having too much monitoring and evaluation. Excessive monitoring can demotivate the team or even waste time and money. Leaders must find the right balance between monitoring and productive work.

Responsiveness

Responsiveness is being willing and able to change a course of action if necessary. If circumstances change during the course of a planned project, it may mean that the project, or its schedule, has to be changed as well. Such changes cost time and money, so the need for them should be carefully assessed before the change is made.

Adaptability

Adaptability – the ability to change if circumstances change – is a useful quality in team members who may have to do many different types of work. It is especially useful in the armed forces, where you have to get used to being in different countries, meeting people from different cultures, and carrying out different roles. It is useful in ordinary teamwork when leaders or team members change, and people find themselves suddenly working with new colleagues.

Consideration of options

This means making choices. Unless the choice has to be made instantly (e.g. in an emergency), it is best to consider all options and weigh them up before making the choice. In theory, choices should be made which benefit the organisation rather than the individual.

Maintaining focus

It is easier to maintain focus if:

- the work is interesting
- you are self-disciplined
- the team is focused
- the aims of the project are worthwhile
- your own reputation is at stake

Fig 4.13 Considering options

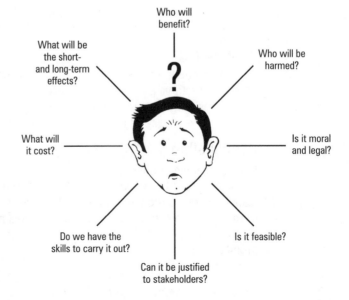

- you have a suitable work environment
- you are in good health
- you have a good work–life balance.

One of the drawbacks of teamwork is that peer pressure (or other pressure) can be put on you to work harder than you should. However, working too hard can undermine your focus and prevent you from thinking clearly. Keep times when you can relax, be with people you like, and do your own thing. Hard work is good: being a workaholic is not!

Openness to criticism

Criticism should always be listened to. You should be prepared to change if it becomes clear that you should do so, but remember that there is, on average, a 50% chance that the critic is wrong. Even in a team you don't necessarily have to do something just because someone else tells you to do it. Keep your cool; give yourself time to weigh up the situation, and do what you think is best.

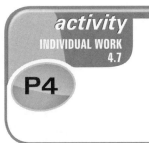

activity

INDIVIDUAL WORK 4.6

D2

1 Carry out a detailed self-appraisal of your performances in the activities you have taken part in.

2 Draw reasoned conclusions as to how you can develop your teamworking abilities in the future.

Importance of personal organisation in teamwork within the uniformed public services

For people working in teams in a uniformed public service there are huge advantages in good personal organisation. It benefits the individual, because the better the organisation, the less stress, hassle and overwork there tends to be. It benefits the team, because teams need dependable and well-organised colleagues who can be trusted to work efficiently. It benefits the service itself, because it can meet its targets. It benefits stakeholders and partners who are not let down by failures in teamwork. Above all it benefits the public who get a good service at surprisingly low cost.

activity

INDIVIDUAL WORK 4.7

P4

Write a job description relating either to a job you do or one done by someone you know. The job must be one which involves an element of teamwork. The description should include a table setting out:

1 the communication skills required for the job (giving examples of when they are used)

2 the personal organisation needed.

Progress Check

1. Think of as many differences as you can between formal and informal teams.
2. In a diverse team, what issues should members be aware of?
3. Why is teamwork often more effective than individual work in a uniformed public service?
4. State the main differences between discussion-based exercises, table-top exercises and live exercises.
5. Outline the strengths and weaknesses of multi-agency or multi-service teams.
6. What are team roles and what effect do they have on the work of a team?
7. Outline Bruce Tuckman's ideas on team development.
8. What are performance indicators, and where do they come from?
9. What are the differences between monitoring, evaluation and review of teams?
10. What are the problems of (a) too much and (b) too little group turnover?
11. How are targets set and used?
12. Explain accountability.
13. State three main reasons why targets may have to be renegotiated or rescheduled.
14. State eight ways to build morale.
15. What factors should be taken into account when considering options?

UNIT 5

Understanding Discipline within the Uniformed Public Services

This unit covers:

- The need for discipline in the uniformed public services
- What conformity and obedience mean, highlighting their place in the uniformed public services
- The importance of self-discipline in the uniformed public services
- The complex nature of authority in the uniformed public services

A uniformed public service is only as good as its discipline, as discipline is essential in the uniformed public services, where success is built on effective teamwork. This unit will tell you what discipline is and why discipline matters in the uniformed public services. It explores the effects of discipline on people's behaviour, feelings and work.

Conformity and obedience are aspects of discipline, and the unit looks at why people tend to conform and obey, and at the implications of this.

The unit also investigates self-discipline, how we can express it in ourselves and how self-discipline in employees benefits the uniformed public services as a whole.

Finally, the unit examines the concept of authority: what it is, its moral and legal basis and how it shapes the work of the uniformed public services.

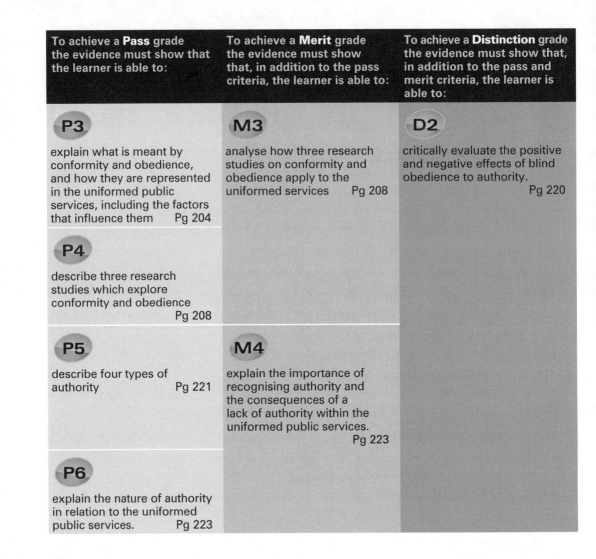

To achieve a **Pass** grade the evidence must show that the learner is able to:	To achieve a **Merit** grade the evidence must show that, in addition to the pass criteria, the learner is able to:	To achieve a **Distinction** grade the evidence must show that, in addition to the pass and merit criteria, the learner is able to:
P3 explain what is meant by conformity and obedience, and how they are represented in the uniformed public services, including the factors that influence them Pg 204	**M3** analyse how three research studies on conformity and obedience apply to the uniformed services Pg 208	**D2** critically evaluate the positive and negative effects of blind obedience to authority. Pg 220
P4 describe three research studies which explore conformity and obedience Pg 208		
P5 describe four types of authority Pg 221	**M4** explain the importance of recognising authority and the consequences of a lack of authority within the uniformed public services. Pg 223	
P6 explain the nature of authority in relation to the uniformed public services. Pg 223		

The need for discipline in the uniformed public services

Discipline is the ability to behave in a controlled, organised way. It is also the art of giving and obeying orders while retaining human dignity and respecting human rights. Although its nature has changed over the years, discipline is still the bedrock of uniformed public service work.

All the uniformed public services in Britain are organised in a way that encourages discipline.

Uniformed services

In the uniformed services, discipline, in the sense of giving and receiving orders, is linked to the rank structure. Rank is based on experience, **managerial** skills and, in some cases, qualifications. People of higher rank are able to give commands, orders or instructions to people of lower rank. They can also determine what work or jobs people of lower rank do, as long as those jobs fit in with the person's job description. There are certain safeguards: if an order is clearly unreasonable, or if it appears that harassment of the subordinate employee by the higher employee is taking place, there are **grievance procedures** and appeal systems. However, on the whole the uniformed public services are run on a rank-based system with a level of trust and expertise which means that orders and commands can be followed promptly, professionally – and more or less willingly.

Fig 5.1 Hierarchical command

The hierarchical command and rank structure of each service

A hierarchy is a chain of command with the 'bosses' at one end and the 'workers' at the other. They are often called 'rank structures' or '**role structures**', and each uniformed service has its own hierarchy with special names for each rank or role within the hierarchy.

Table 5.1 Rank or role structures in the main uniformed public services (2007)

Ambulance	Fire and rescue
Ambulance care assistants	Firefighter
Ambulance technicians	Crew Manager
Call handlers	Watch Manager
Emergency care practitioners	Station Manager
Emergency medical dispatchers	Group Manager
Paramedics	Area Manager
Patient transport services controllers	Brigade Manager
Police	**Army**
Constable	*Non-commissioned ranks*
Sergeant	Private
Inspector	Lance-Corporal
Chief Inspector	Corporal
Superintendent	Sergeant
Chief Superintendent	Staff Sergeant
Assistant Chief Constable	Warrant-Officer 2
Deputy Chief Constable	Warrant-Officer 1
Chief Constable	
	Officers
Ranks above Chief Superintendent in the Metropolitan Police	2nd Lieutenant
	Lieutenant
	Captain
Commander	Major
Deputy Assistant Commissioner	Lieutenant-Colonel
Assistant Commissioner	Colonel
Deputy Commissioner	Brigadier
Commissioner	Major-General
	Lieutenant-General
	General

Royal Navy

Non-commissioned ranks
Rating
Able Rate
Leading Rate
Petty Officer
Chief Petty Officer
Charge Chief Petty Officer
Warrant Officer

Officers
Midshipman
Sub Lieutenant
Lieutenant
Lieutenant Commander
Commander
Captain
Commodore
Rear Admiral
Vice Admiral
Admiral

HM Revenue and Customs

Administrative Assistant
Assistant Officer
Officer
Higher Officer
Senior Officer
Graduate trainee
Grade 7
Grade 6

Maritime and Coastguard Agency

Coastguard Watch Assistant
Coastguard Watch Officer
Sector Manager

MCGA describes the ranks as 'roles'

Royal Marines

Non-commissioned ranks
Marine
Corporal
Sergeant
Colour Sergeant
Warrant Officer Class 2
Warrant Officer Class 1

Officers
Second Lieutenant
Lieutenant
Captain
Major
Lieutenant Colonel
Colonel
Brigadier
Major General
Lieutenant General
General

RAF

Non-commissioned ranks
Aircraftman/woman
Leading Aircraftman/woman
Senior Aircraftman/woman
Junior Technician
Corporal
Sergeant
Chief Technician
Flight Sergeant
Warrant Officer

Officers
Pilot Officer
Flying Officer
Flight Lieutenant
Squadron Leader
Wing Commander
Group Captain
Air Commodore
Air Vice-Marshal
Air Marshal
Air Chief Marshal

Prison Service

Prison auxiliary
Assistant storeman
Storeman
Night patrol
Operational support grade
Prison officer
Senior officer
Principal officer
Manager G
Manager F
Manager E
Senior manager D
Senior manager C
Senior manager B
Senior manager A

Private Security

Ranks and roles depend on employer or job.
With BAA the ranks are:
Assistant Security Officer
Security Officer
Security Officer (Trainer)
There are indefinite and fixed contracts.

All ranks are listed in ascending order.

Career Transition Partnership – a useful website with military ranks and their rough equivalents in civilian life

www.ctp.org.uk

In recent years, there has been a tendency to rename and re-structure uniformed service hierarchies – especially in the ambulance, fire and rescue and prison services.

Employee grades have been changed and renamed in these services. This has been done to change the 'ethos' of the service and 'soften' its public image so that it is more user-friendly, more suitable for a diverse society, and less 'male-orientated'.

Emergency services

All the emergency services have rank or role structures which help to encourage discipline and provide a workable chain of command. Each structure is – to a greater or lesser extent – hierarchical, in the sense that the ranks are arranged in order of seniority or precedence in an unbroken sequence from 'top' to 'bottom'.

The police

Formed by Sir Robert Peel in 1829 and unarmed until relatively recent years, the police have always been considered a civilian force. This civilian character is reflected in the names of their ranks which (apart from 'sergeant') have no military overtones. Their distinctive uniform and rank structure are valuable in terms of public relations and in preserving their 'esprit de corps'. This is a discipline-maintaining feature in all British uniformed services.

The civilian character of the unarmed police makes them more approachable to members of the public – who tell them more because they are unthreatening.

See page 195 for more on *esprit de corps*.

The fire and rescue service

The restructuring of this service was triggered by *The Future of the Fire Service: Reducing Risk, Saving Lives. The Independent Review of the Fire Service* by Professor Sir George Bain (FRS Online, 2002). This hard-hitting report said that, although the fire service (as it was then called) did an excellent job putting out fires and rescuing crash victims, it was living in the past as far as its ethos, staffing policies, disciplinary systems and equal opportunities were concerned. The report claimed that the then fire service was run on militaristic lines, suffered from bullying and harassment, and was not particularly pleasant for women or people from ethnic minorities to work in. So the government decided to overhaul the whole organisation, rename it, change its career structures and discipline codes, and try to bring it closer to the communities that it serves.

The Future of the Fire and Rescue Service (FRS Online)

www.frsonline.fire.gov.uk

In 2003 the necessary changes were brought about with the introduction of a scheme called the **Integrated Personal Development System (IPDS)**.

The rank structure in the fire and rescue service is now called a 'role structure'. The Integrated Personal Development System is less authoritarian than the old system of training and staff development and is more in touch with modern thinking and management theory. It allows young, talented and ambitious firefighters to develop their careers more rapidly and use their potential to the full. 'Officers' are now 'managers'; and discipline is being updated, so that discipline and disputes procedures are up to date and based on best practice.

remember

Discipline is a good subject to discuss with people who actually work in the uniformed public services.

case study 5.1 — IPDS

This year the Government, the employers and the unions have approved a new system of training and development, based on national standards and on a framework of skills and competencies – the 'integrated personal development system' or IPDS. It will apply to all members of the fire and rescue service, including control room staff, non-uniformed staff, and retained and part-time personnel. It will cover all aspects of activity from initial recruitment, selection, training, in-service development and progression through to retirement.

With the introduction of IPDS we intend to:

- replace the 12 ranks of the fire and rescue service with seven 'roles', which reflect the work that fire fighters and other staff actually do;

- introduce **multi-level entry**, so that people can enter the fire and rescue service at a level appropriate to their qualifications and experience, including the most senior levels; and

- introduce **accelerated promotion** and development schemes for those staff who have been identified as having the potential to progress quickly.

(Source: *Our Fire and Rescue Service: A Summary*, www.communities.gov.uk)

activity — GROUP WORK

Do you think that these changes will have helped the fire and rescue service to carry out its work more effectively? Give reasons for your views.

Although these changes have only been running (at the time of writing) for three years or so, it is hoped that they will improve discipline and morale in the fire and rescue service, to the benefit of all concerned.

The ambulance service

The ambulance service is less obviously hierarchical than the other uniformed services. One reason is that it is attached to the NHS and is therefore part of a bigger organisation in a way in which most uniformed services are not. Another reason is that its work has changed very rapidly over the years with the expansion of the paramedic's role. **Primary care** is given to accident and other victims on the spot, or while the ambulance is moving, to take advantage of the 'golden hour' when lives are more likely to be saved. Paramedics and ambulance drivers are both essential, but their roles are so different that there is no point in their having a single chain of command.

Fig 5.2 Horizontal and vertical management

Horizontal management structure

Manager

O p e r a t i v e s

Vertical management structure

Manager

Manager

Manager

Manager

Operatives

A third reason why hierarchical systems are less popular than they used to be in the NHS and elsewhere is that they can be costly. **Horizontal management** systems, with more people doing the work and fewer telling them what to do, get more work done at less expense than vertical systems, which have long and sometimes inefficient chains of command (see Fig 5.2).

The armed forces

The hierarchical system in the armed forces has not changed. The army and the Royal Navy are much older than the other uniformed services, and they have deep-rooted traditions, which people feel strongly about. For security reasons, they are less open to the public than other uniformed forces, and, although they are constantly modernising themselves in other respects and are reflecting changes in society and the public's expectation of them, there appears to be no desire whatsoever to change the basic rank structure.

The prison service

Like the fire and rescue service, this has changed its rank structure in recent years although the process has been more gradual; the change has also been less noticeable because the prison service is less in the public eye than the fire and rescue service. 'Governors' are now 'managers', with many grades. The change in name is probably linked to the growth in the number of privately run prisons; in some ways these are more like businesses than public services (even though their work is basically the same as that of a publicly run prison).

Her Majesty's Revenue and Customs

Her Majesty's Customs and Excise changed its name in 2005 when it was joined with the Inland Revenue (which collects taxes). Like other uniformed services, HMRC is hierarchical in structure. The grades are the same as the civil service.

Hierarchies and discipline

Although hierarchies may change their names and structure, it is likely that they will always exist in the uniformed public services. Their advantages are that:

- They facilitate teamwork, because each team can be led by a line manager who is one 'step' higher than the other team members in rank.

- Managers can themselves be members of teams higher in the organisation.

- It is easy to pass information up the hierarchy and pass orders, commands, policies, etc. down the hierarchy.

- It is fairly clear who is responsible for doing what.

- Hierarchies offer a visible reward for effort and good conduct – through promotion.

- Each team in a hierarchy is a peer group which tends to encourage its members to conform (and **conformity** is an aspect of discipline).

- Hierarchies enable training and disciplinary actions (e.g. verbal warnings) to take place within an organised and accountable framework.

- Hierarchies are traditional – and tradition is linked in people's minds with good discipline.

- There are no obvious disadvantages of a hierarchical system, provided that it is well organised, understood and 'fit for purpose'.

remember

Hierarchical behaviour is natural in humans. We see it in families, gangs, churches and in most other human groups.

Fig 5.3 How teams fit into hierarchies

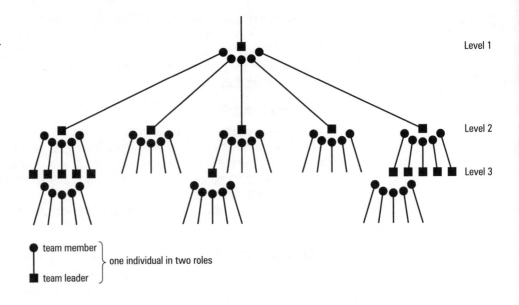

The diagram, of an imaginary uniformed service, shows the relation between teams and hierarchies. Level 1 is at the 'top' of this particular hierarchy.

The need for discipline

Definitions of discipline

The *Collins English Dictionary* (2003) has seven relevant definitions of the word 'discipline'.

Noun

1. Training or conditions imposed for the improvement of physical powers, self-control, etc.
2. Systematic training in obedience to regulations and authority
3. The state of improved behaviour, etc., resulting from such training or conditions
4. Punishment or **chastisement**
5. A system of rules for behaviour, methods of practice, etc.

Verb

6. To improve or attempt to improve the behaviour, orderliness etc. of [people] by training, conditions or orders
7. To punish or correct.

When we talk about discipline in the uniformed public services, we normally mean the orderly way in which members of that service behave. This kind of discipline is linked to smartness, good organisation, self-control, self-respect, and obedience.

'Self-discipline' is the ability to control ourselves so that we do what we ought to do, even when we would rather do something else.

A 'discipline code' is a book of rules (rules of conduct, behaviour, honesty, etc.) that uniformed public service workers are expected to follow. Breaking the rules can lead to another kind of 'discipline' – a series of official punishments ('sanctions' or 'disciplinary measures') that become more severe each time the rules are broken.

In a teaching or training situation, 'good discipline' is the ability of a teacher or instructor to keep order in the class and ensure that the work gets done, but 'good discipline' is also the orderly behaviour of the learners.

The necessity for rules and regulations

Some famous thinkers have said that we have too many rules and regulations and that people should do what they want to do, rather than what other people tell them to do. However, this is not what most people think, and nor is it the view of the government and the uniformed public services. They believe that many people, if not controlled, will – either accidentally or on purpose – do things which are wrong so that they and others suffer.

Throughout history, people have tried to make rules and regulations to stop bad behaviour. Statute laws originated in Ancient Greece, when Solon (d. 559 BC) produced his laws for Athens. Examples, from the Christian tradition, are the Ten Commandments and, from the Muslim tradition, the Five Pillars of Islam.

Ontario consultants on religious tolerance

www.religioustolerance.org

Islam 101

www.islam101.com

Famous non-religious philosophers, such as Immanuel Kant (1724–1804), tried to make universal moral laws which would work even for people who didn't believe in God.

However, it is not just religious leaders and philosophers who have tried to make rules for people to follow. Most of us prefer orderly behaviour (most of the time!). Parents try to discipline their children and teach them how to behave from an early age. Education, religion, the media and our friends also act as '**agencies of social control**' and make rules – **formal** and **informal** – for us to follow. Informal rules are called 'norms'; formal ones are rules and regulations. Every organisation, whether it is a school, a sports centre, a night club or a uniformed public service, has rules and regulations to govern the behaviour of its members – in other words, to create discipline.

Experience teaches that rules and regulations work. Putting up a notice with some rules on it is a lot cheaper and easier than waiting for indiscipline to happen before tackling it.

Rules, regulations and laws are easily confused. Fig 5.4 shows the difference.

The diagram shows that:

- All rules, regulations and laws are forms of discipline.

- Regulations are also laws.

- Rules are not really laws but are often obeyed as if they were.

- There is more to discipline than simply obeying rules, regulations and laws.

> **remember**
>
> Rules and regulations are an effective form of crime prevention.

> *activity*
> **GROUP WORK 5.1**
>
> **P1**
>
> Do a lively presentation suitable for school leavers saying how and why discipline is needed in the uniformed public services.

Fig 5.4 Rules, regulations, laws and discipline

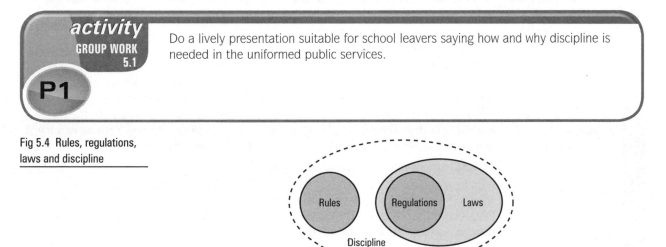

Why orders need to be followed

An order is a written or spoken command.

In private life we can challenge orders or disobey them – for example:

- if we don't want to do what we are being told to do
- if the person has no authority to give the order
- if the order is morally wrong
- if the order is clearly going to harm us or someone else.

However, in the uniformed public services orders must be followed because:

- If they are not, the uniformed service is either paralysed or completely disjointed in its response to any challenge. Orders are a form of communication which results in action, and if the orders aren't followed there can be no meaningful action.

- Apart from making action possible, orders are needed for the management, overall efficiency, morale, values, ethos, image and general well-being of a service. Orders are not only used in fighting or in life-and-death situations; they are also used to ensure that ordinary life runs smoothly, that people are clean and smart, that they keep healthy and in good spirits, and that they give their service a good image. In fact, following orders is an essential form of discipline – in any uniformed service.

remember

Orders are acceptable because they apply to everyone, but they must be issued in a professional manner.

case study 5.2 — The Army's view of discipline

Discipline, comradeship, leadership, and self respect form the basis of morale and of military efficiency. Good discipline within the unit is the foundation of good discipline throughout the Army and is based on good man management. It is therefore essential that every soldier should be brought to understand not only the importance, but the purpose of discipline; that indiscipline has no place in the Army, and that in war it may have serious effects or even lead to disaster. All officers, warrant officers and NCOs are to maintain discipline over officers and soldiers of lower rank than themselves.

(Source: *Queen's Regulations*, www.army.mod.uk)

activity
GROUP WORK

1   What is 'comradeship'?
2   What kinds of 'disaster' can indiscipline lead to?

Maintenance of order

Just as discipline is needed in a school to maintain order, so it is also needed in the uniformed public services. People who join the uniformed services are usually young, fit, active and male. They are proud of their fitness and strength (and are encouraged to be). However, if they are bored or have nothing much to do, there is always the risk that they will use their energy in fighting, going on the rampage, and doing things which will harm themselves, other people, or the reputation of their uniformed service.

The maintenance of order through discipline is a matter of health and safety: horseplay, fighting and bullying result in physical and mental injury. The same is true of racism, sexism, harassment and **victimisation**, which can happen if order is not maintained. Discipline (as its relation with the word 'disciple' implies) has a good deal to do with education and training. Much of the initial training in uniformed services is linked to the building of discipline.

remember

Even if it is not taught directly, discipline can be taught by example or as a **'hidden curriculum'** in other kinds of teaching or instruction.

The rank structure in the uniformed services is used to train discipline. Respect to senior officers has to be shown through salutes and in other ways; and new recruits can see that obeying people of higher rank is a basic rule in the service. The system is such that, by a constant show of respect and by carefully structured and demanding activities, discipline is built up until it becomes almost instinctive.

Discipline is needed to maintain standards and self-respect, and to build morale and a sense of vocation. The high standards of organisation and order for which British uniformed services are famous cannot be achieved without high levels of discipline and self-discipline.

activity

INDIVIDUAL WORK
5.2

M1

You have been put in charge of a group of cadets, several of whom are interested in joining the armed forces or the police. Write a leaflet explaining in depth the importance of discipline and the ways in which it is organised and enforced.

Rewards and punishments

People are complex, and so is discipline. Some people can be disciplined by fear of punishment; others can be disciplined by the promise of a reward for good conduct. Most of us, in fact, can be disciplined by both of these. However, as people get older and more self-disciplined, the rewards and punishments often need to be less obvious until, with a self-disciplined person, the rewards and punishments come from the person's own mind.

This process can be better understood by referring to Maslow's pyramid of human needs.

Link

See page 66 in Unit 2 for a diagram and explanation of Maslow's pyramid of human needs.

Strengths and weaknesses of rewards and punishments

Strengths

Rewards and punishments:

- provide incentives and deterrents which can motivate people to be disciplined
- build disciplined habits in the early stages of training
- encourage obedience.

Weaknesses

However, with rewards and punishments, people:

- are treated like children (or like performing seals)
- do not develop understanding of the reasons for discipline
- develop discipline but not self-discipline
- are not trained to think for themselves.

The consequences of a lack of discipline in the public services

Serious indiscipline in British uniformed public services exists – but it is rare. When it gets into the news, it usually causes a public outcry.

case study 5.3 — Why didn't an officer stop these attacks?

Senior officers were astounded when they were first shown footage of the alleged abuse of Iraqi teenagers on Friday.

What shocked them most was not the sight of British soldiers apparently brutalising unarmed Iraqis but that no officers or senior NCOs stepped in to halt the assaults or reported them later.

But bad as the pictures appear, senior officers were keen yesterday to emphasise that this was not systematic torture and should be placed in the context of Iraq in early 2004.

(Source: Thomas Harding, Defence Correspondent, *Daily Telegraph*, www.telegraph.co.uk last updated: 12:24am GMT 13/02/2006)

activity — GROUP WORK

1 What kinds of damage does this kind of story do to the army?

2 What action do you think should be taken by (a) the army and (b) the government when stories like this come out?

The dire consequences of lack of discipline in the public services are seen most clearly in developing countries, especially during periods of war and civil unrest.

case study 5.4 — Discipline breakdown

Between 2001 and 2006 thousands of families were forcibly evicted from various neighbourhoods in the Angolan capital of Luanda. These forced evictions were typically carried out without prior notification or consultation, without due process and with recourse to excessive use of force. The forced evictions left tens of thousands without shelter. In most cases armed members of the National Police or Armed Forces of Angola (*Forças Armadas de Angola*, FAA), who carried out the evictions, shot indiscriminately at those being evicted, beat them, and arrested those who tried to resist the evictions. Houses were demolished and property destroyed or stolen by those carrying out the forced evictions. In almost all the incidents of forced evictions police arrested human rights defenders, especially members of the local housing rights organization, SOS-Habitat.

(Source: www.amnesty.org)

activity — GROUP WORK

Suggest as many possible reasons as you can why the police and army in Angola behaved in the way described.

Effect on social order

The main effect on social order of a lack of discipline in the public services is that people start to take the law into their own hands. They have no faith that the police will sort out their problem, so they sort it out themselves. The 'punishment beatings' which took place in Northern Ireland in the 1980s happened because Catholic and Protestant communities (particularly Catholic) lost belief in the fairness of the police and tried to enforce 'justice' in their own areas themselves. More recently, in Somalia, the failure of the official government to run disciplined public services led to the establishment of an

Lack of discipline is not the same as effective but evil discipline – i.e. **brainwashing** – which led to the Holocaust in Nazi Germany during the Second World War.

'Islamic Courts' government, based on **Sharia law**. This created a degree of discipline which, however, was brought to an end by the Ethiopian invasion at the end of 2006.

Anarchy

The situation in places like Somalia is one of anarchy (i.e. without leadership). The result is that warlords set up territories, in much the same way as gangs do in some inner cities, and recruit **militia** (unofficial soldiers and police) who patrol in pick-up trucks with machine guns mounted on them. Life for civilians is dangerous and hard. Where so-called public services harass and victimise whole populations, as in Darfur, Sudan, in recent years, hundreds of thousands of people can be killed and millions made homeless.

Amnesty

www.amnesty.org

Human Rights Watch

www.hrw.org

Team spirit is sometimes called 'esprit de corps'.

The role of discipline

There is more to discipline than making people behave themselves. Good discipline has a positive and motivating effect on any organisation where teamwork is used – which of course means all the uniformed services.

Team spirit

Team spirit is a sense of pride in the team, and a belief in the quality and value of its work.

Disciplined people with a good esprit de corps perform well under stress, make fewer mistakes, show courage and optimism, and are usually in good mental and physical shape. They serve others in an honest, generous and unselfish way, and they live up to the high ideals which are expected of a uniformed public service.

See 'Positive synergy' on page 67 in Unit 2 and 'Building morale' on page 175 in Unit 4 for more information on this.

Sense of duty and honour

In Britain there is a long and glorious tradition of public service. On the military side, there have been famous battles such as Trafalgar and Waterloo, and the bravery and suffering of the First and Second World Wars. The armed forces came through this long and bloody history with an excellent reputation and are respected throughout the world for their fighting and peacekeeping skills. This good reputation is not only for their toughness but also for the honour and fairness which they have normally shown. This historic background, and the ideas underlying it, is part of an **ideology** of public service, a series of beliefs and principles based on unselfish collective action for the good of others. Such ideas are expressed in the army publication, *The Military Covenant* (www.army.mod.uk), in the books about the Second World War written by Winston Churchill, and in many present-day service publications. The concept of duty is important: to uphold the honour of the service, to be utterly loyal to colleagues, and to be unselfish in serving the British people.

Concepts like 'duty' and 'honour' are used to build courage, since members of the armed forces are being asked to risk death or disability in the course of their work.

Serving the public

'The public' is a diverse mass of people. Public service discipline demands that everybody is served and protected equally and according to need, whatever their wealth, age, sex, ethnic group or other characteristic. The ethos of public service also demands that a high quality of service is given, efficiently and at the lowest possible cost, and that human rights are respected at all times to the greatest possible degree.

Encouraging discipline in the uniformed public services

Rules

All public services have rules which spell out exactly what standards of conduct and discipline are required. Some of these, such as the police conduct code, are general points of good discipline; others, such as the PACE Codes, are codes of practice explaining exactly what can and cannot be done in different parts of their work.

Procedures

Procedures are the actions taken either to prevent indiscipline or to deal with it after it has happened.

Procedures to prevent indiscipline are often part of the ordinary day's work. They include wearing uniform and carrying out organised tasks throughout the day which leave little time or energy over for undisciplined behaviour. **Drill**, for example in the armed forces, and the morning training activities in the fire and rescue service have an underlying disciplinary purpose in addition to any other skills that are being perfected.

Procedures to deal with indiscipline include a system of reprimands and warnings, **summary justice** (in the armed forces) and legal procedures to deal with major disciplinary infringements. These are designed to ensure that a given offence is dealt with in the same way whoever handles it.

Policies

These are more general than rules and procedures and are to do with underlying principles. For example, the army has a 'no drugs' policy.

remember

Procedures which develop discipline may appear to be carried out for a completely different reason.

remember

The uniformed public services have a zero-tolerance drugs policy, but in some cases they do not automatically discharge offenders.

Link

See page 292 in Unit 7 for information on the classification of drugs.

Legislation

Here, legislation means laws passed by Parliament laying down how the uniformed services should enforce discipline. Laws deal with offences and the procedures by which suspects and those charged are dealt with.

The Armed Forces Act 2006 (relevant sections)
This major new law dealing with discipline in the armed forces merges the three previous laws, known as Service Discipline Acts (SDAs) which governed discipline in each of the

---

case study 5.5   Revealed: hard drug culture among soldiers

Figures released by the Ministry of Defence show that 520 soldiers tested positive for Class A drugs in 2005, massively up on the 350 recorded the previous year and double the 260 caught in 2003.

Defence minister Tom Watson claims those who test positive "are almost always discharged", although the army has an Early Intervention Programme (EIP) designed to re-educate offenders.

(Source: Brian Brady, Westminster Editor, 21 May 2006, www.scotlandonsunday.scotsman.com)

activity
INDIVIDUAL WORK

What do you think the army's policy towards drug-taking and drug-takers should be?

remember

The Armed Forces Act 2006 may lead to changes in the Queen's Regulations.

three armed services. (The laws were the Naval Discipline Act 1957, the Army Act 1955 and the Air Force Act 1955.) From now on, therefore, the disciplinary systems in the army, Royal Navy and RAF are essentially the same. This does not mean that there are huge changes in the individual services – only that illogical and unreasonable differences have been ironed out.

The Act deals with criminal offences (tried by **court martial**) and **military offences**, which are actions that are not against civil law but which are unacceptable in the armed forces – for example, **insubordination** and disobedience to lawful commands.

Dealing with minor disciplinary offences in the armed forces (officially called 'administration') is essentially the job of a commanding officer. It consists of 'summary justice', and there is no need to go through any kind of court or hearing. There is, however, an appeals system.

The whole Act is very long: parts 1–13 deal with disciplinary matters.

Office of Public Sector Information
www.opsi.gov.uk
The British Army
www.army.mod.uk

Code of professional standards for the police

case study 5.6

Police code of conduct

Honesty and integrity
1. It is of paramount importance that the public has faith in the honesty and **integrity** of police officers. Officers should therefore be open and truthful in their dealings; avoid being improperly beholden to any person or institution; and discharge their duties with integrity.

Fairness and impartiality
2. Police officers have a particular responsibility to act with fairness and **impartiality** in all their dealings with the public and their colleagues.

Politeness and tolerance
3. Officers should treat members of the public and colleagues with courtesy and respect, avoiding abusive or deriding attitudes or behaviour. In particular, officers must avoid: favouritism of an individual or group; all forms of harassment, victimisation or unreasonable discrimination; and overbearing conduct to a colleague, particularly to one junior in rank or service.

Use of force and abuse of authority
4. Officers must never knowingly use more force than is reasonable, nor should they abuse their authority.

Performance of duties
5. Officers should be conscientious and diligent in the performance of their duties. Officers should attend work promptly when **rostered** for duty. If absent through sickness or injury, they should avoid activities likely to retard their return to duty.

Lawful orders
6. The police service is a disciplined body. Unless there is good and sufficient cause to do otherwise, officers must obey all lawful orders and abide by the provisions of Police Regulations. Officers should support their colleagues in the execution of their lawful duties, and oppose any improper behaviour, reporting it where appropriate.

Confidentiality

7. Information which comes into the possession of the police should be treated as confidential. It should not be used for personal benefit and nor should it be divulged [told] to other parties except in the proper course of police duty. Similarly, officers should respect, as confidential, information about force policy and operations unless authorised to **disclose** it in the course of their duties.

Criminal offences

8. Officers must report any **proceedings** for a criminal offence taken against them. Conviction of a criminal offence may of itself result in further action being taken.

Property

9. Officers must exercise reasonable care to prevent loss or damage to property (excluding their own personal property but including police property).

Sobriety

10. Whilst on duty officers must be sober. Officers should not consume alcohol when on duty unless specifically authorised to do so or it becomes necessary for the proper discharge of police duty.

Appearance

11. Unless on duties which dictate otherwise, officers should always be well turned out, clean and tidy whilst on duty in uniform or in plain clothes.

General conduct

12. Whether on or off duty, police officers should not behave in a way which is likely to bring discredit upon the police service.

(Source: www.ipcc.gov.uk)

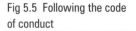

activity

INDIVIDUAL WORK

1   List the main types of disobedience which can happen in the police force – judging by the rules above.

2   Note:
(a) how these could harm the individual officer
(b) how they could harm police colleagues
(c) how they could harm the reputation of the force as a whole
(d) how they could harm the public.

Fig 5.5 Following the code of conduct

What conformity and obedience mean, highlighting their place in the uniformed public services

Conformity means doing what other people want you to do (or what you think they want you to do) without having to be told.

Obedience means doing what you are told.

Both these kinds of behaviour are important in the uniformed public services.

Conformity

Compliance with common practices

Compliance means doing what other people in our social group do in our daily lives. Most people, in most social groups, conform in everyday things like speech, eating habits, dress, and so on.

This kind of conformity is linked to 'social control' – the various pressures that act on us as we grow up which turn us from babies into members of our society. The main agencies of social control are the family, the peer group, education, the media, religion, employment and the law. All of these encourage conformity of one kind or another. The conforming types of behaviour are called 'social norms'.

Social norms

Social norms are the normal types of behaviour for any social group. Social groups include:

- age groups
- colleges and classes in colleges
- people of the same socioeconomic group
- women, men
- ethnic groups
- people with the same interest
- people with the same religion
- teams
- people doing the same job (e.g. firefighters, midwives, rock guitarists)
- people belonging to the same organisation (e.g. a regiment, the Freemasons, the Red Cross)
- people living in the same village, town or area.

The role of self-esteem

Self-esteem is defined as the way we value ourselves: physically, socially, intellectually and emotionally.

Low self-esteem is linked to feelings of insecurity. Research has tended to show that people with low self-esteem, or low feelings of security, are more likely to conform. It is suggested that people with low self-esteem can increase their feeling of security by belonging to a group and adopting its norms because there is 'safety in numbers'.

> **remember**
> Norms are about behaviour – what people normally do; values are people's beliefs. The two are sometimes linked.

For more information, see Kiesler, C. A. and Kiesler, S. B. (1969) *Conformity*. Addison-Wesley, Reading, MA.

case study 5.7

Not-so-useful norms

Today's little rant is about ... Drivers.

1) Why is it, when we're travelling on blues we ALWAYS get stuck behind some muppet who decides that, no, I'm not going to get out of the way of that big police car with blue flashing lights, I was on the road first and my weekly shopping trip is more important than whatever they're running too – Newsflash pal, BLUE LIGHTS MEAN GET OUTTA FLIPPIN WAY!

We don't put them on because "we're going for our tea break" or "it's home time". If we did, we'd be hauled up in front of people who get paid lots more money than I do and be given such a rollocking that we'd not be able to sit down for a week, we'd lose our driving authorisation and we'd probably get "stuck on".

So please, if you see a police car/ambulance/fire engine/coastguard/can't think of any more blue light response service, please, move over to the LEFT and stop so we can get past safely. (Notice I put LEFT in big letters, that's because some people think it's clever to swing their car into the RIGHT hand lane when we approach on blues!)

2) When you see a police car blocking a road with its blue lights flashing and a police officer standing in the road wearing a big yellow jacket, waving their arms about and re-directing traffic, please follow the directions of that officer and DON'T drive [past] the "ROAD CLOSED" signs, almost hit the officer, drive around the cones and past the police car and then carry on up the CLOSED ROAD!

We only close roads when we REALLY have to, not because we think it'd be fun to close a major road during rush hour and see how much hassle we can cause...

God help me if I ever get my response course!

OK rant over!

(Source: probationerpc.blogspot.com)

activity
GROUP WORK

What does this extract tell us about (a) police probationer norms and (b) norms for 'muppets'?

The causes of low self-esteem are not fully understood. They are related to the way a person has been brought up, to their perceived performance at school, and to their economic and family background.

Low self-esteem can be changed – either by increasing maturity or by achieving successes and getting respect from others.

The purpose of uniforms

The wearing of uniforms by the uniformed public services has the following effects:

- It encourages esprit de corps by allowing members to identify with their service; this increases loyalty, raises morale, and increases job satisfaction.

- It identifies the members of the service in situations such as warfare where it essential to be able to distinguish friend from enemy.

- For civilian uniformed services, the uniform generates trust in the public because the uniform identifies the police officer/firefighter/ambulance person, etc.

- Uniform shows that the individual is acting not as an individual but for an organisation which has been set up to serve the needs of society.

- Uniform is designed with health and safety in mind (e.g. fireproof) and protects the employee.

- Uniform hides the social and other differences which might cause discrimination or inequality in an organisation.

- Uniforms are used to show the rank of individuals in a uniformed service, and are therefore part of the discipline structure, where precedence (the right to command) is determined by rank.

- The correct wearing of uniform and the responsibility to keep it clean and neat is part of the discipline training in a uniformed service.

The relevance of conformity in the uniformed public services

The uniformed public services encourage conformity among their members in various ways: uniform and rank structures, working in teams, esprit de corps, and by having social clubs, sports clubs and other activities which encourage employees to mix outside working hours. The message is that conformity is a good thing for the work of the service and for its image in society.

Conformity is a powerful bonding force in the uniformed services, but if it becomes too strong it brings with it certain dangers. In a diverse society people are different, and they are often proud of the differences. People have criticised the uniformed public services in Britain for being too full of white males – good at their job, but testosterone-driven, 'laddish', and not very welcoming of female or ethnic minority recruits, let alone gays and lesbians. The idea is that employees have been conforming with each other in a way which excludes the rest of society and puts off new recruits.

In recent years, there has been a move away from this type of conformity. The National Black Police Association (NBPA) and the Gay Police Association signal the fact that what matters is conformity to the professional and public service **ethic**, not the 'white male club' conformity of the past. In a fast-changing world, it is better if public service employees are open-minded and original in their thinking. After a speech to the NBPA in 2006, Assistant Commissioner of the Metropolitan Police Tarique Ghaffur quoted these words from Steve Jobs, head of Apple Computers:

'Your time is limited, so don't waste it living someone else's life. Don't be trapped by dogma – which is living with the results of other people's thinking. Don't let the noise of others' opinions drown out your own inner voice. And most important, have the courage to follow your heart and intuition. They somehow already know what you truly want to become. Everything else is secondary.'

(Source: www.nationalbpa.com)

Too much conformity can slow down career progression in the public services. Not enough conformity can get people labelled as 'snobs', 'square pegs' or 'troublemakers'.

Obedience

Obedience as an act, practice or quality

Obedience is the *act* of carrying out an order. As a *practice*, it means that orders are followed regularly and dependably. As a *quality*, it is the habit that some people have of following orders without delay or complaint.

Obedience differs from conformity. When someone conforms, they do what others do without having to be asked or told (often, it is a form of imitation). When someone obeys, they do what they are told.

Following orders

The ability to follow orders promptly and correctly is an absolute necessity in a uniformed public service. This is not to say that employees are zombies, automata, or never able to disagree with an order, but the bottom line is that when orders have to be obeyed they have to be obeyed. For this reason people who are not prepared to follow orders, for whatever reason, are unlikely to be employed – or to want to be employed – in a uniformed public service.

However, just as people in the uniformed services have a duty to follow orders, so the people giving the orders have an equally binding duty to make sure that the orders are justified. The long and thorough training that officers receive in the armed forces is intended to ensure that their orders are justified as far as is humanly possible.

Orders given in a military establishment involve not just actions in training or combat. Since people often have to live in close proximity in barracks they receive orders about general duties and 'housekeeping' to control behaviour such as untidiness and prevent people from getting on each others' nerves. Orders can be written as well as spoken, and orders are part of the general drive towards discipline which has to exist in a military establishment.

Conscious and unconscious obedience

If someone who has little experience of following orders joins a uniformed service, they may at first have to force themselves to obey. However, after a while they get used to obeying orders, and it becomes second nature. They move from conscious to unconscious obedience.

In the uniformed public services, both conscious and unconscious obedience are necessary: the first so that the work can be done in a disciplined and organised manner; the second in emergencies, when an instant response is needed.

Unconscious obedience is not the same thing as blind obedience.

> **remember**
> There is no way of being absolutely sure whether a person's action is conscious or not.

Link   See pages 219–220 for more information on blind obedience.

Compliance

Compliance is doing what others want us to do. Although in certain phrases, such as 'compliance with common practices' (used on page 199 above) it means conformity, in other contexts, such as 'compliance with a demand, order, etc.', it means obedience.

Depending on the context, compliance can be willing, cheerful obedience, or there can be some feeling that the obedience is being forced. Recently, compliance has also come to mean obedience to rules, regulations and laws.

In the uniformed services, willing, cheerful obedience is a good thing; it suggests that a team is working well.

Status as a factor in obedience

In the uniformed services, as in ordinary life, people are more likely to obey orders if those orders come from someone of higher status. Status usually means rank, and orders are almost always passed from someone of higher to someone of lower rank.

Exceptions can occur, on a temporary basis, if someone of lower rank is seen as an expert in a task which is being done. In these circumstances authority can be delegated, formally or informally, so that for the duration of a particular task the expert, rather than the person of higher rank, is effectively the boss. An example of this is seen at road accidents. The police are usually in charge of the scene and give orders if they need to be given, but, if vehicles are on fire, the fire and rescue service can issue the orders – because they are the experts.

Link   See pages 156 and 165 in Unit 4 for information on team roles and the 'manoeuvrist' style of leadership.

Influences can sometimes be called stimuli.

Influences

These factors can change the nature of orders – or change the way in which people respond to them.

Fear

Fear – of punishment, loss of rank, accusations of cowardice, a physical beating or of peer-group ridicule and disapproval – may cause people to obey orders that they would not otherwise obey. Fear of a team leader or commanding officer should not be the main motivating factor in whether or not an order is obeyed. If people obey an order out of fear, it suggests that relationships within a team are poor, levels of understanding are low, or that some form of bullying, harassment or victimisation is taking place. These are potentially serious problems in a uniformed service, as the allegations of bullying surrounding the deaths of four young soldiers at Deepcut Barracks between 1995 and 2000 have demonstrated.

Reward

Rewards are a **stimulus** for obeying orders, but they should take the form of praise and approving looks, not gifts. Giving obvious rewards for following orders lays a commander open to charges of favouritism and corruption. Corruption is always illegal, by definition, while favouritism is against equal opportunities law and is also illegal (if it can be proved). Both are extremely harmful to morale and undermine the authority of a leader.

Love

'Love' sometimes means intense admiration, and soldiers, for example, may feel intense admiration for their commander and what he or she stands for. They may also love the ideas or the country they are fighting for. This kind of love can produce high levels of obedience and even self-sacrifice.

Sexual love, or 'falling in love', may happen in the uniformed public services. This has traditionally been considered bad for obedience. In the armed forces the ban on women, which is only gradually being relaxed, and the ban on homosexuals, which eventually ended in 2000, originally existed because it was felt that love (and other things related to love, such as jealousy) undermined service discipline.

case study 5.8 Personal relationships in the armed forces

In the area of personal relationships, the overriding operational imperative to sustain team cohesion and to maintain trust and loyalty between commanders and those they command imposes a need for standards of social behaviour which are more demanding than those required by society at large. Such demands are equally necessary during peacetime and on operations. Examples of behaviour which can undermine such trust and cohesion, and therefore damage the morale or discipline of a unit (and hence its operational effectiveness) include: unwelcome sexual attention in the form of physical or verbal conduct; over-familiarity with the spouses or partners of other Service personnel; displays of affection which might cause offence to others; behaviour which damages or hazards the marriage or personal relationships of Service personnel or civilian colleagues within the wider defence community; and taking sexual advantage of subordinates. It is important to acknowledge in the tightly knit military community a need for mutual respect and a requirement to avoid conduct which offends others. Each case will be judged on its merits.

(Source: *The Armed Forces Code of Social Conduct* (2000), www.mod.uk)

activity
INDIVIDUAL WORK

What are the arguments for and against allowing gays and lesbians to join the armed forces?

Respect

There are two kinds of respect in the uniformed services:

- the respect due to rank – e.g. saluting a senior officer
- personal respect for other people as individuals.

Both act as a stimulus for obedience and conformity – and do so without undermining morale.

Respect is different from the other influences mentioned above, since it is of vital importance that people in the uniformed services treat each other with respect – in both the senses given above.

The ways of showing respect due to rank differ according to whether the respect is being shown by a person of lower rank to one of higher rank, or the other way round. Through a system of salutes and conventional ways of addressing superiors, respect for rank is built into the system. People in the uniformed forces are expected to show respect to people of higher rank at all times, and that respect should not depend on whether there is a personal feeling of respect. Commanders and team leaders can show respect to their subordinates by thanking them for work done, by listening to their concerns, by appraising them fairly, by doing what is right and proper to advance their careers, and so on.

Personal respect is the kind of respect that all of us should show to others in our day-to-day lives. It should not take the form of favouritism.

activity
GROUP WORK
5.3

P3

Produce a wallchart outlining:

1 what is meant by conformity and obedience
2 how they are shown in the public services
3 what influences them.

Research studies

As conformity and obedience are such important factors in people's lives – especially their working lives – it is not surprising that they have been closely studied.

Interestingly, however, the most famous studies have dealt with the way that conformity and obedience can undermine our judgement and lead to human rights abuses. The reason for this emphasis was the horrors of the Second World War and the need to understand why the Germans under Hitler were able to send six million Jews to their deaths.

Asch

Solomon Asch carried out a famous experiment on conformity in 1951. He collected together a large number of American college students and divided them into groups of 8–10. In each group, one student was the real subject of the experiment; the others secretly collaborated with Solomon Asch.

He sat each group of students down in a room and showed them a card with four lines on it.

Each student was asked to say, aloud, which of the bars on the right-hand side of the card was the same length as the bar on the left.

All the students except one had been told by Asch to give the same wrong answer. The one who had been told nothing (the real **participant** in the experiment) was positioned so that they had to give their answer next to last – i.e. after all but one of the 'coached' students had given theirs.

Fig 5.6 Diagram of a card
used in Asch's experiment

A B C

The experiment was repeated 18 times with different groups of students. Different sets of bars were used, but the same basic procedure was followed. The 'coached' students were told to give the wrong answers in 12 of the 18 experiments.

Despite the fact that the answers were fairly obviously wrong, many of the uncoached students (the unknowing participants in the experiment) gave the same wrong answer that was given by the 'coached' students who answered before them. The number was far higher than had been predicted following tests using the cards on individual students before the experiment started. Thirty-seven of the 50 genuine participants conformed to the majority at least once, and 14 of them conformed on more than 6 of the 12 trials. Asch said:

'That we have found the tendency to conformity in our society so strong that reasonably intelligent and well-meaning young people are willing to call white black is a matter of concern. It raises questions about our ways of education and about the values that guide our conduct.'

(Source: Asch, S. E. (1955) Opinions and social pressure. *Scientific American*, 193, 31–35)

After the experiment, the genuine participants were interviewed to find out why they had conformed with the majority even when they knew the answer that the majority was giving was wrong.

Most said that they had agreed with the majority because they were afraid of being ridiculed or thought strange. A few genuinely thought that the majority's answers were correct.

Factors influencing conformity

- Conformity was greater when the questions and answers were given aloud, i.e. publicly. When the experiment was done so that the participants were allowed to write their answer down after the others had spoken theirs aloud, their conformity rate went down considerably.

- Conformity was not influenced by the size of the majority. It was as great if the majority was only three or four as it was if it was 15.

- If one other 'coached' student gave the right answer, conformity with the majority dropped greatly, because the participant had an ally. It is much easier not to conform if someone else is also not conforming.

remember
Some psychology websites use the word 'subject' instead of 'participant' for a person taking part in an experiment.

Milgram

In 1961–62, Stanley Milgram wanted to see how far people would obey unreasonable and inhumane commands. He rigged up a laboratory which consisted of two rooms. He then advertised for volunteers (whom he paid) to take part in an experiment which he said was about the effects of punishment on memory and learning.

When the experiment started he asked two people to come into the laboratory and called one of them the 'learner' and the other the 'teacher'. Although they didn't know it, only the people taking the role of teacher were volunteers. The people taking the role of learner were actors employed by Milgram to take part in the experiment. One other person was present: the experimenter.

The experimenter strapped the learner into what looked like an electric chair and fixed an electrode to the person's wrist. The learner was told they would be read a series of word-pairs and tested on their ability to remember the second word of the pair when read the first one again. If the learner made an error, the learner would be given electric shocks of increasing intensity.

After the teacher had watched the learner being strapped in and given instructions, the experimenter made the teacher sit before a 'shock generator'. This machine was a fake, but it looked real and had 30 levers attached, each of which was labelled with voltages ranging from 15 to 450 (well over the lethal limit). The levers were grouped and labelled 'Slight Shock', 'Moderate Shock', 'Strong Shock', 'Very Strong Shock', 'Intense Shock', 'Extreme Intensity Shock', and 'Danger: Severe Shock'.

The experimenter gave each teacher a real 45-volt shock using this equipment, as a result of which the teacher was more likely to believe that the machine really would give the learner electric shocks. The experiment then began with the learner failing to remember words and the teacher giving what were believed to be electric shocks. The learner had been told by Milgram before the experiment to grunt when the 'shocks' reached 75 volts, complain loudly at 120 volts, demand to be released from the experiment at 150 volts, then increase the level of protests until, at 285 volts, he would produce an agonised scream. After that, he made no more sound.

Before the experiment, Milgram described the planned experiment to many people and asked them at what voltage they thought people would refuse to go on with the experiment on the grounds that it was causing too much pain, and health risk, to the 'learner'. Hardly any thought that the 'teachers' would go up to the highest level of electric shock.

In the event about 60% of the people tested, from all walks of life, went all the way, obeying the experimenter till they reached the highest voltage. When the experiment was tried at other universities and in other countries, the obedience rates were even higher than they had been at Yale – the university where the experiment was first carried out. Obedience rates also varied somewhat from country to country: one of the higher levels of obedience – 85% – being recorded at Munich in Germany.

Milgram tape-recorded the verbal interactions between the experimenter and the participants and interviewed the participants after the experiment to try to find out what they had felt during it.

Factors influencing obedience
Milgram found that:

- The participants (people taking part as 'teachers' in the experiment) were more obedient if the experimenter was physically present and standing close to them.

- If there were two experimenters and they disagreed at a certain shock level about the wisdom of going on, the participant did not go on.

Fig 5.7 Milgram's 'shock generator'

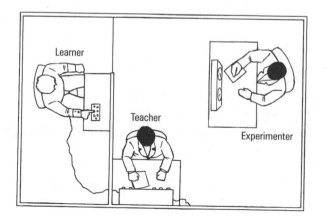

- If two other 'teachers' were present who had been coached to refuse to go on at a certain point, the participant usually did not go on.
- If a person other than the 'teacher' gave the shocks, the participants were more likely to obey the experimenter right up to the highest voltage.
- If the experimenter gave instructions on the phone, the obedience rate dropped.
- If the teacher had to physically put the 'learner's' hand on an 'electric shock plate', the obedience level dropped.
- If the teacher had to decide the shock levels, hardly any went to the top of the voltage scale.
- If the experiment was conducted in a nondescript office instead of at Yale University (widely considered one of the world's best universities), the obedience level was lower.

case study 5.9 — Milgram's conclusions

Even Eichmann [the man in charge of exterminating Jews in Nazi Germany] was sickened when he toured the concentration camps, but he had only to sit at a desk and shuffle papers. At the same time the man in the camp who actually dropped Cyclon-b into the gas chambers was able to justify his behaviour on the ground that he was only following orders from above. Thus there is a fragmentation of the total human act; no one is confronted with the consequences of his decision to carry out the evil act. The person who assumes responsibility has evaporated. Perhaps this is the most common characteristic of socially organized evil in modern society.

(Source: 'The Perils of Obedience' as it appeared in *Harper's Magazine*. Abridged and adapted from *Obedience to Authority* by Stanley Milgram. Copyright 1974)

activity
GROUP WORK

1 Researchers have seen obedience and conformity as dangerous things. The uniformed public services encourage and train for them. Who is right?
2 Experiments like Milgram's are not often done nowadays. Why not?

Hofling

In 1966, Charles K. Hofling carried out an experiment in an American psychiatric hospital to test obedience. He met nurses on 22 different wards to warn them of the dangers of a supposedly new drug called 'Astroten' (which was actually harmless glucose tablets). The maximum dose – 10mg – was clearly labelled on the box.

Later a man posing as a Dr Smith – who was not known to the nurses – phoned a nurse on each of the 22 wards instructing them to give 20 mg of Astroten to a 'patient' who was 'in urgent need of the drug'.

'Dr Smith' had asked the nurses to break three basic rules:

- never to give more than the maximum permitted dose of a drug
- never to give drugs without written authorisation ('Dr Smith' said that he would 'come round in 10 minutes' and do this)
- never to accept instructions from a stranger on the phone.

The nurses were observed in the experiment, and 21 out of 22 nurses followed 'Dr Smith's' instructions.

The experiment appeared to show that public servants working in a hierarchical and authoritarian setting would obey unreasonable or illegal orders if they thought that they

came from someone in authority. As with Milgram's experiment, it suggests that people can be easily manipulated, as a result of their training in obedience, to do things which are wrong.

Zimbardo

Philip Zimbardo carried out the Stanford Prison experiment in 1971. In essence, it was an extended role-play which was organised carefully in advance, had the cooperation of the police, and was elaborately staged using a fake prison which had been constructed in Stanford University. 'Prisoners' and 'guards' were volunteers; real police officers arrested the 'prisoners'; the 'guards' were given total control over the prison environment. Zimbardo and his colleagues watched the behaviour of the participants and discovered that the 'guards' rapidly entered into their role and became brutal in their efforts to humiliate and 'break down' the 'prisoners'. As the guards' behaviour became more extreme, Zimbardo had to halt the experiment.

The behaviour that Zimbardo observed was an illustration of the saying: 'Power corrupts, and absolute power corrupts absolutely'. Its relevance to the uniformed services has been highlighted by the widely publicised behaviour of American soldiers at Abu Ghraib Prison in Baghdad, in 2004, when Iraqi prisoners were systematically abused.

activity
GROUP WORK 5.4
P4

You are volunteers in a human rights organisation.

1. Perform three short role-plays, suitable for a training session of police cadets, demonstrating experiments on conformity and obedience which have relevance to the work of the uniformed services.
2. Give short presentations outlining what the experiments show.

activity
INDIVIDUAL WORK 5.5
M3

Write an article suitable for a public service magazine analysing how the findings of three research studies on conformity and obedience apply to the uniformed services.

Fig 5.8 A disciplined service – fortunately

The importance of self-discipline in the uniformed public services

Self-discipline

This is to do with self-control and with behaving in the correct manner without having to be told. The discipline of initial training, which comes from other people (**supervisory officers**, instructors, mentors, etc.), becomes 'internalised'; in other words the trainee develops a sense of duty and 'tells themselves' what to do.

In the uniformed public services, self-discipline is seen as a very good quality, and people who want a career in the uniformed public services should make every effort to understand and to develop self-discipline.

Personal grooming and presentation

Grooming is to do with hair, nails, teeth and general cleanliness. Presentation is to do with clothes, footwear, posture and overall appearance.

There are rules in the uniformed services about how to wear the uniform, and about the standards of appearance that have to be maintained. These rules are more demanding in the armed forces and are most demanding on **ceremonial occasions**, when the aim is to provide an impressive spectacle of smartness and good drill.

New recruits in the armed forces are given instructions on how to keep clean and be well groomed and properly dressed for their new role. This is important for:

- health and hygiene
- the development of disciplined habits
- morale and esprit de corps
- the public image of the unit or the service.

> **remember**
> Posture and bearing: standing, sitting and walking properly, and making appropriate eye contact: all these can matter in uniformed service work.

> **remember**
> The uniformed services are sensitive about certain kinds of tattoo.

---

case study 5.10 — **Making a good impression**

Her Majesty added: "Many talented young people can learn the principles of management; but effective leadership is far more demanding."

The Queen wished all the cadets success in the future and spoke of how they could be deployed on operations within just weeks.

"I know that everyone here today has been deeply impressed by your smartness and bearing on this parade."

(Source: www.princeofwales.gov.uk)

activity
INDIVIDUAL WORK

Speak to someone who works in a uniformed service and ask them what their feelings are about personal presentation and its importance.

 Link See Unit 13 in *BTEC National Public Services Book 2* for more information on self-discipline.

Punctuality

Punctuality means doing things when you are supposed to do them. Punctuality matters because:

- It enables you to organise your time.
- It prevents other people's time from being wasted.
- It shows respect and consideration for others.
- It can be a safety issue.

Time management

This means using your working time well. Good time management allows a worker to do the maximum amount of work in the shortest possible time with the minimum of effort. A person whose time management is good doesn't seem rushed off their feet; they appear relaxed and unstressed, and if an emergency crops up they are able to deal with it because the rest of their workload is well under control.

See pages 74–75 in Unit 2 for more information on time management.

Reliability

This important attribute means doing what you have agreed to do in the agreed way, at the agreed time. It is linked to punctuality and good time management. Reliability creates trust, and shows that you consider your work to be important.

Reliable people don't skimp their work: they do it properly and thoroughly. This is good for safety, and it saves work in the long run, because a job done well means that there is no need for someone else to come along afterwards and clear up the mess!

Attendance

This means turning up to work. Attendance is a complicated subject because poor attendance can happen for a variety of causes (e.g. sickness, injury, stress, 'pulling sickies', family problems, and so on). The cause is not always what it seems, because stress can make people feel ill, or they may take time off because they find the job boring or are being harassed at work.

Civilian public services, including the uniformed ones, are considered to be stressful places to work. The absentee rates are higher than in the private sector. In 2004, the absence rate in the ambulance service was the highest in the NHS: 6.2% compared with an average of 4.5% for all NHS jobs and around 3.7% for all UK workers. Attempts are being made to reduce the absentee rate in the ambulance service by discouraging short-term sickness and introducing **flexible working contracts**. Ambulance workers have to do a lot of **manual handling**, which means that they are more likely than most to suffer from back and other injuries. Their job is stressful – sometimes traumatic – and they work with people who may pass on infectious illnesses to them.

Like all employees, workers in the uniformed public services have a duty to turn up for work unless there is a good reason why they shouldn't. This means that they also have a duty to look after their health in their own time. As the Police Code of Conduct says, 'Officers should attend work promptly when rostered for duty. If absent through sickness or injury, they should avoid activities likely to retard their return to duty.'

If a uniformed service employee is off sick, they (or someone else) should contact their place of employment and let them know that they will not be coming in – so that their work can be covered.

See page 216 for more on the Police Code of Conduct.

Composure

This means keeping calm under stress. It is mainly a by-product of good training and preparation. Panic, which is the opposite of composure, usually results from a crisis for which we are unprepared. Building skills and competence, and getting plenty of relevant experience, is good for composure. Composure is also helped by being part of a team which gets on well together and knows its job.

Attitude

remember

Racism, sexism and discriminatory behaviour show attitudes that are not accepted in public service work.

Attitude is the effect of personal emotions or beliefs on behaviour. It is shown in our facial expressions, in the things we say without thinking, in our body language, in the decisions we make, and in our relationships with other people. 'Attitude' does not necessarily mean being aggressive or 'stroppy', but it can do. There are good attitudes and bad attitudes. A self-disciplined and professional person keeps their personal feelings in check and does not let their attitudes show unless there is some good, work-related reason for doing so.

Performance

Self-discipline is good for performance, and a self-disciplined person will get more work done, of a better quality and in less time, than a similar person who is not self-disciplined.

These days, performance is measured in the uniformed public services in two main ways:

- by setting targets and recording whether not those targets are reached
- by year-on-year comparisons of performance.

Target setting

Target-setting is considered psychologically motivating – because many people are goal-oriented and need to feel that they are achieving something worthwhile in life. A team that performs well meets or exceeds its targets; a team that performs badly falls short of its targets.

Targets define both the quantity and the quality of work which a team is expected to carry out. If set correctly by the government or by the leaders in a public service, the targets are challenging but not impossible. They can be reached – but only by a disciplined effort.

Table 5.2 Examples of targets for HMRC

3a. Reduce the availability of illegal drugs by increasing the proportion of heroin targeted on the UK which is taken out 2005–06 target: 5,300 kg YTD profile: 3,975 kg	Slippage. 1,842 kg taken out (46% of YTD profile). This is a joint outturn [total] of all CIDA* agencies. HMRC contribution 774 kg (42% of CIDA outturn)
3b. Reduce the availability of illegal drugs by increasing the proportion of cocaine targeted on the UK taken out 2005–06 target: 13,200 kg YTD profile: 9,900 kg	Ahead 11,721 kg taken out (118% of YTD profile). This is a joint outturn of all CIDA agencies. HMRC contribution 5,269 kg (45% of CIDA outturn)

* Concerted Inter-agency Drugs Action Group

(Source: *Spring Departmental Report 2006, HM Revenue & Customs*. Presented to Parliament by the Paymaster General and the Chief Secretary to the Treasury by Command of Her Majesty, June 2006)

Year-on-year comparisons of performance

This is similar to target setting in that the aim is to do better than in the previous year. An example of this is shown in the following statistics from the West Yorkshire Police.

Table 5.3 Statistics from West Yorkshire Police Annual Report

	2004–2005	2005–2006	Improvement
Robberies per 1000 population	0.9	1.2	No
Domestic Burglary per 1000 households	20.8	18.7	Yes
Vehicle Crime per 1000 population	18.6	16.8	Yes
Criminal Damage per 1000 population	29.6	27.3	Yes
Total Violent Crime per 1000 population	24.9	26.1	No
Total Crime per 1000 population	122.7	122.4	Yes

(Source: West Yorkshire Police *Annual Report 2005–2006*)

Self-discipline is needed to meet targets if they have been properly set. Self-discipline is required not only to work hard, but also to become more effective and efficient by learning new strategies, the use of new equipment and of better methods of working, and so on.

activity
INDIVIDUAL WORK
5.6

M2

Research and write a report on what people who work in the uniformed public services think about the importance of self-discipline. Your report should be suitable for trainers of new recruits to use as an information source.

Personality

Personality is shown in many aspects of people's behaviour: the way they tackle a job, the way they relate to other people, and the way they respond to the various problems and challenges that life throws in their path.

Everybody is different, and the fact that the uniformed services wear uniform does not mean that they expect people to be like clones with identical personalities. In a diverse society, differences should be appreciated. We can enjoy, and learn from, the differences in other people. If everybody was exactly the same, nobody would have anything to learn from anyone else.

> **remember**
>
> Assertiveness is not the same as aggression.

Self-discipline is sometimes needed, however, when dealing with people whose personalities we don't like. When there is a personality clash or a conflict of attitudes or opinions, it should be dealt with *assertively*. Brief guidelines for **assertiveness** are given in the next case study.

activity
INDIVIDUAL WORK
5.7

P2

Design and produce a poster suitable for a public service training suite describing why self-discipline is important in the uniformed public services.

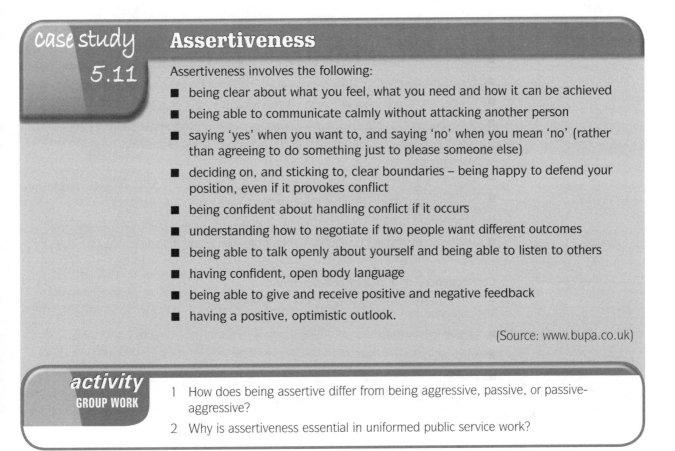

case study 5.11

Assertiveness

Assertiveness involves the following:

- being clear about what you feel, what you need and how it can be achieved
- being able to communicate calmly without attacking another person
- saying 'yes' when you want to, and saying 'no' when you mean 'no' (rather than agreeing to do something just to please someone else)
- deciding on, and sticking to, clear boundaries – being happy to defend your position, even if it provokes conflict
- being confident about handling conflict if it occurs
- understanding how to negotiate if two people want different outcomes
- being able to talk openly about yourself and being able to listen to others
- having confident, open body language
- being able to give and receive positive and negative feedback
- having a positive, optimistic outlook.

(Source: www.bupa.co.uk)

activity
GROUP WORK

1. How does being assertive differ from being aggressive, passive, or passive-aggressive?
2. Why is assertiveness essential in uniformed public service work?

The effects of self-discipline and the consequences on the individual and organisation of a lack or total absence of self-discipline

In our working lives – and especially if we are working for a uniformed public service – self-discipline is always a good thing.

The effects of self discipline in a uniformed service

The effects of self discipline in a uniformed service are as follows.

For the individual working in the service
- It saves time, effort and stress.
- It improves working relationships.
- It helps us to keep calm, think clearly and act decisively in an emergency.

For the organisation
- It improves productivity: the quality and quantity of work done.
- It reduces **absenteeism** by reducing stress, harassment, unsafe working practices, etc.
- It limits discrimination and promotes harmony in a diverse workforce.
- It gives a good image to the public and to members of other services.
- It raises morale.
- Organisation is better.
- There is less waste of time and money.

For the public/community/people served

■ They are protected and served more efficiently and more effectively.

■ They are treated with respect and in a fair, organised manner.

■ They trust and admire the service because its members are self-disciplined.

■ The service is a good role model – especially for young people.

■ In peacekeeping activities, a disciplined service is a good ambassador for the country.

For enemies, criminals, etc.

■ They are deterred from attacking the service or the country to which it belongs.

■ They are deterred from breaking the law.

■ Enemies are more likely to be defeated, and criminals are more likely to be caught.

■ There can be respect for fair play even from the enemy, if soldiers obey the rules of international law.

Consequences of a lack of self-discipline

For the individual working in the uniformed service
The consequences are:

■ lack of job satisfaction

■ frustration

■ stress

■ failure to develop good professional skills

■ low morale

■ low workrate

■ poor quality work

■ poor attendance record.

For the organisation
The consequences are:

■ low morale; tendency to panic or to act without thinking

■ missing targets

■ low levels of efficiency and productivity

■ poor attendance of staff

■ money wasted (or little to show for the money spent)

■ poor paperwork; high level of errors

■ friction between staff; bullying, harassment and discrimination

■ low health and safety levels

■ bad publicity

■ high level of complaints, civil lawsuits, etc.

For the community served
The consequences are:

■ dissatisfaction with the service; complaints

■ raised levels of crime, insecurity, etc.

■ lack of confidence in the authorities generally

■ the possibility of people 'taking the law into their own hands'.

For enemies and criminals
The consequences are:

■ good news! – they can exploit weaknesses in the services

■ more crime or increased danger of enemy attack.

Total absence of self-discipline
Large-scale absence of self-discipline is virtually unknown in the British uniformed public services. Individuals who show a total absence of self-discipline are weeded out, or turn up in the civil courts or at courts martial.

The effects of a total absence of self-discipline in a uniformed service are catastrophic and lead to large-scale human rights abuses.

Link

See page 195 above.

activity

INDIVIDUAL WORK
5.8

D1

Make a collection of news reports on examples of good and bad discipline in uniformed public services in a range of countries. Use these as the basis for an article for a public service magazine giving a balanced assessment of the importance of good disciplinary systems and standards in the uniformed services.

The complex nature of authority in the uniformed public services

Authority
Authority is defined as 'the power or right to enforce obedience'. It is complex because of:

■ the variety of forms that it takes

■ the range of people, both inside and outside the services, who have authority over the services and their staff.

Within a range of different public services
In the uniformed public services, authority is built into the system through the rank structure and the rules and regulations that govern each service. As we have already seen, this authority is deeply rooted and traditional in nature having been built up – especially in the army and the Royal Navy – over hundreds of years.

Everyone working in the uniformed public services has to comply with a discipline code which has the force of law. Most breaches of discipline are not 'serious' and do not end up in court or a court martial.

Armed forces
In the armed forces, minor breaches of discipline are dealt with in a summary way (quickly, with minimum fuss, by a commanding officer).

For more information see *Queen's Regulations*, Chapter 6
Armed Forces Act 2006
www.opsi.gov.uk
The British Army
www.army.mod.uk

Police

In the civilian uniformed public services, disciplinary codes keep changing. The most recent Code of Conduct for the police came out in 2004.

See Statutory Instrument 2004 No. 645 *The Police (Conduct) Regulations 2004* – read the Notes immediately before Schedule 2

www.ipcc.gov.uk

The Police Code of Conduct reflects the special nature of police work and the need to maintain public confidence in the police at all times. The authority comes from Parliament – i.e. the government. The power to enforce this authority is delegated to the police authorities, which supervise local police forces, and to the police themselves where there is a relatively minor infringement that can be dealt with internally without reflecting on the honesty or integrity of the police.

The Police Code of Conduct deals with personal behaviour; the PACE Act Codes of Practice cover police powers in dealing with suspects and investigating crimes.

Independent Police Complaints Commission

Because sensitive issues can arise from police work – especially when a person dies as an apparent result of police activity (e.g. in police custody, during a police car chase, or while resisting arrest) – the government has set up the Independent Police Complaints Commission (IPCC). Both the police and the public have the right to refer a case to the IPCC. The IPCC does not determine the punishment, but its recommendations are likely to be followed up by the courts if necessary. Even if the IPCC decides that there are no grounds for charging the police with **manslaughter** etc., the courts have the authority to try the officer(s) if someone else brings a prosecution.

Prison service

HM Chief Inspector of Prisons

Independent teams of inspectors funded by the government are employed to inspect civilian uniformed services and make sure that they are giving a high-quality service. They can carry out announced or unannounced inspections and produce reports which are publicly available on government websites. They do not have direct powers to enforce changes themselves, but the sponsoring government departments (e.g. the Home Office for the police and the Ministry of Justice for the prison service) can enforce the necessary changes by contacting chief constables, prison directors or others who have the authority to make sure that the changes are carried out. Where police forces, prisons, etc. are well below standard there is often a series of inspections to ensure that the required improvements really are taking place.

> **remember**
> Inspection reports are available on the internet and make interesting reading!

> **Link**
>
> See pages 26 and 27 in Unit 1 for more on HM Chief Inspector of Prisons and the IPCC.

If a shocking incident takes place which brings discredit on a service, such as the racist murder of Zahid Mubarek at Feltham Young Offender Institution in 2000, the government (usually after a lot of agitation from the media, pressure groups and MPs) will hold an official inquiry. The one on the murder of Mubarek criticised the institution and some of its employees very severely in a 700-page report and produced 88 recommendations for change.

The Zahid Mubarek Inquiry – especially the recommendations at the end of the Appendices

www.zahidmubarekinquiry.org.uk

Fire and rescue services

HM Chief Inspector of Fire Services

There is at present no Chief Inspector of the fire and rescue services in England and Wales, although there is one in Scotland. Fire and rescue services are therefore inspected internally and, locally, by their own fire and rescue authorities. Financial management and value for money can also be inspected by the Audit Commission. There are plans to make new arrangements for fire and rescue service inspection, according to the *Parliamentary Select Committee on Communities and Local Government Fourth Report* (2006, www.publications.parliament.uk).

Extent of authority; power or right to enforce obedience

Officially, no uniformed service in Britain is above the law, so – within Britain – none of the uniformed public services is allowed to take actions which are against the law. They have no authority to enforce obedience either among their own personnel or among the public at large by means which infringe human rights as laid down in the Human Rights Act of 1998.

See pages 109–110 in Unit 3 for more on the Human Rights Act 1998.

However, there are certain activities carried out by the uniformed public services where they have been accused (mainly by human rights organisations) of exceeding their authority and going beyond what is allowed in the law. The following are examples:

- the imprisonment of so-called 'terror suspects' for long periods without trial, then attempting to deport or repatriate them to countries where they are likely to be tortured

- the secret introduction of 'Operation Kratos' – a shoot-to-kill policy to be used against terror suspects (so far this has led to the death of the innocent Brazilian Jean Charles de Menezes at Stockwell Tube Station in July 2005)

- the failure to remove DNA samples of innocent people from the police database.

See page 220 for more on the case of Jean Charles de Menezes.

Fig 5.9 Extraordinary rendition – is it legal or not?

Outside Britain, the uniformed services have been involved in other possibly illegal acts:

- the invasion of Iraq, condemned in 2004 by the then Secretary General of the UN, Kofi Annan, as 'illegal'
- 'extraordinary rendition' – the practice of secretly taking 'terror suspects' to interrogation centres in countries such as Poland or Bulgaria, in contravention of international law and with no safeguards that they will not be tortured.

The government has insisted that all of these are legal activities, but there is still considerable disagreement about the true extent of the authority of the uniformed services.

Nature of authority

Authority = Power + Moral rightness.

Power

Power by itself is not true authority. An armed robber who points a gun at you has the power to shoot you – but not the authority. This is because the robber is morally and legally in the wrong. To be in a position of true authority it is necessary to have both power and moral and legal rightness.

However, the word 'powers', as in 'police powers' does mean 'authority' – in the form of legal backing.

Position

Position is linked to power, and it is therefore a factor in determining whether a person has authority. In the uniformed public services, a person of higher rank has authority over a lower-ranking person. Since this is generally agreed, the higher-ranking person also has moral rightness on their side.

Status

This is almost the same thing as position, so a person of higher status is likely to have authority over a person of lower status, provided that they are in the same uniformed public service and there is some kind of chain of command between them. However, a person of high status in one service does not have authority over a person of lower status in another service unless they are involved in some kind of joint operation, and the authority has been agreed beforehand (e.g. in a multi-agency response to a major incident).

Influence

A verb is about doing something; a noun is the name of a thing or idea.

'To influence' (verb) means to affect someone's behaviour (or thinking), but without enforcement. Often 'influence' (noun) – the ability to change people's behaviour by example or persuasion – is linked to power, wealth, charisma, status, past achievements, expertise or moral standing. Influencing someone is not the same as giving a direct order, but it still requires a kind of authority. An example of a famous person with this kind of authority was Pope John-Paul II, who was very influential in world politics even among people who were not Catholics. This is the kind of authority that a 'role model' has over their admirers.

However, influence is not always good, and it is possible to influence people through tempting them (e.g. by bribery or illicit gifts) or by threats such as blackmail. This kind of influence is called corruption.

Corruption

There is always a risk that people in authority can be tempted to make money dishonestly through corrupt practices. If a 'drug baron' pays a top police officer so as not to get arrested, this would be a simple example of corruption. Corruption is something that can happen at the highest level, and at the time of writing (2007) the police are investigating possible sales of honours (places in the House of Lords) by the government to people who have given money or loans to the Labour party, which is in power. Corruption undermines the authority of a public service, whether it is the police or the government, and has a bad effect on the rest of society, which sees no reason why it should obey the rules if the uniformed services or the government do not.

case study 5.12

Leaked report accuses 1000 prison officers of corruption

Offences include taking bribes and drug smuggling.

Service head says problem is being tackled.

There are at least 1,000 corrupt prison officers who smuggle drugs and mobile phones into prisons, and a further 500 staff are involved in "inappropriate relationships" with inmates, according to a confidential internal police and Prison Service report.

The study, leaked to the BBC, says the vast majority of the 45,000 prison staff in England and Wales are honest and operate with integrity, but a small minority are involved in corrupt practices, which include accepting bribes to facilitate transfers to less secure prisons.

(Source: Alan Travis, Home Affairs Editor, www.society.guardian.co.uk, Tuesday 1 August 2006)

activity
INDIVIDUAL WORK

1   List as many reasons as you can why a prison officer might become corrupt.

2   What measures do you think could be taken to reduce corruption in prison officers?

ODPM (2006) *A Model Code of Conduct for Local Government Employees: A Consultation Paper* – about risks of corruption; see Communities and Local Government website

www.communities.gov.uk

Disobedience

This means refusing to obey an order. It can lead to disciplinary action of varying seriousness, depending on the situation. Large-scale disobedience is called a **mutiny** – a rare event in the British uniformed services. Strike action is also a form of disobedience. Strikes are illegal in the armed forces, the police and the prison service but legal in the fire and rescue service, which has a trade union. When firefighters go on strike, cover (up to a point) is provided by the army.

Blind obedience including both positive and negative aspects

This means obeying a command without question, however unreasonable or bad the command might be. It is not the same as the kind of unconscious obedience which happens in an emergency.

It is hard to think of any positive aspects of blind obedience. In times of great danger (e.g. warfare) orders may have to be obeyed immediately and without question. However, this is not blind obedience if the soldiers, for example, obey their commanding officer whom they know to be well trained. Instant obedience is forced on them by the urgency and danger of the situation and by the need to maximise their chances of success and survival.

True blind obedience is behaviour which is suicidal, such as going 'over the top' in the First World War, or murderous, like the behaviour of the Auschwitz officials who, when they were later tried by the Americans and British at the Nuremburg trials, said that they were 'only obeying orders'. Such blind obedience is often the result of months or years of propaganda or 'brainwashing' by a government and its media. Occasionally, in individuals, it is the result of a personal obsession with another person which leads to their being obeyed slavishly – in which case it is a psychological disorder called 'automatism'.

activity
INDIVIDUAL WORK
5.9

D2

Write a leaflet for a human rights group explaining, with examples, what blind obedience is and examining in depth its good and bad effects.

Moral dilemmas and responsibility for decisions taken

A moral dilemma is a hard choice, usually between two evils. A classic case was the killing of Jean Charles de Menezes by armed Metropolitan Police officers in July 2005. They had authorisation to kill terrorist suspects on sight but had no real proof that de Menezes was a terrorist or that he was armed. Should they shoot him and kill him, or not? If he was a terrorist, he could blow them and many other people up. If he wasn't a terrorist, they would kill an innocent man. They made a hard choice and killed an innocent man. The Independent Police Complaints Commission held an inquiry and decided that the officers could not be charged with manslaughter. The officers later returned to armed duties. The Metropolitan Police Commissioner, Sir Ian Blair, took the responsibility and defended the force's shoot-to-kill policy. Had the officer who killed de Menezes acted without authorisation then he would probably have been charged with manslaughter, and Sir Ian Blair would not have taken responsibility.

These hard choices happen from time to time in the uniformed services, and the circumstances dictate who takes responsibility. Often it is not easy to get at the truth when such incidents take place, and it may be that sometimes they are covered up and the people who ought to take the responsibility never do.

Types of authority

These are to do with styles of leadership.

Link   See pages 50–54 in Unit 2 for more about styles of leadership.

Authoritarian

Authoritarian discipline is based on a strict hierarchy with a wide 'power gap' between ranks. There is little chance to question orders, appeal against decisions or discuss things in a democratic way. There is an authoritarian element in all uniformed services – perhaps there has to be – but in its extreme form the authoritarian approach has serious drawbacks. Leadership, management and discipline in the armed forces was highly authoritarian during the First World War, and this resulted in gross abuses of power such as shooting British soldiers for cowardice when they were, in fact, suffering from **post-traumatic stress disorder (PTSD)**.

Dictatorial

This is leadership and discipline by decree – 'You will do it because I say so!' – with no valid reason given. The commanding officer has absolute power and cannot be questioned. Dictatorial leadership leads to low morale and, in an army, desertion, brutality, and human rights abuses.

Consultative

A consultative system is fairly democratic and works well most of the time. Leaders obtain the opinions of others before making decisions. This makes good use of individual ability and teamwork skills, and it is good for discipline because it enables fair systems to be set up and a consensus (agreement) between people as to the right level of discipline in an organisation. At times of crisis, the consultative system may have to give way to a more authoritarian one (e.g. when a state of emergency is declared in a country due to war or a major threat).

Participative

This system is freer than a consultative one: the **participative leadership** system is more truly democratic and means that as many people as possible have a leadership role or play an active part in decision-making. This system is rather individualistic and difficult to organise, and it may lead to problems of discipline in that it can seem like a free-for-all, where anything goes. However, if it is well organised and people understand and respect the system, it can lead to good discipline and performance.

How these forms of authority are applied to the public services

Authoritarian

This is the basic, traditional, old-fashioned British system. We are still moving away from it – slowly. It is more deeply ingrained in the armed forces than in the civilian uniformed services.

Dictatorial

This is not generally used in Britain.

Consultative

This is very much used in civilian public services, including the police, the teaching service, and so on. Teamwork, bureaucracy and the wide use of meetings are aspects of a consultative system. It is somewhat authoritarian because the power to make decisions and enforce discipline still rests firmly with people in leadership roles.

Participative

This is increasingly used in some sectors, especially teaching and social work. The Integrated Personal Development System of the fire and rescue service is much more participative than the old rank system, and it may be a model for the future. Participative authority involves the sharing and delegation of decision-making and is used in military command and control, especially when a rapid response is needed.

---

activity
GROUP WORK
5.10

P5

1 Form groups of four or less. Each group member should deliver a short teaching session to the rest of the group (less than 5 minutes) – or run a short activity – on a subject relevant to the uniformed public services. Each group member should use one of four different kinds of authority.

2 Then, individually, write a brief teaching assessment of yourself and three other people who have all used different types of authority, describing the type of authority you used and the effects that it had on your 'class'.

Legislation

Armed Forces Discipline Act 2000

This Act begins the process, which ends in the Armed Forces Act 2006, of merging the discipline (legal) framework of all three armed forces into a single system. It standardises the rules about keeping military personnel in custody, the right to choose a court martial trial or not, and the appeals system for summary (fast) justice.

Armed Forces Act 2001

This modernises the system of discipline in the armed forces and makes it more equal between the three main services. It ensures that the system of military justice is fully in accordance with the Human Rights Act. It preserves the system of courts martial, and the ability of commanding officers to carry out summary justice for relatively minor offences. The system remains separate from the civilian justice system of courts which applies to the rest of us. However, there are more rights of appeal than there used to be, through a new Service Complaints Panel, and a Court Martial Appeal Court. There is an independent Joint Service Prosecuting Authority which deals with prosecutions using evidence collected by the Royal Military Police. The Armed Forces Act will be fully implemented by the end of 2008.

The Armed Forces Act 2006 completely replaces the Armed Forces Discipline Act 2000 and most of the Armed Forces Act 2001. It finalises the changes those Acts began, by merging the discipline and legal system of all three armed forces. As they were fairly similar to begin with, the changes are not enormous. Some links are made with the civilian law system, for example in the role of the Criminal Cases Review Commission, which can refer cases tried in courts martial to the (civilian) appeals courts.

> **remember**
>
> The word 'discipline' refers to criminal offences in the Armed Forces Act 2006.

See more on the Armed Forces Act 2006 in Unit 6, pages 251–252.

Police and Criminal Evidence Act 1984

This deals with the authority of the police over suspects and witnesses and lays down strict rules on what they can and cannot do. These rules are in the forms of Codes of Practice, and they are updated from time to time to take new policing needs, technology and working methods into account. The rules exist partly to ensure that the evidence that the police collect will stand up in court, and partly to ensure that suspects are not discriminated against or victimised. They make the processes of stopping, searching, arresting and questioning much more open and accountable than they were before 1984. Section IX explains the correct way to run ID parades so that the evidence gained is as valid as it can be and the police themselves cannot be accused of bending the rules.

Police Act 1997

This Act set up the National Criminal Intelligence Service and the National Crime Squad. These were authorities set up to deal with large-scale and organised crime. They have been merged in the Serious Organised Crime and Police Act (SOCPA) 2005 to form the Serious Organised Crime Agency. SOCPA strengthens the powers of the police, by modernising the Police and Criminal Evidence Act, but at the same time makes it possible to discipline police officers who are under investigation before the investigation is completed.

Fire and Rescue Services Act 2004

This sets up new fire and rescue authorities with greater powers than the old ones. Non-metropolitan county councils, district councils, metropolitan counties and the London Fire and Emergency Planning Authority are all fire and rescue authorities.

Their members consist of people appointed by the Secretary of State and people locally appointed – usually elected councillors. They have wide powers to set budgets and facilitate fire prevention, firefighting, accident and civil defence work in the area. Their responsibility for dealing with large-scale emergencies, and for helping in the event of terrorist attacks, is increased. They also have a duty to liaise with other fire authorities and other public services in order to enable a combined response to a major incident.

Subsequent amendments

Amendments are slight changes made in the law, or clarifications of it set out in Regulations, sometimes called Statutory Instruments (small precise laws). Laws such as PACE are updated nearly every year, which is why the Codes of Practice keep changing.

Search the British Army's website for a section on 'discipline and military law' For a copy of the *Queen's Regulations for the Army*, search the website for 'Queen's regulations for the army'

www.army.mod.uk

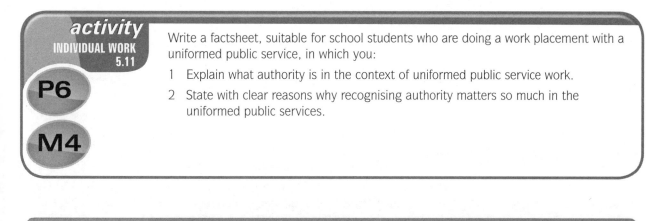

activity
INDIVIDUAL WORK
5.11

P6

M4

Write a factsheet, suitable for school students who are doing a work placement with a uniformed public service, in which you:

1   Explain what authority is in the context of uniformed public service work.

2   State with clear reasons why recognising authority matters so much in the uniformed public services.

Progress Check

1. Give the hierarchy (ranks) for three uniformed public services.
2. What are the advantages of hierarchical management structures?
3. Explain the difference between rules, regulations and laws.
4. Name six parts of the Police Code of Conduct and say why they are important.
5. Explain six reasons for wearing a uniform.
6. How do conscious obedience, unconscious obedience, blind obedience and compliance differ?
7. Outline the significance of Stanley Milgram's experiment on obedience.
8. What attitudes are unsuitable for a person working in a uniformed public service?
9. Explain six things that an assertive person does.
10. In what ways does a uniformed public service benefit from having a disciplined workforce?
11. What are the limits of the authority of any two of Britain's uniformed services?

UNIT 6

Diversity and the Public Services

This unit covers:

- 'Diversity' within a historical context
- Relevant legislation that protects the human rights of individuals
- The role of the public services and their duty to provide equality of service to all members of the community
- How national and local policies, strategies and procedures address diversity issues within a chosen public service

The development of a diverse society in Britain in the last 60 years has changed our idea of Britishness and has had major effects on the work of the public services. This unit investigates what diversity is, and how society is coming to terms with it. It explains the ideas and terms which are linked with diversity.

After looking at recent laws passed to protect minority groups and ensure better social justice, the unit examines the role of the public services in a diverse society and their responsibility to fulfil those roles in a fair and even-handed manner.

Finally you will learn about the ways in which the public services have themselves become more diverse, and how they look after the needs of different groups of employees.

grading criteria

To achieve a **Pass** grade the evidence must show that the learner is able to:	To achieve a **Merit** grade the evidence must show that, in addition to the pass criteria, the learner is able to:	To achieve a **Distinction** grade the evidence must show that, in addition to the pass and merit criteria, the learner is able to:
P1 outline the historical developments which have made the UK a diverse society Pg 232		
P2 outline the composition of your local and national community in relation to ethnicity, religion, gender and age Pg 243		

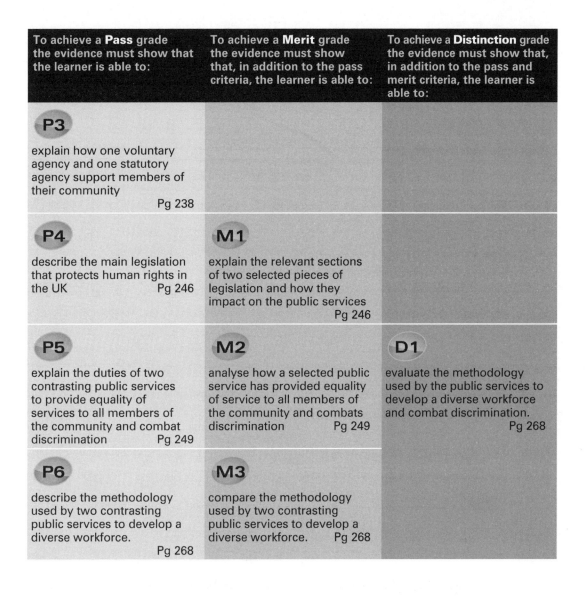

To achieve a **Pass** grade the evidence must show that the learner is able to:	To achieve a **Merit** grade the evidence must show that, in addition to the pass criteria, the learner is able to:	To achieve a **Distinction** grade the evidence must show that, in addition to the pass and merit criteria, the learner is able to:
P3 explain how one voluntary agency and one statutory agency support members of their community Pg 238		
P4 describe the main legislation that protects human rights in the UK Pg 246	**M1** explain the relevant sections of two selected pieces of legislation and how they impact on the public services Pg 246	
P5 explain the duties of two contrasting public services to provide equality of services to all members of the community and combat discrimination Pg 249	**M2** analyse how a selected public service has provided equality of service to all members of the community and combats discrimination Pg 249	**D1** evaluate the methodology used by the public services to develop a diverse workforce and combat discrimination. Pg 268
P6 describe the methodology used by two contrasting public services to develop a diverse workforce. Pg 268	**M3** compare the methodology used by two contrasting public services to develop a diverse workforce. Pg 268	

'Diversity' within a historical context

'**Diversity**' can be defined as the presence in **society** of many different kinds of people, all living and working close to each other. In the modern British context, the word refers to factors such as ethnicity, **gender**, religion, **sexual orientation**, age, disability and occupational background (job).

Although in this unit we shall be looking at diversity as a modern feature of society, beginning around 1950, Britain has in some senses always been a diverse country.

Historical developments and social attitudes

From the invasion of the Romans onwards (AD 43), waves of people have come into Britain and settled here. By the Middle Ages (1400), Britain was actively involved in overseas trade and in trying to gain territory in Europe and beyond. As a result of trade (including the slave trade) and colonisation, Britain was a wealthy country by 1800. The **Industrial Revolution** was getting under way; there were foreigners living in places such as London and Bristol; the British Empire was being developed, and there were the beginnings of modern social attitudes.

Historical perspective since 1800

Successive waves of invaders and refugees from prehistoric times gave the country an ethnic mix. **Colonialism** and the slave trade added to this. By 1800, the Industrial Revolution was in progress and, even at that date, the world was beginning to experience an early form of globalisation.

Table 6.1 Historical perspective since 1800

Immigration and date	Comments
1772	End of slave trade; by this time, around 14,000 Africans are living in England
1801	First census: total population of England and Wales is 9 million; Scotland's population is 1.6 million
1820	More Chinese arrive
1840 onwards	Many workers from Europe come to the new industrial towns in the north of England
1845–1850	Around 200,000 Irish come to Britain to escape the Potato Famine
1880–1910	100,000 Jews arrive in Britain after persecution in Russia
1890	Chinatown established in east London
1914–1918	60,000 refugees from mainland Europe stay in Britain, mainly in **internment camps**; most leave at the end of war
1916	People come from the Caribbean to work in factories – some race riots after 1918
1938	Jewish refugees arrive from Germany, Austria and Czechoslovakia
1941	60,000 more Irish come to help war effort
1948	Immigration from the Caribbean begins
1950–1952	350,000 Germans, Poles, Ukrainians, etc. come
1955	Immigration from South Asia begins – 15,000 from India and Pakistan by 1955
1955–1962	250,000 arrive from Caribbean
1971–1972	28,000 Ugandan Asians and many Kenyan Asians arrive – fleeing discrimination and persecution
1974	20,000 Greek Cypriots arrive, following Turkish invasion of north Cyprus
1983–1992	Large-scale immigration – 240,000
1990	First refugees arrive from Somalia
1998–2000	Arrivals from Kosovo, Iraq, Afghanistan and Zimbabwe
2001	Around 150,000 more people in the country every year
2002	103,000 people seek asylum in Britain
2004–2006	375,000 people arrive to work from the new 'accession' EU countries such as Poland, the Czech Republic, Slovakia, Estonia, Hungary, Latvia and Lithuania. Between 310,000 and 750,000 illegal migrants are said to be in the country in 2005 (figures from the Home Office and MigrationWatch)

In these successive arrivals from other countries, there were pressures (usually persecution and economic deprivation) pushing the people out of their own countries and other forces (the hope of a better or freer life) pulling them into Britain. These forces are sometimes called '**push and pull factors**'.

Society's attitude

Society's reaction to the large-scale **migration** into the country over the past 50 years has varied from anger and outrage to approval and optimism. Anger or outrage arises from feeling that the country is already overcrowded and that jobs are going to be lost. Approval comes from economists, business people, or people who like the idea of freedom of movement. It is said that at a time when more and more British people are retiring, yet the economy is doing well, there is a need for more workers, especially young, skilled and well-motivated people.

The main problems have been **racism** – conscious or unconscious hostility towards people of other **races**. Sometimes this hostility has taken the form of condescension ('they're primitive, naïve' etc.). Sometimes it takes the form of physical and social stereotyping (e.g. about the sexual abilities of other races, their morality or lack of it, their marriage customs, their cruelty towards women, etc.). Some of this stereotyping is about imagined lack of intelligence (black people); imagined greed or wealth (Jews). Some stereotypes seem favourable, but are stereotypes nonetheless (e.g. that all black people love music). Many stereotypes involve sport: Asians can play cricket but not football; black people can play football but they can't manage teams. A trigger of racism is fear: 'they're going to take our jobs' (a particular fear at present linked to the arrival of skilled workers from eastern Europe); 'house prices will drop like a stone'; 'they aren't clean and we might catch diseases off them', and so on. Societal attitudes like these, myths which have no basis in fact, have been hard for British people to get rid of.

Ethnic diversity is not the only kind of diversity. Various kinds of cultural diversity have increased, not only because of immigration but also – and just as importantly – from the globalisation of the media, the importing of **culture** (e.g. films and music) from America and elsewhere, and the vast increase in tourism, business travel, and so on.

Ethnicity

Ethnicity is the shared cultural background of people who originate from a particular geographical area. Race is the classification of large groups of people on the basis of genetically inherited characteristics such as skin colour and facial appearance. Ethnicity and race are often confused. Strictly speaking ethnicity has nothing to do with race; but in practice there is a link, because people who come from the same area are usually of the same race.

Fig 6.1 Reality – but also a stereotype

Culture is to do with people's behaviour and beliefs. Behaviour includes things like dress, food, language, etc. Beliefs centre on religion and shared moral ideas. The behavioural aspects of culture are called 'norms', while the belief aspects of culture are called 'values'.

Link

See page 199 in Unit 5 for information about social norms.

> **remember**
>
> We all have our roots in a particular culture, with its own norms and values.

Religion

Until the occupation by the Romans starting in AD 43 Britain was a pagan country with Druidic religions, as we can see from Stonehenge and other ancient sites. Around 200 years after Christ, Christianity was introduced by the Romans and it gradually took over. In the Middle Ages, Britain was Catholic, but in the Reformation (around 1540) the Catholic Church was replaced by the Church of England, which, to this day, remains the established ('official') church. However, since 1600 other Christian churches such as Methodism, Baptism, Congregationalism, Unitarianism, and Quakerism grew up, and as a result British Christianity became fragmented. Also, although Britain is not a Catholic country, there has always been a large Catholic population. Up to the Second World War, there were few non-Christian believers apart from the Jews who followed Judaism. However, since the Second World War other religions have become established, as a result of the influx of people from other Commonwealth countries: the main ones are Islam, Hinduism, Sikhism and Buddhism. Rastafarianism is practised by some people of African-Caribbean descent, and there are people of African origin who practise various **animist** religions. In addition, there are many people from all religious backgrounds who don't practise their religion – and there are also agnostics (who don't know if they believe in a god or not) and atheists (who believe that there is no god).

Society's attitudes to religion have changed in recent years. The outcry in parts of the Muslim world against the novel *The Satanic Verses*, by Salman Rushdie (published in 1988), dismayed many non-Muslims and sowed the seeds of so-called 'Islamophobia' in the British media and elsewhere. Political events, such as the first Gulf War in 1991 and further bombings of Iraq in 1998 by Western powers, gave Muslims the feeling that they were being unjustly attacked, as did the support of the West for Israel at the expense of the Palestinians. '**Radicalisation**' of young Muslims in Britain was therefore beginning well before 11 September 2001, and this 'Islamist' movement, wrongly identified with the Muslim religion as a whole, has led both to the London bombings of 2005 and to the general tension surrounding religious issues at the present time.

Fig 6.2 A diversity of religion

Sexual orientation

For much of British history, homosexuality has been 'the love that dare not speak its name'. Until recently, homosexuals were not allowed to enter the armed forces (or at least they had to lie about their sexual orientation to get in). Fifty years ago, they were liable to entrapment by plainclothes police officers in public toilets, and they have often suffered harassment in the workplace or 'gay-bashing' attacks in the street. Homosexual acts between consenting men, even in private, were illegal. (Sex between women was never a criminal offence.) However, in the last 40 years there have been big changes.

Table 6.2 Legislation relating to sexual orientation

1967	Sex between consenting men is legalised (but the age of consent was 21, not 16 as for heterosexual sex)
1988	Section 28 of the Local Government Act bans the 'promotion of homosexuality' by local authorities
1994	Age of consent for gay male sex is lowered to 18
1999	European Court of Human Rights declares that gays should not be banned from joining the armed forces
2000	Government lifts ban on lesbians and gay men in armed forces
2001	Age of consent for gay male sex is lowered to 16
2002	Equal rights are given to same-sex couples applying for adoption
2003	Repeal of Section 28.
	Employment Equality (Sexual Orientation) Regulations become law: it is now illegal to discriminate against lesbians, gay men and bisexuals in the workplace
	Criminal Justice Act 2003 gives tougher sentences to perpetrators of crimes motivated by the victim's sexual orientation
2004	Sexual Offences Act abolishes crimes of buggery and gross indecency (which had targeted male homosexuals)
	Civil Partnership Act gives same-sex couples the same rights as married heterosexual couples
2006	Equality Act makes discrimination against gays and lesbians in 'the provision of goods and services' illegal

Disability

Disabled people have been able to benefit from the tide in public opinion moving against discrimination of almost all kinds. Disabled people now have a higher media profile, take part in the Olympic Games and are beginning to be helped and protected by sympathetic laws.

Table 6.3 Legislation relating to disability

1995	Disability Discrimination Act (DDA)
2000	The European Framework Directive
2003	DDA 1995 (Amendment) Regulations 2003
2005	Disability Discrimination Act (replaces and upgrades the 1995 Act)
2006	Public Sector Disability Equality Duty

TUC – *Advice for Unions on the 2006 Public Sector Disability Equality Duty*
www.tuc.org.uk

Definitions of disability

Impairment of ...

■ mobility

■ manual dexterity

■ physical coordination

■ continence

■ ability to lift, carry or otherwise move everyday objects

■ speech, hearing or eyesight

■ memory or ability to concentrate, learn or understand

■ perception of the risk of physical danger.

(Source: www.tuc.org.uk)

activity
GROUP WORK

Discuss the problems that each of the above could cause for a person carrying out an average day's work or study with you.

Age

Age is a complex issue, both for young people who are on the brink of adulthood and for older people who are either not far off retirement or find themselves considered too old to do certain jobs. Both the young and the old sometimes feel themselves to be discriminated against on age grounds; this form of discrimination is sometimes called '**ageism**'. As young people are well aware, there are plenty of regulations about the ages at which certain things cannot be done.

See page 246 for regulations relating to age.

The rights of older people are now covered by the Employment Equality (Age) Regulations 2006. The main **provisions** are:

■ Age discrimination is unlawful unless objectively justified.

■ It is illegal to set conditions of employment etc. which discriminate against a particular age group.

■ Any harassment or victimisation on age-related grounds is outlawed.

■ Upper age limits on unfair dismissal and **redundancy** are removed.

■ There will be a standard retirement age of 65.

Acas – *Age and the Workplace: Putting the Employment Equality (Age) Regulations 2006 into Practice*

www.acas.org.uk

Gender

'Gender' is the word used to describe issues relating to the politics of sex, or to the way we talk about male and female roles in society. **Women's rights**, for instance, are a gender issue, but discrimination against women – or men – is called 'sex discrimination'.

In British society, as in nearly all others, women have traditionally been discriminated against in anything relating to power and money, whether inside or outside the home. Following women's rights movements throughout the twentieth century, both in Europe and America, social attitudes have tended to change and laws have been brought in to protect women and give them a higher level of social and economic justice. The main British laws of this kind are shown in Table 6.4.

Table 6.4 Legislation relating to gender

1970	Equal Pay Act: women are to get the same pay as men for the same work
1975	Sex Discrimination Act: it is unlawful to discriminate against women
1989	Employment Act: this provides extra protection for women at work
1996	Employment Rights Act: this gives rights to **maternity and parental leave**
1999	Sex Discrimination (Gender Reassignment) Regulations (for people who have changed sex)
2002	Employment Act: flexible working hours for parents of young children
2005	The Employment Equality (Sex Discrimination) Regulations

These laws have not eliminated all discrimination against women, but they have made a difference, strengthened women's legal position, and reduced the very obvious discrimination that existed in the past.

The Chartered Institute for Personnel and Development – look up 'sex discrimination'
www.cipd.co.uk
Department for Business, Enterprise and Regulatory Reform – look up 'sex discrimination'
www.berr.gov.uk
Office of Public Sector Information – all the laws are on this site; some are under 'Acts' and some are under 'Statutory Instruments'
www.opsi.gov.uk

Media representation

Diversity and the media representation of it are complex issues. The situation is a chicken-and-egg one, in that it is hard to know whether the media have taken the lead in encouraging diversity and society has followed, or whether society has taken the lead and the media have followed. In Britain the issues have been:

- Are minority views, culture and interests adequately covered on TV, radio, in music, film, literature, art and advertising?

- Are women and people from ethnic and other minorities physically shown in the media (or are the media full of white male faces talking 'English' English)?

- Do the media perpetuate stereotypes (e.g. black people are only good at sport and music; all gays have limp wrists) or do they give a balanced, truthful view of people?

- Do the media contain propaganda, hidden racist messages, etc. that attack minorities and their culture, or encourage hatred?

- Should the media have real freedom of speech and say whatever they like on any subject (e.g. religion) or should they be regulated in 'sensitive areas' and made **'politically correct'**?

The British media are controlled by:

- the Public Order Act 1986 ss 17–29 (racial hatred), which prohibits threatening, abusive or insulting material if it is intended to (or does) stir up racial hatred

- the Obscene Publications Act 1959, which has been used to ban gay literature, art, photographs, films, etc.

The media are also controlled, up to a point, by a number of **voluntary codes**.

Language

Abusive language relating to black people, gays, women and disabled people is generally not used in the media. It is worth noting that many words previously used are now considered to be insulting and have been replaced by other words. Some people dislike this trend, considering it to be 'political correctness gone mad', but the view of most people, and of the public services, is that such words and expressions are racist or 'xenophobic' (against strangers), or sexist or 'misogynistic' (anti-women), or simply unacceptable because of the hurt and hassle they cause, and the bad reputation they can bring.

The current view of politicians and of most of society is that people who come to live in Britain from other countries should be able to speak English to a usable standard. The ability to speak a certain amount of English is now a citizenship requirement.

See page 93 in Unit 3 for information about requirements for becoming a UK citizen.

Art and literature

British art and literature of the past tended to ignore people from non-British backgrounds; Shakespeare (1564–1616) was an exception and so was Kipling (1865–1936). Modern arts and literature are reflecting an increased awareness of diversity, for example the art of Tracey Emin and novels such as *White Teeth* by Zadie Smith and *Brick Lane* by Monica Ali. Popular music, such as that of Bob Marley, has been more important than art or literature in helping people accept diversity.

---

activity
GROUP WORK
6.1

P1

Produce a wallchart suitable for a community centre showing the history of diversity in Britain.

Concepts

Integration

Integration refers to the idea that people who are different from the majority should 'fit in'. It normally relates to people who come to live in Britain from overseas. People who believe in integration think that immigrants should learn to speak English and live as British people do. They need not drop their religion and culture, but they should mix with British people and think of themselves as British.

Tolerance

This relates to the idea of 'live and let live' or 'let's agree to differ'. A tolerant person is relaxed about other people's differences from themselves.

Multiculturalism

Those who believe in a **multicultural** society believe that it is a good thing if people from different cultures (ethnic groups, religious beliefs, lifestyles, etc.) live together in towns or communities.

The rights and responsibilities of individuals in society

Rights are anything that a person is entitled to by law or custom, for example the right to work. Responsibilities are duties: anything that a person should do for the benefit of other

Groups of people such as companies and public services also have rights and responsibilities.

people, for example obey the law. The individual – that is, every person – has rights and responsibilities. 'Society' means within the **community**, or within Britain as a whole.

Equal opportunities

Equal opportunities legislation is a collection of laws designed to ensure that all groups which have been discriminated against in the past are treated fairly and equally at work.

Positive action to find solutions for greater social inclusion and representation without lowering standards in favour of race or gender or disability

Positive action is any action designed to help people from minorities, and women, have the same opportunities and life chances that white males enjoy in British society. The idea is based on the fact that there is still an element of **prejudice** against minorities which risks making it less easy for, say, a Muslim of Bangladeshi background to get on in a uniformed public service than a white male with the same abilities etc. Positive action by the public services is intended to help recruit people from minority groups so that there is, eventually, the same proportion of those minorities in, say, the police, as there is in society as a whole. It is against the law to discriminate by accepting applicants simply because they are black, female or gay. It is equally against the law to lower standards for ethnic minority candidates, women, or disabled applicants. Positive action tries to ensure that these groups get the encouragement and training they need to be able to apply on a fair footing in the first place.

Corporate social responsibility

This is the duty of uniformed public services to work towards the elimination of discrimination in their own organisations and in the way they treat the public.

Diversity

Definition of diversity

Diversity means people from different backgrounds living and working together, on equal terms, in the same community.

As used by the public services

In the public services, diversity is often linked with equal opportunities.

As used by local communities

A local community refers to the people living in an area such as a housing estate, part of a town, a suburb, a village or a group of villages. It can be defined either by the people living in it, by local government, or by central government. Although the community may be (and often is) diverse, it has a geographical unity and some degree of social unity (i.e. people mix with each other at work, school or recreationally).

A local community may regard itself as diverse, especially if members of that community see people of different ethnic backgrounds living in their own streets, or attending their local schools. For most people, the word 'diverse' suggests ethnic or racial differences rather than differences in occupation, education or social attitudes – even though all of these are aspects of diversity. Whether the community welcomes diversity depends on economic and social factors: if jobs, house prices or culture seem threatened, ethnic tension may result.

Composition of the local and national community within the borough/local authority area

This refers to the mix of people in the local community, as revealed in census figures.

Ethnicity, religion, gender and age

The mixture can be of ethnic groups, religious belief, gender, ages, or any other way of classifying people for which statistics have been collected.

case study 6.2

Equal opportunities

Equal Opportunities legislation is aimed at protecting minority groups.

Equal Opportunities and Diversity policy goes beyond the application of that legislation, and extends the right of fair treatment to everyone, including the elimination of unlawful discrimination, harassment and bullying.

It recognises that everyone is unique, respects them for that, and offers them the opportunity to develop their potential. Most importantly it stresses the need for everyone to be able to function as part of a team and makes teamwork and cohesion a priority. It places a responsibility not only on leaders but also on the individual to take action when they are treated unfairly.

(Source: *Soldier Management: A Guide for Commanders.* © Ministry of Defence 2004)

The MPA [Metropolitan Police Authority] is required, under Section 404 of the Greater London Authority Act 1999, to promote equality of opportunity for all persons irrespective of their race, sex, disability, age, sexual orientation or religion and to eliminate unlawful discrimination. The Authority will not seek merely to follow the law but to exceed it. It will operate to a "Gold Standard", applying the highest standard of the law to all the equality strands (race, gender, disability, sexual orientation, religion or belief and age). This is best illustrated in the application of the principles of the Race Relations (Amendment) Act 2000 to eliminate discrimination, promote equality of opportunity and promote good relations between persons of different groups in relation to all equality strands. This will benefit all staff and all Londoners.

(Source: www.mpa.gov.uk)

activity
INDIVIDUAL WORK

Comment on these two 'definitions' (or descriptions) of diversity as seen by the army and the Metropolitan Police Authority.

1 What differences are there between them?

2 Which do you prefer – and why?

Statistics of this kind are collected in each national census – a detailed count of people living in Britain which is done every 10 years. It is compulsory to fill in the census form with information about the people in each house or household. The system relies on people's honesty: they are asked and have to state their own ethnic group, religion, etc. The personal information on the form is said to be completely confidential. The last census was carried out in 2001 and the next will be in 2011.

Census statistics are available on the National Statistics website. Not only do you get statistics for each area – you can also see comparative figures and/or percentages which show you what the area is like compared with bigger areas, and with the whole country.

National Statistics – see website for all the information you want and more, about the people living in your local area

www.statistics.gov.uk

case study 6.3

Ethnicity and district

Table 6.5 Ethnicity and district

		Dewsbury South	Kirklees (Metropolitan District)	Yorkshire and the Humber	England
Ethnic Group – Percentages; White; British (Persons)	%	64.06	83.73	91.67	86.99
Ethnic Group – Percentages; Asian or Asian British (Persons)	%	33.73	11.35	4.48	4.58

(Source: www.statistics.gov.uk)

activity
INDIVIDUAL WORK

What does this table tell you about the white British and the Asian or Asian British populations of South Dewsbury and of Yorkshire and the Humber as compared with the population in England as a whole?

Support groups

A feature of Britain's diverse society is the huge number of support groups which exist to service the social, economic, religious, aesthetic (artistic), cultural, physical, educational, security, and recreational, sporting, caring and medical needs of different groups of people.

Local provision

> **remember**
> If you have difficulty finding this kind of information, ask at your college or local library.

Most support groups are locally based although they may be local branches of a national organisation. If you look in the brochures or website of any local government area you will find long lists of voluntary and other organisations which cater for the diverse needs of a diverse society.

Voluntary and statutory agencies

A voluntary agency is an organisation run by private individuals on a charitable basis. It gets its money from appeals or membership fees, and it is likely that many of the people who work for the agency are not paid. Workers in such groups are called volunteers because they work of their own free will (they think the work is worth doing and enjoyable for its own sake).

A statutory agency is one which has been set up by law. All the main public services and all agencies set up by the government are of this type. They are wholly or partly paid for by the taxpayer, and most of the people who work for them are paid.

> **remember**
> Local authorities help to fund some voluntary organisations, and many local organisations work in partnerships.

The dividing line between voluntary and statutory is not always clear cut (except, of course, to the officials of the agency). The users of the agency's services may neither know nor care about its legal basis. In addition, voluntary and statutory agencies often work together in partnership. Neighbourhood Watch schemes, for example, are voluntary and must be started by volunteers, but they get plenty of help and support from the police which is, of course, a statutory organisation.

Link

See pages 119–120 in Unit 3, for information about volunteer working in public services and in the community, and page 236 below for more on statutory organisations.

Family centres, community centres, charities and religious support groups

There is a bewildering variety of support groups.

Family centres

These are places where mothers and children can go to relax, play and meet.

Community centres

Community centres are buildings where there are recreation facilities, or where films can be shown, meetings held, and night classes and cultural groups run, and so on.

Charities

These are non-profit organisations mainly staffed by volunteers which try to satisfy a social, medical or humanitarian need which is not met by the government. Many national charities such as Oxfam or Save the Children have local branches or shops; others help local people: for example, Citizens Advice is an important source of free legal advice for many people.

Charities with an annual turnover of more than £1000 must be registered with a statutory agency: the Charity Commission. They get tax relief, but are also monitored. This is mainly to avoid 'scams'. You will find lists of registered local charities on the Charity Commission website.

Religious support groups

These are often based in places of worship and are linked to the main religion practised there. Some have a social function; others are used for discussion and educational purposes; others are for prayer, meditation and worship, and others (e.g. the Salvation Army) do good works for local people.

Statutory organisations

These are set up by central or local government. They can be:

- central government organisations which have local branches (e.g. Neighbourhood Renewal, a section of the Department of Communities and Local Government)

- partnerships where the local authority works with other public and private bodies to carry out a major social duty (e.g. Crime and Disorder Reduction Partnerships)

- set up by the council but receive money from departments in central government (e.g. **Pathfinder** Schemes).

---

case study 6.4   Examples of local charities

502900 Healey Community Association 10 Jan 1974

529338 Heavy Woollen District Manufacturer's Scholarship Scheme 01 Apr 1971

524710 Heavy Woollen District Scout Council 10 Dec 1963

529241 Hirst Cup Trust 14 Dec 1965

502739 Howden Clough Community Association 20 Nov 1973

1054131 Islamic Cultural and Welfare Association 29 Mar 1996

1110670 Learn Org UK Limited 01 Aug 2005

(Source: www.charity-commission.gov.uk)

---

activity
GROUP WORK

1 From the information available, what roles do you think the above charities carry out?

2 Choose any 30 charities from your own local area and group them into types, according to the work that they do.

Community support actions by statutory and non-statutory partners in a Crime and Disorder Reduction Partnership (CDRP)

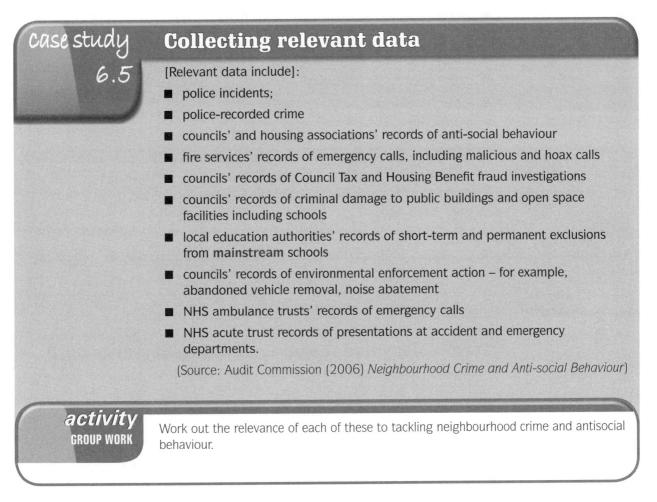

case study 6.5

Collecting relevant data

[Relevant data include]:

- police incidents;
- police-recorded crime
- councils' and housing associations' records of anti-social behaviour
- fire services' records of emergency calls, including malicious and hoax calls
- councils' records of Council Tax and Housing Benefit fraud investigations
- councils' records of criminal damage to public buildings and open space facilities including schools
- local education authorities' records of short-term and permanent exclusions from **mainstream** schools
- councils' records of environmental enforcement action – for example, abandoned vehicle removal, noise abatement
- NHS ambulance trusts' records of emergency calls
- NHS acute trust records of presentations at accident and emergency departments.

(Source: Audit Commission (2006) *Neighbourhood Crime and Anti-social Behaviour*)

activity
GROUP WORK

Work out the relevance of each of these to tackling neighbourhood crime and antisocial behaviour.

A CDRP's responsibilities are to:

- analyse anti-social behaviour problems in their neighbourhoods
- collect the views of **frontline** workers
- respond rapidly to local concerns
- record anti-social behaviour using the National Standard for Incident Recording
- draw up detailed neighbourhood profiles of information on victims, offenders and crime hotspots and workable solutions to connect concerns with incidents
- share personal data on offenders
- communicate with local people
- let them know when action has been taken and why
- evaluate performance
- develop targets.

Within the CDRP, council responsibilities are to:

- gather information, data and community **intelligence** at the neighbourhood level
- empower CDRP to take rapid and effective action to deal with local issues
- develop communication between the council and local people

There is probably a CDRP in your local area. Try to talk to someone who works in it.

- inform residents of action taken
- work with builders and town planners
- encourage residents' associations and ward councillors.

The responsibilities of the police are to:

- support neighbourhood working by deploying people in targeted areas
- collect data relating to antisocial behaviour
- work with other local agencies
- provide intelligence and rapid responses to antisocial behaviour.

activity

GROUP WORK 6.2

P3

Give a presentation to a community forum explaining how one voluntary agency and one statutory agency support members of their community.

Link

See page 250 below for more on CDRPs.

Terminology and meaning of different words used

Terminology means specialised words – often linked with work or a particular field of study. Diversity has its own terminology, and this should be learned and understood by people working in the public services, as the wrong use of some words can give rise to misunderstanding or offence.

Below are explanations of some of the terminology used in discussing diversity and discrimination.

Racism

Racism has two main meanings: one is concerned with what people think (a), and the other is concerned with what people say or do (b).

(a) Racism is the belief that any race or ethnic group is biologically, intellectually, emotionally, morally or spiritually superior to other races or ethnic groups.

(b) Racism is discrimination against a race, ethnic group or its culture.

Because (a) is a belief, it is a private matter which goes on in someone's head, but (b) is not a private matter because it shows itself in words or actions which can harm other people and which, in Britain, are against the law. In this book, and in the public services, racism usually has meaning (b) – but see '**institutionalised racism**' below.

A 'race' is a group of people who have visible genetic features (e.g. skin colour, hair type) which distinguish them from other races. Because the word itself has racist overtones, it is no longer used in public service work.

Racist

A racist (noun) is a person who is hostile to, or discriminates against, people of other races or ethnic groups.

A racist (adjective) action is an action which discriminates against one or more races or ethnic groups.

A racist law is one which discriminates against any race or ethnic group.

Institutionalised racism

This term became famous following the Macpherson Report (1999) into the murder of the teenager Stephen Lawrence in 1993. Lord Macpherson of Cluny, who led the inquiry, accused the Metropolitan Police of 'institutionalised racism' because he found that the officers concerned had failed to investigate the murder properly because the victim was black.

The idea is that people who work in an institution (any large organisation of people such as a police force, a college or a government department) share certain unthinking beliefs, and that people working in a place which is institutionally racist can be racist without knowing it. Lord Macpherson recommended that the police and other organisations should examine all aspects of their activities to see if they contained some racial bias of which they were not aware. He also recommended that workers in such places should be trained in race and **diversity awareness**. His report is one of the reasons why there is now a diversity unit in your course and why diversity plays such a large part in the training of the police and other public services.

Multiculturalism

See page 232 above for more information on this.

Ethnocentricity

Fashions change with words related to diversity. 'Multiculturalism' is a word that is probably going out of fashion, as it means different things to different people.

This is related to racism. It means seeing everything from the viewpoint of your own traditions and culture, and regarding other traditions and culture as being worse than your own.

The word is not often used, and it does not have the same force as 'racism'. There is no law or regulation which forbids ethnocentricity. The British media tend to be ethnocentric (not surprisingly, since many people like to read or hear about their own countries and communities). The coverage of the wars in Iraq and Afghanistan is ethnocentric because it concentrates on the activities of the British military. Newspapers such as the *Daily Mail* are more ethnocentric than, say, *The Guardian*. TV stations such as OBI and BEN and newspapers such as *The Voice* cater for ethnic minority groups in Britain, but these are not usually described as ethnocentric.

The Voice

www.voice-online.co.uk

Sexism

Although the word looks as though it could be used for either sex, in practice it refers entirely to the beliefs or behaviour of men who think of, or treat, women as inferior. Rather like racism, sexism can be either conscious or unconscious, and it can be institutionalised (as it used to be in the old fire service before its name and identity were updated after 2004).

Sexism is deeply rooted and is found in almost all world societies. Throughout history it appears that men and women have had different roles in the family and in society. This is presumably based on the biological differences which have always been there and which affect us from earliest childhood. Parenting, as many psychologists have shown, has an enormous effect on our behaviour and thinking, and it is thought that sexual identities are learned from an early age and reinforced by stereotyped parenting behaviour. Little girls still play with Barbie dolls and little boys still play with toy tractors. In Western society, the famous people of the past are almost all men. In modern employment, women are still far more likely to be nurses and teachers, while men become engineers and soldiers. Whereas over 90% of British men drive, the figure is about 57% for women.

Sexism can express itself in abusive behaviour – including physical attacks, harassment, unwanted sexual advances and 'humour' which is degrading to women.

Gender pay gap

Also, over 30 years after the Equal Pay Act, the average earnings of women working full time are still significantly less than men's.

---

case study 6.6

Gender pay gap

The gender pay gap of 12.6% expresses the difference between men's and women's median full-time hourly earnings.

Although this is perhaps due to the different jobs that men and women occupy within the public services, it does mean that women working full time are currently paid, on average, 87.4% of men's hourly pay. Since 1975, when the Equal Pay Act came into effect, the full-time pay gap has closed considerably – from 20.7% in 1997 to 17.2% in 2006, using the mean. Using the median, the full-time gender pay gap has closed from 17.4% in 1997 to 12.6% in 2006. However, the public services is one area where females get the same pay as their male colleagues in the same job role.

(Source: www.womenandequalityunit.gov.uk)

activity
INDIVIDUAL WORK

1 What is the difference between mean and median?
2 Do you think more should be done to get true equality – and, if so, what?

Reasons for the pay gap are:

- differences in education, qualifications and work experience
- breaks from work due to caring for children and others
- a disproportionate amount of low-paid work (especially low-paid part-time work) is done by women
- travel patterns – women work nearer to home
- women's work is concentrated in low-paid occupations – '60% of working women work in just 10 occupations' (www.womenandequalityunit.gov.uk)
- women are less likely to be promoted: there are fewer in the higher jobs.

Heterosexist

This word is sometimes used to describe actions, words, or thinking which promote the idea – or contain the assumption – that heterosexual love (i.e. between a man and a woman) is the 'best', 'right' or 'most acceptable' form of love. British society and culture, like that of – probably – every other nation is mainly heterosexist. The mass media and the churches are largely heterosexist, as their reaction to gay marriage shows. Heterosexism is not a crime, but it is (intentionally or not) an attack on diversity.

Homophobia

This word, which has appeared in the last 20 years or so, has been put together from Greek words which mean 'fear of the same [sex]', but its actual meaning is hostility and violence towards homosexuals and same-sex relationships. Homophobia therefore means:

- any violence, harassment or threats towards homosexuals
- in a wider sense, society's hostility towards and fear of lesbians and gay men.

Homophobic crime is violence towards or harassment of homosexuals. Homophobia in the wider sense is a common social attitude in many cultures. In 85 countries out of 192 homosexuality is still illegal, sometimes punishable by death. In Western countries, with laws allowing homosexuality and banning discrimination, homophobia is slowly declining.

Gay Police Association
www.gay.police.uk
The Professional Trades Union for Prison, Correctional and Secure Psychiatric Workers (POA)
www.poauk.org.uk
HM Prison Service
www.hmprisonservice.gov.uk

Equal opportunity

This is more often seen in the plural form: 'equal opportunities'. It refers to all the laws, regulations and rules of the workplace which prevent discrimination on the grounds of:

- sex
- race
- disability
- colour
- nationality
- ethnic or national origin
- religion or belief
- sexual orientation
- age.

 See page 242 below for an explanation of direct and **indirect discrimination**.

Equality

This means 'having the same as other people', and it is used when talking about rights, earnings, standard of living, and opportunities. Equality is fair treatment, the absence of discrimination and social justice.

The old communist idea of absolute equality – trying to make everybody the same in wealth, power, benefits, etc. – is, these days, generally considered to be an impossible dream.

Prejudice

This is defined as 'irrational suspicion or hatred of a particular group, race or religion'. It shows itself in sexism, racism or homophobia and in any unreasoning bias against minority groups. It is linked to the formation of negative stereotypes, and sweeping statements of the 'all Belgians are thick' type. It comes from the Latin for 'before the judgment' (i.e. deciding that a person is guilty before the trial has even taken place).

Harassment

Harassment is defined as:

'... any behaviour, which an individual finds unacceptable, unwelcome or unreasonable. It may be non-verbal or verbal and may be motivated by gender, race, religious beliefs, disability or physical appearance.'

(Source: www.bfpo.mod.uk)

It can take the form of persecution or bullying of individuals or small groups of people, physical or verbal abuse, unfair treatment at work, threats, or attacks on the victim's friends and family. Whether this behaviour is intentional or not, it is now illegal.

The British Forces Post Office (BFPO) *Equality and Diversity Action Plan 2004/2005*

www.bfpo.mod.uk

Victimisation

This is the same as harassment, but is used more in the context of attacks on larger groups or classes of people (e.g. in ethnic cleansing, or any other large-scale harassment or discrimination).

Disability

See the case study on page 230, where this is defined.

Direct and indirect

These words are used to describe two different kinds of unlawful discrimination.

Direct discrimination is discrimination which clearly and explicitly targets a particular group of people. In the 1950s, boarding houses sometimes had notices saying 'No Blacks' in the window. This was direct discrimination. It would still be direct discrimination if a café owner didn't employ a black waiter for the reason that, 'it would upset my customers'. If a man was refused a nursing job simply because he was a man, that too would be direct discrimination.

Indirect discrimination is discrimination where conditions are set which unfairly target a particular group of people. If a girls' school said, 'All pupils must wear skirts' that would be indirect discrimination, since it would in effect target Muslim girls (probably from Asian backgrounds). If an employer only gave training to full-time workers, this would discriminate against women because women are more likely to be part-time workers.

In specific circumstances, **lawful discrimination** is allowed.

Fig 6.3 A community is the people who live in it

Write and design a leaflet outlining the composition of your local and national community in relation to ethnicity, religion, gender and age. Your leaflet should be suitable for trainee community support officers.

Relevant legislation that protects the human rights of individuals

Legislation

This section looks at current UK legislation. Legislation is laws, and 'current' means that the laws are in force now.

The Sex Discrimination Act 1975 (Amendment) Regulations 2003

> **remember**
> Sex discrimination still exists. There are many college courses – and careers – which attract mainly male or mainly female students.

The Sex Discrimination Act 1975 outlaws sex discrimination in employment, education, advertising or when providing housing, goods, services or facilities. It applies to both direct and indirect discrimination. The Act outlaws discrimination against married people, in employment or advertisements for jobs. It prohibits employment discrimination on the grounds of pregnancy, maternity or gender reassignment, and it bans harassment in employment, vocational training and further education.

The 2003 Regulations which have been added to the Act mainly affect the police. If a police officer behaves in a sexist manner, the Chief Constable is ultimately responsible. The Regulations also ban discrimination resulting from the ending of a relationship.

Human right protected: prohibition of discrimination

Equal Pay Act 1970

> **remember**
> There are still major differences between the average earnings of men and women in the UK.

This Act makes it illegal to pay a woman less than a man for doing the same job. It also says that men and women must have the same terms and conditions, with regard to, for example, piecework (where pay is according to the amount of work done, rather than hourly), output and bonus payments, holidays and sick leave.

Since 1970 the European Union has added other benefits to this Act, so women are now equal in redundancy payments, travel concessions, employers' pension contributions and occupational pension benefits as well.

Human right protected: prohibition of discrimination

Human Rights Act 1998

This Act puts the UK in line with the rest of Europe where human rights are concerned.

See pages 109–110 in Unit 3 for more about the Human Rights Act.

Race Relations (Amendment) Act 2000

This Act lays down race relations duties for what it calls 'public authorities'.

Public authorities include:

- government departments
- national assemblies of Scotland and Wales
- armed forces
- NHS

case study 6.7 — The Human Rights Act 1998

The Human Rights Act 1998 gives legal effect in the UK to certain fundamental rights and freedoms contained in the European Convention on Human Rights (ECHR). There are 16 basic rights taken from the European Convention on Human Rights. These rights not only affect matters of life and death like freedom from torture and killing but also affect your rights in everyday life: what you can say and do, your beliefs, your right to a fair trial and many other similar basic entitlements. The rights include:

- right to life
- prohibition of torture
- prohibition of slavery and forced labour
- right to liberty and security
- right to a fair trial
- no punishment without law
- right to respect for private and family life
- freedom of thought, conscience and religion
- freedom of expression
- **freedom of assembly and association**
- right to marry
- prohibition of discrimination
- protection of property
- right to education
- right to free elections
- abolition of the death penalty.

(Source: www.direct.gov.uk)

activity
GROUP WORK

1 Discuss cases where one or more of these rights has been infringed in your own experience. What did you do about the infringement – and would this law have helped you?

2 Some people feel that this law should be repealed (got rid of). Find out what their reasons are and say whether you agree.

- local government
- fire and rescue authorities etc,
- schools, colleges and universities
- police and policing agencies such as the Serious Organised Crime Agency (SOCA).

The Act does not cover situations to do with immigration and asylum. The House of Commons, the House of Lords, the Security Services, the Intelligence Services and the Government Communications Headquarters (GCHQ) are also exempt.

Public authorities have a duty under the Act to:

- eliminate unlawful racial discrimination
- promote equality of opportunity and good relations between persons of different racial groups.

This adds to the duty of simply not practising discrimination, as laid down in the Race Relations Act 1976.

Human right protected: prohibition of discrimination

Public Order (Amendment) Act 1996

This Act changes one word of the Public Order Act 1986: 'Section 5(4)(a) of the Public Order Act 1986 shall be amended by leaving out the word "the" and inserting the word "a"'. The Public Order Act 1986 was drawn up:

'to abolish the common law offences of riot, rout, unlawful assembly and affray and certain statutory offences relating to public order; to create new offences relating to public order; to control public processions and assemblies; to control the stirring up of racial hatred; to provide for the exclusion of certain offenders from sporting events; to create a new offence relating to the contamination of or interference with goods; to confer power to direct certain trespassers to leave land'. It made it an offence to cause 'harassment, alarm and distress.'

Protects: right to respect for private and family life

Attacks: freedom of assembly and association by controlling assemblies and mass trespass

The preamble to the Public Order Act 1986

See www.webtribe.net

Disability Discrimination Act 2005

This extends the Disability Discrimination Act 1995.

The 2006 Act states that all local and public authorities (e.g. the police) must not discriminate against or harass disabled people and must make adjustments to accommodate their needs.

Public authorities must:

■ eliminate discrimination that is unlawful under this Act

■ eliminate harassment of disabled persons that is related to their disabilities

■ promote equality of opportunity between disabled persons and other persons

■ take account of disabled persons' disabilities, even where that involves treating disabled persons more favourably than other persons

■ promote positive attitudes towards disabled persons

■ encourage participation by disabled persons in public life.

Transport providers must make transport accessible. Clubs with more than 25 people must make arrangements for disabled people. So must qualifications bodies such as examining boards (e.g. BTEC).

The **Disability Rights Commission** will set up conciliation services if there is a dispute. The Act also sets up a system of helping disabled people to obtain their rights.

Human right protected: prohibition of discrimination

Freedom of Information Act 2000

The Act gives people a right to obtain information held by a wide range of public authorities including local government, the National Health Service, schools, colleges, the police and other public bodies and offices. People can apply to a commissioner for access to documents, or copies of documents, as well as for the information itself. If information is refused, a reason must be given.

Some information is not covered by the Act. This includes information which can be obtained by means other than applying through the commissioner, information which it is later intended to publish, information linked to security, defence, the national interest, criminal proceedings, legal and government matters, health and safety issues, some environmental information, and personal information covered by the Data Protection Act 1998.

The right to officially held information is not included explicitly in the European Convention of Human Rights.

Human right protected: probably 'freedom of thought, conscience and religion'

Employment Equality (Age) Regulations 2006

These regulations apply to all employers, training providers, trade unions, professional organisations, etc. They cover recruitment, terms and conditions, promotions, transfers, dismissals and training.

The regulations make it unlawful on the grounds of age to:

- discriminate directly or indirectly against anyone
- subject someone to harassment
- victimise someone who is going to complain of age discrimination, or who is going to support a **complainant**.

Employers must not allow their employees to discriminate on age grounds.

The regulations set a national retirement age of 65, making compulsory retirement below 65 unlawful unless objectively justified. However, there are exceptions:

- An older person can be laid off if there is a clear economic or health and safety reason (not just saving money).
- Where there is a genuine occupational requirement (e.g. the need for a young or old actor to play a particular part), discrimination is still lawful.

Human right protected: prohibition of discrimination

Protection from Harassment Act 1997

This law states: 'A person must not pursue a **course of conduct** (a) which amounts to harassment of another, and (b) which he knows or ought to know amounts to harassment of the other.'

It is directed at racial harassment, sexual harassment and **sectarian** or religious harassment. The 'course of conduct' includes speech, and the offence carries a maximum prison sentence of six months.

Human right protected: respect for private and family life

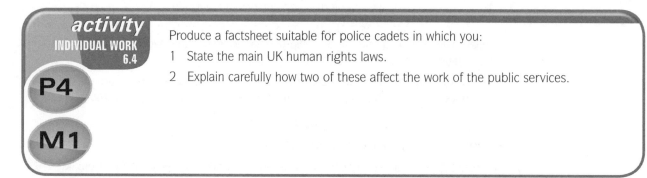

activity

INDIVIDUAL WORK 6.4

P4

M1

Produce a factsheet suitable for police cadets in which you:

1 State the main UK human rights laws.

2 Explain carefully how two of these affect the work of the public services.

EU Legislation – EEC directive on equal treatment

The first EU Equal Treatment Directives were Council Directives 76/205/EEC and 76/207/EEC (1976). These have now been updated by the Council Directive 2000/78/EC of 27 November 2000 establishing a general framework for equal treatment in employment and occupation. The basic idea is that all anti-discrimination employment law comes under one law, instead of being scattered about in a number of different Acts which have inconsistencies in them, in that they offer more protection for some minorities than for others. Directive 2000/78/EC states that:

'Any direct or indirect discrimination based on religion or belief, disability, age or sexual orientation as regards the areas covered by this Directive should be prohibited throughout the Community.'

The areas covered by the Directive are:

'... both the public and private sectors, including public bodies, in relation to: (a) conditions for access to employment, to self-employment or to occupation, including selection **criteria** and recruitment conditions, whatever the branch of activity and at all levels of the professional hierarchy, including promotion; (b) access to all types and to all levels of vocational guidance, vocational training, advanced vocational training and retraining, including practical work experience; (c) employment and working conditions, including dismissals and pay; (d) membership of, and involvement in, an organisation of workers or employers, or any organisation whose members carry on a particular profession, including the benefits provided for by such organisations.'

(Source: www.ec.europa.eu)

The points in this Directive are basically covered by UK law, but it may suggest that UK laws will eventually be amalgamated into a single, big anti-discrimination law.

Human right protected: prohibition of discrimination

The Chartered Institute for Personnel and Development – a useful website containing good stuff on discrimination law

www.cipd.co.uk

Business Link – an excellent website for regulations on discrimination at work

www.businesslink.gov.uk

Department for Business, Enterprise and Regulatory Reform

www.berr.gov.uk

Women and Equality Unit

www.womenandequalityunit.gov.uk

Equality Challenge Unit

www.ecu.ac.uk

remember

Many British laws are brought in as a result of laws being passed in the EU.

The role of the public services and their duty to provide equality of service to all members of the community

The purpose of the anti-discrimination laws, which target 'public authorities', is to try to ensure that the public services give an equal service to all members of the community.

Role

See Unit 16 in *BTEC National Public Services Book 2* for information about the roles of different public services, both civilian and military.

Services to individuals

Public services serve us, the public, at a number of levels. If we take as an example the fire and rescue service, they:

- are there if we need them and so reassure us all by their very existence, even if we never have to ring 999 or 112

- serve individuals by rescuing them, putting out their fires, or giving safety advice on an individual basis

- serve groups because they are based in communities (which are groups of people) with whom they have links. They give fire safety advice to schoolchildren, companies, etc. (themselves communities) and make links with the community by setting up outreach schemes and by having fire stations staffed by retained firefighters in towns which are too small to warrant a full-time presence.

If we ring the fire and rescue service, they don't ask us what colour our skin is, what our nationality is, how much our house cost, or what our religion is. Although they may serve us as individuals, they treat us all the same. They put out a fire in someone's back kitchen with the same energy and professionalism as they put out a fire at Windsor Castle, and they don't charge us afterwards.

The other uniformed services have the same approach – and on the rare occasions when they don't, we usually get to hear about it because all these services are **legally accountable** to the public.

See pages 28–32 in Unit 1 for more information on accountability.

Aims and objectives of key organisations in the public sector

'Key organisations' are any major public service.

The 'public sector' is all the government, government agencies and public services that are paid for by the taxpayer. (The private sector consists of privately run businesses which need to make a profit, and whose customers pay them.)

Emergency services, armed forces and other public services

The emergency services must protect and rescue people irrespective of who they are and without discrimination, and treat everybody with the same degree of respect and consideration. They must be genuine equal opportunities employers. The armed forces are a special case in that they have to discriminate between 'friend' and 'enemy' in warfare. **Rules of engagement** should at least attempt to protect civilians, but as these rules are secret it is hard to know what this protection is. There are still some no-go areas for women in the armed forces; otherwise the forces are equal opportunity employers. Other public services should be non-discriminatory both in their treatment of the public and in their own employment policies.

Links to statutory and non-statutory services

A statutory service is one which has been set up by passing a law. Laws which set up a statutory service can be either Acts (which are large, wide-ranging laws) or Statutory Instruments, which are often called Regulations and are narrow and specific.

All the main public services are statutory, as are many other more specialised services or bodies which are attached to them, such as the Serious Organised Crime Agency, the Forensic Science Service, the Meteorological Office, and hundreds of others which are less well known.

Non-statutory services may be charities, such as Citizens Advice, the Duke of Edinburgh's Award Scheme, or the Red Cross. They may also be private companies, such as Group 4.

> **remember**
>
> Aims express the wish or intention of the service; they are often introduced by the word 'to'. Objectives are more practical; they deal with essential parts of the job, and are usually measurable (e.g. through keeping statistical records, or by being officially inspected).

case study 6.8 — Aims and objectives of the prison service

The aim of the prison service is:

- To provide the very best prison services so that we are the provider of choice.

[It works] towards this vision by securing the following key objectives:

- holding prisoners securely
- reducing the risk of prisoners re-offending
- providing safe and well-ordered establishments in which we treat prisoners **humanely**, decently and lawfully.

(Source: www.hmprisonservice.gov.uk)

activity
INDIVIDUAL WORK

Using the internet, or other publicity and recruitment material, find out the aims and objectives of a range of uniformed public services.

Local government is statutory in itself, but many of the organisations which work with local government, in partnerships and in other ways, are non-statutory.

In recent years, politicians have used a catchphrase: 'joined-up government'. At one level (like 'joined-up writing') it is meant to convey maturity in the way the government runs the country. It also conveys the idea that there is an agency or organisation to cater for every need, so that no one falls through the net. (People who 'fall through the net' may be terrorist suspects who are not tracked, vulnerable old people who risk dying of cold, or abused children who are missed by the child protection agencies and the police.) Most importantly of all, for our purposes, joined-up government means improving the ways in which public services, agencies, volunteers and the public and private sectors all work together. The aim is to benefit the overall quality of service – and to prevent so-called 'cock-ups' when, for example, large numbers of failed asylum seekers or released paedophiles suddenly go missing, and the Home Office has no idea where they've gone.

The effect of joined-up government on the public services is that they now work in partnership much more than they used to. A common example of this is in Crime and Disorder Reduction Partnerships, which were set up under the Crime and Disorder Act 1998 (see page 250).

activity
GROUP WORK
6.5

P5

Give a presentation using visual aids showing how two public services support everybody in the community. Include information on ways in which the services fight discrimination.

activity
INDIVIDUAL WORK
6.6

M2

Write a report suitable for a human rights group, examining in detail how one public service provides an equal service to the whole community and fights discrimination.

case study 6.9

CDRPs and CSPs

These statutory partnerships are known as Crime and Disorder Reduction Partnerships (CDRPs) or Community Safety Partnerships (**CSPs**) in Wales.

The responsible authorities as set out in [section] 5 of the Crime and Disorder Act 1998 are:

- police
- police authorities
- local authorities
- fire authorities
- local health boards (LHBs) in Wales, and
- primary care trusts (PCTs) in England …

At present, responsible authorities are under a statutory duty to ensure that the key agencies come together to work in partnership in a CDRP/CSP, and carry out an audit of local crime, disorder and misuse of drugs every three years. Using the information arising from this audit and based on consultation with local communities they then formulate a strategy for combating crime, disorder and the misuse of drugs including substance misuse (in Wales) in the local area.

(Source: www.crimereduction.gov.uk)

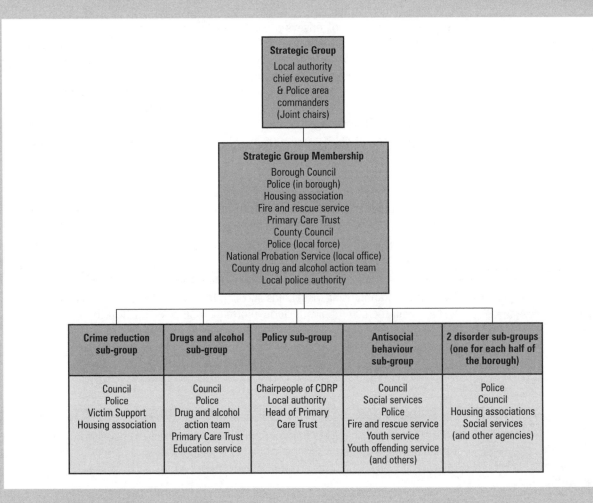

Fig 6.4 Organisation of a Crime and Disorder Reduction Partnership

activity

INDIVIDUAL WORK

1 What is meant by an 'audit' of local crime?

2 What 'strategy' would you propose for tackling crime or antisocial behaviour within a local community?

Links to statutory requirements

Since statutory public services are created by laws, it is not surprising that their work is governed by laws. The responsibilities and duties of statutory public services and the way they carry out those responsibilities and duties are covered by major Acts (the laws which are passed by Parliament), by Regulations (attached to the Acts but not themselves debated in Parliament), and by Codes of Practice. Codes of Practice are strict and specific instructions on how particular tasks should be carried out

remember

PACE Codes of Practice change nearly every year; new and significantly changed versions are likely to come out in 2008.

Police and Criminal Evidence Act 1984

The Police and Criminal Evidence Act (PACE) was introduced in 1984 to regulate the way that the police dealt with suspects. It abolished various old 'stop and search' laws, which were seen as outdated, discriminatory and unreliable, and replaced them with strict and thorough procedures which were to be used at all stages of dealing with suspects.

The PACE Act is backed up with Codes of Practice, booklets which give detailed instructions on searching, arresting, etc. These are shown in Table 6.6.

Table 6.6 Codes of practice for PACE

Code	Police powers covered
A	Searching a person or a vehicle without first making an arrest Making a record of a stop or search
B	Searching buildings etc. Seizing and keeping property found
C	Detention, treatment and questioning of suspects in police custody
D	Identification Keeping accurate and reliable criminal records
E	Tape-recording interviews of suspects in the police station
F	Video-recording interviews of suspects
G	Powers of arrest
H	Detention, treatment and questioning of terrorist suspects

The PACE Codes support the duty of police to provide equality of service to all members of the community by instructing police not to stop and search people without 'reasonable grounds for suspicion'.

Brixton Disorders 10–12 April 1981: Report of an Inquiry by the Rt. Hon. the Lord Scarman, OBE (The Stationery Office, 1981)

Armed Forces Act 2006

The Armed Forces Act 2006 is an Act of major importance. It replaces the Naval Discipline Act 1957, the Army Act 1955 and the Air Force Act 1955 with a single Act which covers discipline and related matters in all three armed services.

The Act therefore provides 'equality of service to all members of the [service] community' by treating Royal Navy, RAF and Army personnel equally in all matters of discipline.

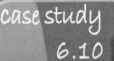

Reasonable suspicion

case study 6.10

Reasonable suspicion can never be supported on the basis of personal factors alone without reliable supporting intelligence or information or some specific behaviour by the person concerned. For example, a person's race, age, appearance, or the fact that the person is known to have a previous conviction, cannot be used alone or in combination with each other as the reason for searching that person. Reasonable suspicion cannot be based on **generalisations** or stereotypical images of certain groups or categories of people as more likely to be involved in criminal activity. A person's religion cannot be considered as reasonable grounds for suspicion and should never be considered as a reason to stop or stop and search an individual.

(Source: Code A 2.2. www.homeoffice.gov.uk)

activity
INDIVIDUAL WORK

What kinds of discrimination are prohibited in this extract?

In many ways, however, discipline in all three services was already similar, so as the Overview of the Act points out:

'The key elements of the discipline systems will remain, in particular a **jurisdiction** for COs to deal with less serious offences, with more serious offences being required to be tried by court-martial. Accordingly it should not be assumed that the provisions of the Act are new. Most of it is based on existing provisions, but updated, and modified to achieve harmonisation between the Services.'

(Source: www.opsi.gov.uk)

The Armed Forces Act 2006 takes measures to prevent harassment on grounds of sexual orientation (241), race (240), religion (240) and disability (241). Figures in brackets refer to sections of the Act.

The armed forces are broadly covered by the Sex Discrimination Act, although some kinds of discrimination (e.g. exclusion of women from the infantry) are allowed. Sexual harassment as such is not mentioned by name in the Act.

Fire and Rescue Services Act 2004
This Act has much to say about the duties and roles of firefighters and the fire and rescue service, but it does not deal with diversity or equal opportunities in the fire and rescue service, or with the way in which it gives equal and non-discriminatory service to the community.

In the past, as the Bain Report (2002) made clear, diversity and equal opportunities has been a difficult area in the fire and rescue service, with complaints of discrimination and harassment being made from time to time. The fire and rescue service comes under the same anti-discrimination laws as other British employers, and therefore the legal measures to encourage diversity and protect minorities are already in place. There has not been the need for anti-discrimination laws specifically targeted at the fire and rescue service, in the way that certain sections of the Armed Forces Act 2006 address these issues in the military. This is mainly because the fire and rescue service comes under civil law, whereas the armed forces have their own system of military law involving courts martial and summary justice which is different from civilian law.

The statutory requirements of the fire and rescue service to provide equality of service to all members of the community therefore come under the Race Relations Act 1976 and its updates, especially the Race Relations Amendment Act 2000; the Sex Discrimination Act 1975 and its updates; the Disability Discrimination Act 2005; and the EEC Directive on Equal Treatment.

On top of this, the government has brought in a more flexible approach to 'equalities' in the fire and rescue service by introducing the *Fire and Rescue Service National Framework 2004/5* (which is likely to be revised and updated before long). This sets priorities for the fire and rescue service both in its work and its staffing policies. In its introduction it says:

'This document is not a national blueprint. Giving Fire and Rescue Authorities the flexibility they need to meet the specific needs of their local communities remains at the heart of the Government's approach. The Framework is designed to give authorities a firm foundation on which to build local solutions.'

(Source: www.merseyfire.gov.uk)

What this means is that the government wants fire and rescue services to have local control over their affairs as far as possible, and therefore does not want to make a set of equal opportunities laws for the fire and rescue service alone.

It does, however, say in the framework that:

'5.2 Fire and Rescue Authorities must ensure that all members of staff are treated fairly and afforded equality of opportunity. Authorities should ensure that all staff are developed in a way which takes account of the differing needs of the individual, in order to deliver the Fire and Rescue Service's aims and objectives effectively.'

The National Framework also introduced the Integrated Personal Development System of staff development in the fire and rescue service, the system of having roles rather than ranks, and generally makes the structure more attractive to women and people from ethnic minorities who might not welcome being in a traditionalist and overly 'macho' workplace.

The government gives further advice and guidance on issues such as **community cohesion** through FRS Circulars sent out by the Department of Communities and Local Government. Examples of the titles are given below:

- FRS Circular 36/2005 – *Consultation on Draft Regulations to Outlaw Age Discrimination*
- FRS Circular 43/2005 – *Minority Ethnic Faith Fire Safety Awareness Campaign*
- FRS Circular 39/2005 – *Stonewall Diversity Champions: Joint Letter to Fire and Rescue Service*
- FRS Circular 37/2005 – *Community Cohesion*.

All these measures help the fire and rescue service in its duty to provide equality of service to all members of the community.

Office of Public Sector Information
www.opsi.gov.uk
FRS National Framework (Department of Communities and Local Government)
www.communities.gov.uk
Stonewall (Equality and Justice for Lesbians, Gay Men and Bisexuals)
www.stonewall.org.uk
Fire Brigades Union
www.fbu.org.uk
Women and Equality
womenandequalityunit.gov.uk
Equal Opportunities Commission
www.eoc.org.uk
London Ambulance Service – see website for *London Ambulance Service Disability Equality Scheme (2006–2009)* and *Race Equality Scheme* (May 2005)
www.londonambulance.nhs.uk

Responsibilities

> **Link**   See Unit 15 in Book 2, where these are covered in more detail.

The diagram outlines how public services fulfil their responsibility to give equal service to all members of the community. They do not do this on their own: the links between public services, local government, central government and other organisations all help them to perform their duties well and with a minimum of discrimination in a diverse society.

Fairness

Fig 6.5 Responsibility of the public services to provide equal service to all members of the community

This means equality of treatment. It also means that the service is of good quality. Fairness inside the service is ensured by equal opportunities policies and systems, and fairness towards the public is developed by diversity training (increasingly important in initial training), codes of conduct which uphold standards, and anti-discrimination laws which public services have to follow. Additional factors which can promote fairness are local government input (through police authorities, fire and rescue authorities, etc.), media pressure and independent inspections (e.g. by Her Majesty's Inspectorate of Constabulary).

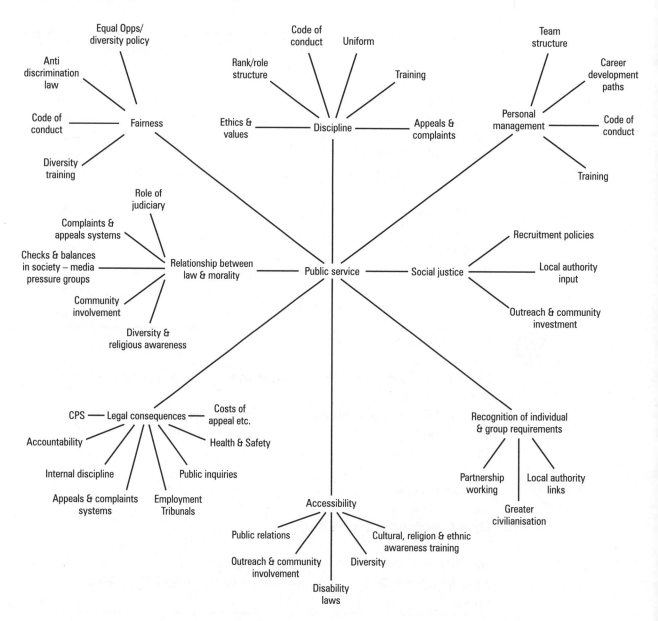

Discipline

Public service discipline follows a code of conduct, backed up by sanctions (punishments) and a discipline system. There are also appeals systems, to try to ensure that disciplinary decisions are fair. Discipline is built into the ethos and traditions of uniformed public services: the uniform, badges and rank or role structure all being conducive to discipline.

Personal management

This rather vague phrase can be confused with personnel management, but in practice there is not much difference in meaning. The fire and rescue service has an integrated personal development system to support its new role structure and make it more 'civilian' in ethos. Good personal management means that employees are treated fairly and without discrimination – and are more likely to show the same good qualities when working with the public. It is achieved using good team structures, training in teamwork, systems of review and appraisal to make sure that people are doing their jobs well and are happy in them, and that their career hopes for the future are being considered.

Social justice

Social justice means treating the public fairly and being responsive to local needs. Public services work towards this by engaging with the community through outreach schemes (e.g. visiting schools, putting on exhibitions of fire safety, etc.). Local authority involvement (e.g. through the police authority) also helps to ensure that they are treating all sections of the community fairly and are working where there is most need of their service. Recruiting from all sections of the community, using **family-friendly** work systems, getting involved in partnerships and supporting youth activities such as the Duke of Edinburgh's Award all help the public service to be a factor in improving social justice in the area where it operates.

Relationship between law and morality

At one level this is the responsibility of Parliament, as its laws should be based on morality (the upholding of good against evil). It is also the duty of the judiciary – judges and magistrates – who must apply the law fairly and honourably, punishing offenders but not victimising them. The judiciary must interpret the law with humanity and in the public interest. In public services and in the law, there must be fair and affordable complaints, grievance and appeals systems – because there is always the risk of **miscarriages of justice** when any legal or discipline system is operated. An ethical (moral) system of laws should have arrangements for correcting its mistakes. The system must be accountable (open for scrutiny and inspection). Where necessary these arrangements should be completely independent of the public services – as with the Independent Police Complaints Commission, the Prisons Ombudsman and the Northern Ireland Police Ombudsman. A further dimension of the relationship between law and morality (not always appreciated by the public services) is the role of the media, and the 'separation of powers' in government. Finally, links with organised religion – e.g. the employment of **chaplains** and **imams** in the armed forces – may help the public services and the people who work in them to be more introspective and understanding about the moral aspects of their work.

 See page 7 in Unit 1 for an explanation of 'separation of powers'.

Legal consequences

This is linked to legal accountability. Discipline, appeal and complaints systems should be transparent, fair, independent where necessary, and should, ideally, never prevent the complainant or accused from obtaining justice in a civilian court. This could be a county court or an employment tribunal, if there has been perceived injustice at work. This is not quite the case in the armed forces where certain offences such as desertion

Fig 6.6 An imam (2rd from right) for the British army: making the link between religion, morality and the armed services

are crimes in a military context but not a civilian one. The court-martial system has been criticised (notably by the European Court of Human Rights) for being too different from the civilian British courts – and therefore not promoting 'equality'. Another system of legal consequences which can affect all uniformed public services is action by the **Health and Safety Executive**. This does not take '**Crown Bodies**' (which include public services) to court, but it is active and effective in promoting health and safety in what can be dangerous work environments.

See pages 28–32 in Unit 1, for more information on accountability, and page 248 above for legal accountability.

Accessibility

This has two sides to it: accessibility for the public as a whole, and accessibility for disabled people. Clearly, in a just and equal society, public services should be easily accessible to both groups. Accessibility for the general public is helped by having clear methods of calling for help, such as 999, and the various methods of reporting crimes which the police post on their websites. Having plenty of well-staffed police stations, officers patrolling their beats, community constables, community support officers, and volunteers such as special constables – in fact a visible presence on the streets – helps to make the police more accessible. Outreach centres used by the fire and rescue service have similar benefits. Work placement schemes, cadet schemes, visits to schools and colleges: all these help to make the services more accessible and user-friendly. Recruiting a diverse workforce gives services a much friendlier and more credible face in a diverse society, and it inspires more confidence among the service's users. For disabled people, accessibility has been improved by new disability laws.

See page 229 above to remind yourself about disability legislation.

Recognition of individual and group requirements

This refers to the need to protect the rights of individuals and yet to satisfy the needs of society as a whole. An example is countryside access: farmers in general would like to keep the public out, while the rambling public would like to go wherever they want. A compromise has to be reached, as it was with the Countryside and Rights of Way Act 2000. Football fans have a right to enjoy themselves, but not when it causes fear and upset to passers-by. Balanced laws, partnership working which takes account of the needs of different sections of society, and good links with local government all help in this.

How national and local policies, strategies and procedures address diversity issues within a chosen public service

Since the 1970s, all the public services have become much more aware of diversity and the need to draw their workforce from all the sections of the population who are willing and able to work. New laws, such as the Equal Pay Act 1970, the Sex Discrimination Act 1975 and the Race Relations Act 1976, caused (or reflected) a major shift in public opinion on these issues. Since that time other anti-discrimination laws have been passed, as well as the Human Rights Act 1998, and the effect of all this is that such issues are now high on the agenda of every British uniformed (and non-uniformed) public service.

Policies, strategies and procedures

These are the planning and methods that go into developing diversity and diversity awareness in the public services.

- Policies are aims, for example to treat everybody equally and without unfair discrimination.
- Strategies are long-term objectives, for example to set up a system of targets and evaluation to ensure that 'equal opportunities' is being put into practice in a particular type of organisation.
- Examples of procedures are training programmes, grievance systems or systems for recording racial incidents, which are used to ensure fair treatment for all. The purpose of procedures is to help put a strategy into practice and make sure that its success can be measured.

Equal opportunities

This is the name given to all the measures taken to prevent discrimination in the workplace on grounds of sex, marital status, ethnic background, age, disability, sexual orientation or any other circumstance irrelevant to work. Public services are required by law to set these measures out in the form of a policy, in order to show their genuine commitment (support) to equal opportunities.

Equal opportunities in Britain are monitored and backed up by several organisations. One is the Equal Opportunities Commission (EOC) which was set up to support and monitor the Equal Pay Act 1970 and the Sex Discrimination Act 1975. The EOC is 'an independent, non-departmental public body, funded primarily by the government'. It deals with 'sex discrimination and inequality related to gender, including good practice in the fair and equal treatment of men and women'. Issues relating to race and ethnicity are covered by the Commission for Racial Equality, set up to support the Race Relations Act 1976. Disability issues are now dealt with by the Disability Rights Commission, which supports the Disability Discrimination Act of 2005.

case study 6.11 — Equal opportunities policy

The main points of the force's Equal Opportunities Policy are as follows:

- Equal opportunities shall mean fairness for all; the recognition, development and use of everyone's talents;

- This fairness will run through recruitment, selection, training, promotion, specialisation and career development generally. It should also govern the relationship of all employees to each other;

- Equality of opportunity does not just relate to race, sex or marital status, but the fact that people can be particularly disadvantaged for those reasons is reflected in legislation;

- No job applicant or employee shall receive unfavourable treatment directly or indirectly on the grounds of gender, sexual orientation, marital status, race, nationality, ethnic origin, religious beliefs and, where applicable, trade union membership, age or disability;

- Selection criteria and procedures will be frequently reviewed to ensure that individuals are selected, promoted and dealt with on the basis of merit, fitness and **competence**, subject only to the restrictions imposed by law;

- Training is an important part of the implementation of the Equal Opportunities Policy. Training programmes will be arranged to ensure that staff are fully aware of their roles and responsibilities and have the opportunity to develop and progress within the organisation.

(Source: www.west-midlands.police.uk)

activity
INDIVIDUAL WORK

Why is it important that the police take equal opportunities seriously?

Equal Opportunities Commission
www.eoc.org.uk
Commission for Racial Equality
www.cre.gov.uk
Disability Rights Commission
www.drc-gb.org

remember
Your own college or workplace will have an equal opportunities policy. Get a copy and look through it.

As far as the public services are concerned, equal opportunities means all the things mentioned in the case study and some other issues such as gender reassignment (sex change). They have equal opportunities officers and diversity awareness training; the latter is an important part of initial training and continues, from time to time, after the **probationary period** is over. Public services set targets for the employment of women, people from ethnic minorities, and other minority groups. Statistics are collected from the public services by the government departments overseeing them (e.g. the Home Office or the Ministry of Defence). These figures are posted on the departments' websites.

Grievance procedures

A **grievance** is a complaint or a problem which an employee has about work, especially unfair treatment at work. Grievance procedures are methods by which an organisation deals with complaints from its own workforce. Public services have well-developed grievance procedures. This is because:

- They have such large numbers of employees that they have plenty of grievances!

- Public services have to set good standards of staff care because they are publicly accountable.

- If grievances are ignored, they can lead to poor relations between staff and management, lawsuits and (e.g. in the fire and rescue service) **industrial action**, including strikes.

- A staff member with a grievance does not necessarily work to the level of their ability and may leave the service altogether. This is wasteful of money and human resources – it costs a great deal to train a replacement.

Grievance procedures follow this pattern:

1. Inform the employer of the grievance in writing.

2. Be invited by the employer to a meeting to discuss the grievance, where the right to be accompanied will apply, and be notified in writing of the decision. The employee must take all reasonable steps to attend this meeting.

3. Be given the right to an appeal meeting, if the employee feels that the grievance has not been satisfactorily resolved, and be notified of the final decision.

Records must be kept during the grievance process and should include:

- the nature of the grievance raised

- a copy of the written grievance

- the employer's response

- action taken

- reasons for action taken

- whether there was an appeal and, if so, the outcome

- subsequent developments.

If serious grievances cannot be settled under the normal procedures, it is possible for an employee in a public service to go to an employment tribunal.

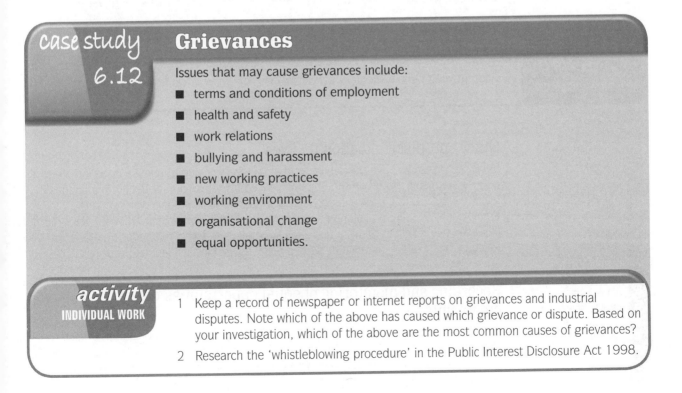

case study 6.12

Grievances

Issues that may cause grievances include:

- terms and conditions of employment
- health and safety
- work relations
- bullying and harassment
- new working practices
- working environment
- organisational change
- equal opportunities.

activity
INDIVIDUAL WORK

1 Keep a record of newspaper or internet reports on grievances and industrial disputes. Note which of the above has caused which grievance or dispute. Based on your investigation, which of the above are the most common causes of grievances?

2 Research the 'whistleblowing procedure' in the Public Interest Disclosure Act 1998.

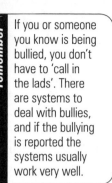

Bullying and harassment at work

Bullying and harassment are very similar. They concern unwanted behaviour from colleagues, managers or other employees and usually involve picking on an individual. They take many forms: verbal bullying, 'sniping', sarcasm, sexual innuendo or unwanted approaches, abusive language, sexist or racist remarks, ostracism (not speaking to someone or excluding them from group activities), unreasonable or public criticism, attempting to humiliate someone in public, hostile gestures and looks, discriminatory behaviour (e.g. giving someone unpleasant or boring jobs to do), backbiting and rumour-spreading, threats of violence and actual violence.

---

case study
6.13

Harassment policies

Public services have harassment policies. These:

■ give examples of what constitutes harassment and intimidating behaviour – it is also useful to define positive and supportive behaviours

■ explain the damaging effects and why it will not be tolerated

■ state that it will be treated as a disciplinary offence

■ clarify the legal implications of harassment

■ describe how to get help and make a complaint, formally and informally

■ undertake that allegations will be treated speedily, seriously and confidentially

■ promise protection from victimisation for making a complaint

■ clarify the responsibilities of line managers, HR [human resources] departments and the role of union or employee representatives

■ make it the duty of supervisors/managers to implement policy and ensure it is understood

■ emphasise that every employee carries responsibility for their behaviour.

(Source: www.cipd.co.uk)

---

activity
INDIVIDUAL WORK

Find out what people should do about harassment at your workplace or college.

Other anti-discrimination policies

Public services now have policies to combat harassment due to religion or belief. These policies are mainly based on the Employment Equality (Religion or Belief) Regulations 2003 (SI 2003/1660), which apply across England, Scotland and Wales, and the Employment Equality (Religion or Belief) (Amendment) Regulations 2004 (SI 2004/437). However, two religions, Sikhism and Judaism, have protection too under the Race Relations Act 1976 – because these two religions are closely identified with particular ethnic groups in a way that, say, Hinduism, Buddhism, Christianity and Islam are not.

Recording and monitoring of equal opportunities data and complaints

Specific complaints should be recorded in writing by an equal opportunities officer, together with relevant details and action taken, and then should be followed up. The amount of following up depends on whether the complainant thinks the problem has been dealt with adequately and the seriousness of the complaint.

Fig 6.7 Bullying in the army – how to deal with it (adapted from *Basically Fair*, an advice booklet, www.army.mod.uk)

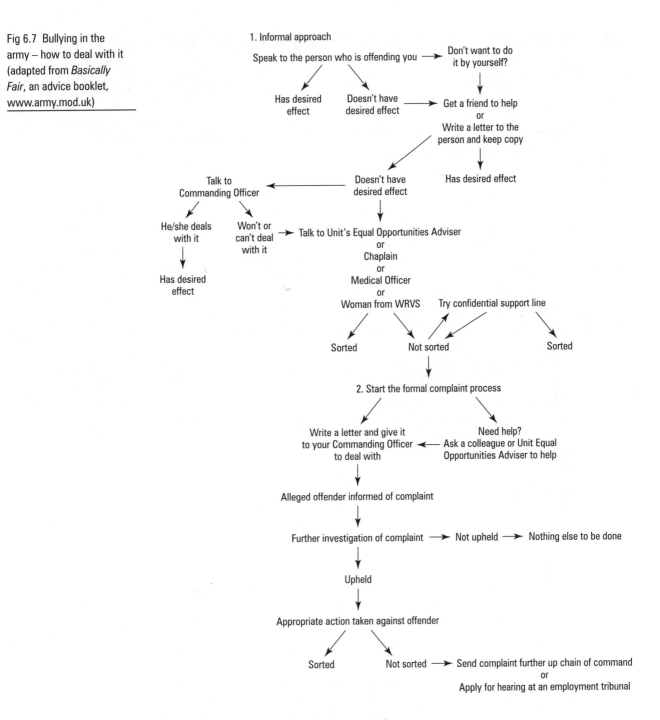

Complaints procedures for service users

These are systems for dealing with complaints from people who feel that they have been discriminated against by a public authority such as the police. Procedures for police complaints are laid down in the Police Reform Act 2002:

- The complainant complains to the police and the complaint is recorded.
- The complainant is interviewed using open questions (e.g. 'Tell me about ...' or 'What did ...?')
- The police officer is interviewed.
- A senior officer decides.
- The investigation can also be carried out by the local police authority, or by the Independent Police Complaints Commission.

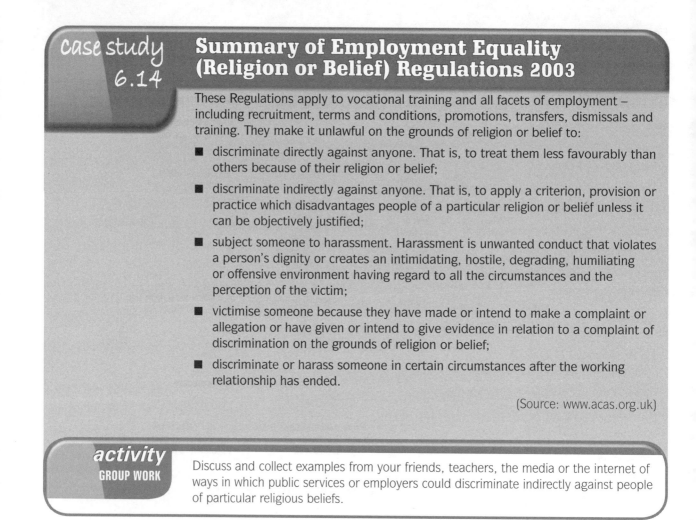

case study
6.14

Summary of Employment Equality (Religion or Belief) Regulations 2003

These Regulations apply to vocational training and all facets of employment – including recruitment, terms and conditions, promotions, transfers, dismissals and training. They make it unlawful on the grounds of religion or belief to:

■ discriminate directly against anyone. That is, to treat them less favourably than others because of their religion or belief;

■ discriminate indirectly against anyone. That is, to apply a criterion, provision or practice which disadvantages people of a particular religion or belief unless it can be objectively justified;

■ subject someone to harassment. Harassment is unwanted conduct that violates a person's dignity or creates an intimidating, hostile, degrading, humiliating or offensive environment having regard to all the circumstances and the perception of the victim;

■ victimise someone because they have made or intend to make a complaint or allegation or have given or intend to give evidence in relation to a complaint of discrimination on the grounds of religion or belief;

■ discriminate or harass someone in certain circumstances after the working relationship has ended.

(Source: www.acas.org.uk)

activity
GROUP WORK

Discuss and collect examples from your friends, teachers, the media or the internet of ways in which public services or employers could discriminate indirectly against people of particular religious beliefs.

Diversity issues

There are certain problems which need to be tackled in order to successfully develop a diverse workforce in a public service. These include:

■ the history and reputation of the service – it may not have been diverse in the past

■ the 'canteen culture' of the service – what the **rank and file** really think about diversity.

Link

See page 164 in Unit 4 for more on 'canteen culture'.

Employment within public services

Some uniformed public services have fewer women, gays, lesbians and people from ethnic minorities than they should and are a long way from reaching their targets.

Problems affecting recruitment include:

■ the negative image of the service among minority groups and women

■ a failure to meet and get to know and understand minority communities

■ not advertising in media used by minorities

■ possible indirect discrimination in the recruiting programme (e.g. inappropriate physical tests).

case study 6.15 — Monitoring

Monitoring is a process that involves collecting, analysing and evaluating information, to measure performance, progress and change. It can be done in several ways, including questionnaires, surveys, consultation and feedback.

Monitoring, by racial group, will allow employers to:

a. determine the composition of their workforce, by racial group, and compare this information with benchmarks, such as census data;

b. know how their workforce is distributed across the organisation, by location, type of job and grade;

c. uncover any disparities [inequalities] between racial groups, in the workforce as a whole and at different levels of the organisation, and investigate the underlying cause

d. find out whether people from certain racial groups are typically taking longer to obtain promotion;

e. examine whether the practices, provisions, criteria, requirements or conditions used to select candidates for employment, training and promotion might be indirectly discriminatory, and why, and consider how they might be changed to avoid any negative effects on candidates from a particular racial group (or groups);

f. set realistic targets and timetables for reducing any significant racial disparities, both within the workforce as a whole, and at different levels of the organisation;

g. send a clear message to its workers, and to job seekers, that the organisation is serious about achieving fair and equitable participation, and encourage them to cooperate fully; and

h. judge whether the equal opportunities policy is achieving its aims.

3.27 Monitoring, by racial group, should cover the following:

a. applications for jobs, temporary and permanent, advertised and nonadvertised, and success rates at each stage of the process;

b. distribution of workers in the organisation, by type of job, location, and grade;

c. applications for promotion, transfer and training, and success rates for each;

d. results of performance appraisals;

e. grievances and disciplinary action, including the results, and tribunal decisions involving claims of racial discrimination or harassment; and

f. terminations of contract (for whatever reason).

(Source: CRE (2006) *Statutory Code of Practice on Racial Equality in Employment*)

activity — GROUP WORK

Go through each of the above measures and decide how it helps to ensure equal opportunities.

Problems affecting **retention** include:

- unsuitable initial training, lack of mentoring, unfriendly attitudes among established staff

- failure to develop the careers of women and people from ethnic minorities (e.g. poor promotion prospects)

- outdated shift, uniform and discipline systems which are not family-friendly, or are unsuited to believers of certain religions

- poor accommodation, unsuitable canteens, poor sleeping facilities, lack of toilets, child care, etc.

All uniformed public services are working hard to reduce these problems. They are also inviting disabled people to apply for some posts.

Development of a diverse workforce

Developing a diverse workforce is a complex task, which takes many years. People may work in a public service for 25 years, so that older employees may not be 'diverse' even though the new intakes are. For this reason, it is extremely difficult to reach government targets of (usually) 7% ethnic minority people in, say, a police force. It suggests that unless people are disproportionately recruited from minority groups, using a quota system (which is illegal), it will be at least 20 years before the ethnic profile of the police matches that of the society they serve.

Fig 6.8 shows examples of what needs to be worked on to achieve a diverse workforce in a uniformed public service.

Recruitment and staff selection

Some uniformed services, such as the ambulance service and the NHS, have a good balance of minorities among their staff. Minorities are under-represented in the armed forces, the police and the fire and rescue service.

Home Office – see website for employment targets
www.homeoffice.gov.uk

To achieve greater diversity the main issues with recruitment are:

- how to recruit more women

- how to recruit more people from ethnic minorities.

Fig 6.8 Five sides to developing a diverse workforce

Recruitment
Advertising
Entry requirements
Entry procedures
Training for potential applicants from minority groups

Institutional culture
Awareness training in sexism, racism, diversity and non-discrimination
Clear and well-publicised policies
Senior people have responsibility for diversity issues
Staff monitoring

Development of a diverse workforce

Retention
Promotion prospects
Initial training
The will to develop a diverse workforce at all levels
Mentoring
Staff development

Support groups
Associations
Federations
Trade unions
These need to be in favour of diversity

Tackling indirect discrimination
E.g. – Systems which are family friendly
Child care
Toilets & accommodation for both sexes
Arrangements where needed for holidays, religious festivals, fasting, praying

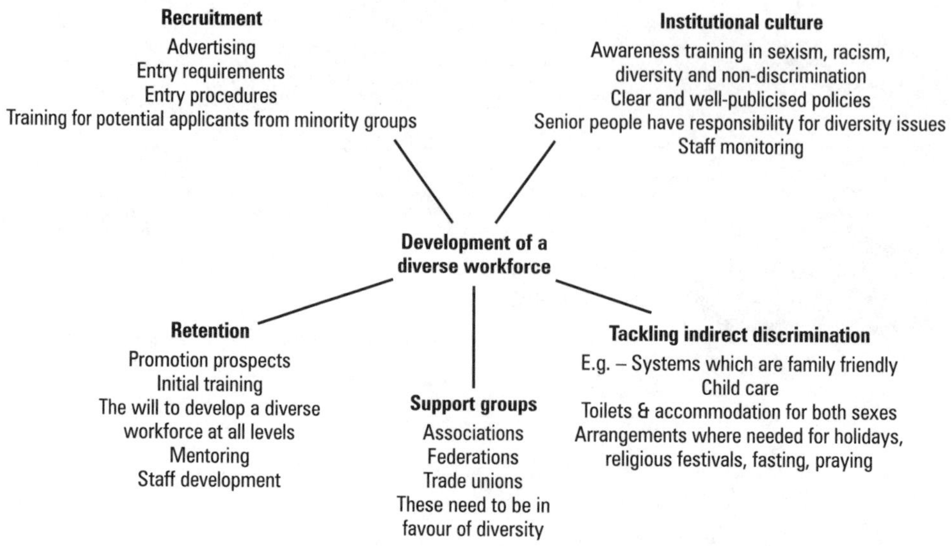

There appears to be no intention to recruit 54% women (their proportion in the population). Gender equality is, however, monitored. In the British Transport Police, 31.5% of officers were women in 2007, but they were not well spread through the ranks. The British Transport Police say:

'Representation for both women and black and minority ethnic (BME) officers is highest at the level of police constable, and work is being undertaken in the Diversity Unit and across the Force to stimulate progression to higher ranks.'

(Source: *Draft Combined Equality Scheme (Disability, Gender and Race) 2007–2010* www.btp.pnn.police.uk)

Ethnic minority recruitment is more of a pressing issue because of their obvious under-representation in some uniformed public services.

case study 6.16

Minority ethnic representation in the police

Here is a table showing the proportion of ethnic minority people in the police over the years 1999–2005

Table 6.7 Minority ethnic representation in the police service nationally

	1999	2000	2001	2002	2003	2004	2005	2004 milestone	2009 target
Police Service	3%	3%	3.1%	3.5%	3.8%	4.3%	4.6%	4.6%	7%
Police Officers	2%	2.2%	2.4%	2.6%	2.9%	3.3%	3.5%	4%	7%
Special Constables	2.9%	3.2%	3.5%	3.6%	4.4%	5%	6%	5%	7%
Police Community Support Officers	–	–	–	–	–	–	14%	–	–
Police Staff	5%	4.7%	4.8%	5.3%	5.5%	6%	6.5%	6%	7%

(Source: *Race Equality: The Home Secretary's Employment Targets, Report 2005*, www.homeoffice.gov.uk)

activity

INDIVIDUAL WORK

1   Why do you think the minority ethnic proportion among police officers is lower than in the other groups given on the table?

2   Comment on the data for police community support officers.

Catering for employees' needs through support mechanisms
Catering for employees' needs includes:

■ monitoring their pay and conditions of service

■ giving professional help and advice

■ supporting people who are sick, suffering from stress, or injured in accidents

■ supporting people who have grievances, or are suffering from discrimination

■ representing the needs of employees to employers

■ working in partnership with employers to improve health and safety

■ providing a social and recreational life.

Fig 6.9 Still under-represented

Unions

Of the main uniformed public services only the fire and rescue service has a full right to join a trade union (the Fire Brigades Union), take industrial action and go on strike. The armed forces and police officers do not have trade unions and are not allowed by law to strike.

Many support staff in, or linked to, public services belong to trade unions. Here are some of them:

Table 6.8 Trade unions

Union	Membership
AMICUS	NHS; Voluntary sector
GMB:	Security workers
NAPO:	Probation Officers
PCS:	Government departments and public bodies
Prospect	Law and order
TSSA	Port authorities
UNISON	Police support staff

Professional associations

The police, who do not have the right to strike, nevertheless have an organisation which looks after the interests of all police officers: the Police Federation. Although the Police Federation has few direct powers, it is able to influence government policy if that looks as if it is going to cause problems for the police. Prison officers also have an association: the Prison Officers Association. Although it is considered by its members to be a trade union, it has not, since the Criminal Justice and Public Order Act 1994, had the legal right to take industrial action. However, it is still fighting for the restoration of full trade union rights.

The Army

The armed forces cannot go on strike but they do negotiate with the Ministry of Defence for improvements in pay and conditions. (At the time of writing, there is a campaign to try to improve army accommodation.)

The following wide range of organisations looks after the welfare of people in the armed forces and people who have left:

- Army Benevolent Fund
- Army Welfare Service
- Forces Pension Society
- HIVE (info for soldiers being transferred)
- Joint Service Housing Advice Office
- Marriage and Relationship Support Directory
- Royal British Legion
- Veterans' Agency (set up by government).

The British Army – see website for information on soldier welfare

www.army.mod.uk

The police

The police have organisations for minority groups within their ranks: for example, the National Black Police Association and the Gay Police Association, both of which work against discrimination in the workplace and support their members.

---

case study 6.17 — Miasma

How many people from minority communities go to work each day in the police service with the anticipation of running up against misperceptions and distorted accounts of their behaviour from colleagues? This murky atmosphere of misconception and distortion in which we work is a condition that has come to be called 'miasma'. It operates like an ever-present toxic fog, consuming people and creating extra burdens that are not directly related to the work itself. An important goal for minority managers therefore is to discover how to work through miasma and not be impeded by it.

(Source: 'The impact of culture, customs and race in contemporary policing', Tarique Ghaffur, Assistant Commissioner, Metropolitan Police. National Black Police Association Keynote Address, Manchester 7 August 2006, www.nbpa.co.uk)

activity
INDIVIDUAL WORK

What is the meaning of 'miasma' and what do you think the police service should do about it?

Aspects of public service work which may impact on individual beliefs

'Beliefs', in this context, are mainly religious beliefs. In our diverse society, large companies and the public services are increasingly trying to make the workplace and the working day fit in more with the requirements of religious believers who work there.

For religious believers employed in a public service any of the activities described under the following headings may be a possible source of difficulty. Most of these points are covered by the Employment Equality (Religion or Belief) Regulations 2003, which recommend that all reasonable efforts are made to accommodate people's religious beliefs. However, the Regulations do not expect employers to go to great expense (e.g. building a special prayer room); that might be considered unreasonable. A more insurmountable religious issue involves the armed forces, where **pacifists** would not be able to join up because they might have to take human life, and Muslims may be unwilling to fight in countries such as Iraq and Afghanistan. In 2007, there were only 330 Muslims out of 100,000 personnel in the British army (www.personneltoday.com).

Shift work impinging on religious festivals
The Employment Equality (Religion or Belief) Regulations 2003 guide the attitude of public service employers. All reasonable efforts should be made to accommodate people's religious needs and practices. Recruitment days and interviews for jobs should not be held during religious festivals. Staff, staff representatives and, if they exist, trade unions should be consulted and a policy drawn up which attempts to avoid clashes between shift work and festivals.

Days of rest or fasting
Again, efforts should be made to accommodate the wishes of workers where possible. Prayer rooms should be provided.

The wearing of a specific style of clothing
Some clothing may not be compatible with the uniform or the requirements of the job (sometimes for health and safety reasons, sometimes because it might affect the 'image' of the service). Over issues such as Sikh turbans and knives, agreements have been made which satisfy both employers and Sikhs. To date, the wearing of veils does not appear to have been an issue in the uniformed public services.

Dietary need
This is catered for in uniformed public services.

Advisory, Conciliation and Arbitration Service – website contains very useful information, particularly on resolving disputes and on equality and diversity
www.acas.org.uk

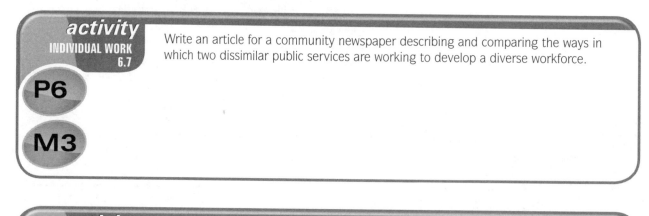

activity
INDIVIDUAL WORK 6.7
P6
M3

Write an article for a community newspaper describing and comparing the ways in which two dissimilar public services are working to develop a diverse workforce.

activity
INDIVIDUAL WORK 6.8
D1

Write a research paper for a local civil rights group, examining in depth the methods used by the public services to develop diverse workforces and fight discrimination.

Progress Check

1. Give three reasons for large-scale immigration into the UK since 1980.

2. Name as many kinds of diversity as you can.

3. Are integration and diversity compatible?

4. List all the individual differences that are covered by the idea of 'diversity'.

5. Why are support groups needed in a diverse society?

6. What is a statutory organisation and in what ways is it likely to differ from a voluntary organisation?

7. What is institutionalised racism and why is it a problem?

8. Why is the average pay of women less than the average pay of men?

9. Explain, with examples, the difference between direct and indirect discrimination.

10. State six rights which are protected by the Human Rights Act.

11. Why do the uniformed public services need to know about the Human Rights Act?

12. What are 'sensitive personal data'?

13. What are public authorities and what are their duties under the Race Relations (Amendment) Act 2000?

14. Name five things that public authorities must try to do under the Disability Discrimination Act 2005.

15. Explain how a Crime and Disorder Reduction Partnership works.

16. What is meant by social justice and how do the public services try to put it into practice?

17. Define 'equal opportunities'.

18. Explain the main points in the Employment Equality (Religion or Belief) (Amendment) Regulations 2004.

19. Why do public services have difficulty meeting their ethnic minority staffing targets?

20. What is the difference between a trade union and a professional association?

Physical Preparation and Fitness for the Uniformed Services

This unit covers:

- The major human body systems
- The effects of lifestyle factors on health and fitness
- Planning a fitness training programme to prepare for uniformed public service
- Undertaking a fitness training programme to prepare for uniformed public service

Most uniformed public service work demands high levels of fitness. Fitness is not something that can be developed overnight, nor is it simply a matter of training and exercise.

This unit shows you how to develop your fitness in a healthy and structured way, beginning with a look at the biology of fitness, i.e. the parts of the body which determine fitness and how they work. You will also learn about healthy eating and the kind of lifestyle that is good for fitness.

After outlining the fitness requirements for the uniformed public services, the tests that are used and how these fit in with the needs of the job, the unit considers different kinds of fitness and how these can be developed by proper training. There is also a section on the ways in which fitness is tested.

Finally, the unit gives you the background needed to enable you to plan, carry out and monitor your own fitness training programme, one suited to your individual needs and, where appropriate, to the service that you may wish to join.

grading criteria

To achieve a **Pass** grade the evidence must show that the learner is able to:	To achieve a **Merit** grade the evidence must show that, in addition to the pass criteria, the learner is able to:	To achieve a **Distinction** grade the evidence must show that, in addition to the pass and merit criteria, the learner is able to:
P1 describe the muscular-skeletal, cardiovascular and respiratory systems Pg 282	**M1** explain the effects of exercise on the muscular-skeletal, cardiovascular and respiratory systems Pg 282	

To achieve a **Pass** grade the evidence must show that the learner is able to:	To achieve a **Merit** grade the evidence must show that, in addition to the pass criteria, the learner is able to:	To achieve a **Distinction** grade the evidence must show that, in addition to the pass and merit criteria, the learner is able to:
P2 describe the lifestyle factors that can affect health and fitness, and the effects they can have Pg 291	**M2** explain the effects that lifestyle factors can have on health and fitness, when applying for a uniformed public service and long-term employment Pg 291	**D1** evaluate the effects that lifestyle factors can have on health and fitness, when applying for a uniformed public service and long-term employment Pg 308
P3 describe the fitness requirements and tests of three different uniformed public services Pg 299		
P4 plan a personal fitness training programme to prepare for a selected uniformed public service, with support Pg 308	**M3** plan a personal fitness training programme to prepare for uniformed public service Pg 308	
P5 undertake a personal fitness training programme to prepare for a selected uniformed public service Pg 315		
P6 describe the strengths and areas for improvement of the personal fitness programme. Pg 316	**M4** explain the strengths and areas for improvement of the personal fitness programme. Pg 316	**D2** evaluate the personal fitness training programme making recommendations for improvement. Pg 316

The major human body systems

Body systems are groups of organs which work together for a collective purpose.

Muscular-skeletal system

This is the name given to the arrangements of bones and muscles which hold us together and enable us to move.

Skeletal system (structure and function)

Bones are composed of calcium, phosphorus (both minerals) and collagen (a protein that helps to give bones strength and resist breakages). They also contain nerves and blood vessels. Different bones have different structures; in large bones the outer part is made of dense, tough, compact bone, and the inner parts are made of spongy bone. There are 206 bones in the human body; nearly all of them are attached to other bones in an arrangement that is called the skeleton. Our skeleton gives us our underlying shape and our ability to move.

Bones are the same in everybody, and they all have names. The main names are useful to know as they are related to health and fitness **training**.

Fig 7.1 The human skeleton

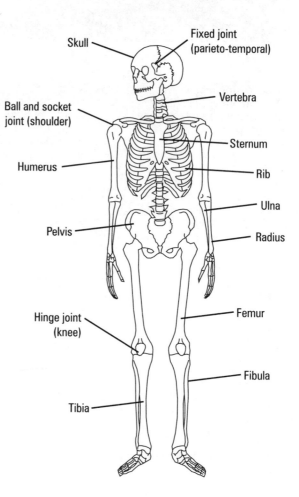

Bones have a number of functions:

- to enable the body to move
- to protect vulnerable parts of the body
- to produce red blood cells in the **marrow**
- to conduct sound (in the ear).

Joints

The bones which enable us to move – and most bones have some role in movement – are linked to other bones by joints. Joints are classified by the way the two bones fit together and by the type of movement they produce. The main kinds of joint are described below.

Fixed

Fixed joints are places where bones meet and cannot move. The main ones are in the skull and are called sutures.

Sutures are interfaces between two bones, but they can't move at all so they are not joints in the normal sense. They look like small irregular cracks, and they join together the bones of the skull to make a safe container for the brain.

Slightly moveable

These are found in the spine, which is a chain of 33 bones, some linked by fixed joints and some separated by cushions of cartilage (a gristle-like substance made of protein) called intervertebral discs. They are tied together with **ligaments** but can move slightly. The vertebrae (individual spinal bones) also have some facet joints, which are synovial.

Fig 7.2 Suture

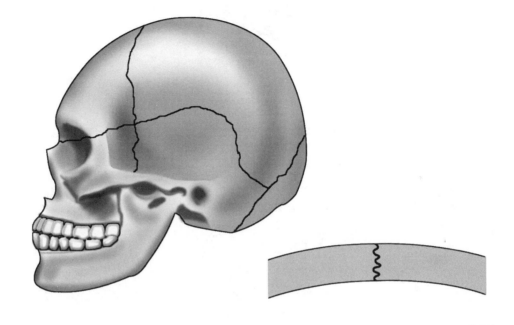

Spine Universe
www.spineuniverse.com

Synovial

These are moveable joints enclosed by a sac of synovial fluid which protects and lubricates the joints.

■ Ball and socket – these are found at the shoulder and hip and allow the bones to move in any direction. Both ball and socket are almost round.

Fig 7.3 Ball and socket joint

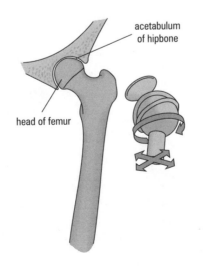

acetabulum
of hipbone

head of femur

■ Condyloid or ellipsoidal joints – these are found at the wrist and ankle. They are really elliptical ball and socket joints which move better in some directions than in others, although a certain amount of movement is possible in all directions.

Fig 7.4 Ellipsoidal joint

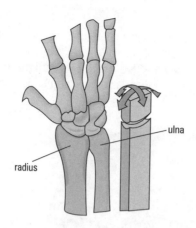

- Saddle joints – these are found at the thumbs. The bones have forked ends and sit on each other like a horse-rider sits on a saddle. They give a range of movements similar to ellipsoidal joints.

Fig 7.5 Saddle joint

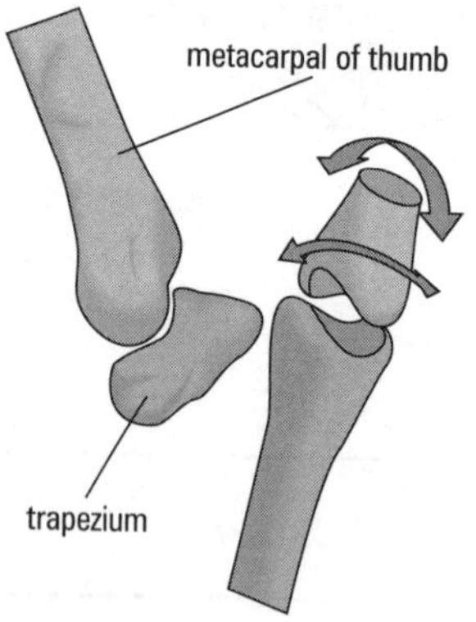

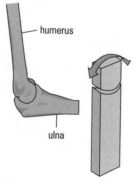

- Hinge joints – these are found at the tops of the elbows and knees. Like a door hinge they allow movement only in one direction.

Fig 7.6 Hinge joint

- Pivot joints – these are found in the week and in the forearms immediately below the elbow. They are able to swivel round.

Fig 7.7 Pivot joint

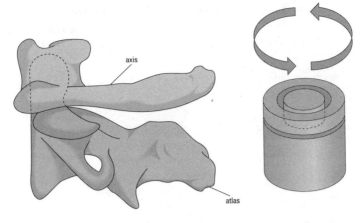

- Gliding or planar joints – these are found between small bones (carpals) in the wrist and (tarsals) in the feet. They only move slightly, but in many directions.

Fig 7.8 Gliding joint

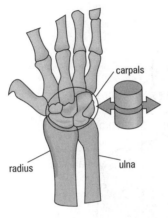

By themselves joints don't hang together very well. The bones are kept in place by ligaments – strong bands of protein (collagen), which are attached to the bones and in some cases wrap around them.

Fig 7.9 Bones and ligaments

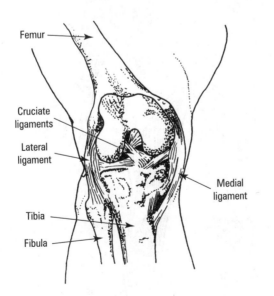

Joints and bones are, however, completely unable to move unless they are attached to muscles. Muscles change the position of bones by pulling at them (never by pushing). They are able to pull because they are attached to the bones by tough cords called tendons.

Tendons (and many other organs, such as the heart and stomach) are held in place by ligaments.

Muscular system

About half the weight of an average person's body is made of muscles; each of us has over 600 of them. Muscles have two roles:

■ to move

■ to generate heat.

Structure

Muscles are arranged in a complex overall structure, linked to bones by tendons, or in flat sheets. Most muscle has a fibrous appearance under the microscope, due to the long, thin muscle cells, but heart muscle and smooth muscle (around the intestines, blood vessels, etc.) are not fibrous in appearance.

Anatomy is the arrangement of organs and the internal structure of the body.

Fig 7.10a Anatomy of the main skeletal muscles

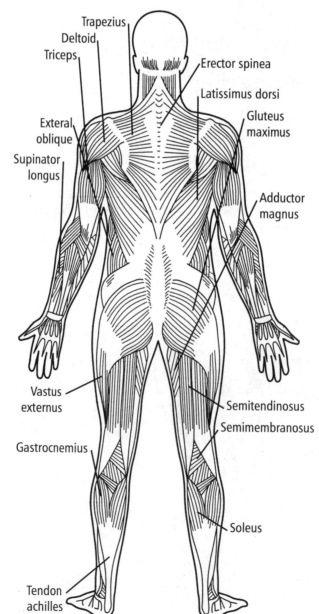

Fig 7.10b Anatomy of the main skeletal muscles

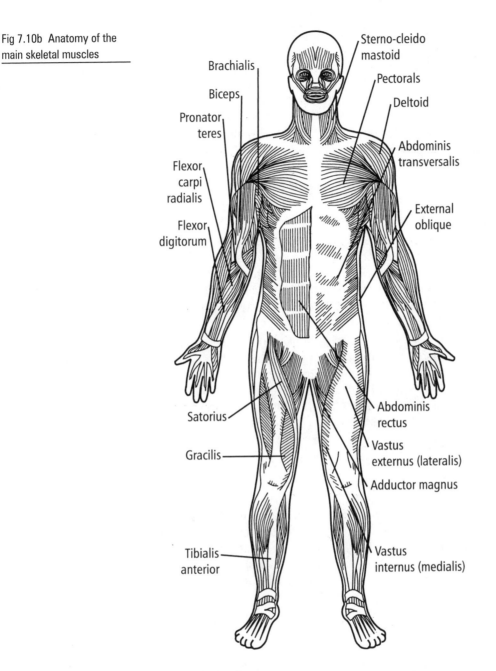

Sterno-cleido mastoid

Brachialis

Biceps

Pronator teres

Flexor carpi radialis

Flexor digitorum

Pectorals

Deltoid

Abdominis transversalis

External oblique

Satorius

Gracilis

Tibialis anterior

Abdominis rectus

Vastus externus (lateralis)

Adductor magnus

Vastus internus (medialis)

Types of muscle

There are three types of muscle in the human body.

Cardiac

Cardiac muscle is found only in the heart. We can't control its movements by will-power; and it doesn't get tired. Heart muscle beats at a fixed rate, governed by part of the heart called the sinus, but this rate can be varied by messages from the brain and by the amounts of **hormones** such as adrenaline in the blood.

Skeletal

This is the kind of muscle that we control and of which we are aware in our everyday lives, especially when we do sport or exercise. It is called skeletal muscle because it is usually attached to our bones. Every intentional movement that we do, down to the twitch of an eyelid, is done by skeletal muscle.

The structure of skeletal muscle is striated – that is, if we look at it closely, it is made up of tiny lines and bands. Skeletal muscle is made of cells (sometimes called **fibres**) which, when they are relaxed, are long and thin.

Smooth

This kind of muscle carries out many of the automatic functions of our bodies. Organs such as blood vessels, the intestines, the stomach and the bladder are formed of this kind of muscle. It is called smooth muscle because it doesn't have the streaks or striations which are visible in skeletal muscle. Like skeletal muscle it works by contracting, but it doesn't have tendons and isn't attached to any bones. Its movements push food through our digestive system by alternately squeezing and relaxing.

When we need a lot of blood in our muscles (e.g. when exercising hard), the smooth muscle in the walls of **arteries** leading to those muscles relaxes and allows the vessels to dilate (get wider) so that more blood can get through. However, if we get into a cold shower the same smooth muscle contracts in our surface blood vessels so that less blood goes to the skin, and our core body temperature doesn't drop.

Muscle movement

Muscle cells are in contact with the nervous system and if they get a message they contract, bunching up to become much shorter. When this happens they pull on the muscle's tendon which is attached to a bone. Thousands of cells acting together are strong enough to move the bone, and, of course, to move our whole body if we want them to.

Many muscles in the body, especially in the limbs, are arranged in pairs which work against each other. This means that if one muscle moves a part of the body out of position, the **antagonistic** (paired) muscle can pull the body part back into position again. The most well-known antagonistic pairing of muscles is the biceps and the triceps. The biceps, at the front of the upper arm, bends the arm at the elbow. The triceps, at the back of the upper arm, pulls the arm straight again at the elbow.

Types of muscle fibres

Skeletal muscle contains two types of cell or fibre: slow-twitch and fast-twitch. The two types are mixed in varying proportions in different muscles and, to some extent, in different people. They get their energy in different ways and act differently.

Slow-twitch fibres are long and bunch up relatively slowly when told to do so by a nerve impulse. They are used for activities requiring **endurance**, such as long walks, **aerobic** exercise and jogging. Distance runner, thanks to their training and their genetic makeup (i.e. their hereditary characteristics), have more slow-twitch fibres than the average person. Their muscles don't bulge but they don't get tired easily either.

Fig 7.11 The antagonistic action of biceps and triceps

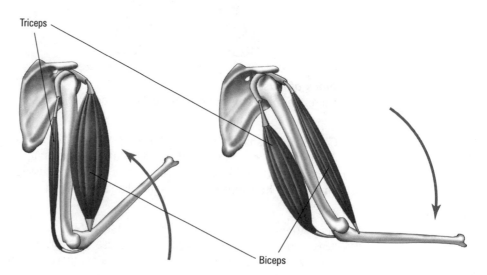
Triceps
Biceps

Fast-twitch fibres are shorter and thicker and respond to nerve impulses with a sudden, violent bunching-up. Sprinters, weight-lifters, shot-putters and heavyweight boxers have more than the average numbers of fast-twitch fibres in their muscles and are able to do sudden, powerful movements. Such athletes and sportspeople can lift much heavier weights than distance runners can, but they get much more tired than a distance runner if they have to run far.

As we shall see, the uniformed public services like to recruit people who have plenty of endurance but are also relatively strong. They don't have to be outstanding athletes. But it helps if they have a good average mix of slow- and fast-twitch muscle fibres … and, of course, if they keep themselves fit and healthy.

Link   See pages 295–300 for the uniformed public services' fitness requirements.

Effects of exercise (short-term and long-term)

Link   See pages 282–285 for information on the effects of exercise.

Cardiovascular system

'Cardiovascular' means relating to the heart and the blood vessels. It is a system because the heart and the blood vessels are linked and have clearly defined roles.

Structure of the heart

The heart is a pump about the size of a fist in the left-hand side of the chest. It contains four muscular chambers: the two top ones are called atria, and the two bottom ones are called ventricles. The heart has a left side and a right side, each with one atrium and one ventricle.

The two sides of the heart do different jobs. The right side deals with blood coming in: the left side deals with blood going out.

Blood coming into the heart is dark red in colour because its oxygen has been used up on its journey round the body. It flows into the right atrium through two big **veins** called the superior vena cava and the inferior vena cava. When the right atrium is full, it squeezes blood into the right ventricle through the tricuspid valve, which, like all valves, only allows blood to flow one way. The right ventricle then squeezes the dark-red blood into the pulmonary artery and pumps it to the lungs. In the lungs the blood gets refilled with oxygen; then it comes back through the pulmonary veins into the left atrium. This blood, now bright red, is squeezed through the mitral (aka bicuspid) valve into the left ventricle, then pumped out into the body via the aorta, the biggest artery, which soon splits so that some blood goes up towards the head, and the rest goes down towards the feet.

When a person is resting the average heart beats at about 70 times a minute, but it can rise to double this at times of high activity and stress. When a person's blood pressure is measured, two figures are given, one for the maximum pressure at the height of the beat, and the other for the minimum pressure which comes between two beats. The maximum pressure is the systolic pressure; the minimum pressure is the diastolic pressure. Blood pressure is expressed as a fraction. If the figure when a person is relaxed is above 120/80, the blood pressure is high.

Blood vessels

These are tubes lined with muscle along which blood flows. Vessels carrying blood away from the heart are called arteries, while vessels carrying blood back to the heart are called veins. In the bigger arteries you can feel your pulse; in veins you cannot. The countless tiny vessels which supply blood to the cells in the muscles and the organs of the body are called capillaries. Blood vessels can dilate (get wider) or constrict (get thinner) according to the needs of the particular parts of the body they supply: for example, blood vessels supplying muscles dilate during exercise, so that the muscles can get more blood.

The Children's Heart Institute – see website for information about the heart
www.childrensheartinstitute.org

Function of blood

An 'average' person contains about 6 litres of blood. The amount rises after drinking water, and goes down when a person is dehydrated. Blood is made up of a large number of cells suspended in a liquid called plasma. The main types of blood cells are:

- red blood cells which carry oxygen and nutrients round the body
- white blood cells (leukocytes) which defend the body against bacteria and viruses
- platelets which help the blood to clot when there is an injury.

MSN Encarta
www.encarta.msn.com

Delivery of oxygen and nutrients

These are transported in the red part of the blood, which is called haemoglobin, in special cells called red corpuscles (red blood cells). The cells are able to turn the complex chemicals in haemoglobin into energy, or use them in tissue repair or the making of other chemicals.

Removal of waste products

Waste products from cells get into the bloodstream and are carried mainly to the liver and kidneys. Much of the waste is turned into urea, which is soluble in water and leaves the body as urine. White blood cells identify and attack bacteria and viruses, as do antibodies (chemicals created in the liver and other organs).

Thermoregulation

This means keeping the body at the right temperature of 36.5–37 °C. When blood flows into the skin and cheeks it cools us down, which is why some people go red when they get too hot. When we are too cold blood vessels near the skin constrict so that less blood gets chilled, and the core body temperature remains as it should be. Body temperature is kept up by muscular movement (changing chemical energy into mechanical and heat energy) and by chemical reactions in the liver.

Effects of exercise (short-term, long-term)

See pages 282–285 for information on the effects of exercise.

Respiratory system

Structure

The respiratory system is a series of linked organs connected with breathing. Air enters the nose or mouth, passes through the pharynx and larynx (which produces sounds for speech), then carries on down the trachea (windpipe). When it gets down into the chest the windpipe splits into two tubes called bronchi, which go into the lungs. The lungs are large spongy organs containing millions of little sacs called alveoli.

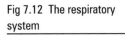

Fig 7.12 The respiratory
system

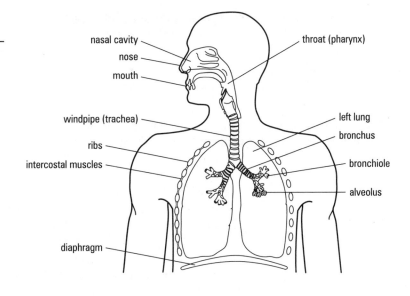

The lungs, which are soft and delicate, are protected by the ribs. The ribs are joined
by sheets of intercostal ('between the ribs') muscle which enable them to rise and
fall. Underneath the lungs, positioned horizontally like a table mat, is another sheet of
muscle called the diaphragm which rises and falls as we breathe, pushing air out of the
lungs and pulling it in again.

Function

In the walls of the alveoli are countless tiny blood vessels with walls so thin that gas can
be released and absorbed through them. The blood that arrives in the lungs from the
heart is full of carbon dioxide, which is a waste produce from the body's **metabolism**.
This is released into the lungs in the form of gas. Once this has happened, the blood
absorbs the oxygen we have breathed in and carries it off into the body, where it
is needed. This exchange of oxygen for carbon dioxide is the main function of the
respiratory system.

Other functions are:

■ to enable us to make sounds which we use in speech (As we breathe out we can
generate sounds in the vocal cords of the larynx. These sounds vary in pitch and are
modulated by the throat, lips, teeth, tongue and soft palate to make speech.)

■ to help to keep us cool.

Mechanics of breathing (inspiration and expiration)

Breathing consists of inspiration (breathing in) and expiration (breathing out). The basic
principle is that, when we make more space in our chest, air flows in, and, when we
make less space in our chest, air flows out again. We make space in our chest by two
methods:

■ by moving the diaphragm downwards

■ by moving the ribcage outwards.

The diaphragm is a sheet of muscle which lies roughly horizontally under the lungs.
When it pushes downwards, it makes more space in the chest cavity; this allows air to
flow into the lungs and inflate them. After several seconds, when the oxygen has been

taken from the air and replaced with carbon dioxide, the diaphragm rises and squeezes the 'used' air out again, so that it can be replaced with fresh, oxygen-rich air.

It is also possible to breathe by pushing the ribcage upwards and outwards, using the intercostals, muscles which lie between the ribs. This makes more space in the chest cavity. Once again, air flows into the lungs, inflating them to fill the extra space, and the exchange of oxygen for carbon dioxide takes place in the lungs.

Under normal conditions, breathing with the diaphragm is more effective than breathing with the ribcage, although we usually do a combination of both. 'Breathing exercises' often concentrate on making proper use of the diaphragm. It is interesting that, although breathing is an automatic process which goes on even when we are asleep or unconscious, we do have conscious control of it, for example when we speak or sing.

When we breathe in, air passes through the nose and nasal cavity, or the mouth. This has the effect of humidifying (moistening) the air and warming it, so that it is less likely to damage the delicate lining of the lungs. Inside the bronchi and trachea, cilia (microscopic hairs) and a coating of **mucus** trap dust and other foreign bodies so that they cannot lodge in the lungs. The movements of the cilia gradually push this trapped dust out of the respiratory system altogether.

activity
GROUP WORK
7.1

P1

M1

1 Produce wallcharts showing (and labelling) the muscular-skeletal, cardiovascular and respiratory systems; the charts should be suitable for a gym used by students.

2 Produce posters for the same gym, explaining the effects of exercise on these body systems.

Effects of exercise on the systems

Exercise has both short- and long-term effects on the muscular, cardiovascular and respiratory systems.

Short-term, immediate effects

The effects on the muscular system are that there is rapid, forceful movement which generates heat; at the same time, energy is generated in the muscles by metabolic (chemical) processes that turn fat and glucose into energy. When the exercise is over, there may be muscular shakiness or pain caused by depletion of glucose and other chemicals, a build-up of lactic acid, or tiny muscular injuries. Excess heat is got rid of mainly by sweating.

Link

See page 284 below for a description of the processes that turn fat and glucose into energy.

When we exercise, the behaviour of the heart and the blood vessels automatically changes in order to give each part of the body what it needs. This means changing the flow of blood to different parts of the body – a process which is called redistribution.

When we are resting, blood goes to the digestive system, the urinary system, the liver, and various other organs and glands which keep the body functioning properly. However, when we exercise the body has different priorities. Blood flows faster to the lungs because we need more oxygen in our blood. It flows faster to the muscles because they are doing extra work and need extra oxygen to keep going. Blood also flows faster to the skin because muscular movement generates more heat than the body needs, and if the blood is in the skin it cools down because it is close to the air. Not only that: the blood in the skin stimulates sweat glands that cool us down by moistening our skin, which then loses heat as the moisture evaporates.

Raised heart rate
A person's resting pulse rate is typically around 70 beats per minute (bpm), but sportspeople and others who get a lot of exercise may have slower resting pulse rates – down to 55 bpm or below.

Whatever the resting pulse rate, it accelerates as soon as we move, and a young person who is really working at it can raise the **heart rate** to nearly three times the resting rate.

The fastest pulse rate that a person can achieve is called the maximum heart rate. For a healthy person, the maximum can be found by using this formula: 220 – (age). A healthy person of 17 therefore has a maximum heart rate of 220 – 17 = 203. (This maximum can only be maintained for a short time.)

Increased respiration
Breathing gets faster and deeper when we exercise, to supply the oxygen that muscles need to generate energy. In aerobic exercise, we get energy from chemical reactions between oxygen and glucose, which comes from carbohydrate foods or from 'fat-burning' during exercise. The high energy needs of active muscles mean that extra oxygen is needed.

Differences between aerobic and anaerobic respiration
'Aerobic' means 'using air'; '**anaerobic**' means 'without using air'. The words are now connected with two different kinds of training. Aerobic training involves activities that last a long time, such as distance running, jogging, long-distance swimming, fast walking, aerobics and the kind of energy you might use in digging a garden. Anaerobic training consists of short bursts of powerful activity, such as weightlifting (when the weights are heavy) shot-putting, javelin-throwing, high-jump and the 100-metre sprint. In the two kinds of training, different '**energy pathways**' send energy to the muscles. They also involve the use of different kinds of muscle cell: aerobic training uses the slow-twitch cells, while anaerobic training uses the fast-twitch cells.

Energy is stored in the body in two forms:

- fat
- glycogen.

Fig 7.13 Fat vs. glycogen

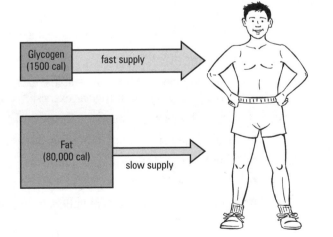

Glycogen is stored in smallish amounts in muscles and liver, and comes from eating carbohydrates. Fat is slowly produced in the body from all the calorific foods we eat, and if the energy isn't used up the body stores it.

Glycogen acts quickly and can be used even when the body is getting no extra oxygen. Fat acts slowly and cannot be turned into energy without the addition of large amounts of oxygen. Thus, in anaerobic activity the body 'burns' glycogen, and in aerobic activity it 'burns' fat.

If we want a sudden burst of energy, we burn glycogen. It creates more energy than fat, but only for a short time. If we want a steady supply of energy for hour after hour, or even day after day, we use fat.

Energy pathways
Using the anaerobic pathway, glycogen energises the muscles in 2–3 seconds. Through the aerobic pathway, fat takes 20 minutes to be broken down into a form where it can be used by the muscles as an energy source. However, the total amount of aerobic energy available in the human body is vast. It gives people huge reserves of endurance, and it has been said (although not proved) that, if a person and a horse set out to walk round the world, the horse will drop dead of exhaustion first.

With gentle or moderate physical activity lasting over 20 minutes, nearly all the body's energy needs are satisfied by the aerobic energy pathway. In this pathway, fat is changed with the help of oxygen into glucose, then glycogen, then adenosine triphosphate (**ATP**).

When physical activity is above a certain intensity (e.g. in power lifting), the aerobic energy pathway alone cannot supply the body's needs. At this point (when the heart rate is around 80–90% of its maximum) the so-called 'anaerobic threshold' is reached, and the anaerobic energy path starts working. Glycogen which is already in the blood and the muscles is then rapidly changed (using a different chemical reaction) into ATP without the need for oxygen. This produces a quick rush of energy, as the muscles use this sudden supply of ATP. In fact, however, the total amount of energy provided by the glycogen, when it is changed to ATP anaerobically, is much less than if it was changed more slowly into ATP using the oxygen in the bloodstream. It is a case of less energy being released more quickly, giving a few valuable seconds of power.

There is a third pathway by which energy reaches the muscles. This is also anaerobic and uses a combination of ATP and another chemical called creatine phosphate. Creatine phosphate gives extra energy in the first few seconds of a major effort if the ATP in the muscles is getting used up. Once again, the amount of energy is small compared with aerobically produced energy, but it gets into the muscles much more quickly.

Blood flow
Faster and more powerful beating of the heart during exercise increases the blood flow to the muscles, where it is urgently needed. The heart also sends more blood to the lungs through the pulmonary artery to pick up more oxygen, more quickly. To fulfil these needs, blood pressure rises during exercise. However, in a healthy, fit person both heart rate and blood pressure go down again once the exercise stops.

Long-term effects

The long-term effects of regular, suitable exercise are very beneficial to health. Research in the USA has shown that regular exercise:

- reduces the risk of dying prematurely
- reduces the risk of dying from heart disease
- reduces the risk of developing **diabetes**
- reduces the risk of developing high blood pressure
- helps reduce blood pressure in people who already have high blood pressure

- reduces the risk of developing colon cancer
- reduces feelings of depression and anxiety
- helps control weight
- helps build and maintain healthy bones, muscles, and joints
- helps older adults become stronger and better able to move about without falling
- promotes psychological well-being (www.cdc.gov).

Improved muscle tone

Good muscle **tone** means that the same mass of muscle works more efficiently and/or powerfully than it does if muscle tone is poor. This is related to the ability of the muscle to **metabolise** glycogen and ATP to produce energy. Regular exercise builds up this ability by allowing tiny, energy-producing bodies called **mitochondria** to multiply inside the cell and increase the energy supply. Muscle tone is then good.

The improved tone is linked to greater efficiency; this is thought to come from an increase in the number of mitochondria, which convert the chemical adenosine triphosphate (ATP), which comes from glycogen, more rapidly and effectively into energy.

Lowered heart rate and blood pressure

Regular exercise strengthens the heart and enables it to pump more blood with each beat. The heart rate slows down, but the muscles still get the same amount of blood. Exercise lowers blood pressure in the long term by widening the blood vessels and making them work more effectively.

remember Regular exercise is good for fitness and has no bad health effects.

Improved strength

Regular anaerobic (intense) exercise together with a good **diet** increase the quantity and effectiveness of fast-twitch muscle cells, which increases muscle strength.

Stamina

Regular aerobic exercise improves stamina by making the heart and blood vessels work better, and by developing lung capacity and efficiency. A further advantage is that it encourages the development of mitochondria and slow-twitch muscle cells.

Weight

Aerobic exercise uses up **calories** and then changes the body's stored fat into glycogen. The effect of this 'fat burning' is to reduce body weight if, over a period of time, the number of calories used is greater than the number of calories taken in with food. Exercise is a healthy way of maintaining a steady body weight, if the calories used match the calories eaten.

Cholesterol

This is a kind of fat which occurs in animal fats, saturated (hard) fats, and '**trans fats**'. Many people eat too much of these kinds of fat and exercise too little. As a result, some people suffer from deposits of fat in the arteries; this raises blood pressure and inhibits the flow of blood to the parts of body where it is needed. In the long term, this is bad for health and increases the risk of heart attacks and **strokes**.

remember We all need some saturated fat, but some people eat too much of it.

Digestion

Moderate exercise is good for digestion and is thought to reduce the long-term risk of bowel cancer.

The effects of lifestyle factors on health and fitness

Lifestyle factors

People who have been recruiting into the armed forces over many years often claim that today's young people are less fit than their predecessors of 20 or more years ago. Whether this is true is hard to prove, but there is general agreement among medical experts that young people in Britain are, on average, not as healthy and fit as they should be. A number of reasons for this are put forward, related to **lifestyle**.

Physical activity

It is believed that many people do not do enough physical activity to be as healthy and fit as they should be. Activity is good for health and essential for fitness (see above and below).

Smoking

Medical research and statistics show that smoking is bad for your health and fitness. The biggest single collection of information about the health effects of smoking is found in *The Health Consequences of Smoking*, a 460-page report produced by the Surgeon General in the USA in 2004. It contains the statements shown in the following case study.

The statistics in the report relate to the USA, but the underlying message appears to be true of smoking everywhere.

Passive smoking

Another US government report has this to say on passive smoking:

'Secondhand smoke is similar to the mainstream smoke inhaled by the smoker in that it is a complex mixture containing many chemicals (including formaldehyde, cyanide, carbon monoxide, ammonia, and nicotine), many of which are known carcinogens. Exposure to secondhand smoke causes excess deaths in the U.S. population from lung cancer and cardiac related illnesses.'

(Source: www.cdc.gov)

Fig 7.14 Are people less fit than they used to be?

Health is defined by the World Health Organization as 'a state of complete physical, mental and social well-being and not merely the absence of disease or infirmity'. Fitness is defined as: 'good health or physical condition, especially as the result of exercise and proper nutrition'.

case study 7.1 — The health consequences of smoking

(a) Smoking harms nearly every organ of the body, causing many diseases and reducing the health of smokers in general.

(b) Smoking causes cancers of the mouth, throat, larynx (voice box), lung, esophagus, pancreas, kidney, and bladder.

Smoking causes cancers of the stomach, cervix, and acute myeloid leukemia, which is a cancer of the blood.

Cigarette smoking causes most cases of lung cancer. Smokers are about 20 times more likely to develop lung cancer than nonsmokers. Smoking causes about 90 percent of lung cancer deaths in men and almost 80 percent in women.

(c) Cigarette smoking during childhood and adolescence produces significant health problems among young people, including cough and phlegm production, an increased number and severity of respiratory illnesses, decreased physical fitness, an unfavorable lipid profile, and potential retardation in the rate of lung growth and the level of maximum lung function.

(d) Smoking harms your whole body. It increases your risk of fractures, dental diseases, sexual problems, eye diseases, and peptic ulcers.

If you smoke, your illnesses last longer and you are more likely to be absent from work. In a study of U.S. military personnel, those who smoked were hospitalized 28 percent to 55 percent longer than nonsmokers. And the more cigarettes they smoked, the longer their hospitalization.

(Source: *The Health Consequences of Smoking: The 2004 Surgeon General's Report: What it Means to You*. Statements (a), (b), and (c) come from the report itself; (d) comes from a leaflet giving the main findings.)

activity
INDIVIDUAL WORK

1 Why are doctors and scientists now so certain that smoking is harmful?

2 Does the government have a right to try and stop people from smoking?

Alcohol

Research on alcohol has produced plenty of evidence that – in large amounts – it is harmful to health. Most of the concern has centred on binge drinking – often among young people – and the effects of regular heavy drinking over a long period of time.

There is disagreement among the experts as to whether or not small amounts of alcohol are harmful to health. There is no evidence that it produces any benefits to health or fitness among young people.

Heavy drinking can lead to accidental or other deaths in young people. Special risks are accidents, especially road accidents, and manslaughter and suicide. Young people are not at high risk of dying, but those who do die are relatively likely to do so as a result of drinking too much. In addition, heavy alcohol use is likely to be linked to heavy smoking and drug abuse, as part of a pattern of risky behaviour. Alcohol and drugs are a dangerous combination which can lead to accidental death, choking, etc. In later life, alcohol abuse can lead to diabetes, heart disease and liver disease, including cancer of the liver.

Unbiased advice on the health effects of alcohol is relatively hard to find in the UK. Research by teams partly sponsored by the drinks industry, and cooperation in government policy by the Portman Group, also sponsored by the drinks industry, together with the fact that advice on alcohol use by the US government is stricter than similar advice given by the British government, means that viewpoints appear contradictory. If you are investigating this topic, obtain information from a number of sources before making up your mind.

Drugs (recreational, performance-enhancing)

From a scientific or medical point of view, it is quite hard to discover the true effects of recreational drugs and steroids on health and fitness. This is because the substances are mainly illegal; and, although many trials have been carried out (sometimes on animals) to determine their **toxicity** or whether they cause cancer, these have not always been conclusive and relate to health rather than fitness. Surveys are also likely to be inconclusive since these can depend on people's feelings and opinions, rather than medical facts. Research is often carried out by organisations which may be biased, either for commercial or political reasons, and results can be contradictory. For example, the downgrading of cannabis to a class C drug in 2004 was followed by a rush of research suggesting that cannabis was much more dangerous than previously thought. Was the research politically motivated by a desire to prove the government wrong – or had the government really made a mistake? These are the kinds of questions that get asked about recreational drug research.

People who work with recreational drug users report the following negative effects:

- Barbiturates cause about one-third of drug-related deaths, mainly due to overdose or suicide. The addiction is psychological, but **withdrawal** is difficult.

- Cannabis causes **psychological addiction**; it impairs judgement and can lead to accidents; it may affect mental powers of concentration; it may damage sperm quality. When cannabis is smoked with tobacco, there are serious health risks from the tobacco.

- Cocaine – there is risk of agitation, paranoia and violence in the short term; and hallucinations, delusions, and loss of interest in sex.

- Ecstasy – short-term effects include increases in heart rate and blood pressure; and feelings of paranoia. There have been a few sudden ecstasy-related deaths due to **hyperthermia**, excessive water intake or from unknown causes. Long-term effects are not well known.

- Heroin – the main risks are overdose (because the purity varies); HIV and **hepatitis** B and C infection from sharing needles. It is dangerous for pregnant women and their babies. The drug is extremely addictive.

- LSD – is a hallucinogenic; it impairs judgement and can cause accidents.

- Methadone is highly addictive, with a risk of overdose.

- Psilocybe ('magic') mushrooms can cause vomiting, nausea or stomach pains.

- Tranquillisers are addictive; they cause drowsiness, and therefore accidents; risk of overdose leading to death (www.recovery.org.uk).

Recreational drugs are said to produce feelings of well-being, but not the 'complete well-being' of the WHO definition of health (see page 286).

remember

Research on many of these drugs is incomplete – especially as regards their long-term effects. They are all classified.

Link   See page 292 for drug classifications.

Anabolic steroids

These are body-building drugs which are taken not primarily for pleasure but to increase muscle bulk and improve athletic performance. **Anabolic** steroids are related to hormones, which are produced naturally in the human body, and for this reason can be hard to detect. Since the hormones that they resemble are sex-linked hormones, their alleged negative effects tend to be sex-linked.

Taking steroids is illegal and unsporting.

As with some other drugs, there is a lack of certainty about their long-term consequences and side effects. Anabolic steroids are said, among other things, to reduce fertility in men and cause excessive growth of body hair in women. The drugs cause short stature (height) if taken by people who haven't finished growing. There is an increased risk of liver disease and heart attacks with prolonged use.

Since anabolic steroids increase muscle bulk, they increase strength; and it is possible (judging by steroid abuse in the sporting world) that they enhance performance.

Cyswllt Ceredigion Contact

www.recovery.org.uk

National Institute on Drug Abuse

www.nida.nih.gov

How Much is Too Much? Drinking and You (Department of Health, 2005)

www.dh.gov.uk

Action on Smoking and Health (ASH)

www.ash.org.uk

Stress

This is the name given to a series of illnesses, or levels of ill health, linked to such factors as overwork, anxiety, low self-esteem or a perceived lack of control over our lives. The word is confusing because it is used in many different ways. Stress can sometimes show itself in bad temper or worry, where the sufferer is conscious of being under stress. However, it can also show itself in things like asthma and skin conditions, where the sufferer is not necessarily aware of being under stress. A related condition is post-traumatic stress disorder (PTSD); this affects some people after a shocking event, when, usually about six months later, they begin to experience panic attacks, flashbacks, nightmares and other unpleasant symptoms.

Stress has bad effects on health, because good mental health is needed if a person is to have good physical health as well. Long-term stress is thought to contribute to cancer and heart disease, and it may be a factor in alcoholism, drug abuse and some mental illnesses.

Conditions that result from a mental state are sometimes called '**psychosomatic**' illnesses, and stress could be described as one of these. Curing stress is not easy. Possible approaches are:

- eliminating the stressor (cause of stress) by, for example, changing jobs, changing work habits, achieving a better work–life balance, tackling a problem of harassment, etc.
- using meditation and other thinking techniques
- taking up rewarding leisure pursuits
- taking up a sport or regular exercise
- having counselling
- taking medicines prescribed by a doctor.

Diet

A good diet is essential for good long-term health.

Requirements

The main requirements of a good diet are that it should be balanced and in the right quantity for the individual's needs. A balanced diet is one which has the right amounts of different kinds of food to cover the body's needs. Food is divided into groups, all of which are needed by the body, but the groups must be in the right relative quantities.

Recommendations

Nutritionists have identified five food groups which are needed in a healthy diet. If all five food groups are present in the right amounts, then we have a good balanced diet.

Group 1: Bread, cereal and potatoes

These unrefined carbohydrates should make up nearly 50% of a healthy diet. They provide energy which, because the carbohydrates are complex, is released at a steady, sustaining pace. These foods also provide plenty of fibre. Fibre is not a nutrient, but it helps in the digestion and absorption of food, and it helps to keep the intestines healthy (e.g. by lowering the risk of bowel cancer).

Group 2: Fruit and vegetables

These should be the next largest part of a healthy diet after Group 1. British experts recommend five pieces of fruit/portions of vegetables a day (i.e. five in all, including both fruit and vegetables). They are a necessary source of vitamins, minerals and fibre, contain only natural sugars and are relatively low in calories.

Group 3: Meat, fish, eggs and alternatives

These foods should make up 10–15% of a healthy diet. They are needed for protein, which helps the body to grow and repair itself, and promotes natural muscle development. The 'alternatives' are vegetarian foods such as beans and nuts, but these should be supplemented with milk, eggs or cheese for a top-class protein intake. These foods also contain some necessary vitamins and minerals.

Group 4: Milk and dairy

These are a source of protein and fats. The equivalent of one pint of milk provides the body's calcium needs (calcium is essential for healthy bones). Younger people may need more dairy foods than older people. Semi-skimmed or skimmed milk contains the same amount of protein and calcium as whole milk.

Group 5: Fats and sugars

These are a source of energy, and fats contain some vitamins. Hard (saturated) fats increase the risk of heart disease, so vegetable or fish oils are better from a health point of view. Fats/oils are needed by the body so must not be excluded from the diet. In the USA, the recommendation is that 27% of calories should come from fats/oils (which means a small amount of fat, because fat is highly calorific). Sugar is a luxury, and white sugar, although providing a 'rush' of calories, has little nutritional value.

Table 7.1 Rough proportions of food groups for a balanced diet (British)

Food group	Quantity
Bread, cereal, potatoes, rice	11
Vegetables, fruit	9
Meat, fish, eggs and alternatives	7
Milk and dairy	3
Fat and sugar	5
Total	35

Water and salt

Water and salt are not nutrients in the strict sense, as they are not broken down chemically in the body as, say, fats and carbohydrates are. However, both are essential for life. Water makes up more than half a person's weight and is the medium in which most of the body's metabolism (chemical reactions) takes place. All the body systems depend on water (e.g. the lungs could not absorb oxygen if their lining was not moist, and blood would not be liquid without water). Water is used in digestion, temperature regulation, and as a solvent for nutrients and other chemicals. For a 'normal' day an 'average' adult needs to drink two litres of water (either as water itself or as nonalcoholic drinks). Additional water comes in food. In hot weather, or when taking part in strenuous activity, people need to drink extra water to replace water lost by sweating.

Salt (sodium chloride) is necessary for life. It is through salt that the body controls its water content and maintains the right amount of water in the cells. Messages pass through the nerves and the brain thanks to the movement of electrically charged sodium ions – from dissolved salt – through cell membranes. The UK government recommends that adults eat 6 gm of salt per day, but many of us eat much more than this. The result of eating too much salt (much of which is added to manufactured food) can be raised blood pressure and, in the long term, increased risk of heart attacks and kidney disease.

Nutrition

This is the study of the chemicals in food and the effects that they have on the human body. 'Chemicals' here include carbohydrates (sugars and starches), proteins (meat, fish, beans, etc.), fats, vitamins and minerals. Different lifestyles have different nutritional needs. Young active people benefit from eating plenty of protein because it helps growth and develops muscles. Athletes need plenty of carbohydrates while they are training to replace the energy lost. Older people who take little exercise should cut down on fats and sugars. Vitamins (e.g. vitamin C) are **organic compounds** which are needed for good health; their best source is natural foods although some people take them in supplements. Minerals are a complex subject: examples are calcium, magnesium and iron (in the form of naturally occurring compounds); they are mainly needed in small amounts. Food packaging often has minerals listed with a **Referent Nutrient Index** giving guidance on how much of that mineral is provided in the product, in relation to the recommended daily needs.

Personal hygiene

A reasonable level of personal hygiene is needed for good health. This includes eating clean, fresh food; washing your hands fairly often; avoiding contact with health hazards, such as infected blood or toxic chemicals; wearing protective clothing, etc. when necessary; and visiting the doctor and dentist at sensible intervals, or if anything appears to be wrong with your health.

> **remember**
>
> Diets which are not balanced damage health and fitness.

---

activity

INDIVIDUAL WORK 7.2

P2

M2

1 Produce a factsheet, PowerPoint presentation or similar teaching aid, outlining the lifestyle factors that can affect health and fitness, and the effects that these can have.

2 Use the aid in giving a presentation suitable for school leavers, explaining the effects that lifestyle factors can have on health and fitness when applying for a uniformed public service and in long-term employment.

Effects

Physical activity

Physical and psychological health benefits

See pages 282–285 above for physical effects on health.

Psychological benefits are that physical activity relieves stress and gives enjoyment and a sense of achievement. It is also a creative way of getting rid of spare aggression, and it uses and encourages the development of many intellectual skills.

Social benefits

Games and sports are natural social activities which help us to learn about ourselves and other people, and to make friends. They are an enjoyable way of improving our social, communication and teamwork skills.

Smoking, alcohol, drugs (health risks)

See pages 286–289 above for the effects on health.

Policies of the uniformed public services

The uniformed public services allow the consumption of legal drugs such as alcohol, tobacco and caffeine, but they do not allow their members to use the drugs listed in Table 7.2.

Table 7.2 Drug classification (Classes A–C)

Class	Drug
A	Ecstasy, heroin, cocaine
B	Amphetamines
C	Cannabis, stimulants, tranquillisers, some painkillers

In addition, many prohibited drugs come under the heading of steroids: some are classified as A, some as B and some as C.

The army, for example, has compulsory drug testing, and encourages soldiers to secretly report their comrades if they think that they are taking illegal drugs. Soldiers found guilty of drug-taking are liable to be **discharged**. Applicants tested and found to have drugs in the bloodstream will not be accepted.

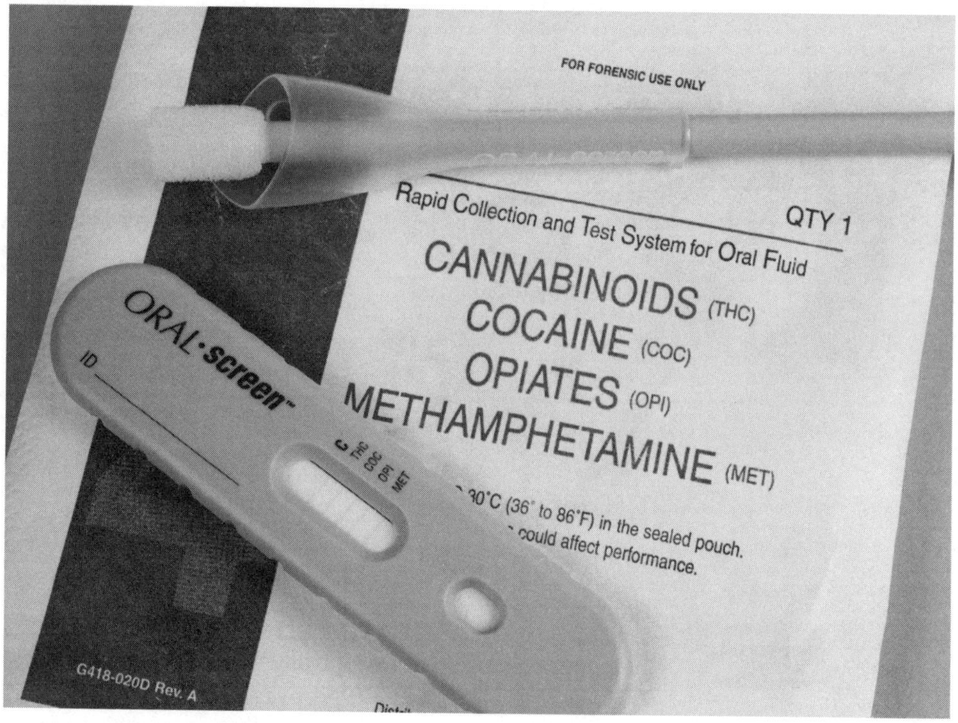

Fig 7.15 Drug test

FOR FORENSIC USE ONLY

Rapid Collection and Test System for Oral Fluid   QTY 1

CANNABINOIDS (THC)
COCAINE (COC)
OPIATES (OPI)
METHAMPHETAMINE (MET)

ORAL·screen™

ID

G418-020D Rev. A

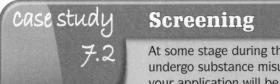

case study 7.2

Screening

At some stage during the recruitment process all applicants will be required to undergo substance misuse screening. If the outcome of such a test is positive then your application will be terminated.

(Source: www.westyorksfire.gov.uk)

activity
INDIVIDUAL WORK

What scientific or medical reasons justify this approach by the West Yorkshire Fire and Rescue Service?

Stress, e.g. physical and mental health risks; post-traumatic stress disorder

See page 289 above.

Diet

The benefits of a healthy diet are feeling well and tending to be in better health. It is easier to become fit and indeed strong on a good diet. People who eat a balanced diet are likely to live longer, are less likely to suffer from heart disease and some kinds of cancer, and are better able to be the weight they want to be. The effects of poor nutrition include tiredness, lack of vitality, inability to get fit, weight problems, problems with mental concentration and health problems in later life. People who eat a healthy diet are not certain to be healthy, but people who eat poor nutrition are certain to suffer from it.

Personal hygiene

See page 291 above for personal hygiene in general.

Possible infections while on public service operations include tropical diseases, such as malaria and various **water-borne infections**, and a risk of sexually transmitted diseases such as HIV-Aids, syphilis, gonorrhoea, hepatitis, etc. Precautions can and should be taken to avoid all of these, since they are seriously damaging to long-term health and can be fatal.

Importance of body weight

Although the uniformed services have abolished height restrictions, they still expect applicants to be roughly the right weight for their height.

The 'right weight for height' is calculated using a formula which gives a number called a **Body Mass Index** (**BMI**). The calculation can be done online (see www.cdc.gov), or you can use the following formulae.

Metric measurements	weight ÷ (height)^2
Imperial measurements	weight ÷ (height)^2 × 703

The other way to find out if you are the right weight for your height is (a) measure your own height and weight and (b) compare them with ideal (not average) heights and weights on a chart, like the one published by the **Food Standards Agency** (www.food.gov.uk).

Table 7.3 Body Mass Index for a person of 5′ 9″

Height	Weight range	BMI	Considered
5′ 9″	124 lbs or less	Below 18.5	Underweight
	125 lbs to 168 lbs	18.5 to 24.9	Healthy weight
	169 lbs to 202 lbs	25.0 to 29.9	Overweight
	203 lbs or more	30 or higher	Obese

(Source: www.cdc.gov)

Obesity is defined as having a BMI of 30 or above (i.e. about 40% above the ideal weight).

The ideal weight is a weight determined by life-expectancy figures gathered over many years. In Table 7.3, the weight range considered 'healthy' is the range of weights at which people of that height have the longest life expectancy.

Body composition
It is possible for people who are overweight to improve body composition (i.e. the BMI) by a combination of aerobic exercise and some form of diet. The diet should be balanced, and in no way should it be a 'crash diet', as this is bad for health and fitness. The aim should be to reduce weight slowly, but in such a way that it won't be put on again. Usually, this isn't a matter of eating less but of eating more healthily, replacing sweets with fruits and eating 'complex' carbohydrates, such as potatoes, instead of sugary foods. Cutting down (but not completely) on fat is also a good idea. People with a low BMI who wish to join a public service should probably get advice from a professional on the best way to get into the 'acceptable' range.

See pages 301 and 302 for more on body composition.

Centres for Disease Control and Prevention – see website for general fitness information
www.cdc.gov
The University of New Mexico – see website for general fitness information
www.unm.edu
Better Health – see website for quality consumer health information for Australians
www.betterhealth.vic.gov.au
The President's Council on Physical Fitness and Sports
www.fitness.gov

Planning a fitness training programme to prepare for uniformed public service

The armed forces, the fire and rescue service, the police and the prison service all have fitness tests for applicants. All members of the services have to take and pass these tests. This is not normally the case for civilian employees of these services, who simply have a medical examination – even though some (for example community support officers and many ambulance staff) do require a good level of fitness and, sometimes, strength.

Since most people can greatly improve their fitness by suitable training, it makes sense to know how to train and prepare beforehand and to work out a training **programme**.

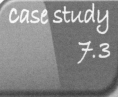

Entry fitness requirements for uniformed public services

Here is an outline of some of the main fitness tests for uniformed public services.

Police

The police fitness test is very simple, and has two elements.

The test should be run in the following order and to the following standards:

Endurance fitness (bleep test)	Level 5/4
Dynamic strength test	Push 34 kgs; pull 35 kgs.

The standards apply to both male and female candidates (*Home Office Circular 2*, August 2004).

Prison service

---

case study 7.3

Fitness tests for the prison service

The tests are:

1. Height and Weight

We'll measure your height and your weight to find out your Body Mass Index, which will tell us if you're overweight or not. If you are overweight, we'll let you how much weight you need to lose to join us and advise you on the best way to reach your target. This is as much in your interest as ours because being within the right weight limits will make you healthier as well as helping you pass the next tests.

2. Grip Strength

For this test, we'll measure the strength of your forearm muscles by asking you to squeeze a measuring device as tightly as you can in one hand at a time.

3. Endurance Shuttle Run

To find out how well your energy lasts, we'll ask you to run faster and faster over a 15-metre course until you reach your target level.

4. Dyno

Here, we want to know how strong your upper arms and upper body are. So we'll ask you to do some pulling and pushing.

5. Speed Agility

Prison Officers have to be able to run from one part of the prison to another. So, to test your ability to do that, we'll ask you to run round an obstacle course and change direction quickly.

6. Shield

This test involves holding a 6-kilogram shield and practising control and restraining techniques.

(Source: www.hmprisonservice.gov.uk)

---

activity
INDIVIDUAL WORK

1   Which of these are tests of **health-related fitness** and which are tests of job- or **skill-related fitness**?

2   Which of these tests might discriminate against women applicants?

Armed forces

Soldier entry tests have two parts to them: the Physical Selection Standards for Recruits (PSSR), which are carried out in the gym, and a 1.5-mile run which is done on the next day. The PSSR tests are partly tests of fitness and strength, including weightlifting, and partly **job-related fitness** (e.g. a 'jerry can carry'). The 1.5-mile run has to be done in under 14 minutes. The PSSR tests can vary in order to suit the kind of work done in the unit that the entrant is applying for.

Army Officer entrants have to do a 500-m run and a 'beep test' (multi-stage fitness test). They also have to do 50 sit-ups in two minutes. Males have to do 44 press-ups while female entrants have to do 21 press-ups. Entry fitness tests for army officers are the same whatever unit they are going into.

Reasons for differences between entry requirements for different public services

The reasons for the differences are quite complex, and some are traditional. Before 2003, for example, there was no physical entry test for Royal Navy applicants. In June of that year, a Pre-entry Joining Fitness Test (PJFT) was introduced, similar to the entry fitness test for soldiers, with a 1.5- (2.4-km) mile run on a running machine. Pass times vary according to the age and gender of the applicant. The same test is used for 'Other Ranks' in the Royal Marines.

Differences in the fitness entry requirements for different public services depend on:

- the traditions of the service
- the importance of physical fitness in the work of that service
- the nature of the work done
- the need to avoid discriminatory testing (e.g. between male and female applicants)
- the fact that a few branches of the armed forces, such as the Royal Marines and the Infantry, are still all-male.

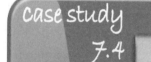

case study 7.4   RAF entry fitness test

When you attend the Officers and Aircrew Selection Centre (OASC), you will take a fitness assessment.

The first stage of the fitness assessment consists of completing as many 20-metre shuttle runs as you can – at a steadily increasing speed. The pace is set by a series of electronic bleeps, and for this reason the assessment is often called the 'bleep test'.

You will then have to perform as many press-ups and sit-ups as you can in one minute.

(Source: www.raf.mod.uk)

activity
GROUP WORK

1 Officers and aircrew have the same fitness assessment. Why do you think this is the case?

2 What is the relevance of physical fitness to the work of the RAF?

3 Why do you think there are no job-related fitness elements in this test?

Royal Airforce
www.raf.mod.uk
South Yorkshire Police
www.southyorks.police.uk
HM Prison Service
www.hmprisonservice.gov.uk
Fire Gateway
www.fire.gov.uk

The different stages of the fitness tests and any differences between entry levels

Fitness tests are broken up into stages. Each stage tests a different aspect of fitness. Many tests are divided into health-related **components of fitness**, where the fitness being tested is to do with the applicant's endurance or strength (see more below), and skills-related fitness, where learnable abilities such as agility and dexterity are tested.

The difference between soldier and officer entry in the army

See above, page 296.

Reasons for the inclusion of particular tests within public services

Public service fitness tests are intended to be job related; in other words, they test abilities which are of practical use in that service.

It is also important for civilian public services that the physical entry tests are not discriminatory, either against women or against people from ethnic minorities who may have (on average) different physiques from most white male applicants. This is why height restrictions were abolished in the 1990s. More recently, a police agility test was dropped, both because it appeared to discriminate against women and because it was hard to prove that policing, as a job, required special levels of agility.

The main reasons for including particular tests are:

- Relevance to the job – if the test tests health-related fitness, it has to be a kind of fitness which would help the applicant to do the job well. If it tests job-related or skill-related fitness, the test is really an **aptitude test**, testing how well the applicant is likely to pick up certain necessary skills in initial training.

- Health and safety – over the years, public services have sometimes been criticised for using test items which are dangerous and put applicants at risk of injury. These tests have largely been eliminated (and applicants are reminded that they should have their own medical examination, and fitness training, before they reach the application stage).

- Equal opportunities – some services used to have fitness tests which discriminated against women applicants (e.g. by being easier for tall people to do). These have been phased out, and test items are now less '**gender specific**'.

> **remember**
>
> Fitness tests for the armed forces and the fire and rescue service are more difficult than the others.

Strength tests are included for soldiers because their work requires physical strength as well as endurance. They have to carry heavy packs, unload lorries and handle machinery. Young applicants who are physically fit but have not yet reached their full potential strength are sometimes told to develop their strength and reapply in a year or so.

Individual assessment of entry fitness for a chosen public service

To assess your own fitness against the fitness required to enter a chosen public service you should get the help of a qualified physical training (PT) instructor, or someone who

case study 7.5

Fire and rescue service

Physical tests

This section consists of six different tests which assess an applicant's **physical competence** and their confidence and ability to follow instructions.

Ladder Climb

This is a physical test of confidence and the ability to follow instructions. Applicants must ascend a 13.5 metre (45 foot) Fire & Rescue Service ladder to a point two thirds of the full working height, take a leg lock and remove their hands from the ladder and look down to the assessor to identify a symbol placed flat on the ground at the foot of the ladder. Applicants will be assisted if necessary by the safety officer.

Casualty Evacuation

This is a physical test of upper and lower body strength and co-ordination. A 55 kg (8½ stone) dummy is dragged backwards around a 30 metre (100 foot) course around four cones guided by a safety officer. Applicants will need to complete this exercise in a given amount of time.

Ladder Lift

This is a physical test of upper and lower body strength and co-ordination. The bar of a ladder lift simulator weighing 30 kg (4½ stone) is to be raised to a height of 182 cm (6 foot) assisted if necessary by the safety officer.

Enclosed Space

This is a physical test of confidence, agility and identification of **claustrophobic** tendencies. Applicants wear a breathing apparatus facemask and negotiate a crawl and walkway with clear vision. Halfway through the route their vision is obscured and they retrace their steps to the start/finish point. A safety officer will provide assistance if necessary. Applicants will need to complete this exercise in a given amount of time.

Equipment Assembly

This is a physical test of manual dexterity. Applicants must assemble and then disassemble a portable pump following a demonstration by the safety officer.

Equipment Carry

This is a physical test of aerobic fitness, stamina, upper and lower body strength and co-ordination. Applicants will need to carry items of equipment over a 25 metre (82 foot) course around two cones. This is not a test of memory as the safety officer will remind applicants of the sequence of events. The equipment will consist of one 30 metre (100 foot) hosereel tubing on a drum, two coiled 70 mm soft suction hoses, one 100 mm hard suction hose and suction strainer in a basket and one 33 kg (5 stone) barbell. Applicants will need to complete this exercise in a given amount of time.

(Source: www.fire.gov.uk)

activity
GROUP WORK

1 To what extent is each of these fitness tests and to what extent are they aptitude tests?

2 Contact your local fire and rescue service and see if they will let you practise these tests.

3 Do you feel that any of these tests discriminate against female applicants and – if so – is the discrimination justified?

is involved in this stage of recruitment into a uniformed public service. In particular you may be able to get help, or arrange some practice tests, through the army, the fire and rescue service or the police. You need someone to make sure that you have the equipment you need, that the environment is safe, and that your scores are recorded. You also need to be sure that you are in good health and reasonably fit before you even start assessing your own fitness against the levels demanded by a public service. If you do a practice test, make sure that you warm up correctly before it, so that you can give of your best and reduce any risk of injury.

Tests you may have to do include 'bleep tests' (otherwise known as 'beep tests', the 'multi-stage fitness tests' or 'shuttle runs'), sit-ups and press-ups.

activity
**INDIVIDUAL WORK
7.3**

P3

Write an email to a friend who is about to leave school and wants to join a uniformed public service, outlining the entry fitness requirements and entry tests for three different uniformed services.

Components of fitness

Fitness is divided into components, or types of fitness. These types of fitness are divided into health-related fitness, which is to do simply with the efficiency of your body mechanisms and biological processes, and skill-related fitness, which is to do with your mind's ability to control what your body does.

Health-related components of fitness

A brief explanation of the health-related components of fitness is given in Case study 7.7.

These sites contain general fitness information

Top End Sports

www.topendsports.com

American Sports Medicine Institute

www.asmi.org

BUPA

www.bupa.co.uk

Department of Health

www.dh.gov.uk

National Institutes of Health

www.nih.gov

Sports Coach

www.brianmac.demon.co.uk

BBC

www.bbc.co.uk

Aerobic capacity

This is the respiratory part of '**cardiorespiratory** endurance' in Case study 7.7 on page 301. It is linked to the aerobic energy pathway. **Aerobic capacity** is the ability of the body to use oxygen.

case study 7.6 — Beep test, sit-ups and press-ups

Beep test

The test has 23 levels where each level lasts approx. one minute. Each level has a series of 20 m shuttles where the starting speed is 8.5 km/hr and increases by 0.5 km/hr at each level. On the tape a single beep indicates the end of a shuttle and 3 beeps indicates the start of the next level. The test is conducted as follows:

The place where the test is carried out must have two lines 20 m apart marked on the floor. You start at one line. The first of a pre-recorded series of beeps tells you when to start. You run back and forth ('shuttle') between the two lines. Your foot has to cross the line by the end of each shuttle. If you reach the line before the beep, you have to wait for it before you start running again.

When you are unable to reach the line you drop out, and the number of levels and shuttles completed gives you a score. Using a conversion table gives you a measure of your aerobic fitness.

Sit-ups

Lie on your back with your legs bent, knees together and feet flat on the floor.

Rest your hands on your thighs.

Sit up until the palms of your hands touch your knees.

Return to the starting position.

Press-ups

Start in the front-support position with your hands and toes on the floor and trunk, hips, arms and legs extended. Bend your arms and lower your chest to the floor. Then push your body upward as you straighten your arms, returning to the front-support position. Repeat this action rhythmically and continuously without stopping for the allotted time.

Fig 7.16 Sit-ups

Fig 7.17 Press-ups

(Source: www.brianmac.demon.co.uk).

activity
INDIVIDUAL WORK

1 What are the scientific drawbacks of the beep test as a way of assessing aerobic fitness?

2 What are the practical advantages of the beep test as a way of assessing fitness for the uniformed public services?

3 What are the advantages of press-ups and sit-ups as a way of assessing fitness?

The health-related components of fitness

Cardiorespiratory endurance – the ability to deliver oxygen and nutrients to tissues and to remove wastes, over sustained periods of time. Long runs and swims are among the methods employed in measuring this component.

Muscular strength – the ability of a muscle to exert force for a brief period of time. Upper-body strength, for example, can be measured by various weight-lifting exercises.

Muscular endurance – the ability of a muscle, or a group of muscles, to sustain repeated contractions or to continue applying force against a fixed object. Push-ups are often used to test endurance of arm and shoulder muscles.

Flexibility – the ability to move joints and use muscles through their full range of motion. The sit-and-reach test is a good measure of flexibility of the lower back and backs of the upper legs.

Body composition is often considered a component of fitness. It refers to the makeup of the body in terms of lean mass (muscle, bone, vital tissue and organs) and fat mass. An optimal ratio of fat to lean mass is an indication of fitness, and the right types of exercises will help you decrease body fat and increase or maintain muscle mass.

(Source: www.fitness.gov)

activity
INDIVIDUAL WORK

Choose a public service which interests you and note down examples of work in that public service, identifying in each case which of the above components of fitness is/are relevant.

Link See page 284 for information on the aerobic energy pathway.

A person with high aerobic capacity is particularly good at long-distance running, swimming, cycling, hill-walking and other activities requiring a steady output of energy by large muscle groups (e.g. thighs and legs) for a long period of time.

Aerobic capacity is assessed using the multi-stage fitness test. It can be given a figure by measuring VO_2 max – the maximum volume of oxygen the person is able to use while carrying out aerobic exercise.

Cardiac and vascular systems

Cardiac relates to the heart, and vascular relates to the blood vessels. Both need to be in good working order if a person is to be described as fit.

Cardiac fitness means that the heart:

- can pump a large volume of blood with each stroke
- beats relatively slowly when at rest
- beats slower than the hearts of most other people during a given **intensity** of exercise
- returns rapidly to a resting rate after exercise.

Vascular fitness means that:

- The blood vessels are wide, unclogged and able to carry the blood round the body.
- The muscles are well supplied with blood.
- Blood pressure (when the person is resting) is 120/80 or less.

Fig 7.18 Cardiovascular
fitness

Both good aerobic capacity and good cardiac and vascular systems are needed if a person is to be good at endurance activities such as distance running, long-distance cycling and hillwalking.

Strength

Strength is the ability of a person to exert a powerful force using the muscles. It is linked to the numbers of fast-twitch muscle cells that the person has, the size of the person's muscles, and the amount of training or strenuous activity the person has done. It is also linked to the number of mitochondria in a person's muscle cells. These tiny hair-like 'organelles' (bodies inside each cell) change a chemical called ATP into energy and can be developed by the right kind of training. Strength, unlike endurance, is developed by anaerobic training (and high-protein diets) and, at its maximum, involves the metabolising of carbohydrates such as glycogen into ATP without the use of oxygen.

Muscular endurance

This is the ability of the muscles to go on working for long periods of time. The main requirements for muscular endurance are:

- slow-twitch muscle cells
- large muscles
- plenty of mitochondria to generate energy.

Flexibility

This is a measure of how easily a person can bend at the joints. Exceptional flexibility is needed to reach the top in many sports, especially sports such as gymnastics, swimming and some athletic events. Unlike the other health components of fitness, flexibility is rather difficult to train, and training should be done only with professional advice, as there is a risk of permanent injury.

Body composition

For public service purposes this means the ratio (relationship) between the amount of fat in the body and the rest of the body, i.e. muscles, bones and vital organs. It is related to the Body Mass Index. There are various ways of measuring it: the skinfold test using callipers is the traditional one, although it is not 100% accurate. For fitness it is generally best if body composition falls within the 'normal' range (e.g. a BMI of 18–28), but some fit people are outside this range.

Skill-related components of fitness

These are aspects of fitness linked to the control that we have over our movements. They are connected with the health of the brain and the nervous system and of the mind (learned skills, motivation, etc.).

remember

If you are seriously interested in fitness and sport, it is worth trying to understand the basics of sports science.

Speed

Speed in running, swimming, cycling, etc. is linked to aerobic stamina, anaerobic strength, coordination, skill and motivation. Speed can be improved by training.

Reaction time

Some reactions (e.g. the kick we give if someone taps our knee or the shrinking of the eyes' pupils in bright light) are outside our control and are not components of fitness. Others – as when a runner leaves the blocks on hearing the starting pistol – are conscious and, like all skills, can be improved by practice. A quick reaction time depends on good physical health and fitness as well as on motivation, but there is probably a genetic (inborn) element as well.

Agility

This is the ability to run and change direction quickly – the quality which is shown by top footballers when dribbling past opponents. It is linked to strength, speed, motivation and balance.

Balance

Balance is controlled by the fluid in the cochlear in the inner ear. In some ways, it is a sense like hearing and sight. As a skill-related component of fitness it can be trained by practice, and it can be tested on army assault courses.

Coordination

This is the ability to string movements together or to do a number of different, controlled movements at the same time. It is learnable.

Power

Power means sudden, violent movements. A combination of strength, speed and coordination, it can be developed through training and practice.

Fitness tests

Fitness tests are measurable activities used to determine how fit someone is. There are two main approaches:

- The testing of single components – for such tests, the activities chosen use only one component of fitness, so that they give a clear result for that component. Examples are push-ups, sit-ups and 'sit and reach' tests, where a simple action produces a measurable result (e.g. the number of sit-ups you can do in one minute). Single-component tests are best adapted to measuring health-related components of fitness.

- Skill- or job-related fitness tests assess a number of components simultaneously. The fire and rescue service test of crawling round a confined space tests several components of fitness (e.g. speed, agility, strength) but also tests aspects not directly linked to fitness such as motivation and tendencies towards claustrophobia. The primary purpose of such tests is not to test physical fitness itself, but to test fitness for a particular job.

Link See page 298 for the fire and rescue service test.

To understand the principles behind fitness tests it helps to have a basic understanding of how the body generates energy.

Movement uses energy which comes from the food we eat and the oxygen we breathe. The energy reaches our muscles by two mechanisms: aerobic and anaerobic. The body uses a number of different chemicals and metabolic systems (chemical reactions) to get energy to the muscles; their nature depends on the kind of energy needed.

Aerobic capacity

This is the ability to carry out moderate physical activity such as jogging for a long time without getting tired. The body uses the aerobic energy pathway. Aerobic capacity is often measured using the multi-stage fitness test (beep test) and is given as VO$_2$ max (maximum volume of oxygen used).

Aerobic training checklist

- Have a medical first, if you are not used to training, or think that you are unfit for a medical reason.
- Plan your training, and set yourself realistic but challenging targets.
- Warm up before you start each session, and make sure that you are properly equipped.
- Try to get your heart rate above 65% of the maximum but not above 80%. (If you get above this, your training will become anaerobic, and your aerobic fitness could actually decline as a result.)
- Train using aerobic activities such as jogging, distance swimming, fast walking, or aerobics.
- If you start off unfit you will make fast progress at first. If you are already fit, progress will be slower.
- As aerobic capacity increases, increase the duration but not the intensity of your training.
- Unless you are aiming to lose weight, you should increase your carbohydrate intake.
- Avoid **dehydration**.
- Measure your improvement using a method such as the Harvard step test.
- Keep a record of your progress.

Multi-stage fitness tests

See page 296 for more information on multi-stage fitness tests.

Strength

This is the ability to act with great physical force. It uses anaerobic energy pathways. For a strength test the person being tested must use maximum effort for a short period of time.

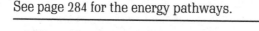

See page 284 for the energy pathways.

Fig 7.19 Aerobic fitness should come first

Endurance and muscular strength checklist

- Plan your training and set yourself targets.
- Do not start strength training unless you have reasonable aerobic fitness.
- Circuit training, using weights or press-ups for the anaerobic parts and the treadmill or running for the aerobic parts, will give balanced development in both endurance and strength.
- To some extent, endurance training undercuts strength training, and vice versa; on the other hand, doing the two kinds of training together is good preparation for a public service fitness test.
- To make progress in strength, you should increase intensity by gradual stages.
- All safety principles should be observed.
- Avoid overtraining.
- Monitor your progress and keep a record (www.betterhealth.vic.gov.au).

Wingate test

This was devised at Wingate University in the USA. The equipment needed is an exercise bike and an ergometer (a device for measuring energy output). The resistance of the ergometer must be set so that it is equal to three-quarters of one per cent of the body weight of the person being tested. As a formula this is expressed as follows.

Body Weight (kg) $\times$ 0.075 = Ergometer Resistance

Muscular endurance

This is the ability of muscles to work for long periods of time without getting tired.

Sit-up test

Link

See page 300 for more information on sit-up tests.

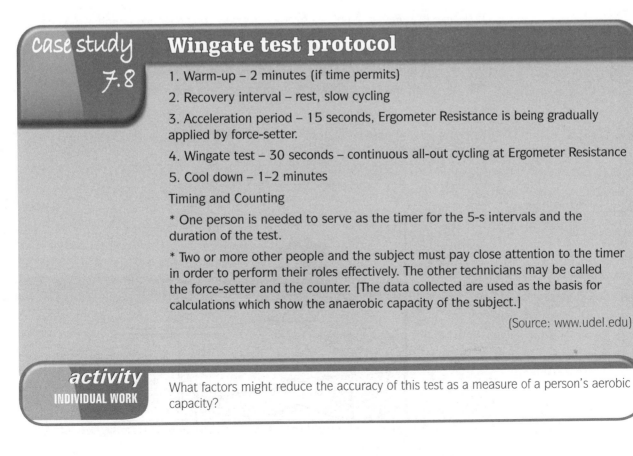

case study 7.8

Wingate test protocol

1. Warm-up – 2 minutes (if time permits)

2. Recovery interval – rest, slow cycling

3. Acceleration period – 15 seconds, Ergometer Resistance is being gradually applied by force-setter.

4. Wingate test – 30 seconds – continuous all-out cycling at Ergometer Resistance

5. Cool down – 1–2 minutes

Timing and Counting

* One person is needed to serve as the timer for the 5-s intervals and the duration of the test.

* Two or more other people and the subject must pay close attention to the timer in order to perform their roles effectively. The other technicians may be called the force-setter and the counter. [The data collected are used as the basis for calculations which show the anaerobic capacity of the subject.]

(Source: www.udel.edu)

activity
INDIVIDUAL WORK

What factors might reduce the accuracy of this test as a measure of a person's aerobic capacity?

Flexibility

Sit and reach tests

Required:

- bench marked on top with a line showing the position of the soles of the feet; the bench should have an overhang of 15 cm
- ruler (cm).

The aim is to test the flexibility of the lower back.

1. Sit on the floor without shoes, legs straight, feet flat against base of bench.
2. Reach forward and push fingers along the top of the bench as far as possible.
3. Record the distance between marker line and fingertips, then add 15.

Table 7.4 Typical sit and reach test scores for 16–19 year olds

Gender	Excellent	Above average	Average	Below average	Poor
Male	>14	11–14	7–10	4–6	<4
Female	>15	12–15	7–11	4–6	<4

(Source: Davis, B. et al. (2000) *Physical Education and the Study of Sport*. Cited on www.brianmac.demon.co.uk)

Speed

This is tested in push-ups, sit-ups, the 60 m sprint, the beep test and in the Illinois agility run (see page 307).

Reaction time

A reaction time test measures how long it takes for a person to respond to a stimulus such as the flashing of a light or the dropping of a ruler.

In the ruler test, Person A holds a ruler loosely between finger and thumb at 30 cm, while B puts a finger and thumb close to but not touching the 0-cm mark on the same dangling ruler. A lets the ruler fall without warning, and B catches the ruler between finger and thumb. The lower the reading on the ruler, the faster the reaction time.

There are online reaction tests which are more accurate and sophisticated.

Agility

The police used to have an agility test but it has been discontinued. An example of this kind of test is given on page 307.

Fig 7.20 Sit and reach test

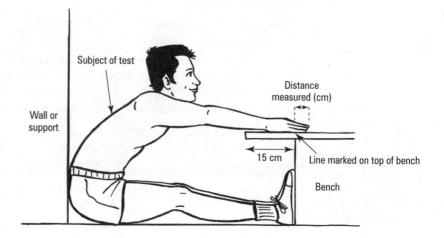

Illinois agility run

A course is set up on a flat surface, 8 metres by 10 metres, using four traffic cones.

1. Lie face down at Start.

2. On the command, jump up and run round the cones on the path shown.

3. The time is recorded.

Table 7.5 Typical scores for 16–19 year olds for the Illinois agility run

Gender	Excellent	Above average	Average	Below average	Poor
Male	<15.2 secs	15.2–16.1 secs	16.2–18.1 secs	18.2–18.3 secs	>18.3 secs
Female	<17.0 secs	17.0–17.9 secs	18.0–21.7 secs	21.8–23.0 secs	>23.0 secs

(Source: Davis, B. *et al.* (2000) *Physical Education and the Study of Sport*. Cited on www.brianmac.demon.co.uk)

Balance

This is tested (to some extent) by the fire and rescue service:

'Ladder Climb – Testing Confidence at Height

'The test will consist of you ascending a fully extended 13.5 metre ladder to approximately two-thirds of its extended height. At this position you will take a 'leg lock', remove your hands from the ladder, look down and identify a symbol on the ground and then descend the ladder.

'You will have to perform this within a specified time.'

(Source: www.westyorksfire.gov.uk)

Balance on a board

Army assault courses use beams and other devices to test balance. The aim is to walk along a narrow beam confidently without falling off.

Coordination

This is tested in many skill-related fitness tests. An example is this item from the prison service entry fitness test:

'6. Shield

'This test involves holding a 6-kilogram shield and practising control and restraining techniques.'

(Source: www.hmprisonservice.gov.uk)

Fig 7.21 Course for the Illinois agility run

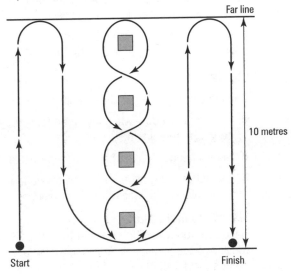

Power

The standing jump involves standing behind a line and then, without any run-up, jumping as far forward as you can. This used to be used in some public service fitness tests but appears to have been discontinued.

An example of a test that requires power, from the fire and rescue service, is:

'Casualty Evacuation – Testing Muscular Strength and Stamina

'You will be required to drag a 55kg casualty walking backwards (guided by an assessor) around a 30 metre course. You will have to perform this within a specified time.'

(Source: www.westyorksfire.gov.uk)

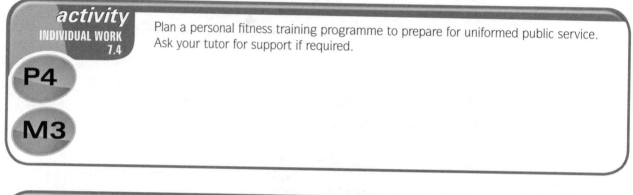

activity
INDIVIDUAL WORK
7.4

P4

M3

Plan a personal fitness training programme to prepare for uniformed public service. Ask your tutor for support if required.

activity
INDIVIDUAL WORK
7.5

D1

Write an article for a uniformed services recruitment magazine evaluating the effects that lifestyle factors can have on health and fitness, when applying for uniformed public service and in long-term employment.

Training programme

Every component of fitness can be improved by training. This is true for any healthy adult.

Fitness training is a complex subject, and you are advised to research it in some depth if you are serious about becoming very fit. For the purposes of this unit, you should be able to show an improvement in fitness and reach levels which would get you through at least some public service entry fitness tests.

Training for fitness is essential if you want to maximise your fitness – and if you want to maximise your chances of getting into the uniformed services.

Goals

Training can be done for three main reasons:

■ individual needs – when a person feels they want or ought to become fitter, in order to get more enjoyment out of life

■ sports needs – to get better at a particular sport or athletic activity

■ job needs – e.g. when applying to a uniformed public service which has a fitness entry test, or in which fitness is needed.

Specific to individual

Since everybody is different, and their training needs are different, training should be specific to the individual. A training programme that is suitable for one person could be useless, or downright harmful, for another.

Fitness tests

If you are intending to join a uniformed public service which has a fitness entry test, you should research the kind of test they do and train for that test. If the service uses a beep test, then you need to put some aerobic training into your training programme. If the service tests upper body strength, then you need to include training activities which improve upper body strength. If there are skill-based components in the test, you should find out what they are and practise similar manoeuvres; if possible, visit their fitness centre and practise appropriate exercises there.

Link

See pages 295–300 for examples of fitness-testing activities.

Principles of training

These are overload, specificity, **progression**, variation, reversibility, frequency, intensity, time and type. What they mean, and how they are relevant to your training, is shown in Fig 7.22 below:

Fig 7.22 The principles of training

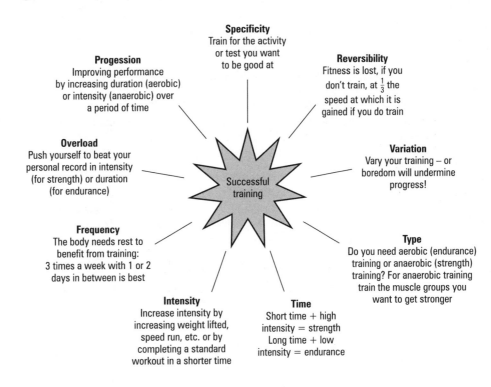

Specificity
Train for the activity or test you want to be good at

Progession
Improving performance by increasing duration (aerobic) or intensity (anaerobic) over a period of time

Reversibility
Fitness is lost, if you don't train, at $\frac{1}{3}$ the speed at which it is gained if you do train

Overload
Push yourself to beat your personal record in intensity (for strength) or duration (for endurance)

Variation
Vary your training – or boredom will undermine progress!

Successful training

Frequency
The body needs rest to benefit from training: 3 times a week with 1 or 2 days in between is best

Type
Do you need aerobic (endurance) training or anaerobic (strength) training? For anaerobic training train the muscle groups you want to get stronger

Intensity
Increase intensity by increasing weight lifted, speed run, etc. or by completing a standard workout in a shorter time

Time
Short time + high intensity = strength
Long time + low intensity = endurance

Overload

Overload means that you must push any training activity beyond the limit that you normally reach in everyday life. If you're training flexibility, you should stretch slightly further; if you're lifting weights, you should lift the heaviest that you can for the type of exercise you are doing.

Specificity

Specificity means training for one muscle group (e.g. arms, abdominals). This is strength training, in the anaerobic zone, and it will only develop the parts of the body that you are training. This means, for example, that if you train your thighs using these anaerobic methods it will have no effect on the strength of your arms.

Progression

Progression is the principle that your training programme should become gradually more difficult as you get fitter or stronger. An increase of 10% per week in either duration (aerobic training) or intensity (anaerobic training) is about right.

Variation

You should vary your training activities, to reduce the risk of training injuries, to avoid **disproportionate** development of certain muscle groups, and to avoid boredom.

Reversibility

Reversibility means that if you stop training for more than, say, a week, your strength and fitness gains will go into reverse and you will start becoming weaker and less fit. After about six months, you will be back to the level you would have been at if you had never exercised at all.

FITT Principles

The four principles that follow can be remembered by using the acronym FITT.

*F*requency

This is how often you train in a week. Three times a week is a good level of frequency to aim for.

*I*ntensity

If you are aiming at aerobic training, the intensity should be below the anaerobic threshold (i.e. heart rate less than 80% of maximum). If you are doing anaerobic training, the intensity should be very high and your heart rate should be above 80% of maximum.

*T*ime

The time spent on a training session depends on the type of training you are doing. Endurance training (aerobic) could last for an hour or even more. Strength training (anaerobic) should last for 30 minutes a session. Training that is a mixture of the two should last 30 minutes or slightly more.

*T*ype

The type of training depends on the purpose of the training. For aerobic fitness, the training should use the aerobic energy pathway and therefore be of moderate intensity. For strength training, the anaerobic energy pathway is used, and the training is of high intensity. For skill-related fitness, the training should include agility, balance, coordination, etc. as required.

Periodisation (macrocycle, mesocycle, microcycle)

Periodisation is the process of splitting fitness training into blocks of various lengths. The aims of periodisation are to:

- produce meaningful and achievable long-term plans
- maintain motivation
- make it easier to monitor and evaluate progress
- achieve higher maximum levels of fitness.

A macrocycle is a long-term fitness plan lasting six months to one year. Its purpose is to work up to a peak of maximum fitness. A mesocycle lasts from three to four months. Its purpose is to reach strength or fitness milestones on the way to your final target which should be achieved at the end of the macrocycle. A microcycle is a planned training block of one to four weeks. Its purpose is to learn a new skill, lift a heavier weight, or achieve some other stage of progression.

Training techniques

There's a wide range of training techniques for different sports and for different types and levels of fitness. These can be divided roughly into those that are suited to aerobic training and those suited to anaerobic training. However, it is worth remembering that the uniformed public services normally want people with a good level of both aerobic fitness and strength. They aren't looking for marathon runners or weightlifters, so much as people who come in between.

Fig 7.23 Training techniques related to anaerobic/aerobic fitness (The techniques become more 'aerobic' as you move from left to right.)

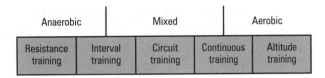

Resistance training
This is training against a force, such as weights, or a machine with built-in resistance. It is useful for strength training – although it can be used in endurance training too. In practice it means weightlifting, or using your own weight as the force that has to be overcome. Resistance training aims to increase strength, not aerobic fitness. It uses the anaerobic pathways, and progresses by increasing intensity (e.g. the weight that must be lifted) rather than repetitions.

Repetitions
This means performing the same action a number of times. In weight training it is normal to repeat the lift, but to increase strength it is necessary to increase the intensity (the weight lifted), not the number of lifts. Increasing the number of repetitions rather than the intensity leads to an increase in aerobic fitness but not an increase in strength.

Continuous training
This is training such as jogging or swimming which lasts for, say, half an hour or more; it is used for endurance training.

Interval training
This is hard training with short breaks in between; it is particularly useful for strength development.

Circuit training
This is varied training with short rests in between. Typically it is done in a gym and involves moving from one activity to the next. It is a good way of exercising a wide range of muscle groups, or of mixing aerobic and anaerobic training. Case study 7.9 shows a circuit which would exercise most muscle groups. Although as it stands it is anaerobic, if two or three aerobic activities were interspersed the whole circuit would be much more aerobic in nature.

An example of circuit training

1. Chest press (pectorals, anterior deltoid, triceps, coracobrachialis, subscapularis)
2. Squat or leg press (hamstrings, quadriceps, gluteals)
3. Row pull (latissimus dorsi, middle and posterior deltoid, rhomboids, infraspanatus, teres minor)
4. Lunge (hamstrings, quadriceps, gluteals)
5. Shoulder press (anterior deltoid, upper trapezius, pectorals-clavicular, coracobrachialis)
6. Lat pull (latissimus dorsi, teres major, pectorals-sternal)
7. Biceps curl (biceps brachii, brachialis, brachioradialis)
8. Triceps extension (triceps brachii, anconeus)
9. Heel raise (gastrocnemius, soleus)
10. Seated ab (machine) (rectus abdominals, internal and external obliques)

(Source: *The Fitness Professional's Complete Guide to Circuits and Intervals* by Len Kravitz, PhD www.unm.edu)

activity
INDIVIDUAL WORK
Find an anatomical diagram showing muscles and identify each of these muscle groups.

Training diary e.g. progression, attitude, motivation, linked to goals

A training diary is needed to monitor, review and evaluate your training programme. It should include your plan, which should be set out like a calendar with the dates and times of each training session, your intermediate goals and progressions, and your final targets.

There should be space in your diary to record:

- your progression – for example lifting heavier weights or increasing the duration of aerobic activities

- attitude – an honest appraisal of how you feel your training is going

- your motivation – the methods you use to maintain or develop your enthusiasm; motivational problems you may come across, and suggested solutions

- goals – these are the targets you have set yourself, and your progress, attitude, etc. should be seen in relation to how well you are moving towards your goals.

Undertaking a fitness training programme to prepare for uniformed public service

When developing a personal training programme you need to go through a number of planning stages, and take various things into consideration.

Considerations

Health and safety

Warm up and cool down

Before any workout or any other bout of serious physical activity you should warm up for five minutes. Here are some warm-up exercises suggested by the fire and rescue service.

'Arms and Shoulders: shoulder circling and shrugging, arm circling, arm swinging, arm shaking, wrist rotate and shake. Start gently and gradually build up the intensity.

'Trunk and Back: side bends, hip circling, toe touching, trunk arching.

'Legs: gentle knee bends and leg lunges, ankle point, circle and flex, walking and slow jogging.'

(Source: www.westyorksfire.gov.uk)

The aim of warming up is, first, to raise your heart-rate and, secondly, to increase flexibility in order to lessen the risk of injury. Activities should be gentle, especially at first.

A cool down consists of 5–10 minutes of gentle jogging and stretching, to help your muscles and joints recover.

Fig 7.24 Nine considerations for healthy, safe training

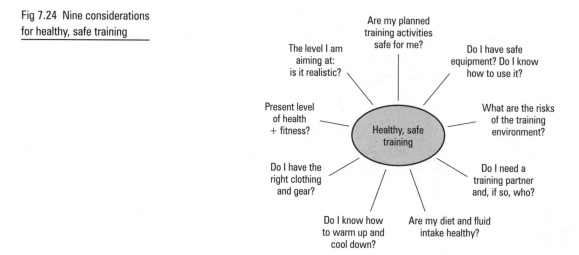

Equipment related

Make sure that you know what sort of equipment you are going to use. Find out how it works, check (or get an expert to check) that it is safe and in good working order. Always use the equipment in the way that it is designed to be used.

Facility related

Is the venue safe? Carry out a risk assessment (e.g. for cross-country runs etc.). Are there dangers from other people (e.g. horseplay)? Are drinks available if there is a risk of dehydration?

Injury

What will happen if you have an accident? Is there a first aid box? Are there first-aiders around?

Illness

Don't train if you are ill. Stop training if you feel ill. Get a fitness check from a doctor before you start if you are not used to training. Make sure that your training plan fits in with your capabilities.

Type of training programme

Ask yourself:

- What am I training for?
- How long have I got?
- What is my present level of fitness?
- What are my training needs?
- What facilities are there?
- What kinds of physical activity do I enjoy?
- What planning do I need to do?

To develop your programme:

> **remember**
>
> It is possible to do serious training without joining a gym or spending any money: running, jogging, walking, sit-ups, push-ups, etc. will combine into an effective programme.

1. Decide on your training needs (e.g. because you are having a fitness test in one month; because you want to improve your overall fitness; because you have joined a football team etc.). If you need to develop aerobic fitness, devise an aerobic programme. If you need to develop strength devise an anaerobic programme (as long as your basic fitness is good enough – otherwise you should start with aerobic exercise whatever your final aims are).

2. Make a list of exercises or activities which you wish to include in your training. If you want to do circuit training, you may include some of the items given above on page 311. Then draw up a timetable for a month giving yourself three main training sessions a week of, say, 1–1½ hours each, with rest-days in between. Write down the activities you will do at each training session.

3. Decide how you will make your training progressive. If you want to increase aerobic fitness, you should gradually lengthen your training sessions and increase the number of repetitions of each exercise. If you want to increase your strength, you should progressively increase the intensity of your activities by small degrees (perhaps at the end of each week) by, for example, lifting heavier weights, or doing 15 push-ups in a shorter time. Note these progressions down on your training timetable.

4. Plan any changes of diet and/or lifestyle that you think may be beneficial during your training programme. Decide how you will record your progress during and after your training programme. Check that you have the equipment and back-up you need and that your safety arrangements are adequate.

5. When you have made all these basic decisions and are happy with the result, draw up a finished version of your training programme. Leave space on it to keep a brief log of your training, including your feelings about it and your progress.

See Tables 7.6 and 7.7 for a possible layout.

Comparison of entry requirements of relevant public services

Compare the different public service fitness tests and choose one which is feasible (doable) for someone of your capabilities. If you are unfit, don't try to get up to the level of a Royal Marines commando in one month. If you are already fit, choose a fitness test which will give you a bit of a challenge.

Other considerations

If you play a sport, consider if – or how – you should incorporate it into your training. Alternatively, you may want to confirm in some way that your training programme will help your sporting performance.

A training programme for a specific purpose such as a fitness test normally lasts a month or six weeks. You should plan it so that it will help you in the test items, timing it to finish two days before the test itself.

To reduce the mental pressure of a fitness assessment you should:

- Take part in practice fitness assessments whenever possible so that you know what to expect.
- Prepare yourself well by getting enough rest and food in the days before, and by arriving at the testing centre in plenty of time.
- Remember that many public service fitness tests can be retaken – and that in any case there is no point in getting a job which is too physical for you!

Monitoring

Monitor test results, training, feedback

It is essential to keep a detailed fitness log (or diary) to record all aspects of your training. In it you should include:

- your fitness test results (before, during and after your training)
- your training diary with dates and details of sessions (see example below)
- feedback from your coach or instructor.

Your log should be incorporated into your training timetable so that you can put your comments in context, and so that they are easily available for any self-assessment at the end of your training programme. It might look like the one in Table 7.6.

Table 7.6 Self-assessment of your training programme

Week No.	Monday	Tuesday	Wednesday	Thursday	Friday	Saturday	Sunday
1	Circuit 1		Run			Circuit 1	
Notes							
2	Circuit 2		Circuit 2			Run	
Notes							
3	Run		Circuit 3			Circuit 3	
Notes							
4	Circuit 4		Run			Circuit 4	

Your log will go where it says 'notes'.

Circuits 1, 2, 3 and 4 are progressions, so Circuit 2 is slightly longer (if aerobic) or more intensive (if anaerobic) than Circuit 1. See Table 7.7 below.

Table 7.7 Circuits 1 and 2

	Press ups	Standing squats	Lunges	Triceps press	Jog on spot	Dorsal raise	Sit-ups
Circuit 1	10 reps followed by 10 step-ups	10 reps followed by 10 step-ups	10 reps followed by 10 step-ups	10 reps followed by 10 step-ups	30 seconds	10 reps followed by 10 step-ups	10 reps followed by 10 step-ups
Circuit 2	15 reps followed by 15 step-ups	15 reps followed by 15 step-ups	15 reps followed by 15 step-ups	15 reps followed by 15 step-ups	40 seconds	15 reps followed by 15 step-ups	15 reps followed by 15 step-ups

activity

INDIVIDUAL WORK 7.6

P5

You are going to apply for a uniformed public service in three months' time. Carry out a fitness training programme to prepare you for that service's physical entrance test.

remember
A person who is fit to begin with may well show smaller gains in fitness while doing a training programme than a person who is unfit to begin with.

Review

This is appraisal – where you look at what you have done and comment on your progress, your successes, your difficulties and the level of your achievement. This should be done in an honest and systematic manner.

Fitness training programme

Here you review how suitable your programme turned out to be. Did it achieve what you set out to do? Did you find it enjoyable or useful doing it? Were there practical problems which you hadn't foreseen? Did you suffer injuries or illness because of it?

Results achieved

Was there a measurable improvement in fitness or strength? Did you meet your targets? Were your systems and frequency of fitness assessment/measurement adequate?

Strengths

What did you do well? What were the strengths of your training programme? Could you recommend it to someone else?

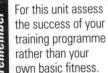

remember
For this unit assess the success of your training programme rather than your own basic fitness.

Areas for improvement

These should relate to the design and carrying out of your training plan, as well as to your actual fitness.

Extent to which training programme achieved identified goals

The main goals are your targets, and the extent of the achievement is how well the targets were met. For your training programme to have been a real success, the targets should have been fairly difficult and your increase in fitness fairly significant. If your goals were also to feel better, enjoy the training, etc., these aspects should be reviewed too.

Evaluation

This means assessing how successful your training programme was overall. It is a summing up of your review points under headings such as:

1. Was it achievable?
2. Did I find it worthwhile?

3. Did I meet my targets?

4. What did I find difficult?

5. Were there problems in my planning and preparation?

6. What would I do differently if I did it again?

7. Where do I go from here?

Modifications and improvements to programme

These should be put forward in the light of your answers to the seven questions above and should include some suggested plans for maintaining your fitness or improving it in the future.

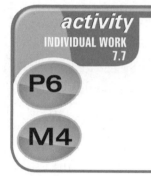

activity
INDIVIDUAL WORK
7.7

P6

M4

Carry out an appraisal of your own fitness training programme from the beginning of the planning process to the completion of the training programme itself. Explain what you did well, and what you should have done differently.

activity
INDIIDUAL WORK
7.8

D2

Write an analysis of your training programme, assessing what you got out of it in relation to the time, effort and expense that you put into it. Explain what you could have done to improve your programme both in planning and execution, and make a list of recommendations as to how you could continue to develop your fitness.

Progress Check

1. Name six types of moving joint, and give an example of each.

2. Explain the difference between slow-twitch and fast-twitch muscle fibres.

3. What happens in the alveoli?

4. Outline the differences between the aerobic and anaerobic energy pathways.

5. Name 10 parts of the body in which cancer can be caused by smoking.

6. How do you calculate your body mass index?

7. Name the five food groups.

8. What happens in a beep test?

9. List the health-related and skill-related components of fitness.

10. What percentage of the maximum heart rate should be reached in (a) aerobic training and (b) anaerobic training?

11. Name the nine principles of training.

12. How can you make sure that a training programme is progressive?

Outdoor and Adventurous Expeditions

This unit covers:

- A range of different expeditions
- Planning expeditions
- Undertaking expeditions
- Reviewing the planning and undertaking of expeditions

Expeditions started in the Stone Age – when people spread over the surface of the planet and settled in all continents except Antarctica – and have been going on ever since.

This unit pays its respects to famous expeditions of the past then moves on to modern expeditions, and the great variety of expedition types and reasons for going on expeditions.

As the main purpose of the unit is to enable you to go on expeditions of your own, the unit deals in detail with planning, preparation, equipment, organisation and finance. It also looks at the practicalities of travelling on foot in mountainous areas, and of camping, sleeping out and navigation.

The last section is about reviewing the successes and failures of expeditions, and how to learn from them.

grading criteria

To achieve a **Pass** grade the evidence must show that the learner is able to:	To achieve a **Merit** grade the evidence must show that, in addition to the pass criteria, the learner is able to:	To achieve a **Distinction** grade the evidence must show that, in addition to the pass and merit criteria, the learner is able to:
P1 describe four different expeditions Pg 330	**M1** compare and contrast four different expeditions Pg 330	
P2 plan a one-day expedition, with support Pg 335	**M2** plan a one-day expedition Pg 335	
P3 plan a multi-day expedition, with support Pg 339	**M3** plan a multi-day expedition Pg 339	

▶

To achieve a **Pass** grade the evidence must show that the learner is able to:	To achieve a **Merit** grade the evidence must show that, in addition to the pass criteria, the learner is able to:	To achieve a **Distinction** grade the evidence must show that, in addition to the pass and merit criteria, the learner is able to:
P4 undertake two different expeditions, with support, demonstrating appropriate skills and techniques Pg 354	**M4** undertake two different expeditions, demonstrating appropriate skills and techniques Pg 354	**D1** undertake two different expeditions, demonstrating advanced expedition skills and techniques Pg 354
P5 review their planning of, and undertaking of, expeditions identifying strengths and areas for improvement Pg 358	**M5** explain identified strengths and areas for improvement and relate them to suggestions made in personal development plan. Pg 359	**D2** justify suggestions made in personal development plan. Pg 359
P6 produce a personal development plan based on identified strengths and areas for improvement. Pg 359		

A range of different expeditions

Expeditions

An **expedition** is usually defined as:

- a journey undertaken by a group of people with a definite objective, such as an expedition against the enemy stronghold or a scientific expedition to, for example, the South Pole

- the group undertaking such a journey.

However, it is possible for individuals to undertake expeditions. They may or may not have a **back-up team**.

Types

There are plenty of ways of classifying expeditions. The one used here follows the one in the 2007 BTEC Specifications.

Individual

This means that a person goes on an expedition by themselves. It doesn't mean that they do all the planning and preparation by themselves. Most people who go on long expeditions (other than, say, lone **backpackers**) have a support team of some sort.

Any reasonably fit individual can go on an expedition without spending much money. In fact it is the cheapest kind of travel holiday. A person who decides to spend the holiday walking the Pennine Way by themselves is going on an expedition. They need no back-up: the person goes to Edale in Derbyshire, carrying food and a tent or **bivvy bag**, and walks the 250-odd miles to Kirk Yetholm near the Scottish border.

Ellen MacArthur

The classic recent example of an individual undertaking a long expedition is the round-the-world solo journey by Ellen MacArthur. It was a sporting, technical and personal challenge, and resulted in her breaking a world record which had been thought to be nearly unbreakable.

case study 9.1

Ellen MacArthur sails into record books

Tuesday, 8 February, 2005,

Ellen's new record:

71 days 14hrs 18mins 33secs

The key facts and figures

Britain's Ellen MacArthur has completed her single-handed round-the-world voyage in record-breaking time.

She crossed the finish line at 2229 GMT on Monday, beating the previous mark set by Francis Joyon of 72 days, 22 hours, 54 mins and 22 secs.

The Isle of Wight-based yachtswoman completed the 27,000-mile voyage in 71 days and under 15 hours.

After achieving the record time, MacArthur said: "I feel exhausted but I'm elated to be here."

She added: "It has been an unbelievable journey.

"The whole voyage has been very draining, and there's a lot of things going round in my head.

"But it's great that I can finally switch my brain off and relax in the company of others, which I've really missed."

The 28-year-old added: "I always believed I could break the record, and Francis agreed it was breakable. But I really didn't think I would do it at the first attempt.

"The whole south Atlantic was terrible and it has just been one big draining event from there onwards.

"When I crossed the line I felt like collapsing on the floor and just falling asleep. I was absolutely over the moon."

Her shore team were waiting to greet her on the navy patrol vessel HMS Severn, which will escort her B&Q trimaran into British water.

MacArthur's project director Mark Turner admitted: "We thought it would be pretty hard – in fact, we thought we might have to have two or three goes at it.

"I'm glad we did it the first time–I'm not sure we could deal with doing it second time.

"It was hard the whole time – there were very few moments of relaxation."

(Source: www.bbc.co.uk)

activity
INDIVIDUAL WORK

1 How far would you say Ellen MacArthur's achievement described above was a team effort?

2 What benefits do expeditions like hers bring to the people involved – and to the rest of us?

Fig 9.1 Single-handed – but with back-up

Groups, teams

There is no obvious difference between a group and a team in this context. They are collections of people who go on an expedition together. They range from a group of people who go camping together for pleasure to well-trained and funded teams who climb in remote mountain ranges, or go down unexplored **potholes**.

The famous expeditions of the past were nearly all group or team efforts. A list of past explorers or travellers is given below. There may be hundreds more – and you can research the main facts about them using the internet.

Table 9.1 Past explorers

Roald Amundsen	Vasco da Gama	Sir Henry M. Stanley	Jacques-Yves Cousteau
Vasco Núnez de Balboa	Leif Ericsson	Gino Watkins	Thor Heyerdahl
Ibn Batuta	Sir Edmund Hillary	F. Spencer Chapman	Alain Bombard
Richard Burton	Henry Hudson	Chris Bonington	Ranulf Fiennes
John Cabot	Ponce de León	Maurice Herzog	Haroun Tazieff
Jacques Cartier	David Livingstone	Heinrich Harrar	Gerald Durrell
Lewis and Clark	Ferdinand Magellan	Norbert Casteret	David Attenborough
Christopher Columbus	Mungo Park	Mary Leakey	Mary Kingsley
James Cook	Robert E. Peary	Jane Goodall	Gertrude Bell
Francisco Coronado	Francisco Pizarro	Junko Tabei	Robin Knox-Johnston
Hernando Cortés	John Speke	Amelia Earhart	Vladimir Peniakoff
Robert Falcon Scott	Marco Polo	Apsley Cherry-Garrard	Richard Branson
Charles Darwin	Sir Ernest Shackleton		

Female explorers

www.femexplorers.com

Distinguished women of past and present

www.distinguishedwomen.com

Enchanted learning

www.enchantedlearning.com

Early explorers

Early explorers lived in the days when the world was not well known to the West. The purpose of their expeditions varied, but most were looking for wealth. Marco Polo (roughly 1254–1324) started in Venice and went as far as Beijing to trade in spices and other things which were valuable at the time. After he returned, he was imprisoned in Italy and dictated the story of his travels in prison. For five or six hundred years his account was the main source of information about the Far East in Europe. A wave of exploration beginning with Columbus in 1492 and, including the likes of Magellan and Vasco da Gama, was again driven by hopes of trade but also provided direct, rather than mathematical, evidence that the world was round.

Another wave of exploration was associated with British colonialism: this included Henry Morton Stanley, John Speke and Mungo Park. They all explored Africa at the time that Britain was colonising the continent, and their energy and determination (some would say greed) is one reason why most of Africa was colonised by the British – otherwise the French and the Portuguese would have got there first. Also in the nineteenth century, there were Christian missionaries, such as David Livingstone, whose main motivation to go on expeditions was to find people who could be converted.

Later, at the beginning of the twentieth century there was a rush to get to the North and South Poles: Peary, Amundsen and Scott were the main names here. This final wave of land-based exploring expeditions was motivated by **prestige** and national pride, although there was some scientific interest too.

Official website of Ellen MacArthur

www.teamellen.com

The Complete Works of Charles Darwin On-line

www.darwin-online.org.uk

Brycchan Carey's website

www.brycchancarey.com

Elizabethan era

www.elizabethan-era.org.uk

BBC

www.bbc.co.uk

With the development of aeroplanes it became possible to see all parts of the world, and with the development of satellites later in the twentieth century the whole world was accurately mapped. Expeditions have therefore changed their purpose. Fig 9.2 outlines some of these.

Groups

Most expeditions are carried out by groups of people. The nature of the groups may vary considerably – often the group is a club or society, but a large number comprise people brought together and led by commercial organisations which run expeditions as a service to the public. These organisations arrange activities such as **trekking** in the Andes or paragliding in Nepal (doing all the planning and organisation and leading the

remember

Expeditions are now big business.

Fig 9.2 Modern reasons for
expeditions

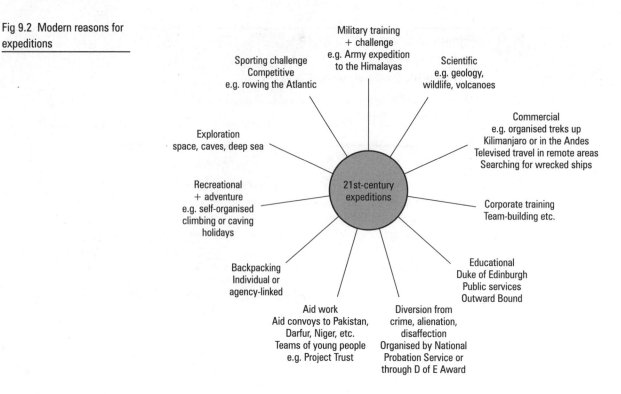

expedition itself), and members of the public pay to go with them, thereby enjoying
an expedition, which is also an adventure holiday, in greater security and probably at
cheaper cost than if they were to arrange the activity themselves.

Teams

A team is a kind of group – probably more closely knit and more used to working
together. (A group that often works together is likely to turn into a team, in time.)

One of the most famous explorers to travel with a team was Sir Ernest Shackleton.
Shackleton and his team attempted a crossing of the Antarctic in 1914 – partly to
recover national pride after Robert Falcon Scott's famous 1912 expedition failed to be
the first to reach the South Pole. (Scott was beaten by 35 days by the Norwegian, Roald
Amundsen, and he and his companions died near the end of the return trek.)

Corporate

Expeditions of the type run by Exodus (see page 323) and Outward Bound®, a
registered charity, are of this type. In many ways they are adventure holidays – to
remote and beautiful parts of the world. Outward Bound® also runs expeditions for
business people as leadership training and team-bonding experiences. In this sense, the
expeditions resemble some of those run by the uniformed public services for the training
of their own personnel.

Students (gap years)

Some students and young people go to the Far East and elsewhere backpacking under
their own steam. These journeys are informal or semi-formal expeditions which vary
in nature from adventurous tourism and extended holidays to long journeys of self-
discovery, or searches for inner fulfilment.

Other young people participate in aid schemes, or schemes which combine foreign aid
and tourism, organised by charities and similar organisations. They might, for example,
carry out teaching or community work in an African village and then spend some
time 'on **safari**' exploring the region and seeing the scenery and the wildlife. These
'expeditions' can last for weeks, months or even longer.

case study
9.2

Expeditions

1. Expedition to Patagonia

Day 1   Start Buenos Aires, afternoon walking tour.

Day 2   Fly south to El Calafate and transfer to El Chalten in Los Glaciares N.P.

Day 3   Daywalk to Cerro Fitzroy **base camp** and Laguna de los Tres.

Day 4   Free morning to relax in El Chalten, further trekking in the area or optional boat trip to Viedma Glaciar. Transfer to El Calafate.

Day 5   Private tour to the incredible Moreno Glacier. Optional boat trip or minitrekking on the glacier.

Day 6   Free day in El Calafate on the shores of Lake Argentina. Many optional excursions including horse riding, Upsala Glacier, icebergs and Estancia Cristina tour.

Day 7   Torres del Paine N.P. Tour of the highlights of the park.

Day 8   Daywalk to the base of the Towers of Paine.

(Source: www.exodus.co.uk)

2. Cambridge University Caving Club

Leader – Overall coordinator and motivator.

Treasurer – Collects deposits to fund gear-buying. Keeps track of accounts and sends out expo bills in the autumn. Provides expo tallies book.

Sponsorship – If you are going to pursue sponsorship, start early (you will be competing with many similar groups and most potential **sponsors** will be more impressed by an air of efficient organisation than one of last minute desperation).

Equipment – This covers more than just rope and hangers. Will need to liaise closely with sponsorship officer and club Tackle Master.

Transport – The logistics of getting 20 or so cavers and half a tonne of miscellaneous gear out to Austria, on a shoestring budget with a limited number of cars, are daunting. Whoever does this probably ought to be a driver themselves, so they know what's involved.

Project officers – If there is a special project which has its own special needs (radios, aerial photos or whatever), it may be best to have one person specifically responsible.

Consultants – Previous expo members can help a great deal, even if they are not going. Don't be afraid to ask questions, solicit suggestions, or ask for help with equipment or training. Keeping older members involved will also make it more likely that they will return to expo in the future. This is particularly useful in view of the amount of information which is still not written down adequately, like where to find cave XYZ etc.

(Source: cucc.survex.com)

activity
GROUP WORK

Based on the information above, what are the similarities and differences between the expeditions run by Exodus and those run by the Cambridge University Caving Club?

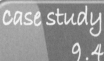

case study 9.3

The Imperial Trans-Antarctic Expedition

The Imperial Trans-Antarctic Expedition was the fourth British Antarctic expedition of the 20th century, and aimed, but ultimately failed, to be the first to cross the Antarctic continent from one side to the other. It is best known for the heroic and successful efforts of its leader, Sir Ernest Shackleton, and its men to save themselves from the remote, frozen conditions of the Antarctic after disaster destroyed their ship thousands of miles from the nearest outpost of civilization. Although wireless radio was available to ships at the time, the expedition's remote location made any such contact impossible, and because World War I was raging, no rescue effort ever left Britain in search of the missing crew. Much of the adventure was captured on film as 28 men endured 22 months in the Antarctic, temperatures of –35 °F (–19.4 °C), with scant provisions, and ultimately produced a life-saving trip across 800 nautical miles (1500 km) of open ocean in a small, 23-foot (7-meter) boat to find a remote whaling station on the island of South Georgia using **navigation** by only a **sextant** and **chronometer**.

(Source: www.answers.com)

activity
GROUP WORK

People such as Shackleton and Scott have often been seen as heroes and **role models**. Do you agree with this assessment?

Disaffected youth

Disaffected youth are young people who either have criminal records or are seen as being at risk of turning to crime. They may be school refusers or have social and educational backgrounds which have led to their being 'antisocial' or at least 'anti-society'. Various organisations use expeditions and adventurous outdoor activities as a positive way of encouraging these young people to raise their self-esteem, develop a sense of social and personal responsibility, and get involved in enjoyable activities which can benefit them (and the rest of society) in the future.

case study 9.4

Dorset Expeditionary Society

Annually, in conjunction with schools the Society's leaders field some sixty residential courses involving over 2000 young people. Almost every week of the year, at least one expedition leaves Dorset. Predominantly groups come from schools, colleges or clubs to work with our leaders. The ventures will take place in the 'wild country' areas of Dartmoor, Wales and Scotland. Youngsters will rock climb, mountain bike, camp, canoe, parachute, cave, hill walk and pony trek. They will learn new skills and raise their physical fitness but more importantly, they will live together in a situation in which co-operation, tolerance and teamwork are essential.

In keeping with its aim to encourage the development of all young people, the Society actively seeks to provide disadvantaged and disaffected youngsters with opportunities for adventure and exploration. In so doing we clearly recognise that those most in need of such experiences are the least able to ask for them, or indeed recognise their worth.

(Source: www.dorsetexp.co.uk)

activity
INDIVIDUAL WORK

Find out what work of this nature is done in your local area.

Dorset Expeditionary Society
www.dorsetexp.co.uk
Youth information
www.youthinformation.com

Educational

Schools, colleges, the armed forces and many commercial organisations provide expedition opportunities for young people (e.g. the Duke of Edinburgh's Award). The aims include:

- developing esprit de corps and 'bonding' the group
- developing teamwork and leadership skills
- achieving part of an academic qualification
- building self-esteem
- providing enjoyable activities outside the classroom
- developing thinking and problem-solving skills
- improving geographical and scientific knowledge
- developing skills in camping, canoeing, skiing, mountaineering, etc.
- inspiring a love of nature and the outdoors.

Military

The military, and especially the army, go on expeditions and encourage them at almost every level. They range from Army Youth Team expeditions for young people right up to major expeditions, such as the army's 2006 attempt on Everest, which got to within a short distance of the summit up a very difficult route. Army expeditions are run by and for the army, but it is possible for other people (e.g. scientists) to accompany them.

Fig 9.3 High point of an army career

remember

There are many different grades of mountain leader award, and anybody who is interested can enrol for a qualification.

case study 9.5 — Expedition opportunity

AML/AMI or above urgently required for high altitude expedition to Kyrgyzstan July/August 07. Will be attempting virgin [unclimbed] peaks up to 5,150m. For more information please contact the Expedition Leader.

(Source: www.army.mod.uk)

activity — INDIVIDUAL WORK

Who would answer this advert – and why?

Adventurous outdoor training and expedition exercises are a part of basic training for soldiers, and a significant part of officer training. After basic training about 33% of military personnel go on to do further expedition-style training. They are also encouraged to gain qualifications such as the Mountain Leadership Award.

The British Army
www.army.mod.uk
The Defence Suppliers Directory
www.armedforces.co.uk
Mountain Leader Training
www.mltuk.org
Mountain Leader Training England
www.mlte.org

case study 9.6 — Adventurous Training

The Aim of military Adventurous Training (AT) is to develop, through authorised challenging pursuits and within an outdoor environment, leadership and the qualities necessary to enhance the performance of military personnel during times of peace and war.

The **Joint Service** Mountaineering Scheme is delivered from dedicated centres both in the UK and overseas, to meet the AT Aim through the delivery of structured courses that seek to develop the requisite skills and techniques necessary to:

Operate in mountainous **terrain** in summer, winter and Alpine terrain. Students will progress from **Proficiency** through Leader to **Expedition Leader** to **Advanced Expedition Leader**.

Develop the requisite skills and techniques necessary, to conduct climbing, the supervision of **single pitch** and **abseiling** activities, then progressing onto winter climbing [climbing on snow and ice].

(Source: www.army.mod.uk)

activity — INDIVIDUAL WORK

In what ways do you think adventurous training could 'enhance the performance of military personnel during times of peace and war'?

Clubs

There are many climbing, walking and potholing clubs which carry out expeditions, both in Britain and abroad. Potholing is an activity in which it is still possible to carry out true exploration and see places that nobody has ever seen before.

case study 9.7

Potholers discover UK's biggest cave

Potholers have discovered the UK's biggest known cave – which is almost as high from floor to ceiling as the London Eye – after following clues left by a Cambridge student in the 18th century.

The cave in Derbyshire's Peak District, known as Titan, is estimated to be a massive 459ft (140m) from floor to ceiling, beating the previous record holder, Gaping Ghyll in the Yorkshire Dales, by almost 200ft (60m).

It was discovered by Dave Nixon and a group of Peak cavers near another huge cavern, Leviathan, after he found an old account in a university library.

The paper, written in 1793 by James Plumtree, described a network of caves which went beyond the well-known Speedwell cave system near Castleton.

Plumtree's account took him down the Speedwell Canal and deep into a nearby lead mine, but his journal described a cave system that went far beyond what had since been explored.

Mr Nixon, a leading underground explorer, realised the entrance must have been blocked by a rockfall and after removing the rocks, eventually discovered a long system of caves leading them to Titan.

The team of cavers then spent a further three years removing another fall of boulders before finally gaining entry to the bottom of the cavern.

Mr Nixon told the BBC: "It wasn't a matter of stumbling, it was a lot of research and a lot of hard work."

His team have now completed a man-made shaft which allows cavers to abseil down in to the cave, saving them a challenging five-hour underground journey.

The cave was carved out over millions of years by water eroding limestone, and contains a massive waterfall which plunges deep below ground level.

Until now, Titan has only been within reach of the relatively small number of expert cavers who knew of its existence.

(Source: Elsa McLaren and agencies (2006), www.timesonline.co.uk)

activity
INDIVIDUAL WORK

Why would Dave Nixon and his colleagues think that the discovery of Titan was worth the effort of digging for three years underground?

Cambridge University Caving Club
www.cucc.survex.com
The University of Edinburgh Expeditions Committee
www.expeditions.ed.ac.uk

Duration

Expeditions can last any length of time from one day to several years (although expeditions lasting several years are rare these days). One of the most famous long-lasting British expeditions was carried out by Charles Darwin. In 1831, at the age of 22, he applied and was accepted, after promising to pay the captain £500, to serve as a naturalist on HMS *Beagle* on a British science expedition around the world. He stuffed animals and collected insects, plants and fossils and sent them in crates back to London. He went to the Galapagos Islands and studied giant tortoises, among other things.

case study 9.8   **Charles Darwin**

I believe it is well ascertained, that the bladder of the frog acts as a reservoir for the moisture necessary to its existence: such seems to be the case with the tortoise. For some time after a visit to the springs, their urinary bladders are distended with fluid, which is said gradually to decrease in volume, and to become less pure. The inhabitants, when walking in the lower district, and overcome with thirst, often take advantage of this circumstance, and drink the contents of the bladder if full: in one I saw killed, the fluid was quite limpid, and had only a very slightly bitter taste. The inhabitants, however, always first drink the water in the pericardium, which is described as being best.

(Source: Charles Darwin (1839) *The Voyage of the Beagle*)

activity
INDIVIDUAL WORK

What is the value of scientific expeditions?

Returning to Britain in 1836, Darwin used his observations to work out his famous theory of evolution, which claims that all species of plant and animal, including ourselves, are descended from a single life form and that the changes happened through random genetic mutation and the survival of the fittest – a process he called 'natural selection'. This theory was publicised in *The Origin of Species* (1859). The book caused outrage at the time because it seemed like an attack on Christianity. Now, 150 years later, Darwin's ideas are still triggering lawsuits and demonstrations in countries as far apart as the USA and Turkey.

Form

Expeditions can be classified by the mode of transport used. They can involve any of the activities listed above, and more. Modern expeditions often use motorised transport (e.g. in the Antarctic), power boats (e.g. on the River Amazon), submarines and even space shuttles – but, to come down to earth, on BTEC courses they use non-motorised transport! For example:

- mountaineering
- trekking
- canoeing/kayaking
- sailing
- caving
- pony trekking
- cycling.

Area

There is no law that says that an expedition has to be in any particular area, but they are normally away from big cities or even towns. A one-day expedition for students is likely to be in the nearest area of open country. In the BTEC Specifications, there is an assumption that you will go on expeditions in 'mountainous' terrain which in Britain limits the choice. The most likely areas are Dartmoor, Wales, the Pennines, the Lake District, the Mountains of Mourne, the Southern Uplands of Scotland and the Scottish Highlands. If there are ways of overcoming the cost barrier, there is no reason why expeditions shouldn't take place in Ireland, mainland Europe, Scandinavia, Iceland, or even further afield. For people who can afford it, and are properly equipped, skilled and motivated, expeditions can be in any part of the world and on land or sea or in the air.

Aims

Some people have a built-in desire to go on expeditions, and 'itchy feet' that make them want to take to the road. The essential aim is often simply to get out and go somewhere different, for an adventure. The official aim is sometimes a reason or excuse to do something that they would probably do anyway.

Having said this, expeditions cost money and have to be justified (e.g. explained to sponsors and shown to be worth doing). If we look back over history, we see that expeditions are carried out for any number of reasons, some of which are briefly outlined below.

Military and conquest

Armies have always marched, and when they have marched to battle the march has been an expedition. When Julius Caesar invaded Britain in 55 BC he came as the leader of an expedition which had heard of a large, fertile, possibly wealthy island off the coast of what was then Gaul. The present occupation of Afghanistan by NATO forces is an expedition on a huge scale, with all necessities – weapons, equipment, clothes, food and everything else – transported in from the other side of the world. The present-day training of British soldiers in places such as Belize, Kenya, Canada and Oman involves expeditions into environments which cannot be found in Britain, but in which British forces may have to fight: savannah, bush, deserts and mountains. Then there is all the adventurous training which, as mentioned above, is used primarily for teambuilding and basic skills and which takes place in Britain itself.

Science

Expeditions to the Arctic, the Antarctic, to tropical rain forests, to archaeological sites, to erupting volcanoes, or to the sea bed, even expeditions into space by shuttle or rocket to land on the moon, repair the Hubble Telescope, or put people on the International Space Station, are all motivated by the need to advance science and technology, on which so much of our civilisation is based. Scientific aims are linked to commercial aims; for example, when drilling teams prospect for oil they are, in effect, expeditions.

Exploration

Although this is a less important motive than it used to be, because the earth's surface is now fully mapped, it is still an aim for cavers and for people examining the ocean floor.

Personal development and teambuilding

These are the main purposes for most educational expeditions and also for expeditionary activities carried out by people in industry, or in the military, who wish to develop their teamwork and leadership skills.

Competition

The exploits of Ellen MacArthur are a good example of expeditions based on competition. She is a sportswoman, but there is a commercial slant too in the sponsorship of her boat by B&Q.

Informative, entertainment, educational

Expeditions as carried out by ordinary people are often a form of active tourism. Travel is said to broaden the mind, and expeditions teach us about places and people. They are entertaining because things happen, and you have to make choices, and sometimes, as in sport, you have to put yourself to the test. As a social experience they are different from most because you see your friends, or your companions, in a new setting, and for that reason you see a different side to their personalities, and your own. They are educational because they are a learning experience.

Commercial

Expeditions are now big business – so they are commercial. As long as air travel is cheap, and the exchange rate is favourable (and thanks to their media portrayal through holiday programmes and celebrity or reality TV), there is keen interest in expeditions. They are seen by many as healthier than lounging on a beach in dangerously ultra-violet sunlight, bingeing on the local plonk, or whatever – and there is a certain snob-appeal in going somewhere exotic and developing a tough pioneering image. Also, even though expeditions may damage the environment, and be yet another sign of globalisation, they bring much-needed wealth to impoverished communities in places like Namibia and Nepal.

Other factors encouraging modern expeditions

A large number of factors connected with technology, modern wealth and affluence, leisure, tourism, holidays and changed social and cultural attitudes have made expeditions easier, less risky and in some ways more attractive than they ever used to be:

- Funding is available – from grants and commercial sponsorship (e.g. B&Q's sponsorship of Ellen MacArthur).

- Increased leisure pound – people have more disposable income, so more money to spend on travel.

- Planning and **logistics** are easier.

- There are more opportunities – gap years for students, more leisure time and more affluence – and it is socially acceptable for women to travel in a way that it used not to be.

- Universal education means that people have more technical skills and organising ability – both of which are needed for expeditions.

- Cheap air travel (the 'shrinking world') makes it easier to get to wild and remote areas.

- Seeing other places on television encourages travel.

- Social changes – people living in developing countries are more welcoming of expeditions, and there is now more tourist **infrastructure** in these countries.

- There is much better equipment than there used to be – of every type.

- Private transport can be used to get to the expedition starting point.

- There are new expeditionary sports such as scuba diving and paragliding.

- Rescue is more likely than it used to be – if something goes wrong!

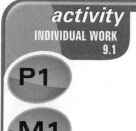

activity
INDIVIDUAL WORK
9.1

P1

M1

Produce a booklet suitable for Scouts, Guides or a similar organisation, describing, with illustrations, four expeditions which are all different from each other. In your booklet, there should be a conclusion, explaining in some detail how the expeditions differ from each other and what they share in common.

Planning expeditions

Planning an expedition properly has the following advantages:

- It increases the chance that the expedition will achieve all its objectives.
- It saves hassle and stress in the run-up to the expedition and during the expedition itself.
- It can save a lot of money.
- It makes the expedition safer.
- It avoids discomfort.
- It makes you feel good about your organising skills and gives you confidence for the future.

Plan

Planning is a process that should be done in stages. It begins with the idea, impulse, invitation, instruction or intention to go on an expedition. On a BTEC course it might be because you know expeditions are a part of the course; in the army you may know it is a part of training which is being planned for a definite date. In these cases you go on the expedition primarily because you have been told to, or because it is part of a wider commitment. If you belong to a club or society of mountaineers, potholers or others who go on expeditions, you and your club-mates will have been thinking on and off about possible destinations and purposes for some time. If you want to go on an expedition-style holiday, you might start trawling through brochures or the internet, or simply look at maps of an area that you have always wanted to visit. If you are a youth leader an instructor or an expedition leader working in the private sector, you might always be on the look-out for ideas for expeditions for the people you lead or for your clients. And, because of the range of expeditions which, as we have seen, takes place, there are many other scenarios (e.g. scientific research or oil prospecting) where people decide that they have to organise an expedition. Whatever the motivation, it is once the motivation is there that the planning has to start.

Appropriate choice of activity

Expedition organisers, who put forward the initial proposal (to get permission, funding, etc.) have to make sure either that:

- the people are right for the expedition or
- the expedition is right for the people.

An expedition to study the volcano on Jan Mayen Island needs to have members with a scientific interest and expertise in volcanoes, but an expedition for a BTEC National group, or any group of young people, has to be tailored to the needs and abilities of the expedition members.

Nevertheless, in each case the activities have to be:

- appropriate to the aims and objectives of the expedition
- appropriate to the interests and abilities of the expedition members
- acceptable to the sponsors and organisers, and to the organisation to which they belong
- acceptable to parents and relatives of expedition members
- as healthy and safe as is reasonably practicable
- **inclusive** for expedition members
- environmentally sound
- acceptable value for money
- as enjoyable as possible to expedition members without undermining any of the above.

Fig 9.4 Expedition planning stages

Initial proposal
Aims, objectives, date(s)
duration, venue, group, cost

↓

Get permission

↓

Logistics and general planning
Travel, accommodation, money,
people, roles, chain of command,
record-keeping, activities

↓

Detailed planning + preparation
Equipment (personal, safety, activities)
Informing expedition members
Tents, sleeping bags, cooking/food
Insurance, Health + Safety, Contingency plans
Organisation of activities
Money matters

↓

Pre-expedition
Finalising finance, insurance, transport plans,
packing, daily activities worked out
All documentation + financial
issues settled
Checking preparations, equipment,
Contingency plans finalised
Expedition members fully informed
Time/place of expedition start – reminders

↓

Expedition

↓

Debrief + review
Learning from the experience

Could be 3 months or more for a 1-week expedition

Appropriate choice of location

For the purposes of the BTEC National in Public Services an expedition is likely to be in a more or less mountainous area. This is because it says in the 'Essential Guidance for Tutors' that Unit 9 'is a practical unit and should be delivered in a practical fashion in an appropriate mountainous environment using the appropriate equipment'.

See page 329 above, where some suitable mountainous areas in Britain are listed.

For other expeditions an appropriate location is one that provides an environment suitable for the expedition's aims and objectives. Caving expeditions are always in limestone areas, because, in Britain, limestone is the only kind of rock that produces explorable caves. For ice-climbing (a dangerous activity for the unskilled and ill-equipped) Ben Nevis, the Cairngorms and a few other places in the Scottish Highlands are the only suitable places in Britain. If an expedition is carried out in order to do an archaeological dig, it has to be to a place where it is believed that archaeological remains will be found.

Factors that affect whether or not a location is appropriate include:

- suitability of the area and the facilities for the aims and objectives of the expedition
- ease and cheapness of travel to the expedition start
- the weather and the time of year
- availability and cost of camp sites
- whether there is something else to do if the weather turns bad
- whether the area has been **risk-assessed** in relation to the planned activities.

remember
Expeditions should be equal opportunity activities!

Aims and objectives

An aim is an aspiration (ambition) or intention; an objective is a statement of what will be done, in a particular context.

Aims are more general than objectives. An aim might be:

■ to walk from Horton in Ribblesdale to Kirby Stephen in three days, camping at Dent and Garsdale on the way.

Objectives might include:

■ Tents are correctly pitched bearing in mind the nature of the ground and the direction of the prevailing wind.

■ The expedition members plan and follow a route from Garsdale to the summit of Wild Boar Fell, using route-cards, map and compass.

Note that aims are often expressed in phrases beginning with 'to', while objectives are more usually expressed in sentences in the present tense.

The purpose of aims and objectives is to give the expedition a clear planning focus, enabling people to carry out **verifiable** or assessable activities. The expedition can be regarded as successful if the aims and objectives are carried out.

Permissions

Where an expedition is carried out by or on behalf of an organisation, or where sponsorship or help is needed, it is normal to get permission for it. This is so that it can be approved by the people who will foot the bill. Getting permission also helps to protect the organisers of an expedition from criticism or prosecution if something goes seriously wrong.

An expedition organised by a college or a public service always has to have permission – sometimes from a number of people. Schools and colleges now have to have educational visits coordinators to oversee activities such as expeditions. The bigger or more ambitious the expedition, the more separate permissions it might need. Such permissions might come from:

■ the organisation – perhaps through a vice principal or head of department

■ the insurers

■ the line manager of the expedition organiser (i.e. the person immediately above the organiser in the chain of command)

■ the governing body (a collection of important local people, councillors, industrialists, etc. who oversee the work of the institution if it is a college or school)

■ the local authority (especially if the school or college is formally run by the local authority)

■ parents or guardians (who need to sign **consent forms** if the people going on the expedition are under 18)

■ participants (who sign their own consent form if over 18; it is unwise to take people on expeditions if it is clear that they don't want to go).

If significant detail is not provided, the organisation may be sued for any accidents that occur. Where appropriate the permission should be signed and in writing.

Landowners

Permission should generally be obtained from anybody on whose land the expedition intends to camp. Often, this is an official camp site, so accepting a booking amounts to giving permission. The law forbids people to do '**wild camping**' in England but allows it in Scotland (since 2003), as long as it is away from houses etc. and causes no nuisance or damage.

Although wild camping is illegal in England, the law is not strictly enforced in Snowdonia and the Lake District, but it is strictly enforced in the Peak District, the North York Moors and any areas (dry peaty moors, for example) where there is a fire risk.

remember

Camping which leaves no mess, and causes no fire risk, is unlikely to get anybody into trouble.

Appropriate administrative bodies

This applies to expeditions organised by the armed forces, for example, where they have their own systems for approving and regulating expeditions. For this purpose, the main administrative structure covering all the armed forces is the Joint Services Adventurous Training Scheme (JSAT).

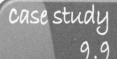

Approval in the armed services

To conduct most types of expedition training, approval will be required from the relevant authorities (primarily CO, Div SO2 AT and HQ ATG (A)). The correct form to apply for authority to conduct expedition training is the JSATFA. The JSATFA provides all 3 Services with a standard expedition application proforma.

(Source: www.army.mod.uk)

activity
INDIVIDUAL WORK

Why do you think adventurous training and expeditions are authorised by a single body for all three armed services?

Logistics

Logistics is a general word meaning transport and supply. Logistics is one of the most important aspects of expedition planning, and if expeditions fail it is often due to logistical problems (e.g. lack of proper equipment, food and other supplies). The reason why logistics is so important is that expeditions often go to remote areas where supplies, even food, cannot be obtained nearby.

The logistical needs of an expedition are determined by many things:

- size and type of group
- remoteness and accessibility of expedition area
- the level of self-sufficiency of the expedition
- length of time the expedition will last
- activities of the expedition
- weather and climate
- nature of the expedition environment
- health and safety back-up needed.

Group size

Expeditions vary in size according to their purpose and other factors. For a BTEC National Public Services expedition, the determining factor is the size of the student group (assuming that they are going on an expedition where they basically remain as a single group). For a Duke of Edinburgh's Award expedition, the group is likely to be smaller – say four to six – and able to fit into one or two tents. Upper limits are often fixed by the size of buses (or minibuses) in which people are transported to the expedition starting point or the base camp.

Staff/group ratios

In an educational expedition, staff members or instructors are usually 'in charge' of a number of students. With any closely supervised expedition there should normally be at least two members of staff. The younger and more vulnerable the students, or the more risky the activities, the fewer students there should be per member of staff. For standard activities, such as hillwalking with people aged 16 and over, a staff:student ratio of 1:10 is normal.

Surrey County Council Guidelines for Educational Visits and Outdoor Activities
www.surreycc.gov.uk

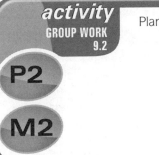

activity
GROUP WORK
9.2

P2

M2

Plan a one-day expedition suitable for a named group of young people.

Transport

Link

See page 336.

Accommodation groups
Expeditions can:

- *Stay at a centre.* If expedition members are young, vulnerable and have never camped, there are obvious advantages in using a centre. Centres – whether youth hostels or commercial outdoor centres – usually have dormitories or bedrooms, often with bunk-beds, and communal kitchens and living rooms. They usually have good showers, toilet and drying facilities, etc. It is possible to self-cater. They provide a degree of home comfort but are less challenging, and there is less freedom of movement than there is with camping.

- *Camp in tents on an official camp site.* This gives much better training in self-reliance and enables people to learn **camp craft**. There is freedom to move from one site to the next, staying in a different place each night. Most commercial sites have basic but adequate washing and toilet facilities. Rain, wind, cold, and flooding are all potential hazards – but skilled, well-organised camping can minimise the discomfort.

- *Camp – but not on an official site.* This is sometimes called 'wild camping' (unless permission has been obtained from a farmer). It is illegal but people usually get away with it. If the camp is pitched at nightfall and taken down at daybreak, and is well away from any houses, the chances are that nobody will notice. It is more of an option for small groups than for large expeditions, and it is essential to avoid fire risks and to clear up any mess afterwards.

- *Bivouac.* This is sleeping out in a **survival bag** or under a plastic sheet. It can be enjoyable in summer, especially for experienced backpackers who like **bivouacking**. It is still necessary to use a sleeping bag and, preferably, a **sleeping mat** too. Bivouacking is not recommended in winter.

Whatever accommodation system is used, young expeditioners need supervising at night. Suitable privacy is needed, and with some groups there may be a risk of illicit drinking or drugs.

Equipment
This important aspect of logistics is dealt with in more detail below.

Food
It is not essential to have cooked food on a summer expedition – but most people prefer it. There is a lot more scope for variety if you have a base camp and don't have to carry on your back the food to be cooked. If you are active and the weather is cold

case study 9.10

Modes of transport to the expedition area – and comments

Public transport (individual). It is theoretically possible for expedition members to travel to the expedition area by local bus and train, individually. The advantage is that it cuts down on arranging, but for a student expedition it is not the best option. Less-motivated students wouldn't turn up; it would be easier for some people to get there than for others; it might be harder to meet up at the expedition area; people could miss the bus, or a connection. The overall expense is likely to be greater than for some other methods such as the college minibus. Some students of driving age would drive there, perhaps with their friends; there is a greater risk of road accidents; the insurance situation would become complex, and the overall discipline of the expedition could be undermined. It would be hard to take head-counts because people might arrive at different places at different times. Besides all of these objections, many expedition areas are poorly served by public transport.

Public transport (group). This system is better because staff can be responsible for students during the journey, and proper head-counts can be taken. Cheap group travel is available on some trains if you book early. The main disadvantage, as stated above, is that expedition areas often have poor public transport, or none at all.

Transport belonging to the institution (e.g. college minibus). This is convenient and cheap, but there have been serious accidents with college-type transport. Drivers must be qualified and able to drive a minibus safely; the minibus must be in good mechanical order, and there should be somebody beside the driver to maintain order and discipline. Minibuses typically only carry about 12 people and their luggage, so unless there are two minibuses there may be a lack of capacity. A big advantage is that minibuses can be used as support vehicles during the expedition, and offer back-up if someone is ill or injured.

Transport belonging to the providers of the expedition (e.g. army transport). This is sometimes (not always) obtainable and is a cheap and easy alternative. It can be used by the providers as a support vehicle during the expedition.

Hired coach. Coaches are large and comfortable, and have skilled, qualified drivers (although they can have serious accidents, and there may be an added risk on long-haul continental routes). The cost varies, but this is a convenient form of transport for fairly large expeditions accompanied by several staff members.

Private cars of expedition members and staff. This is not the most environmentally friendly way to use expedition transport. However, in terms of flexibility of arrangement and dealing with emergencies, there are advantages in having one car driver with an expedition together with a coach. This system works with recreational expeditions run by committed adults but can cause organisational and discipline problems in student expeditions.

Ferries. In expeditions with students aged under 16 going to the continent or Ireland there are some safety risks; young students should not wander about unsupervised on deck.

Air. Good supervision and organisation is needed in an expedition of young people.

activity
INDIVIDUAL WORK

Choose and justify (i.e. support with reasons, arguments and examples) your preferred form of transport to the starting point of an expedition that you will be going on.

(which is usually the case on an expedition) you need plenty of carbohydrates as well as protein and fats. Although excellent for health, vegetables and fruit are heavy (because of the water content) and perish when carried for long distances. Dried fruit is a useful supplement. Tinned food is heavy, so dried food is better for carrying; it can be mixed with water and cooked at the camp site.

Lightweight campers sometimes carry lightweight diets (e.g. oatmeal, dried milk, raisins and cheese) which don't need cooking, save weight and hassle, and last for several days.

Equipment

This is a complex subject: there is only room to go into the basics here. For a camping expedition, the following are needed.

Tent

Tents are widely used in expeditions. They cost anything from about £30 upwards, but a reliable one for expedition purposes usually costs at least £100. You can buy tiny tents for one person, and then a range of different sizes going up to 10-person tents. Lightweight tents are used for backpacking-type expeditions where the tent has to be carried a long way and weight is an issue. Mountain tents are also lightweight but are streamlined and designed to withstand strong winds, snow and heavy rain. Medium tents designed for four people are still light enough to carry and are suitable for most BTEC expeditions. Most tents are of a dome shape and are easy to put up and take down – but it is still a very good idea to practise putting one up and getting it down again before the expedition. Putting up a strange tent in driving rain can leave you sodden and homesick almost before the expedition has started!

Bigger tents are more comfortable than little ones, but they weigh more and can be more difficult to pitch (put up). They are sometimes used for a base camp, where most equipment is kept, and then people use smaller tents if they are going up into the mountains for a few days. Cooking tents can be used in an expedition where the food for the whole party is being prepared under canvas. Bivouac equipment is useful in summer for people who want to sleep out on a mountain without carrying too much weight.

Fig 9.5 Which is the right tent?

Personal equipment

Rucksack

For an expedition where you have to carry your own camping stuff, a rucksack with at least 60 litres' capacity is needed. You may be able to borrow one from your expedition organisers. Before the expedition starts, check that it feels comfortable and adjust it to fit your back.

Sleeping bags

These are essential when camping. They come in different weights, and you should make sure that the one you have is warm enough for the season. If your sleeping bag has too low a tog rating (i.e. is not warm enough), you may find that you have to sleep in all your clothes as well as the sleeping bag. The filling should be Terylene® or the equivalent (although down sleeping bags are said to be the warmest, weight for weight). Get advice before buying one.

Sleeping mat

This is a kind of mat about 2 cm thick which you put under your sleeping bag in the tent to prevent the cold striking up from the ground.

Warm clothes

It is absolutely essential that you take enough warm clothes with you on an expedition. Unglamorous or wimpish as it might seem, it is best to bundle up in several layers of clothing when it is cold.

Base layers

T-shirts and sweat shirts can be put on top of your underwear (up to four or five if the weather is really cold).

Warmth layers

You can put fleeces and an anorak on top of the base layers – in winter weather. Even in hot summer weather you should take more clothes than you need because the nights can be unexpectedly cold.

Waterproof protection

It is usual to wear anoraks or Gor-Tex® or some other breathable waterproof fabric. These are expensive but may, perhaps, be borrowed from an expedition organiser. Cheap waterproof cagoules will do, although they can get damp inside from condensation in cold weather. Some form of waterproof protection is essential in Britain.

Footwear

Proper walking or climbing boots are expensive, but they are needed on rough, steep or boggy terrain, especially in cold weather. Wellingtons are cheap, keep your feet dry and are usable for some kinds of walking. However, they can be dangerous on steep slopes because they slip on mud and wet grass. Ordinary shoes should never be worn for rough walking. Some people wear trainers when walking, but these don't protect the ankles and don't keep the water out.

Other useful stuff

- Water bottle – because of the amount of muck-spreading done by modern hill-farmers, it is not as safe to drink from moorland streams as it used to be. You should therefore carry a bottle of water (up to 1 litre) with you, especially on warm sunny days when there is a risk of hyperthermia and dehydration.

- Bin-bags – these are needed to wrap your dry clothes in, even when in the rucksack or the tent, so that they don't get rained on by day or night.

- Torch – a torch is useful if you have to mess about at night.

See page 342 for discussion of first aid.

Group equipment

Stoves

These are usually of the '**Trangia**' type and consist of a meths burner and a series of nested aluminium pans, which can also be used as stands and **windbreaks**.

To use these stoves it is necessary to carry a bottle of methylated spirits (methanol) as fuel. Methanol should be treated with caution as it is highly flammable, burns with an invisible flame, which can be dangerous, and is toxic.

remember

It is unwise, unsafe, and usually illegal to light fires at a camp site.

Cooking equipment

This should be kept to a minimum if it has to be carried. The Trangia pans ought to be enough. Light metal plates, enamel mugs and a bare minimum of cutlery should be carried. Some implements like a fish slice and a tin-opener are needed.

Ropes

If you are going rock-climbing, potholing or anything else on your expedition, the organisers should supply the equipment you need. If you buy your own climbing rope, take an expert along with you. Activity equipment is expensive and usually made to high technical specifications, so that you get the maximum enjoyment from the activity with the minimum of risk.

activity
**GROUP WORK
9.3**

P3

M3

Plan an expedition for young people that would be suitable as part of basic training for a public service. The expedition should last a number of days. Produce action plans, permission requests, **route cards**, transport arrangements, equipment lists, approximate costings, health and safety arrangements, shopping lists and any other information that you feel would be needed by participants.

Finance

Expeditions have to be paid for, and getting the money together is one of the most difficult parts of expedition planning. The order in which things are done is usually as follows:

Fig 9.6 Trangia stove

1. Costing – produce a clear and itemised statement of what the expedition is going to cost
2. Costing – communicate to expedition members and parents
3. Collection schedule – devise a timetable for collecting money from expedition participants and/or other sources
4. Collection schedule – communicate
5. Receipts – start collecting the money, recording it, giving receipts, keeping the money safe
6. Receipts – end by ensuring that all money is collected; making **contingency** arrangements in cases of financial hardship
7. Bursary – spending the expedition money; paying the providers (if they are being used); paying for transport; equipment; accommodation costs, etc.
8. Account/balance sheet – a clear statement of the money that has come in and the money that has been paid out
9. Refunds – calculate/give out (this is if too much money has been collected).

Budgeting, income and expenditure

This means working out costs, getting money in – and spending it.

Budgeting includes:

- getting quotations from expedition providers (if they are going to be used)
- matching them with the services provided to decide which is most affordable, or best value for money
- working out the cost for expedition members, and how staff members will be paid for
- getting quotations for transport
- finding out other costs such as equipment purchase or hire, fuel for transport (if needed), costs for accommodation including camp sites, etc.

Identifying major cost areas

These are food, transport, fuel and camping fees, and possibly costs charged by expedition organisers and/or costs for the hire/purchase of equipment.

Audit systems

The collection and spending of money must be clearly and properly recorded, so that everybody who wants to know can see that the money has been collected efficiently and honestly, spent wisely, and that expedition participants have had value for money. It is vital that there is a proper **audit system**:

- to ensure that everybody has paid the correct amount (it is not unknown for people to claim that they have paid when they haven't)
- to protect the organisers from accusations of fiddling or incompetence.

Without a proper audit system the organisers are likely to find themselves out of pocket.

A system of receipts coupled with a matching account book, which expedition members sign when money is paid in, is an effective way of collecting money, especially from people who may only be able to pay a bit at a time.

It goes without saying that money should be kept in a safe place after it is collected – ideally in a special college or bank account. This allows a second check to be kept on the amount of money collected.

Working to planned budget

It is important if you are organising the expedition yourself to:

- know how much money you have to spend
- work out costs in advance, ensuring that they do not go over your budget

remember

Income is money paid in and expenditure is money paid out.

- ensure that you are not cutting corners – in what you need or in safety equipment
- keep full records of spending
- avoid overspending.

Planning for emergencies
Sometimes expedition organisers collect a little more money than is needed for the expedition itself in case unforeseen expenses connected with the expedition turn up. If this is done, it should be done openly, and with the agreement of participants.

Surrey County Council Guidelines for Educational Visits and Outdoor Activities – this is a top document!
www.surreycc.gov.uk

Health and safety
There are several sides to health and safety when planning expeditions.

Health
Health considerations include:

- obtaining the names, addresses and phone numbers of expedition members' doctors and contact details of next of kin
- ensuring that any relevant health information about expedition members is known by the organisers (e.g. asthma, recent injuries) and that medication is both known about and taken care of during the expedition (this information should be on medical forms)
- informing parents and guardians – in writing – about all aspects of the planned expedition
- obtaining parental consent (**notification forms**)
- not taking anybody who is ill, or has conditions which would put them at risk
- taking correctly filled first aid kits and a first-aider
- knowing emergency numbers and details of the mountain rescue facilities in the expedition area
- making certain that everybody is properly and fully insured.

Safety
Safety considerations include:

- organising an expedition that is within the capabilities of the expedition members
- carrying out a proper risk assessment of the expedition and its activities, in relation to the people going
- having safe transport to and from the expedition area
- paying attention to weather forecasts – especially heavy rain in relation to streams and caves
- having contingency and escape plans in case of bad weather or anything else that could affect the safety of an activity
- ensuring that, if the expedition involves having separate groups, all groups are effectively monitored
- checking that people are properly dressed and equipped on the hills, and that they have food and water
- teaching navigation skills and ensuring that people can find their way, or know what to do if they get lost
- using route plans which expedition members follow and which those in charge have copies of

- telling groups to keep together – and making sure they do
- making it clear – and keeping a record of – when people should be back at camp
- having enough properly qualified and safety-aware staff and instructors present
- having a clearly understood chain of command, so that people know who is responsible for what
- ensuring that stoves are understood and used safely
- not lighting fires
- organising activities that are exciting but within people's capabilities, relatively risk-free, and don't involve long periods of unsupervised hanging around
- giving instructions and carrying out practice drills, if necessary, on mountain safety
- having written and agreed return dates and times (both for each day and for the whole expedition)
- having activities or measures in place which prevent accidents or indiscipline during 'down time'
- being there to deal with disputes, arguments or other problems between expedition members and, in some cases, depression or homesickness
- taking steps to ensure that there is no risk of unauthorised drinking or of anyone taking any recreational drugs during the expedition.

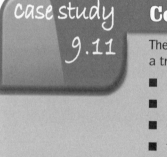

case study 9.11

Contents of a travelling first aid kit

The Health and Safety Executive recommends the following minimum contents for a travelling first aid kit where no special risk has been identified:

- a leaflet giving general advice on first aid;
- six individually-wrapped sterile dressings;
- one sterile unmedicated wound dressing approximately 18cm x 18cm;
- two triangular bandages;
- two safety pins;
- individually wrapped moist cleansing wipes;
- one pair of disposable gloves.

(Source: *Surrey County Council Guidelines for Educational Visits and Outdoor Activities*, www.surreycc.gov.uk)

activity
INDIVIDUAL WORK

Bearing in mind the nature of expeditions in mountainous terrain on foot, what other first aid items might you want to carry?

Health and Safety Executive
www.hse.gov.uk

Undertaking expeditions

remember

This unit is not in itself about teamwork and leadership, but these are an aspect of expedition skills, and you should try to show good teamwork and leadership qualities during the expeditions you undertake.

For this unit you will need to go on expeditions. Your aims are to show skill and understanding both when camping and when travelling on foot. You will be expected to assess yourself, and perhaps others, on how well the expeditions were done.

Skills

Navigation skills

These are to do with finding your way around in open country, perhaps on mountains, possibly in foggy weather or even after dark. As your expeditions may well be in places you have never visited before, you will need to be able to use a map and compass.

Orientation of map

Orientation of map is sometimes called 'setting the map'.

1. Lay the map flat.
2. Turn the compass housing so that north is aligned with the direction-of-travel arrow.
3. Put the compass on the map.
4. Line up the long edge of the compass with a vertical gridline.
5. Turn both compass and map, keeping the long edge of the compass in line with the gridline, until the magnetic needle points to north on the housing.
6. The map is now set. The top edge of the map faces north, and all the vertical blue **gridlines** on the map also point north.

If you do this when you are planning an expedition, or a day's walk, you can then work out the **bearings** of each leg, or section, of the walk. To do this you:

1. Keep the map in position.
2. Place the long side of your compass against both your starting point and your destination point on the map.
3. Turn the compass housing so that N is at the north end of the magnetised needle.
4. Read the bearing at the index line. This is the bearing of your first leg. Note it down.
5. Repeat the process with all the other legs of your expedition.

Direction finding

Setting the map and using it to find bearings is one part of direction finding. The other part is reading the compass and finding direction when you are out on your expedition. The basic method is:

1. Hold the compass close to your chest, where you can keep it steady and see it properly.
2. Point the direction-of-travel arrow in the direction you want to go.
3. Turn the compass housing so that the north end of the magnetic needle is at N on the housing.
4. Read off the bearing of the direction you want to go in at the index line below the housing.

Fig 9.7 'Silva'-style compass

remember

The index line on a compass is just under the housing behind the direction-of-travel arrow.

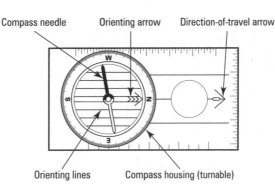

Compass needle   Orienting arrow   Direction-of-travel arrow

Orienting lines   Compass housing (turnable)

Interpretation

A compass gives you magnetic north – the direction of the north magnetic pole. Grid north on the map is, for practical purposes, the same as true north, which is towards the North Pole itself. The difference between magnetic north and true north is 4°, magnetic north being 4°W of true (i.e. grid) north. This is a fairly slight difference, and for practical purposes it usually doesn't matter.

If you want to change one to the other the following rhyme may help to remind you how to do it:

> Grid to mag – add.
> Mag to grid – get rid.

If a hilltop that you're walking towards is at 245° according to your compass, it will be at 241° on the map.

Grid references

Grid references are groups of six figures which are used to identify a position on a map. They are based on the blue squares on your map and the numbers that run along each side of the map.

Figure 9.8 is a simplified map of a place called Maggie's Farm.

To give a six-figure grid reference for the farm:

1. Read *along* the line numbers from left to right ('eastings') and put down the number of the line to the left of the farm. This is 05.

2. Estimate tenths of the distance across the square from left to right, starting at line 05. These are shown on the bottom of the square in the simplified map. Maggie's Farm is six-tenths of the way across the square, so the next figure in the grid reference is 6.

3. You have now done the first half of your grid reference, and it is 056. Write this down.

4. Read up the line numbers from bottom to top ('northings') and put down the number of the line below the farm. This is 17.

5. Estimate tenths of the distance up the square from bottom to top, starting at line 17. These are shown to the right of the square on the simplified map. Maggie's Farm is eight-tenths of the way up the square, so the next figure in the grid reference is 8.

6. You have now done the second half of your grid reference, and it is 178.

7. Put the two halves of your grid reference together and you have the six-figure grid reference for Maggie's Farm, which is 056178.

Figure 9.8 Maggie's Farm

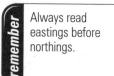

The method is exactly the same whether the Ordnance Survey (**OS**) map is 1:25,000 or 1:50,000.

The squares are 1 km in size, so a six-figure grid reference gives the position of the place you have pinpointed to the nearest 100 m.

Scale and distance

The maps used for expeditions in Britain are usually 1:50,000 or 1:25,000 in scale. The smaller the number on the right, the larger the scale: a 1:25,000 map is a larger-scale map than a 1:50,000 map. A centimetre on a 1:25,000 map equals 250 metres on the ground. A centimetre on a 1:50,000 map equals 500 metres on the ground. This means that a 1:25,000 map gives more detail than a 1:50,000 map but covers a smaller area.

On either map the blue squares of the grid have sides 1 km in length.

To measure distances you measure your planned route in centimetres. If it is 40 cm on a 1:25,000 map, it is 40 × 250 m on the ground – which is 10 km.

Measuring a wiggly route on a map can be done:

- with a piece of thread or thin string
- marking the length of each leg on the edge of a piece of A4 paper (without marking the map!) and then measuring the total with a ruler
- using your fingers if you know their measurements
- judging it by eye (with the help of the grid-squares).

Handrail features

These are features like walls, ridges, paths and streams which help you to find your way without looking too often at the map. They can be identified on your map when you plan your walk and noted on your route card. Often, they lead you to the place you are going to – and they can be very useful, especially in fog.

Use of key

The key is the part of a map which tells you what all the **symbols** mean. It is worth looking at the key and studying the symbols, because if you understand them they will give you a lot of information. Features on the key to which you should pay particular attention are those which tell you about natural hazards and what the ground will be like underfoot. Things to look out for are shown in Table 9.2.

Table 9.2 Map symbols

Feature	Map symbol	Importance for walkers
Streams which are too wide to jump across	Double blue line with pale blue in between	You can't cross them without getting wet
Cliffs	Black wiggly symbol like a broken comb	Risk of falling; possible risk of stones falling on head
Scree (loose stones)	Lots of spots	Risk of broken ankles and serious delay if the stones are large
Rock outcrops	Tiny black caterpillars	Slow progress – you have to walk round them
Bog and marsh	Broken blue lines	Wet feet; slow progress; possible risk of getting stuck in bog
Plantations and bushes	Tree symbols	Obstructions to progress
Walls and farmland (only marked on the 1:25,000 map)	Faint lines for walls, fences and hedges; plain white paper for farmland	Walls, fences and hedges get in the way; walking on farmland is bad for agriculture; risk of stroppy animals (and humans)

Compass skills

It is important to take care of compasses and maps; in particular, compasses should be kept away from magnets. Maps should be folded correctly, kept in waterproof bags, dried out carefully if they get wet, and not drawn on.

See page 350 for information on advanced compass skills.

Camp craft skills

Camp craft skills are those that you need to camp safely, comfortably, and without irritating other people.

Erecting tents

Read the instructions and, if possible, practise putting up the tent before the expedition. Be orderly and systematic. Any **guy ropes** should be tight and pulled outward from the tent at 90°. Pegs should be at 90° to the guy rope, so that they aren't easily pulled out. Don't tread on the tent fabric. Take care not to get water in the tent; ask for help if you're getting in a tangle.

Striking (taking down) tents

When **striking camp**, take the tents down in an orderly way. Put pegs, poles, etc. in the right bags. Check that you haven't left anything out. Roll the tent up properly. *Most important of all: if the tent is wet, dry it out properly as soon as you can.*

Selecting camp site

A good camp site has flat, dry, clean ground, without sticks, stones and lumps. Avoid places which look as though they might flood. Choose a place which is reasonably sheltered but not actually under trees. Pitch the tent with its back to the wind, preferably close to a wall, hedge or other windbreak (if available). Keep away from other tents as much as reasonably possible, and in any case leave two yards between your tent and the next. If the ground slopes, sleep with your head at the top end.

Use of terrain for shelter

It is possible to camp quite high on mountains, but wind can be a problem. The prevailing wind in Britain comes from the west, so the east slopes of hills tend to be less windy. (However, this is not always so. Check the weather forecast and see what the wind is going to be like before you start your expedition.) Cwms, corries, cloughs and combes (small valleys on British mountains) are less windy than ridges and exposed hillsides. Rocks and small hummocks can give shelter and so, of course, can bushes and walls.

Cooking

Cook out of the wind but never inside the tent. If you are on a long, tiring expedition keep the cooking simple and calorific.

Bivouac building

Bivouacs are very enjoyable if you like sleeping out under the stars without a tent. Choose a comfortable, dry bit of ground. If it is likely to rain, you need a waterproof sheet or survival bag. Light tarpaulins or tent groundsheets will do. Some of these can be fastened down with aluminium pegs. Always use a sleeping bag for a bivouac and, unless the night is very warm, put on extra clothes. Dew and condensation can be a problem with a survival bag, so in the morning, if the weather is dry, tie your sleeping gear to the outside of the rucksack and walk with it like that until it has dried off. More elaborate bivouacs can be built using tarpaulins, branches, etc., but it is not very practicable, takes time and energy and limits your choice of site.

Travelling skills

Walking on mountains is a skill. If you have to walk a long way, get into your rhythm and keep going. Don't run downhill: you can break an ankle or injure a knee. It is often easier to zigzag up a steep slope than to go straight up it. If you can see ahead, plan an easy route avoiding outcrops and rough ground. On steep ground, keep an eye above for falling rocks, especially if there are people or frisky sheep around. If you dislodge a stone and it sets off at high speed, shout 'Below!' at the top of your voice, even if you can't see anybody. If you are going up or downhill in a group, keep close together – again to avoid the risk of setting off stones which might then hit another member of the party.

Don't expect to go up hills as fast as you can walk on the flat. If you are going up a hill, every contour adds an extra minute onto the time that you would take to walk the same distance on the flat. Rough or boggy ground also slows you down.

See page 352 for more on calculating walking times.

Pace and rhythm

Pace can mean walking speed, but it can also mean the length of each individual step. A moderately fast walker going across open ground averages 2½ miles (4 km) an hour. Everybody has their own pace, depending mainly on their aerobic fitness. You should aim to walk as fast as you reasonably can without getting short of breath or experiencing discomfort. Breaks should be short (under 20 minutes) if you want to cover a long distance in one day. Rhythm means getting into a steady pace that suits you. Avoid rushing uphill or downhill.

> **remember**
> Unnecessary variations in walking speed are tiring.

Energy conservation

This means finding the best walking speed for you or your group and sticking to it. Monitor your tiredness, and, if you are getting too tired, activate your contingency plan (see below).

Control skills

Don't run on rough ground or down steep hills (unless you are a fell-runner or other expert). If your boots are slippery, take extra care.

Traversing difficult ground

Steep ground, snowy ground, wet ground, screes and stony ground, ground with rushes, swamps, soft peat or hidden holes, frozen or slippery ground: all these must be treated with caution. Go slowly or avoid such areas, especially if the light is poor. Allow more time in your expedition planning if the ground is difficult.

> **remember**
> Expeditions should be inclusive. Talk to the organisers if you think that you are being made to spend money which you or your family cannot afford.

Avoidance of hazards

Hillwalking is not the most dangerous activity in the world, but up to 50 people die avoidably on Britain's hills and mountains each year. Many others are injured or taken ill but are saved by mountain rescue or by the brave and sensible actions of their companions.

Table 9.3 lists possible hazards. Note that more of them are to do with human behaviour than with the mountains or the weather.

Table 9.3 Potential hazards

Potential hazard	Nature of danger	How to avoid the danger
Poor planning	Getting lost, overtired, too thirsty, too hungry, etc; getting benighted	Plan properly. Have an escape or contingency plan for bad weather, injury, etc. Know how to call for help if you need it. Carry a whistle, torch or phone
Dangerous terrain	Steep rocky ground, cliffs, snow, ice, swollen streams, bogs, tiring tussocky grass	Use a 1:25,000 map, which shows relevant terrain features. Change your route if the ground is unexpectedly difficult. Don't climb mountains in snow unless you are properly equipped
Bad weather	Wind, heavy rain, snow, fog, extreme cold, extreme heat, strong sunshine	Listen to the weather forecast and go out properly equipped. Take spare clothes in cool or cold weather, and sunblock and extra water in hot weather
Poor health or fitness of party	Tiredness, feeling ill, dehydration	Plan walks which are not too strenuous. Never go on expeditions when unwell or unfit. Avoid drugs or alcohol on the hills
Lack of walking skills and experience	Not recognising danger, tiredness; being badly equipped; doing something silly	Never split up from the rest of your party. Get advice and listen to it. Don't be too ambitious: climbing mountains can be more tiring and dangerous than it looks. Don't try to show off or take needless risks
Unsuitable equipment	Not protected against the weather or the terrain; results in getting too cold or wet, having blisters, etc.	Obtain the right equipment – if necessary by borrowing it. Unfortunately, good walking gear is costly. Tell your expedition organiser well in advance if money or equipment is going to be a problem. Carry sticking plasters

Fig 9.9 Difficult terrain

British Orienteering
www.britishorienteering.org.uk
The Mountaineering Council of Scotland
www.mountaineering-scotland.org.uk
v-g – the website has information about backpacking in Britain
www.v-g.me.uk

Weather-related skills

The main one is simply to listen to the weather forecast and plan accordingly. It is useful to know how to read a weather map, since these maps give a wealth of information (to someone who understands them) which a satellite picture or radar image cannot provide.

Weather forecasts

The BBC, many national papers, the Maritime and Coastguard Agency, mountain rescue and other organisations all provide weather forecasts. All official British weather information comes from the Met Office. Local people may also give useful weather information.

Visit the Met Office website to get good weather maps and learn how to read them; search under 'Europe: charts'
www.metoffice.gov.uk

Predicting conditions

Table 9.4 Predicting weather conditions

Weather sign	Description	Meaning
Needle on barometer moves left when tapped	**Air pressure falling**	Worsening weather
High cloud getting thicker. Wind strengthening from S or SW	**Warm front coming**	Rain on the way. Low cloud and drizzle after it. Wind is always stronger on hills
Thick dark cloud moving in from W or NW	**Cold front coming**	Heavy rain followed by cool wind and showers
Small heaped clouds or none at all. Not much wind	Fine weather	A good day ahead
Hot with clouds piling up by 11 a.m.	Thundery weather	Risk of storms. Get into a hollow if there is lightning
Both rain and blue sky in sight	A showery day	Showers are often worst around the middle of the day
Cloud moving down over mountains	Risk of fog	Take bearings while you can and make sure you know where you are
Heavy continuous rain	Typical of British mountains	Be careful near swollen streams

Assessing conditions

The more exposed or higher the ground, the worse the weather is. For every 1000 feet (305 metres) temperatures can go down by, say, 3 or 4 °C. On high ground, wind is stronger; rain is heavier; snow is deeper; and fog or cloud may drastically reduce visibility. Always bear this in mind when planning walks over British mountains. Take spare warm clothing and extra food. Very hot weather too can be a hazard, leading to overheating, dehydration and loss of energy. Take extra water, or suitable drinks.

Advanced skills

Navigation skills improve with experience. An interest in geography is useful, because it enables you to notice and remember the shapes of particular mountains and valleys.

Navigation using interpretive features

Being observant can help you to navigate. **Interpretive features** include the lie of the grass, which often shows the prevailing wind (west or south west); cliffs and corries are usually on the northern or eastern sides of mountains; the wind direction on the day helps if you know the weather forecast. The position of the sun at different times of the day is useful. In British Summer Time the sun is at its highest and due south, at 1.30 p.m. Six hours before this it is due east; six hours later it is due west. In winter, with Greenwich Mean Time, the sun is at its highest at 12.30 p.m. Since the sun isn't up in winter for the full 12 hours, it rises in the south east and sets in the south west.

Aiming off using compass bearings

This means setting a course to left or right of where you really want to go, in order to reduce the risk of getting lost. The aim is usually to reach a '**handrail**' and follow it to your destination.

Identification of position by methods of relocation

This means identifying where you are by using a landmark different from the place you are steering towards – because your real destination is hidden. For example, you might be heading for a bothy (mountain hut) but, if it is hidden in a fold in the hills, you steer towards the nearest visible feature (e.g. a crag or ridge above the bothy).

Look out for:

- attack points – landmarks between you and your real destination which help you to avoid getting lost
- collecting features – hills etc. beyond your (hidden) destination which you can steer towards.

Fig 9.10 Aiming off

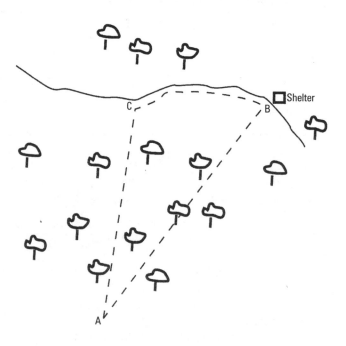

Navigation in poor visibility/darkness

Hilltops are often foggy, in which case you need a compass to navigate with – especially if the hilltop is smooth and featureless. First, you should look at your map or your route card to be sure which direction you ought to be travelling in. Then use your compass to find the bearing. Then walk towards the furthest tuft of grass, or lump of stone that you can see on that bearing. When you reach that tuft etc., look again at your compass, identify the furthest object you can see on that same bearing, and walk to it. Carry on like this until you reach your destination. If it starts getting dark, get down off the mountain as soon as it is safe to do so.

Darkness, especially when there is no moon, or when it is also foggy, is more difficult than fog. Normally, the best thing to do is to get off the mountain before darkness falls. Study the map with a torch and, as long as it appears safe to do so and will not get you too far from your destination, walk downhill to the nearest track or road. If you get caught in darkness on dangerous rocky terrain and can't move further, get into a safe and sheltered place; use your bivouac equipment if you have it; huddle together and have a night out. If the weather is unpleasant and there is any risk of exposure or **hypothermia**, telephone or signal for help: you probably need it.

Navigation with speed and accuracy in all conditions

This is a lot to ask. You need practice and plenty of it – and, even then, mistakes can be made or conditions can be unexpectedly bad. When conditions are really bad, especially in winter, you shouldn't go up mountains at all unless you are fit, experienced, well equipped and know exactly what you are doing.

Elementary interpretation of weather

See page 349 for information.

Techniques

Navigation techniques

Most of these have been discussed in the previous section. Those that weren't covered are outlined below.

Route cards

These are cards or pieces of paper giving details of the route you intend to walk. If you are walking alone or as a member of a separate group, you should keep one copy for yourself and give one to the expedition organiser. This means that, if you or your party go missing, people will know where to look for you.

Fig 9.11 Route card

All details and legs must be completed on your card before you set out. Through lack of space the example on the right is unfinished.

Route Card   Emergency contact 01924 456345

Date 15.07.08
Start time 09.30
Finish time 17.00
Members of party Marion Bartoli, Imran Khan, Jahangir Khan, Kelly Wood
Basic walking speed 2kph
Grid reference for starting point 378032

Leg	To (Grid ref)	Details of route	Bearing	Distance	Height + or −	Time	Rests	Total time	ETA	Escape to
1	364051	Along lane to Gandalf Wood	325	.75 km	+ 50m	27m	10m	37m	10.07	Baggins Bridge
2	358079	Up short steep hill to cairn	316	.25 km	+100m	17m	5m	22m	10.29	Baggins Bridge
3	355104	To summit of Bilbo Pike, then follow ridge to Hobbit Fell	004	2.8 km	+ 485m	2hr 12m	30m	2.42	13.11	Frodo Farm

Calculating time

A fit party crossing open, upland country and not following a path will manage a speed of 4–5 kph (kilometres per hour). This speed can drop sharply if the terrain is rough or boggy, or if the party is walking up or down steep slopes.

Use of rests

It is sensible to take a rest of, say, 10 minutes in any one hour. To cover a long distance, walk as fast as you reasonably can without getting short of breath and take short rests. (Long rests – over 20 minutes – waste time and make you feel lazy.) Small, frequent snacks supply energy for walking better than large, widely spaced meals.

Calculating distance

See page 345 for information.

Counting off features

This is a system used in orienteering to check how far you have gone. In mountain navigation, the same thing is done if you mark your route card as you reach the end of each leg (section).

Camp craft techniques

See also page 346 above.

The main ones are shown below.

Maintaining a dry tent

Pitch your tent in a sheltered, dry place, not too close to other tents. Keep boots and wet clothes off the groundsheet.

---

case study
9.12

Calculating time

The table below shows the time taken to walk 1 km at various speeds. (To convert kilometres to miles, multiply by 3 and divide by 5.)

Table 9.5 Speed/time

1000 m	Speed	5 kph	4 kph	3 kph	2 kph
	Time	12 min	15 min	20 min	30 min

The Mountaineering Council of Scotland says that you should allow 1 minute extra for every contour (10 metres) of ascent.

---

activity
INDIVIDUAL WORK

Time yourself walking a kilometre on the flat at your natural speed. Then go to a steep hill which is a kilometre long and walk up it, again at your natural speed for that slope. Time yourself, and keep a record of that time. How does your own time compare with the norm set by the Mountaineering Council of Scotland?

The Mountaineering Council of Scotland

www.mountaineering-scotland.org.uk

Cooking
Cook outside the tent (to avoid risk of fires and mess).

Waste disposal
Use bins, if available, for cooking waste; otherwise wrap waste in a plastic bag and carry it home or to the nearest bin. Never leave litter at a camp site or anywhere in the countryside. If you have to go to the toilet out of doors, bury the outcome and any tissues.

Personal hygiene
It isn't always possible to wash as well on an expedition as you can at home. At an official camp site there are showers and/or washbasins which are there to be used. Don't carry a lot of heavy or bulky toiletries. Take a towel and dry it whenever possible (e.g. by tying it outside your rucksack while walking).

Packing equipment
Larger and heavier items should be packed first – at the bottom of a rucksack. Clothes should be in bin-bags to keep them dry. Sleeping bags can be carried in their **stuff-bags** and a waterproof bin-bag outside the rucksack, together with a rolled sleeping mat. Soap, meths, etc. should be carried in outer pockets. Food should be well wrapped and should not be kept long in hot weather.

Using equipment
Before setting off on your expedition, check that all equipment is in safe working order and that you know how to use it.

Storing equipment
Tents, ropes, etc. must be cleared of dust and sand, and thoroughly dried and properly packed, rolled, etc. after the expedition. Pegs, stove parts and other items should be checked. Missing bits should be replaced. Climbing ropes should be kept in a cool, dry, dark place.

Advanced techniques

Pacing
This refers to measuring distance by counting your paces and is not normally necessary. However, get to know the normal length of your pace.

Camping in high wilderness terrain
This should only be done by experienced people using the right equipment.

Camping comfortably in difficult weather
Main points are as follows:

- Move the tent if there is a risk of flooding.
- Keep all dry clothes in waterproof bags.
- Always wear waterproof or snowproof (as appropriate) gear outside the tent.
- Keep boots and wet clothes outside the tent and off the groundsheet.
- 'Lock' tent pegs by putting them in crosswise if the tent looks as though it could blow away.
- Wear lots of underwear or pullovers so you don't get chilled.
- Stay in your sleeping bag if there is no point in getting up.
- Ensure that the flysheet is not touching the inner tent.
- Eat plenty of calorific food.
- Keep away from metal poles and pegs during thunderstorms.

If the weather is intolerable, go home.

activity
GROUP WORK
9.4

P4

Take part in two expeditions which have an acceptable level of back-up and monitoring by a support team or by instructors. Use skills which enable you to camp, travel and navigate in safety and reasonable comfort.

activity
GROUP WORK
9.5

M4

D1

Take part in two expeditions without support team back-up or close monitoring by instructors (i.e. carrying all your needs and with occasional checks). Show that you are proficient at camp craft, travelling and navigation.

Reviewing the planning and undertaking of expeditions

As you plan and undertake an expedition you should keep a diary, or log, of everything you do. It doesn't need to be particularly long and detailed, but if you have a record of what you did, when you did it and how it went, it will help you to learn from the experience and will also help you to pass this unit!

Review of planning

Formative and summative

There are two kinds of review: formative and summative. A **formative review** is a review you carry out while you are in the process of doing something. A **summative review** is a review you carry out after the whole activity is completed.

Formative

Formative reviews take place during team meetings at the planning stage. The following questions are usually asked:

- What have we got done so far?
- Are we keeping up to schedule?
- Are there any problems?
- Is there anything we've forgotten to do?
- Do we need to change the next stage of our planning and preparation?

Reviews of this sort are easier if action plans have been written for the expedition members, delegating aspects of planning and preparation to them, and giving them deadlines. Copies of these can be kept by expedition organisers and updated so that they too know exactly how well preparations are going.

Individual expedition members can carry out their own formative review as far as their own personal preparation is concerned. If they have a written action plan, they can check their progress against the plan and ensure that any preparatory tasks they have to do are done on time.

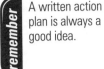

A written action plan is always a good idea.

Summative

Summative reviews are reviews carried out after the expedition is over. Questions asked are:

- How well did it go?
- What did we achieve?
- Did we achieve what we set out to do?
- What were the good bits?
- What were the problems?
- What should we have done differently?
- What did we learn from the experience?

These reviews can take the form of a debrief.

Feedback

Comments on the expedition planning and the expedition itself can be obtained from observers (e.g. instructors who might be monitoring your expedition from a distance) and from peers (members of your own group). Much of this feedback will be informal, but some may take the form of written appraisals.

See pages 71–74 in Unit 2 for more information on debriefs and feedback.

Strengths and areas for improvement

Individual expedition members can do their own summative review by writing a self-assessment, describing what they did and how well they think they did it. They can acknowledge strengths and make suggestions for improvement. A summative review can also contain an element of peer assessment with people assessing the skills and qualities shown by other team members. This is appropriate not only for the skills of camp craft and navigating, but also for teamwork and leadership skills and qualities.

Skills

Many leadership, communication and interpersonal skills are used in group expeditions.

Leadership

Examples of leadership skills are:

- setting a good example
- being well organised
- being inclusive and non-discriminatory
- helping others
- thinking of others' comfort and well-being
- awareness of team safety
- being cheerful, positive and encouraging.

Leadership should be friendly but decisive. No expedition member should be excluded from activities; everyone should be treated fairly.

Communication

Examples of communication skills are:

- giving and receiving instructions and acting on them
- functional communication: encouraging, advising, explaining, discussing, planning, suggesting, listening, etc.

Communication should be clear. Listen to what people say, and make sure that they listen to you if you have something important to say.

Even though teamwork and leadership are not very explicitly assessed in this unit, they are mentioned in the content section of the unit specification. Expeditions provide an excellent setting for showing teamwork, communication and leadership skills, and could be used in providing assessable evidence for Units 2, 4, 6, 13 and 18.

See pages 64–66 in Unit 2 for more on leadership and communication skills.

Decision making

Examples of decision-making skills are:

- assessing the options
- acting in the best interests of the team
- solving problems
- considering contingency plans etc.

Decisions should, in general, be agreed democratically. Expedition groups should not split up, except in *very* rare circumstances when someone has to fetch help.

Review of undertaking

Formative

Commenting and assessing during the expedition: for this part of the process it is extremely useful to keep a log, so that all relevant points can be remembered.

Summative

Commenting and assessing after the expedition: this includes the final debrief and any action or future planning arising out of that. For the summative review too, you and others will find it useful to have kept a log or diary of the expedition experience.

Feedback

Useful feedback can come from many people both during and after an expedition. It is a good policy to listen to feedback, but the decision as to whether or not to act upon it is ultimately yours.

Observers

People who could give you feedback include observers (perhaps instructors who are monitoring your party's expedition skills from a distance, as in the Duke of Edinburgh's Award), tutors and expedition organisers.

Peers

These are fellow students, to whom you will be able to give feedback in your turn. Their feedback may be spoken or written and could include comment and even grading of some aspects of performance.

Strengths

In the review your strengths should be made clear – preferably in a detailed written assessment. These strengths should include:

- camp craft, walking and navigation skills
- planning and organisational abilities
- teamwork, leadership, interpersonal and communication skills.

Areas for improvement

Again you should give a detailed assessment linked to what you actually did – or didn't do – on your expedition. Areas for improvement are not necessarily weaknesses: strengths can be improved too, and developed into real expertise. As with strengths, it may be convenient to divide areas for improvement into the 'hard' skills of camp craft, travelling and navigation and the 'soft', but more important, skills of teamwork, leadership and communication.

Appropriateness of expedition

Was it well thought out and worth doing?

Suitability of area

Was the area suitable for developing expedition skills? For example was it open, hilly, interesting and with suitable camp sites?

Choice of expedition

Was the route taken by the expedition interesting, challenging and worthwhile?

Matching of expedition to participants

Was the expedition the right level of difficulty and interest for you and your party?

Health and safety

Did your planning and the undertaking of your expedition show a good awareness of health and safety issues? Did you carry out a risk assessment on the expedition and the expedition area in relation to the strengths and weaknesses of your own party?

Development plan

Your **development plan** is an outline of the skills and personal qualities that you should develop for the future, based on your strengths and shortcomings during this unit. The skills should be divided into two categories:

First, there are technical skills to do with expeditions; these are:

- navigation skills – such as map-reading; use of the compass; interpretation of weather; planning and use of route cards; estimation of time and difficulty of routes in mountainous terrain; safety awareness and knowing what to do in an emergency

- camp craft skills – pitching tents; keeping the inside of the tent orderly, clean and dry; preparing and cooking food; packing rucksacks; assessing the weight of loads, and knowing what is needed and what isn't; looking after the environment

- walking-related skills – choosing and using suitable equipment; dressing for the season and the weather; aerobic fitness; first aid competence; pacing yourself to cover maximum distance with minimum effort and tiredness; knowing when to take rests, and for how long.

Secondly, there are teamwork and leadership-related skills. These are:

- Thinking skills – these are used when planning the expedition, choosing a venue, calculating distances and routes, deciding on food and clothing; learning navigation and other skills; reading maps; using the compass; observing the weather and the surroundings; picking camp sites, pitching tents and cooking; keeping warm and comfortable; keeping a diary or record of your planning and your expedition and all expedition-related achievements. Working out a realistic, useful and challenging **personal development plan** at the end also requires a range of thinking skills – and will test both your imagination and your powers of reasoning.

- Teamwork skills – you need these when working with your team to make the expedition a success from the early planning right through to the conclusions and the review at the end. These skills include the ability to be assertive while seeing and taking into account the views of others. You should be helpful and supportive to the rest of your team, and you should keep a record of what you learn about teamwork from the expedition planning and the expedition itself.

- Communication skills – these include persuading, encouraging, explaining, etc.

- Leadership skills – these include decision making; negotiating in the case of difficulties; setting a good example to your team and to the general public; showing awareness of wider issues such as health and safety, the environment and, as appropriate, the diversity of your team.

> **remember**
>
> A realistic plan takes into account what is possible, considering money, time and other constraints.

You should carry out an honest and thorough self-appraisal of all your skills and qualities before preparing your personal development plan. Be aware of your faults as well as your virtues, but remember to be positive: personal development is based on the knowledge and belief that you can and will do better if you put your mind to it.

activity
INDIVIDUAL WORK 9.6

P5

Write a review, of a kind suited for basic training in a uniformed service, of your own performance in planning and undertaking expeditions, showing what your strengths have been but also outlining ways in which you could improve.

Aims

These are your overall aspirations, for example:

- to improve my teamwork skills
- to become more practical and organised in my camp craft.

Objectives

These are actions that you intend to be able to do within a certain range of capability. Objectives should be realistic and achievable statements about observable or measurable behaviour, for example:

- I will learn how to read a map properly without having to ask for help from someone else.
- I will learn how to disagree with people without getting sarcastic.

Targets

Targets are objectives which you intend to meet to a particular level, by a given time. The acronym used to memorise this approach to target setting is SMART – i.e. specific, measurable, achievable, realistic, time-based. An example of a target is: 'I will pass my driving test by next May'. This statement is a valid target because it is:

- *specific* – i.e. definite, precise, exact: unlike, say, 'I will become a good driver', which is vague and depends on what you mean by 'good'
- *measurable* – because driving skills are measurable in a driving test
- *achievable* – for a person of normal health and good motivation
- *realistic* – assuming that you are old enough, can afford driving tuition, etc.
- *time-based* – with a fixed deadline; you are going to get it done by next May, which is a clear deadline.

Milestones

Like the milestones on a roadside, milestones in target setting are intermediate markers, between now and the final target, which help you to know how far you have to go to achieve that final target. If your target is to climb eight mountains in two years, you could set yourself a milestone of four mountains for one year. Milestones are useful not only for checking your progress; they can also motivate and encourage you when the main target still seems to be a long way off.

Potential obstacles to development

Obstacles – factors which might have a bad effect on your development plan – should be identified and, if possible, eliminated.

Overcoming obstacles to development, both in expeditions and in life in general, is to some extent a matter for the individual. External obstacles are best dealt with by changing some aspect of your life. Internal obstacles may necessitate changing something in yourself.

Whatever your aim, if you feel that something or someone is undermining your personal development, do something about it. Talk to someone, or change some aspect of your life. Everybody has a right, indeed a duty, to develop and fulfil themselves to the best of their ability.

Resources

Obstacles to development are usually to do with a lack of resources. This lack can take many forms. A few are given below:

Human
Human factors include:

- lack of suitable role models
- lack of motivating friends
- lack of confidence and self-belief
- low self-esteem
- family problems
- relationship problems
- lack of interest in self-development
- stress, depression, worry
- difficulties with your career plans or education.

Physical
Physical factors include:

- lack of time
- too busy
- injuries, illness.

Fiscal
Fiscal factors include lack of money.

activity
INDIVIDUAL WORK
9.7

P6

M5

Write a personal development plan, based on your review of your expedition work, suitable for an appraisal with your line manager in a public service. Explain and give evidence for your strengths and your areas for improvement and link them up with the suggestions that you have made in your personal development plan.

---

activity
INDIVIDUAL WORK
9.8

D2

Having completed the personal development plan and suggestions in Activity 9.7 above, give a reasoned explanation supporting each of your suggestions for developing your expertise mentioned in your plan.

Progress Check

1. Give five reasons why people go on expeditions, and for each name an expedition which has taken place for that reason.

2. In what ways might expeditions help disaffected young people who are at risk of turning to crime?

3. Give five reasons why expeditions should be planned.

4. Explain the difference between the aims and objectives of an expedition.

5. If a college is running an expedition, whose permission is needed?

6. What aspects of an expedition come under the heading of logistics?

7. What kinds of accommodation are used on expeditions, and what are the main advantages and disadvantages of each?

8. What kinds of food should campers eat, how should they cook their food, and what safety precautions should they take?

9. Describe the clothes and footwear that should be worn on expeditions.

10. How do you set, or orientate, a map?

11. How do you work out the bearing of each leg when you are preparing a route card?

12. What do 1:25,000 and 1:50,000 mean?

13. Where should you pitch a tent?

14. How do you navigate in fog?

15. What is the difference between a formative and a summative review?

16. What is a development plan and how should it be used?

UNIT 22

Understanding Aspects of the Legal System and Law Making Process

This unit covers:

■ The hierarchy of the court system

■ The role undertaken by the personnel of the courts

■ How legal rules are created by precedent

■ How statutory rules are made and interpreted

As a number of public services – notably the police, the prison service and the National Probation Service – are parts of the criminal justice system, the law and how it operates determines much of the work that they do.

This unit begins by looking at the civil courts, their work and how they all fit together, before going on to examine the criminal courts in the same way. Next it deals with the people who work in the court system, the different jobs they do and the ways in which they are trained and organised. There is also a section on juries and how they function.

This is followed by a section covering precedent and the systems used to try to make court judgments fair and consistent, so that people convicted of the same crime are given the same sentence and do the same punishment. However, not all court judgments are right, and this section also looks at what happens when there might have been a miscarriage of justice.

The final part of the unit explores how laws are made and how the courts put them into practice.

grading criteria

To achieve a **Pass** grade the evidence must show that the learner is able to:	To achieve a **Merit** grade the evidence must show that, in addition to the pass criteria, the learner is able to:	To achieve a **Distinction** grade the evidence must show that, in addition to the pass and merit criteria, the learner is able to:
P3 outline the role of judges and lawyers in civil and criminal cases Pg 384	**M3** explain the rules of statutory interpretation. Pg 395	
P4 describe how precedents are applied in court Pg 392		
P5 describe the process when making an Act of Parliament and outline the rules for statutory interpretation. Pg 395		

The hierarchy of the court system

A hierarchy is a series of organisations or people arranged in order of importance. It is rather like a pecking order.

This unit explains the legal system in England and Wales. The system in Scotland is rather different; if you want to study it you should go to Scottish sources and Scottish websites.

The court system in England and Wales comprises the various courts and the links between them. It is a hierarchy because different kinds of court deal with different kinds of case. The top courts in the hierarchy deal with the most 'important' cases: i.e. the ones where serious crimes or large sums of money are involved, or where important issues of principle are being considered. The courts lower down the hierarchy deal with small everyday cases; although very important to the people concerned, these are not as important to the country or the public as a whole.

Civil courts structure

Civil courts deal with everyday matters of law – disputes, money transactions, legacies, divorces, claims for **compensation**, and so on. Although they do not normally involve the police, National Probation Service or prison service, they are still an immensely important part of the English justice system.

University of Leeds
www.leeds.ac.uk
Respect
www.respect.gov.uk
University of Kent
www.library.kent.ac.uk
BBC
www.bbc.co.uk
Directgov
www.direct.gov.uk

case study 22.1

Remit of the civil courts

Table 22.1 Examples of kinds of law dealt with by civil courts

Agricultural law	Debt and money advice	Legal aid – civil
Alternative dispute resolution	Disability	Legal aid – immigration
Banking law	Discrimination law	Mediation – family
Business affairs	E-commerce	Mental health and incapacity law
Charity law	Education law	Pensions law
Civil liberties and human rights	Employment law	**Personal injury**
Clinical negligence	Environmental law	Planning law
Commercial **litigation**	Family law	Tax law
Consumer law	Immigration law	Transport, road and rail
Consumer problems	**Insolvency** and bankruptcy	**Tribunals**
Contract law	Landlord and tenant – residential	Welfare benefits
Conveyancing – residential		Wills and **probate**
Costs		

activity
INDIVIDUAL WORK

Choose one of these kinds of law and find out more about it. Explain why it is normally civil law but can, in certain circumstances, become criminal law too.

Much of what the civil courts do is not 'news', so we don't hear as much about their work in the media as we do about the **criminal courts**.

Fig 22.1 Civil courts structure in England and Wales

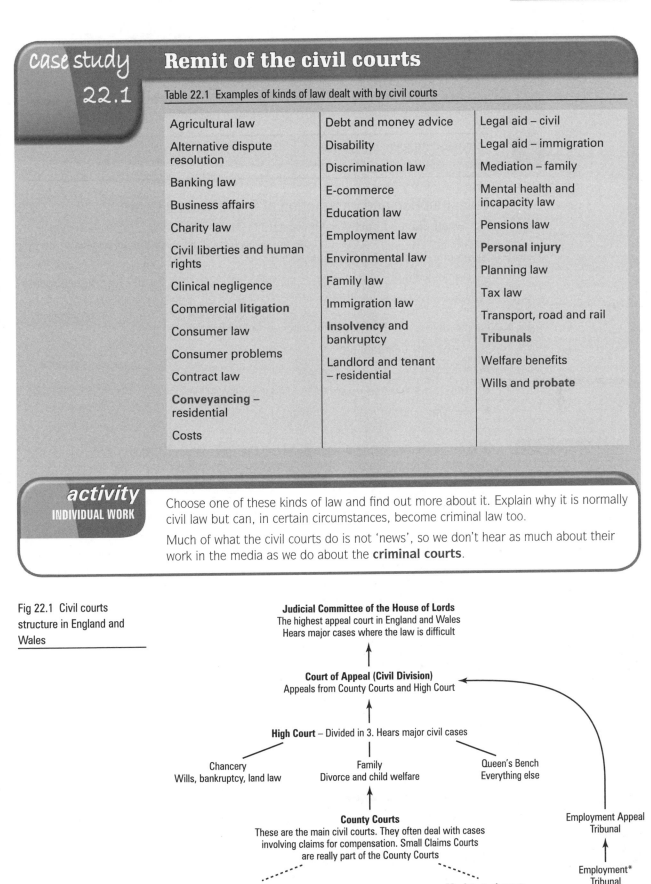

Judicial Committee of the House of Lords
The highest appeal court in England and Wales
Hears major cases where the law is difficult

Court of Appeal (Civil Division)
Appeals from County Courts and High Court

High Court – Divided in 3. Hears major civil cases

Chancery
Wills, bankruptcy, land law

Family
Divorce and child welfare

Queen's Bench
Everything else

County Courts
These are the main civil courts. They often deal with cases involving claims for compensation. Small Claims Courts are really part of the County Courts

Family courts
Most of their work is to do with separation and divorce, and what to do about the children and the property

Magistrates' courts
These are really criminal courts but they do some civil work, such as granting drinks licences, and family court work

Employment Appeal Tribunal

Employment* Tribunal

Magistrates' courts are mainly criminal courts but do some civil work. The Court of Appeal is split into two halves: the Civil Division and the Criminal Division. Employment Tribunals are not really part of the court system but they do hear major civil law cases involving alleged injustice at work, e.g. to do with discrimination and unfair dismissal.

Tribunals employment service
www.employmenttribunals.gov.uk

Role, function and jurisdiction of Small Claims Court

The **Small Claims Court** is not a separate building; it is a series of procedures which take place in a County Court and are designed to deal easily and painlessly with the large number of small **civil cases**.

Small Claims Courts deal with cases brought by people (or firms or other organisations) against other people (or firms or other organisations), usually involving money. The courts can deal with personal injury but only if the amounts of compensation are likely to be less than £1000 (which is not much for a personal injury case).

The cases they deal with are:

■ civil law only

■ simple and straightforward from a legal point of view

■ involving sums of money no greater than £5000.

Civil cases of this sort do not involve the police. It is simply a matter of one person or company having a complaint against another person or company. The people at each side of the case are sometimes called 'parties'. The **party** making the complaint is the complainant, and the party being complained about is the **defendant**. Typical complaints involve problems over goods bought or sold (e.g. not getting what you've paid for), or problems between landlords and tenants (e.g. about rents and property repairs).

There is no need for the person making the claim to have a **solicitor**. However, there is a good deal of form-filling, and what happens depends on the nature of the claim and whether – and how – the claim is defended (in other words, whether the defendant agrees that the claim is justified, ignores the claim, or decides to contest it).

Useful online leaflets from Her Majesty's Court Service:
EX305 *The Fast Track and the Multi-track* (HM Court Service 0806)
EX307 *The Small Claims Track* (HM Court Service 0706)
www.hmcourts-service.gov.uk

The various events that can happen in a Small Claims Court are shown in the diagram below.

The purpose of an **allocation** questionnaire is to help the court to decide the best way of dealing with the case.

Some of the form-filling (e.g. N157 and N160) can be done online.

The costs awarded amount to a few hundred pounds at most.

It is not compulsory for either the complainant or defendant to attend the hearing, but they must provide full documentation to support their case at least a week in advance.

The hearing is usually public but can be private if the judge decides it should be.

County Court

The County Court is the main kind of civil court in England and Wales. Much, but not all, of its work is of the small claims type already outlined above.

There are 218 County Courts throughout England and Wales dealing with all but the most complicated civil law proceedings.

Fig 22.2 Small claims procedure

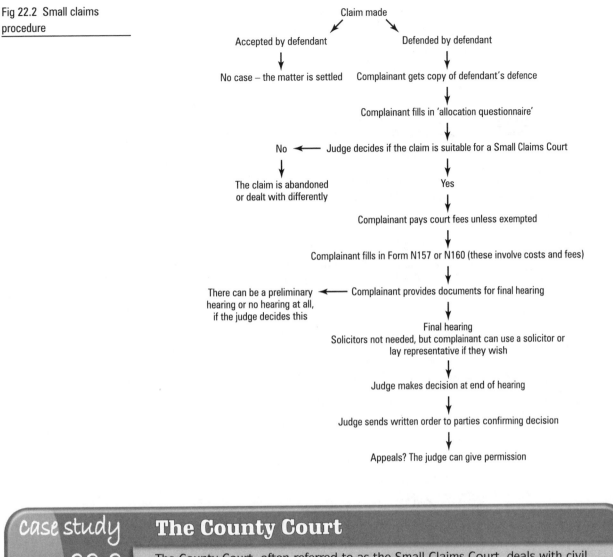

---

case study 22.2

The County Court

The County Court, often referred to as the Small Claims Court, deals with civil matters, such as:

- Claims for debt repayment, including enforcing court orders and return of goods bought on credit
- Personal Injury
- Breach of contract concerning goods or property
- Family issues such as divorce or adoption
- Housing disputes, including mortgage and council rent arrears and repossession.

…

Most County Court cases are between people or companies who believe that someone owes them money. Claims for small amounts are generally straightforward and there is usually no need for those involved to use solicitors.

(Source: www.hmcourts-service.gov.uk)

activity
INDIVIDUAL WORK

Why are most civil cases of relatively minor importance, involving relatively small amounts of money?

Hearings in a County Court are presided over by a **judge**. Because the court deals with civil law, the police and the **Crown Prosecution Service** are not normally involved. Cases are brought, as in the small claims system, by private individuals, companies or other groups who believe that they have been wronged in some way. Normally, there is a fee to be paid to the court, but, as the next case study shows, sometimes no fee is charged.

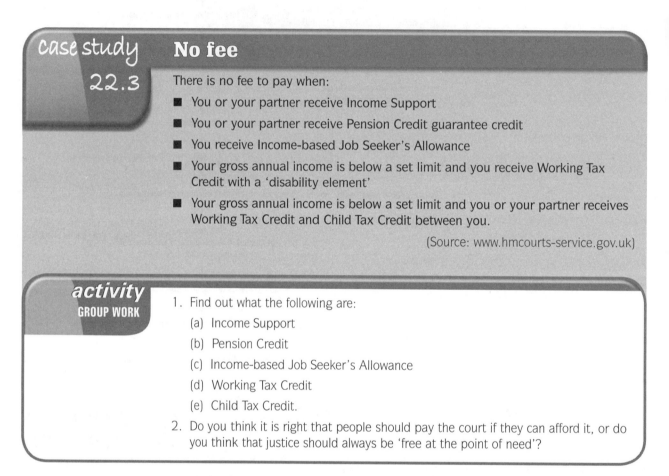

case study 22.3

No fee

There is no fee to pay when:

- You or your partner receive Income Support
- You or your partner receive Pension Credit guarantee credit
- You receive Income-based Job Seeker's Allowance
- Your gross annual income is below a set limit and you receive Working Tax Credit with a 'disability element'
- Your gross annual income is below a set limit and you or your partner receives Working Tax Credit and Child Tax Credit between you.

(Source: www.hmcourts-service.gov.uk)

activity
GROUP WORK

1. Find out what the following are:
   (a) Income Support
   (b) Pension Credit
   (c) Income-based Job Seeker's Allowance
   (d) Working Tax Credit
   (e) Child Tax Credit.

2. Do you think it is right that people should pay the court if they can afford it, or do you think that justice should always be 'free at the point of need'?

Even in other circumstances, if a complainant or defendant can show that the payment of a court fee would involve 'undue hardship', the fee may be waived.

County Court procedure – fast track, multi-track or neither?

Civil lawsuits can vary very much and County Courts have different methods of dealing with them, depending on their complexity and the amount of money involved. Fig 22.3 outlines the procedures.

> **remember**
> Fast track and multi-track procedures are the same at some stages.

Allocation is the process of finding out which track a case should go on. Fast track and multi-track are used only for cases which are too complex, or have too much money involved in them, to be settled by the small claims system.

Ministry of Justice (old site – www.dca.gov.uk – contains material from before 2007)

www.justice.gov.uk

Directgov – Government public services

www.direct.gov.uk

Fig 22.3 Fast track and
multi-track procedures in the
County Court

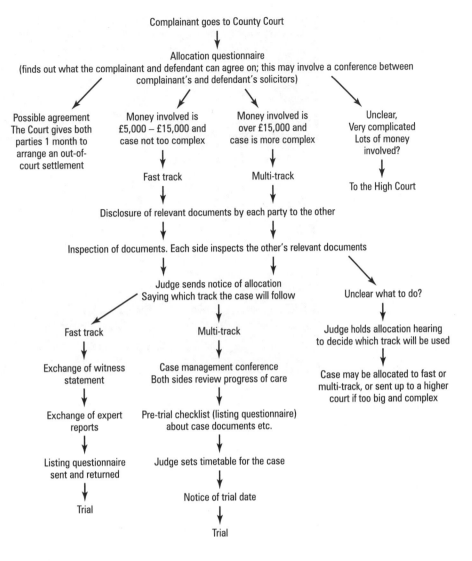

High Court

The High Court is in London and deals only with major civil cases – ones which are too big, too complex, involve too much money or have gained too much publicity for it to be appropriate to hear them in an ordinary County Court. The High Court is divided into three parts which specialise in different kinds of case:

- Queen's Bench Division – this deals with contract law, **tort**, insurance, banking, commercial, shipping, technology and construction, and major disputes involving local authorities. Some types of cases are tried in front of a **jury** (this rarely happens in civil law) and involve fraud, libel, slander, malicious prosecution and false imprisonment.

- Chancery Division – this deals with insolvency, mortgages, **copyright** and **patents**, trust property, probate and **intellectual property** cases.

- Family Division – this specialises in cases about family matters, such as access and custody of children, marriage breakdown, and so on.

Civil Division of the Court of Appeal

The Court of Appeal is, apart from the House of Lords, the highest court in England and Wales to which appeals can be sent. Like the rest of the country's judicial (court) system it is split into civil and criminal divisions.

> **remember**
> The High Court also oversees coroners' courts. These courts inquire about unusual deaths and about treasure. They do not hold trials, but their findings can lead to police investigations.

Fig 22.4 The High Court
– where cases get into the
news

The Civil Division deals with high-level **appeals** that have already been through the High Court or the County Court. It also hears appeals from courts called Appeal Tribunals, which are slightly separate from the main system (see Fig 22.1 above) and which deal primarily with human and individual rights. These tribunals include the Employment Appeal Tribunal, the Immigration Appeal Tribunal, the Lands Tribunal and the Social Security Commissioners.

House of Lords

The House of Lords is sometimes called the Upper House of Parliament, although this is confusing because it actually has less power than the Lower House (the House of Commons). However, besides its **legislative** role in **scrutinising** and **amending** proposed laws, the House of Lords has the judicial role of listening to difficult appeals cases which have not been satisfactorily resolved by the Court of Appeal. Appeals are listened to and decided upon by a group of **Law Lords** who are judges etc. not normally attached to a political party.

At present (2007) the House of Lords is 'the highest court in the land'; however, this situation is likely to change as the next case study shows.

European Court of Justice

The European Court of Justice (ECJ) should not be confused with the European Court of Human Rights; it is a completely different court.

The European Court of Justice has a number of roles:

- to clarify European law for courts in member countries (British courts can contact the ECJ for clarification of points; they have to abide by its judgment, and so do all other countries and courts which make similar inquiries for clarification)

- to take action against governments of member countries for failure to fulfil community obligations

- to make a judgment when member countries demand the annulment of an EU regulation, directive or decision

- to hear appeals against the judgment of the Court of **First Instance**.

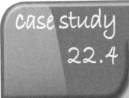

The House of Lords

case study 22.4

[Acting as an appeal court] is an unusual role for a legislative body that is part of Parliament. In most other democracies, the judiciary is separate from the legislature – usually in the form of a supreme court of appeal. For this reason the Government has legislated to establish a United Kingdom Supreme Court that will be constitutionally and physically separate from Parliament ... Until October 2008, when the new UK **Supreme Court** is expected to come into operation, the present system will continue. The reasons for the present set-up are historical – the House of Lords has done this work for more than 600 years as part of the High Court of Parliament. Although the House of Commons was originally part of the High Court of Parliament, it has not been involved in judicial work since 1399. Today only highly qualified professional judges appointed to be law lords take part in the judicial function of the House.

(Source: *House of Lords Briefing: The Judicial Work of the House of Lords*. www. parliament.uk)

activity
GROUP WORK

What is undemocratic about having the House of Lords act as a court of appeal?

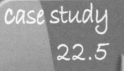

The Court of Justice of the European Communities

case study 22.5

The Court of Justice of the European Communities is the judicial institution of the Community. It is made up of three courts: the Court of Justice, the Court of First Instance and the Civil Service Tribunal. Their main task is to examine the legality of Community measures and ensure the uniform interpretation and application of Community law.

(Source: www.curia.europa.eu)

activity
GROUP WORK

What are the advantages and disadvantages of having European courts which can, in certain circumstances, overrule British courts and even the actions of the British government?

The European Court of First Instance
The Court of First Instance hears:

- direct actions brought against Community institutions
- actions brought by the Member States against the Commission
- actions brought by the Member States against the Council
- actions seeking compensation for damage caused by the Community institutions or their staff
- actions based on contracts
- actions about Community trade marks.

The European Court of First Instance should not be confused with the first instance courts mentioned below.

Difference between first instance and appeal courts

First instance courts are courts dealing with cases which are not appeals: in other words, those that have come to court for the first time. The magistrates' courts are courts of first instance.

Appeal courts deal with cases which have been heard and decided before but which are re-examined when there is evidence to suggest either:

■ that the law was misinterpreted in the first trial or

■ that new evidence/information has appeared which might change the outcome of the first trial.

Criminal courts structure

The criminal courts structure in England and Wales is similar to the civil courts structure in that it consists of lower and higher courts, and that it has systems for hearing appeals. Fig 22.5 outlines the way in which these courts fit into the system.

Role, function and jurisdiction of the Youth Court

Except in the cases of very serious crimes such as rape or murder, or serious crimes which were committed in collaboration with an adult, young people aged 10–17 are tried in the **Youth Court**.

Magistrates' courts

Every person who is going to trial goes to a magistrates' court. If the offence is very serious – i.e. **indictable** – the magistrates' court sorts out any problems to do with **bail** and reporting restrictions, then passes the case on for trial at the **Crown Court**. If the offence is fairly serious it could be 'triable either way', in which case the defendant has the choice of being tried at a magistrates' court or at the Crown Court. The great majority of offences are relatively minor. These are called 'summary' offences and are tried at the magistrates' court.

> **remember**
>
> Magistrates' courts are found in most towns and deal with over 95% of **criminal cases**. They are open to the public, and anybody who is interested in the way the law works should go and check them out.

Fig 22.5 Structure of the criminal courts

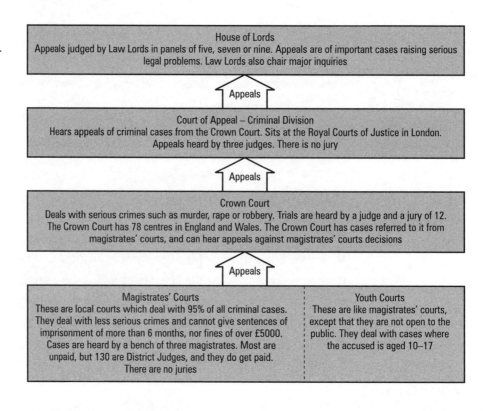

House of Lords
Appeals judged by Law Lords in panels of five, seven or nine. Appeals are of important cases raising serious legal problems. Law Lords also chair major inquiries

↑ Appeals

Court of Appeal – Criminal Division
Hears appeals of criminal cases from the Crown Court. Sits at the Royal Courts of Justice in London. Appeals heard by three judges. There is no jury

↑ Appeals

Crown Court
Deals with serious crimes such as murder, rape or robbery. Trials are heard by a judge and a jury of 12. The Crown Court has 78 centres in England and Wales. The Crown Court has cases referred to it from magistrates' courts, and can hear appeals against magistrates' courts decisions

↑ Appeals

Magistrates' Courts
These are local courts which deal with 95% of all criminal cases. They deal with less serious crimes and cannot give sentences of imprisonment of more than 6 months, nor fines of over £5000. Cases are heard by a bench of three magistrates. Most are unpaid, but 130 are District Judges, and they do get paid. There are no juries

Youth Courts
These are like magistrates' courts, except that they are not open to the public. They deal with cases where the accused is aged 10–17

case study 22.6

The Youth Court

This is a specialised form of magistrates' court. As in the magistrates' court, the case will be heard by **magistrates** or by a **District Judge** (magistrates' courts). The Youth Court is not open to the general public and only those directly involved in the case will normally be in court. The press may attend court and report the proceedings but will not usually be allowed to publish the defendant's name.

A hearing in the Youth Court is similar to one in the magistrates' court although the procedure is adapted to take account of [the] age of the defendant. The Magistrates and District Judges who sit in the Youth Court will receive specialist training on dealing with young people.

(Source: www.hmcourts-service.gov.uk)

activity
INDIVIDUAL WORK

1. Why are Youth Courts not open to the public?
2. What kind of specialist training in dealing with young people would you expect magistrates and District Judges to receive?

Cases are heard by three magistrates, one of whom may be a District Judge. (District Judges are paid and are legally qualified, either as **barristers** or solicitors. **Lay** magistrates are ordinary people, with no legal training, who are trained to be magistrates. They are not paid but receive expenses.) Sometimes the **Legal Adviser** (formerly called the Clerk of the Court), who sits in front of the magistrates, is the only legally trained person present. The Legal Adviser's job is to give advice on the law to the magistrates.

The accused stands in a place called the dock, sometimes with police or prison officers – in case they try to do a runner. If the accused has pleaded not guilty, the case has to be argued to find out who is telling the truth. The prosecution case, explaining the crime that the accused is supposed to have committed – with evidence to support it – is argued by the prosecution solicitor. The defence solicitor argues either that the accused is innocent or is guilty of a lesser crime than they have been charged with, or that they should be treated leniently for one reason or another. Witnesses can be called and questioned. At the end of the arguments and the questioning, the magistrates go into a back room and decide whether or not the defendant is guilty and, if guilty, what the sentence should be. (Their decision may not be based entirely on what they have just heard, because they also get pre-sentence reports from psychologists and social workers, giving more background concerning the accused and the alleged offence.) After making their decision, the magistrates come back into the court and announce both the decision and the sentence, which cannot be more than 6 months' imprisonment or a £5000 fine.

Crown Court

The Crown Court (always in the singular and with capital letters) has 78 centres in various large towns and cities up and down the country. Like the magistrates' courts, the Crown Court is a place that should be visited – if you are interested in life, and if you are interested in the law. Visiting the Crown Court is the best way to learn about crime without doing it.

The Crown Court deals with:

- indictable (serious) offences such as murder, manslaughter, rape, robbery and large-scale fraud

- triable either way offences (slightly less serious) where defendants have chosen to be tried at the Crown Court rather than the magistrates' court

- appeals against decisions made at magistrates' courts

- sentencing people found guilty at the magistrates' court, where the magistrates feel that the sentence should be greater than they are allowed to give (i.e. more than 6 months' prison or £5000 fine).

Trials are run by the judge, who makes rulings on legal matters and arguments, but the guilt of the defendant is decided by the jury, a panel of 12 people selected at random from the electoral rolls (official lists of people eligible to vote). The Crown Court can give any sentence up to and including life imprisonment and can impose fines of any amount.

See pages 380–384 for more information on judges and pages 388–390 for juries.

Criminal Division of the Court of Appeal

This deals with appeals against convictions at the Crown Court. There are about 8000 of these appeals each year. The procedure, which is complex, is carried out by solicitors. Cases that might go to appeal are reviewed by the Criminal Appeal Office before being referred to the appeal courts. **Appellants** must have legal help and advice. In the early stages, the appellant's solicitors have to argue the merits of their appeal, which is likely to be on one (or more) of the following grounds:

- that the law was wrongly applied in the original case

- that the sentence was too harsh

- that new evidence about the case has come to light.

The appellant has to submit transcripts of the original Crown Court hearing. In the first instance, leave to appeal is decided by one judge only. If the 'single judge' allows the appeal to go ahead, a barrister is appointed to represent the appellant and a skeleton argument (case summary) is put forward. When the List Office gets the summary, a hearing date is set. The appeal is listened to by three judges, and a decision is reached. The appeal can (a) be granted so that the original conviction is 'quashed' (disallowed); (b) result in a reduction of sentence if it was the sentence rather than the conviction that was being appealed against; (c) be dismissed, but the appellant can be allowed to

Fig 22.6 The Crown Court – where you can watch serious criminal trials

appeal against this dismissal; or (d) be dismissed without any further leave to appeal. In the case of (c), the second appeal goes to the Criminal Cases Review Commission. If the Commission allows it, the case can go back to the Court of Appeal. If a major legal issue is involved, the next appeal can go to the House of Lords.

Criminal Cases Review Commission

www.ccrc.gov.uk

P1

Produce a wall chart suitable for a citizens' advice centre outlining the civil and criminal court hierarchies and the differences between civil and criminal courts.

Her Majesty's Court Service

www.hmcourts-service.gov.uk

House of Lords

Criminal case appeals in the House of Lords can be considered if the case is complex, difficult, might involve a serious **miscarriage of justice**, or is of major public concern. Criminal appeals from England, Wales and Northern Ireland – but not Scotland – can go to the House of Lords. However, for this to happen there must be a certificate from the previous court, showing that a point of law of public importance is involved; and the appeal must also be allowed by an Appeal Committee of three Law Lords. The Appeal Committee sifts the appeal applications and usually allows about 100 out of 350 to go ahead. The appeals are dealt with by Law Lords: they are paid judges who have had a distinguished career before joining the House of Lords; they work full time on the House's legal work and are rarely involved in politics.

Appeals are heard by a committee of Law Lords called the Appellate Committee. They listen to the Counsel (barrister) for the appellant, the counsel for the **respondent** and then the counsel for the appellant again before making their decision. An appeal hearing usually takes two and a half days, but the decision may take some time after that. The outcome of the appeal is publicly announced in the House of Lords itself.

First instance and appeal courts

The magistrates' and Youth Courts are always courts of first instance: they hear cases themselves, not appeals against judgments in other cases. If someone appeals against a judgment in a magistrates' court, the appeal is heard in the Crown Court. This means that the Crown Court, although usually a court of first instance, sometimes acts as an appeal court. The Court of Appeal and the House of Lords are exclusively appeal courts.

The role undertaken by the personnel of the courts

The courts are a public service employing (with solicitors etc.) around 200,000 people (Home Office (2005) *Statistics on Race and the Criminal Justice System*, www.statistics. gov.uk).

Their roles are many and various, but an outline of the main ones is given below.

The legal profession

Work, training and regulation

If the legal profession was not very well trained and regulated to exclude fraudsters and incompetent lawyers, it would become a minefield for people seeking justice, and the law itself would fall into disrepute. The success of the legal profession is dependent on people trusting it to do an honest and professional job.

Regulation – ensuring that the law professions have a clearly understood and consistent code of professional conduct and the means to enforce it in an effective and accountable way – is a rapidly changing field and is likely to be reorganised when the Legal Services Bill 2006/2007 becomes law.

Barristers

Work

There are about 1200 barristers in England and Wales. Barristers are the most high-profile lawyers. They deal with criminal law and work mainly in the Crown Court and the other higher courts. Their work consists of prosecuting or defending the accused, usually in front of a jury. For this reason, they need not only legal skills and an understanding of criminal law; they also have to be able to influence a jury, which means that they are experts at speaking to an audience. In addition, because they must study large numbers of documents and understand a case at short notice, they have to be good at learning and understanding a lot of information quickly. As well as all this, barristers do a good deal of questioning and cross-examination of witnesses. This means that they have to be able to think on their feet and know how to question people ethically, yet bring out the best – or worst – in them! The job is one which requires confidence, the ability to function well in a high-stress situation, and the assertiveness to cope with the **adversarial** nature of the English legal system, which tends to be confrontational as it is based on the opposition of prosecution and defence.

Training

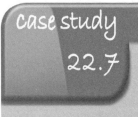

case study 22.7   Barrister training

To qualify as a barrister there are four main stages you must complete:

1. Academic Stage – undergraduate degree in Law, or undergraduate degree in any other subject at the minimum of a 2ii. If you choose the route of an undergraduate degree in a subject other than Law you must take a one year conversion course (Common Professional Examination or CPE).

2. Vocational Stage – You must join one of the four Inns before you commence this stage of training. The Bar Vocational Course, one year full time or two years part time. Once you have successfully completed the BVC you will be Called to the Bar by your Inn. You will also have to undertake 12 qualifying sessions (previously known as "dining") before Call to the Bar.

3. Pupillage – one year spent in an authorised pupillage training organisation (either barristers' chambers or another approved legal environment).

4. CPD – continuing professional development. Barristers are now subject to certain requirements in order to keep their practising certificates. CPD is usually in the form of courses or lectures.

(Source: www.legaleducation.org.uk)

activity
INDIVIDUAL WORK

1 From this information, how many years would it take for a school leaver to become a barrister?

2 Why is it essential to have a degree if you wish to become a barrister?

Fig 22.7 Main routes into the legal profession

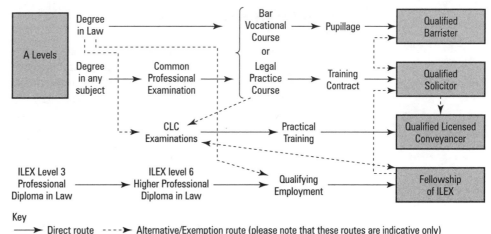

Key
⟶ Direct route   ---→ Alternative/Exemption route (please note that these routes are indicative only)

Regulation of barristers

This is done by the Bar Standards Board which is run by the **Bar Council**. The aim of the Bar Standards Board is 'to regulate the profession in the public interest'. This regulation covers both the qualification of barristers and the way in which they practise at the Bar (in other words, their professional standards while working as barristers). The regulation is carried out by four committees:

- The Rules Committee is responsible for the Code of Conduct and regulations for training.

- The Conduct Committee deals internally with complaints about barristers.

- The Monitoring Committee monitors the regulation itself, to make sure that 'the highest standards of efficiency and diversity' are maintained. It also inspects trainers and course providers.

- The Qualifications Committee ensures that all barristers are properly qualified.

The Bar Standards Board

www.legaleducation.org.uk

The Bar Council

www.barcouncil.org.uk

Solicitors

Work

Solicitors are qualified lawyers. There are about 127,000 of them in England and Wales. Most work in private practice, which means that they work in small firms and partnerships,

The Bar Council

The Bar Council is the professional body for barristers in England and Wales. It has established the Bar Standards Board to deal with the regulation of barristers, while the Council itself provides representation and services for the Bar.

(Source: www.barcouncil.org.uk)

activity
INDIVIDUAL WORK

Think of as many reasons as you can why barristers, solicitors, **paralegals** and **legal executives** all have professional bodies.

giving legal advice and supervising claims, transactions, family law problems, and so on. More solicitors work in the civil law system than in the criminal law system.

Even so, many solicitors work in the field of criminal law. For example, they work for the Crown Prosecution Service, preparing the prosecution cases using the evidence gathered by the police. They prosecute and defend cases in the magistrates' courts, and they do a lot of the legal work for the barristers in the Crown Court, giving them the information that they need to present their cases.

Training
The most straightforward way to become a solicitor is to get a law degree and then go on to the vocational (job-related) training. However, it is possible to become a solicitor with a degree which isn't in law, and it's also possible to become a solicitor without getting a degree at all.

Before their vocational training, solicitors have to study the foundations of law to a suitable level.

At the end of the academic phase of their training (foundations of law), intending solicitors have to get a certificate of completion of the academic stage of training. A good law degree is enough to get this certificate. However, people who have a degree in a subject other than law have to study the foundations of law and pass an examination called the Common Professional Examination (CPE)/Graduate Diploma in Law. If they have no degree at all, they can either study directly for the CPE, which they must pass, or they can gain the necessary legal knowledge by studying with the Institute of Legal Executives (ILEX).

Having gained the right academic standard in law, would-be solicitors can then be accepted for student membership of the **Law Society**. This is followed up by a legal practice course. As the name suggests, the legal practice course is about the practicalities of working as a solicitor. It is mainly skills based and includes:

- compulsory areas (business law and practice; property law and practice; civil and criminal litigation)
- core areas
- pervasive areas (accounts; professional conduct and client care; European Union law; revenue law; human rights)

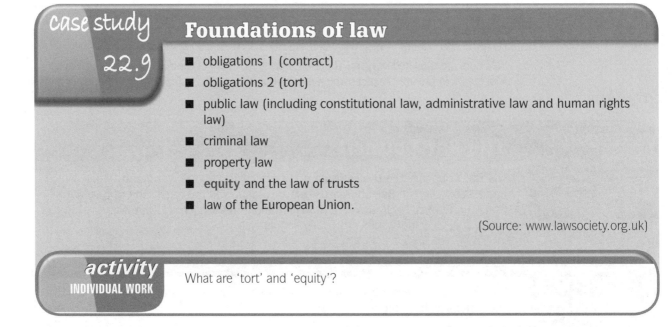

case study
22.9

Foundations of law

- obligations 1 (contract)
- obligations 2 (tort)
- public law (including constitutional law, administrative law and human rights law)
- criminal law
- property law
- **equity** and the law of trusts
- law of the European Union.

(Source: www.lawsociety.org.uk)

activity
INDIVIDUAL WORK

What are 'tort' and 'equity'?

- skills areas (**advocacy**; interviewing and advising; practical legal research; writing and drafting)
- elective subjects.

After passing the legal practice course, trainee solicitors take up a 'training contract' with a firm of solicitors. This lasts two years, if done full time. The trainee is paid around £20,000 a year (although this varies considerably and is less outside the big cities). Around the end of the training contract, the trainee has to take a 12-day Professional Skills Course (PSC). This contains modules on:

- advocacy and communication skills
- finance and business skills
- client care and professional standards.

When the PSC and the training contract are successfully completed, the trainee is at last qualified to begin work as a fully fledged solicitor.

Regulation of solicitors
This was done by the Law Society until 2006, but it has now been separated off from the Law Society and is done by the **Solicitors Regulation Authority**. The actual body doing the regulating is still, however, called the Regulation Board of the Law Society. Specialist committees, such as the Compliance Committee and the Rules and Ethics Committee, are (at the time of writing – 2007) still working out their strategies.

Regulation consists of the following:

- setting the standards for qualifying as a solicitor
- laying down rules of professional conduct
- providing guidance on professional conduct
- setting requirements for continuing professional development
- monitoring solicitors to make sure that they comply with the rules
- dealing with complaints about solicitors and helping to resolve them
- investigating and, if need be, referring solicitors to the independent Solicitors Disciplinary Tribunal
- working with other **regulators** such as the Financial Services Authority.

The work of solicitors is governed by a number of Acts and Regulations passed by Parliament over the years. There is a totally independent complaints procedure through the **Legal Services Ombudsman**.

The Law Society
www. lawsociety.org.uk

Legal executives

Work
There are around 22,000 legal executives in England and Wales. They are legal support workers. In effect, they are non-graduate lawyers who carry out a very wide range of legal work – much of it the same as solicitors do. Legal executives liaise a good deal with the public, dealing with small claims, debt collection and other legal matters. However, they are not allowed to set up independently as solicitors in their own right.

Training
Legal executives qualify through courses run by the Institute of Legal Executives. The first stage of the course is the ILEX Professional Diploma in Law which is level 3 (the same as this unit). The second stage is the ILEX Professional Higher Diploma in Law. This used to be a level 4 qualification but has recently been upgraded to level 6, so, although not a degree, it is now a university-level qualification. The next stages

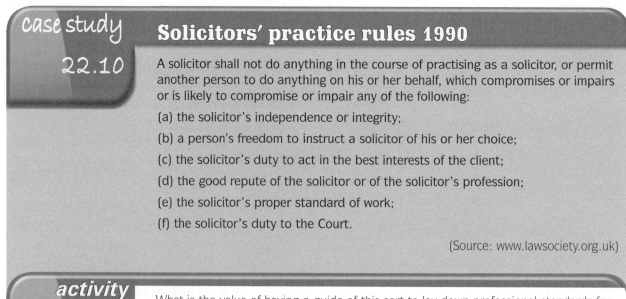

case study

22.10

Solicitors' practice rules 1990

A solicitor shall not do anything in the course of practising as a solicitor, or permit another person to do anything on his or her behalf, which compromises or impairs or is likely to compromise or impair any of the following:

(a) the solicitor's independence or integrity;

(b) a person's freedom to instruct a solicitor of his or her choice;

(c) the solicitor's duty to act in the best interests of the client;

(d) the good repute of the solicitor or of the solicitor's profession;

(e) the solicitor's proper standard of work;

(f) the solicitor's duty to the Court.

(Source: www.lawsociety.org.uk)

activity

INDIVIDUAL WORK

What is the value of having a guide of this sort to lay down professional standards for solicitors?

---

are membership and, optionally, fellowship of ILEX. After this, the progression to full professional status mirrors that of solicitors: potential legal executives do the legal practice course, the training contract and the Professional Skills Course. However, they are exempted from the training contract if they are already Fellows of ILEX.

Regulation of legal executives

Legal executives do not have their own regulatory system and up until now have been regulated under the umbrella of the Law Society which regulates the solicitors with whom legal executives normally work. However, this is likely to change. When the Legal Services Bill 2006/2007 becomes law, a body called the **Legal Services Board** will be set up as an independent regulator to the legal professions. As a result, it is probable that legal executives will be regulated by, and follow, a code of professional conduct laid down by, the Legal Services Board.

The Institute of Legal Executives

www.ilex.org.uk

Paralegals

Work

According to the National Association of Licensed Paralegals, there are around 140,000 paralegals in England and Wales. Paralegals used to be called 'legal assistants' – and sometimes still are. They are, like legal executives, support workers in the field of law, and, also like legal executives, require a good knowledge of law for their work. The difference between paralegals and legal executives is not so much in the work they do, as in the fact that legal executives must be fellows of ILEX in order to have the title 'legal executive'; and, whereas a legal executive has to have had full ILEX training, a paralegal may have no training at all but do a paralegal's work. A 'licensed paralegal' is a paralegal with enough law qualifications to be recognised – i.e. licensed – by the National Association of Licensed Paralegals. Although some people working as paralegals in England and Wales have no training or qualification in the law, this does not mean that they don't do a good job – only that the definition of a paralegal is a complex one, and that paralegals are less easy to regulate than other people employed in legal work.

Most paralegals work for solicitors or for companies which need to know something about the law. They are allowed to do much of the work a solicitor does. However, areas such as the conduct of litigation, rights of audience in the main courts, certain aspects of conveyancing transactions, and the extraction of a Grant of Representation can only be done by solicitors themselves. The areas that paralegals work in include financial services, insurance, banking, building societies, the retail sector, credit control, export, entertainment and the media.

The National Association of Licensed Paralegals

www.nationalparalegals.com

Training

There is no single training route for paralegals. Some have degrees, either in law or in other subjects. Some have started training as solicitors but have not finished: sometimes this may be because it is hard to get a training contract; or it may be because the expense of studying for so many years has been too much. Non-graduate routes into the profession include the following courses:

- Higher Certificate in Paralegal Studies
- Advanced Award in Paralegal Studies for the Voluntary and Community Sector
- Fellowship Award
- Post Graduate Diploma in Paralegal Practice
- Joint Degree Programme.

Regulation of paralegals

Regulation of paralegals has been patchy in the past. They have come vaguely under the umbrella of the Courts and Legal Services Act 1990, but there has been no specific regulation of them as a profession, even though it is clear that the legal system as we know it could not survive without them. Such regulation as there is has been carried out by their employers, by 'market forces' such as the responses of clients, or by the Legal Services Ombudsman (see below). The National Association of Licensed Paralegals was set up in 1987 to represent the interests of this diverse group of workers by enhancing their professional status. Part of this process was to try to make them as accountable and well regulated as other parts of the legal professions. However, a self-regulated profession, and self-regulation is all that the National Association of Licensed Paralegals can provide, is not as transparently well regulated as a profession that has some kind of independent regulatory system to uphold its professional standards, provide universally accepted paths to qualification, and so on. It may be that such regulation will finally be provided when the Legal Services Bill 2006/2007 becomes law.

The Legal Services Ombudsman and complaints

The office of the Legal Services Ombudsman was set up after the passing of the Courts and Legal Services Act in 1990. 'Ombudsman' is the title given to the official who heads the office that deals independently with complaints about a particular public service. (Not all public services have an ombudsman, however.) The role of the Legal Services Ombudsman is to deal with complaints about legal services which – in the opinion of the complainant – have not been dealt with adequately by the profession's regulatory body.

Office of the Legal Services Ombudsman for England and Wales

www.olso.org

case study 22.11

Complaints against the legal professions

Complaints against different legal professions are dealt with by their respective regulatory bodies.

- Solicitor – contact The Law Society (The Law Society deals with service or conduct complaints about lawyers through their Consumer Complaints Service or Conduct Assessment and Investigation Unit);
- Barrister – contact The General Council of the Bar (GCB);
- Licensed Conveyancer – contact The Council for Licensed Conveyancers (CLC);
- Legal Executive – contact The Institute of Legal Executives (ILEX);
- Patent Agent – contact The Chartered Institute of Patent Agents (CIPA);
- Trade Mark Attorney – contact The Institute of Trade Mark Attorneys (ITMA).

(Source: www.olso.org)

activity
GROUP WORK

What are the strengths and weaknesses of having regulation or complaints systems of this type?

The judiciary

remember

The judiciary (from an old word meaning 'judges') is one of the three 'arms' of democratic government, the other two being the legislature (i.e. Parliament) which makes the laws and the executive (government departments and their public services) which carry out government decisions.

The main figures in the judiciary are judges and magistrates. Their job is to interpret the law in relation to the cases they hear: in other words, they have to put it into practice. Also part of the judiciary (in a temporary sense) are juries who are picked to listen to trials in the Crown Court and who (after listening to the judge's summing up) decide whether the defendant is guilty of the offence they have been charged with or not.

Organisation

The organisation of the judiciary is not very tightly controlled, and judges themselves have a degree of **independence**. This is because it is unhealthy for a democracy if governments can tell judges what to do. Nobody, not even a government, should be above the law. Fig 22.8 outlines the organisation of the judiciary.

The bodies in the Ministry of Justice mainly belong to the judiciary since they are concerned with courts and legal processes. The prison service and the National Probation Service are executive, since their job is one of enforcement rather than administering and interpreting the law. Home Office organisations are also executive, but these have to work in partnership with the judiciary if there is to be an effective criminal justice system. The new Office of Criminal Justice Reform is designed to enable the executive and the judiciary to work together effectively while keeping their necessary degree of freedom.

Selection and appointment of judges

People who want to become judges have to have been qualified as a barrister or solicitor for at least seven years, although this is expected to be reduced to five. Normally, such people are barristers or solicitors when they apply to become judges, but lecturers and others who have been correctly qualified for the right period of time can also apply.

The application to become a judge is in some ways similar to applications for the police!

Fig 22.8 Organisation of the judiciary

Home Office: The Home Secretary is in charge of police, immigration and national security	**Ministry of Justice**: The Secretary of State for Justice is in charge of: The Courts Service; the National Offender Management Service (NOMS) – prison, probation, etc.; inspectorates of prisons; Youth Justice Board; Tribunals Service; Legal Aid; criminal and civil law; sentencing; human rights	
Main duties of Home Office Security Counter-terrorism Respect Crime reduction Criminal records Immigration ID and passport	**Office for Criminal Justice Reform** liaises with Home Office and the Attorney General's Office	
	Ministry of Justice Board Ministers of State and Under-secretaries of State help the Secretary of State for Justice in decision and strategy making	
	Departmental Management Board This is composed of senior civil servants in charge of: the Courts Service; judicial services such as training and appointing judges; NOMS; reforming the legal system; legal aid; regional duties	
Main organisations: Border and Immigration Agency Identity and Passport Service Criminal Records Bureau Police	**Lord Chief Justice of England and Wales** Responsible for organisation and work of the criminal courts	
	Attorney General; Solicitor General These are the government's main legal advisers	
	Director of Public Prosecutions: in charge of prosecuting authorities	**Other legal bodies:** Criminal Cases Review Commission Criminal Injuries Compensation Authority (and others)
Bodies paid for by the Home Office, but which are independent or act in an advisory or monitoring role. These include: Serious Organised Crime Agency Independent Police Complaints Commission Police Advisory Board Office of the Immigration Services Commissioner Security Industry Authority	**Prosecuting authorities** The main prosecuting authority is the Crown Prosecution Service. This prepares all the police cases against offenders in both the magistrates' and Crown Courts. Other prosecuting authorities are HM Revenue and Customs, which prepares cases involving tax evasion and illegal international trafficking and the Serious Fraud Office, which deals with complex financial wrongdoings	
	The courts These range from the magistrates' courts up to the House of Lords. There are both civil and criminal courts. A Supreme Court will probably be set up to replace the work done by the House of Lords in dealing with the most major cases and appeals	
	Judges Run trials in the Crown Court, other higher criminal courts, and in civil courts, tribunals, appeal courts and in the House of Lords	
	Barristers Work in higher courts – especially in criminal law	**Solicitors** Work mainly in civil law. Some do criminal law work in the magistrates' courts, and some assist barristers in preparing their cases
	The Bar Council The body that represents and monitors barristers	**The Law Society** The body that represents and monitors solicitors
	District Judges Formerly stipendiary magistrates; paid and qualified to supervise some hearings at magistrates' courts.	
	Magistrates No legal training but, with advice, they too interpret the law	
	Juries Members of the public who judge guilt in Crown Court and some other serious cases	
	Legal Services Ombudsman for England and Wales Leads an independent organisation which deals with complaints about the legal system which cannot be resolved within the judicial system.	
	Prisons etc. HM Prison Service National Probation Service These are both part of NOMS and moved from the Home Office to the Ministry of Justice in 2007	

Stage 1 Application and shortlisting

1. Respond to advertisement or recruitment roadshow/outreach activity; obtain application form and pack

2. Complete application form 10 pages

3. Eligibility tests and character check

4. Sifting based on track record, references

5. Qualifying test – written technical test and/or case study

Stage 2 Assessment

6. References taken up and examined by selection panel

7. Interview and face-to-face assessments. Role plays; formal structured discussion

Stage 3 Decision

8. Selection panel produce a paper on the candidates for the Judicial Appointments Commission's Selection and Character Committee

9. Final checks including medical and health – for all except judicial office holders.

You be the Judge: Career Opportunities in the Judiciary in England and Wales (Department for Constitutional Affairs, October 2005)

www.judiciary.gov.uk

Roles in civil and criminal cases

The main roles of judges in both civil and criminal cases include:

- case preparation
- case management
- hearing actions
- considering and deciding on legal issues
- giving directions to the jury (in criminal cases)
- summing up proceedings
- determining applications
- sentencing
- giving judgments.

Judges also have to ensure that trials are carried out in an orderly, effective, humane and efficient manner. In a criminal case, they have to prevent barristers from saying things that are unacceptable (e.g. not based on the evidence; designed to bias or mislead a jury, etc.). Judges have to ensure that the members of the public present in the court do nothing to disturb the trial (even if they are relatives of the accused), and they have to be aware of the special needs of vulnerable witnesses and take steps to protect them when necessary.

In a civil court, judgments are made 'on the basis of probability', which is a lower standard of proof than that required in a criminal court where the standard of proof is 'beyond reasonable doubt'. So in a civil court, judges themselves decide the rights and wrongs of the case; whereas in a criminal court the guilt or innocence of the defendant is decided by the jury.

Judicial independence and immunity

When they are appointed, judges swear an oath which says, 'I will do right to all manner of people after the laws and usages of this Realm, without fear or favour, affection or ill-will'.

case study 22.12 — Qualities needed by judges

1. *Intellectual capacity*

   High level of expertise in your chosen area or profession

   Ability quickly to absorb and analyse information

   Appropriate knowledge of the law and its underlying principles, or the ability to acquire this knowledge where necessary

2. *Personal qualities*

   Integrity and independence of mind

   Sound judgement

   Decisiveness

   Objectivity

   Ability and willingness to learn and develop professionally

3. *An ability to understand and deal fairly*

   Ability to treat everyone with respect and sensitivity whatever their background

   Willingness to listen with patience and courtesy

4. *Authority and communication skills*

   Ability to explain the procedure and any decisions reached clearly and succinctly to all those involved

   Ability to inspire respect and confidence

   Ability to maintain authority when challenged

5. *Efficiency*

   Ability to work at speed and under pressure

   Ability to organise time effectively and produce clear reasoned judgments expeditiously

   Ability to work constructively with others (including leadership and managerial skills where appropriate)

   (Source: www.judicialappointments.gov.uk)

activity — INDIVIDUAL WORK

1 Rate yourself from 1 to 10 in these qualities.

2 Note down an action plan for improving in some or all of them.

Fig 22.9 Making sense of the law: a judge

remember

As well as being independent, judges also have to be impartial, have integrity (be honest and incorruptible), show propriety (decent, dignified behaviour), ensure equality of treatment and be competent and hard-working.

What this means is that judges must be free to act independently of any pressure from other people – such as the government, the police, local government, business interests, and so on. They must make their judgments based on their knowledge of the law and in the public interest.

This duty of independence is based on the democratic concept of the separation of powers. This is the idea that a democratic country such as Britain has three arms of government – the legislature, which makes laws; the executive which carries out and enforces the will of the government, and the judiciary, which interprets the laws and applies them to particular cases. A judge is part of the judiciary and must be free of undue influence from the two other arms of government, otherwise the country would be at risk of turning into a police state. Without this independence, we would not be able to claim that people in Britain are 'equal under the law', and there would be little defence against the government or the police if they abused their powers.

Immunity

Judicial **immunity** is immunity from pressure, undue criticism and harassment from other powerful people such as government ministers. There is a feeling that politicians should not criticise judges for their decisions, although sometimes they do. On some occasions, if politicians disapprove of a judge's decision, they suggest that the law itself should be changed.

In fact, judicial immunity is a complex subject, and the immunity of judges is very limited. They are not immune at all from prosecution for offences against the law (e.g. in 2007 a judge was arrested for 'flashing' on a train).

Removal from office

It is not easy to remove a judge from office unless they have been convicted of a crime. In cases where complaints have been received the actions taken (see Fig 22.10) may lead to dismissal (depending on the nature and seriousness of the complaint). Judges can only be sacked by the **Lord Chief Justice** and the Secretary of State – who must agree on the action.

The only truly independent person in the process is the Legal Services Ombudsman – and the Ombudsman is not necessarily involved. The judge who is undergoing the disciplinary procedure can appeal to the Ombudsman.

However, the process is a painstaking one, with various safeguards for the judge accused of wrongdoing; it is in any case very rare for a judge to be removed from office.

Office for Judicial complaints

www.judicialcomplaints.gov.uk

activity

GROUP WORK
22.2

P3

Design a mock criminal trial for your class or group. Include role-sheets for 'judges' and 'lawyers', explaining how they will behave and what their roles will be during the mock trial.

Lay people

Lay people (people without legal training) play a vital role in the legal process. Both magistrates and juries are essential in the criminal justice system. This is not in order to save money, but to uphold a very important principle of the law: that the law acts in the name of the people, and that we are (or should be) all equal before the law. The

Fig 22.10 Removal of judges

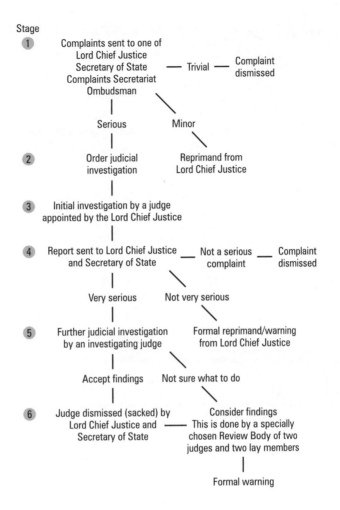

law exists **in the public interest**, serves the public, and the public must be involved. Crimes – in the English system – are crimes against the state (meaning all of us), which is why criminal cases are always referred as R (Regina = the Queen, or Rex = the King) v X (Name of defendant).

> **remember**
> A magistrate is sometimes called a Justice of the Peace (JP).

Magistrates

Traditionally there are two kinds of magistrates – lay magistrates and those who are paid. The paid ones used to be called stipendiary magistrates but are now called District Judges.

Selection and appointment

Lay magistrates are ordinary people who apply for the post. To apply, they have to be aged between 18 and 65; they can carry on working to the age of 70.

Magistrates do not have to be British Nationals, but they have to be prepared to sign the **oath of allegiance**.

Police officers and politicians cannot become magistrates. A history of bankruptcy or previous criminal offences may also prevent appointment.

The selection process for magistrates is a thorough one. The stages are:

1. Application form

2. First interview

3. Second interview (discussing practical examples of likely cases)

4. Background checks (including close relatives, spouses and cohabitees)

5. References.

> ## case study 22.13 — Requirements for magistrates
>
> - Good character: to have personal integrity and enjoy the respect and trust of others
> - Understanding and communication: to be able to understand documents, identify relevant facts, follow evidence and communicate effectively
> - Social awareness: to appreciate and accept the rule of law
> - Maturity and sound temperament: to have an awareness and understanding of people and a sense of fairness
> - Sound judgement: to be able to think logically, weigh arguments and reach a sound decision
> - Commitment and reliability: to be committed to serving the community, willing to undergo training and to be in sufficiently good health to undertake your duties on a regular basis.
>
> (Source: *Serving as a Magistrate: A Detailed Guide to the Role of JP*, www.magistrates.gov.uk)

> ### activity
> **INDIVIDUAL WORK**
>
> Explain why you think each of these qualities is needed in a magistrate's work.

The Ministry of Justice is keen to have more magistrates from minority groups, which are still under-represented in the service.

Training

Training is based on a competence framework similar to the National Occupational Standards: in other words, the job is broken down into tasks and processes and you learn each one.

In initial training, magistrates:

- learn about the role and responsibilities of a magistrate
- undergo induction and core training
- have at least three court observations
- visit a prison, Young Offender Institution and probation service facility
- have two days' consolidation training after a year.

Magistrates also get training in:

- communicating
- listening
- team work
- structured decision making
- awareness of community needs
- respect and lack of bias or prejudice
- problem solving.

In addition to these there are systems of mentoring and appraisal, periods of 'update training' to learn about new developments and procedures, and the possibility of additional training for specialist roles such as Youth Court work. The organisation of training (e.g. whether it is done in small sessions during evenings, or at a residential centre) varies from area to area.

Role and powers

Magistrates sit on the 'Bench' hearing cases for an average of 35 half-days a year. They sit in threes and are helped in legal matters by a Legal Adviser. The magistrate sitting in the middle is the Court Chairman; he or she may be paid and helps to guide the lay magistrates. Mostly, magistrates deal with relatively minor criminal cases such as theft, criminal damage, assaults, public disorder and motoring offences. They can also specialise in the work of the Family Proceedings Court, which deals with family issues, or the Youth Court which hears cases involving young people aged 10–17.

Jurisdiction in civil and criminal cases

All this is criminal law work, but magistrates are involved in the civil law as well if they deal with licensing applications (these come mainly from places where drinking or betting will be done).

activity
**INDIVIDUAL WORK
22.3**

P2

1 Visit the Crown Court and write a guidance leaflet for prospective jurors, explaining what their role will be before, during and after a trial.

2 Visit the magistrates' court and produce a leaflet for offenders, explaining what magistrates do in criminal cases and how they do it.

Removal from office

The removal of a magistrate is similar to, but simpler than, the removal of a judge. It can happen because of some wrongdoing in the magistrate's work, because the magistrate has been convicted of a crime, or because the magistrate has stopped sitting on the Bench. Fig 22.11 shows the procedures.

Fig 22.11 Removing magistrates

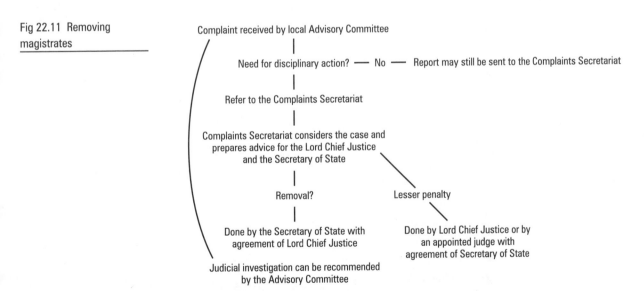

Complaint received by local Advisory Committee

Need for disciplinary action? — No — Report may still be sent to the Complaints Secretariat

Refer to the Complaints Secretariat

Complaints Secretariat considers the case and prepares advice for the Lord Chief Justice and the Secretary of State

Removal?

Lesser penalty

Done by the Secretary of State with agreement of Lord Chief Justice

Done by Lord Chief Justice or by an appointed judge with agreement of Secretary of State

Judicial investigation can be recommended by the Advisory Committee

At any stage, at the request of the magistrate or anyone else involved, the independent Legal Services Ombudsman can be brought into the process.

Advantages and disadvantages

Table 22.2 Advantages and disadvantages of magistrates' courts

Advantages	Disadvantages
The magistrates' court is a well-established institution and everybody knows and understands how it works	For reasons not well understood, magistrates' courts appear to be stricter than the Crown Court, when hearing triable either way cases
The process is cheap compared with the Crown Court because magistrates are paid expenses, not a salary. Although they are well trained, they do not have legal training, which is expensive and takes a long time	The process is time consuming and expensive compared with summary justice, e.g. fixed payment penalties
Magistrates are local people who, ideally, come from a range of social, occupational and ethnic backgrounds, and include both men and women. They represent the diversity of society and should not be prejudiced against offenders (or anybody else)	The theory is that magistrates are diverse and represent all of society; in practice they tend to be white, middle class and middle-aged. They are accused of having a narrow-minded attitude towards justice
Like the jury system, they represent ordinary people and show that justice is a community affair, not something handed down from above, by 'experts'	Their lack of legal knowledge may be a handicap in reaching a fair judgment (although this is not what most people think)
There are many magistrates' courts and people do not have to travel far to go to them	

Magistrates are trained to take a 'holistic' view of crime and think about:

- punishment of offenders
- reduction of crime
- reform and rehabilitation of offenders
- protection of the public
- making of reparation by offenders
- those affected by their offences (www.dca.gov.uk).

Juries

Juries are groups of 12 citizens aged between 18 and 70 who are called to observe and pass judgment on a trial in a Crown Court or, sometimes, in civil cases in the County Court.

Qualification and disqualification

A person can serve on a jury if they are:

- registered as a parliamentary or local government elector
- not less than 18 and not more than 70 years of age
- ordinarily resident in the UK, the Channel Islands or the Isle of Man for any period of at least five years since attaining the age of 13
- not a mentally disordered person
- not disqualified from jury service because of criminal convictions.

Table 22.3 Excused or deferred?

Summoned in past 2 yrs E*	Shift work D	Armed forces D or E (depends on commanding officer)
Insufficient English E	Student hardship holiday work E or D	
Care responsibilities D	Teachers or students in term time D	Work commitments D
Closed religious orders E		Physical disability D or E
Religious festival D	Important public duties D	
Court hard to reach – offer another court	MPs D	
Holidays D	Judiciary D (change from 1974)	
Valid business reasons E		

* Based on guidelines suggested by the Department for Constitutional Affairs: E = excused; D = deferred (put off to a later date).

Selection and role

Potential jurors are selected randomly from the electoral role and are compelled by law to do their jury service unless there is very good reason why they should be excused. At present, jury service is governed by the Juries Act 1974, but some changes were made in the Criminal Justice Act 2003, and guidance was put out by the Department for Constitutional Affairs to make it more difficult for people to get out of doing jury service. According to the government, the chances of being called for jury service in a person's lifetime are only one in six.

The jury's role is to listen to the evidence and the judge's summing up in a case involving a serious crime, then go into a private room to discuss whether the defendant is guilty of the offence with which they have been charged. They appoint a leader or spokesperson who will give the results of their 'deliberations' (thinking and discussing).

Summoning

Juries are summoned randomly by computer. They are asked to take an unbiased approach to the cases that they hear. Jurors receive a letter, to which they have to reply in seven days, instructing them to be at a certain court at a certain time and date.

Criminal Justice System for England and Wales

www.cjsonline.gov.uk

Vetting and challenging

Vetting is the process of checking a jury to ensure that there are no unqualified people (especially people with serious previous convictions or suspected terrorist links, etc.) in the jury. Vetting involves a police check with the Criminal Records Office.

Challenging is carried out by barristers for the prosecution or the defence, or by the judge. It consists of asking a juror to 'stand by' – in other words leave the chosen group of 12 and be replaced by someone else. It happens either because the judge thinks that the person is unsuitable for some reason (e.g. they appear to be drunk or drugged) or because prosecution or defence lawyers have a demonstrable reason to think that the person might be biased in a particular case. There are clear legal guidelines for challenging, to prevent lawyers exploiting the process to obtain an unfair advantage in the trial.

Advantages

The advantages of the jury system are that:

- It is generally popular with the public.
- It empowers ordinary people to make decisions about crime, instead of leaving justice to experts who might be out of touch with what ordinary people think.

- It demonstrates that a sense of justice is inherent in ordinary people.

- The system is relatively cheap, as it doesn't involve employing extra people.

- It is a link between the administration of justice and the community.

Disadvantages

The disadvantages of the jury system are that:

- Juries have to reach unanimous or majority decisions – but the majority isn't always right.

- Jurors who are more forceful or articulate may pressure other jurors into agreeing with them when they don't really agree.

- It is inconvenient for jurors.

- Some crimes (especially fraud) can be so complex that jurors don't understand them properly.

- Jurors can be 'nobbled' (threatened etc.) by criminals and in some cases may be at risk after the judgment.

- As the deliberations of a jury are secret, there is a lack of openness in the system.

- There is a risk that juries in major cases can be influenced by heavy media coverage of the case.

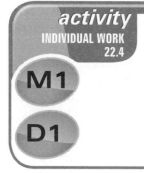

activity

INDIVIDUAL WORK 22.4

M1

D1

You are involved in setting up materials for an exchange project between your community and a similar community on the continent. Research and write a report on the work of judges, lawyers and lay people in the English court system, showing the similarities and differences between what they do and the way they do it. In your conclusion assess carefully what lay people do in the system, explaining the advantages and disadvantages of their involvement.

How legal rules are created by precedent

'**Precedent**' comes from Latin words meaning 'falling before'. It refers to previous decisions made in court.

Judicial precedent

Judicial precedent is the use of decisions in previous cases to guide judges in their decisions in present-day cases. It is, in a sense, a form of 'quality control' in the law because it helps to keep decisions fair and consistent over a period of time and from one court to another.

Development of the system

Precedent was developed under 'common law', the ancient system of law which was the only form of law before Magna Carta in 1215 and continued to be the main form up to the later part of the seventeenth century. Common law was established by custom, and the only way to keep some form of consistency and fairness was to refer back to previous cases, where records had been kept. The basic idea was that, for example, a peasant stealing a goose in Kirkham would get the same punishment as the peasant who had stolen a goose in Mudthorpe five years before.

Crimes which have always been crimes, and are considered to be crimes the world over, in almost every society, are common law crimes. Murder, rape, robbery and theft were all crimes in the Middle Ages, and, although in fairly recent times these have been defined and put on the statute books by Parliament, precedent is still used when determining some penalties (as it was in the old days of common law). This is especially so where the legal sentence for a crime can come anywhere between two widely spaced limits, depending on the exact circumstances.

Law reporting

The use of precedent, sometimes called '**case law**' because it depends on studying the judgments in old cases, is made possible by vast collections of old law reports to which lawyers can refer when deciding what the main issues of a case really are, and what a suitable sentence might be.

Not all cases are reported: only the ones which, in the opinion of the editors of the various lists of reported cases, demonstrate some useful point of law which can be used as a precedent.

Cases are referred to by the main people/bodies contesting them, for example:

- *Blunkett* v *Quinn* [2004]
- *Regina* v *Abu Hamza* [2006].

In the first example, the case was a civil one, and both sides of the case carry the names of people. In the second the case was a criminal one; this is shown by the use of Regina. 'Regina' (or 'R') appears in all criminal cases because the prosecution is carried out by the Crown (as in Crown Prosecution Service). The 'v' means 'versus' (against), just as it would do in a boxing match, and shows the adversarial nature of the English court system.

When lawyers speak about cases they do not use 'v' and 'Regina' as they do when writing. Instead they would say, for example, 'Blunkett and Quinn' (for a civil case) and 'the Crown against Abu Hamza' (in a criminal case).

British and Irish Legal Information Institute

www.bailii.org

Binding authorities

A **binding authority** is a judgment made in a senior court (often a higher appeal court) which is declared (by the court in question) as a model which must be followed in similar cases. In other words these are precedents that other courts have to follow. The Latin name, which is still sometimes used, is '**stare decisis**'.

The binding authority must be based on the reasoning behind the decision, not the decision itself or other, irrelevant, circumstances of the case.

Persuasive authorities

These are precedents which courts may follow, but they don't have to – as they do with a binding authority. **Persuasive authorities** have less force than binding authorities for two main reasons:

- because they are not declared by the judge of the court to be binding authorities but are expressed more as recommendations or 'good ideas'
- because they sometimes come from lower courts, and, although the judgment may be legally valid and adopted by higher courts, a lower court can never compel a higher court to follow its judgments.

Ratio decidendi

This is a Latin phrase meaning 'the reason for the decision'. It refers to the reasoning behind the decision in a case which is then declared to be a binding authority. This same reasoning should be used to decide all later cases where the same basic issues are involved.

The famous case of *Donoghue* v *Stevenson* [1932] and the snail in the bottle of ginger beer established that a manufacturer had a duty of care to the buyers or consumers of their product. In this case, a woman had got gastroenteritis because she drank the ginger beer which had a dead snail at the bottom of it. The **ratio decidendi** is nothing to do with snails or ginger beer; it is to do with the essence of the case, which was that the manufacturer had a 'duty of care'. This principle is the *ratio decidendi* which courts now have to follow when judging cases of negligence by the providers of goods and services.

Respect

www.respect.gov.uk

Obiter statements

Obiter statements are sometimes called '*obiter dicta*'; they are statements made by judges in higher courts which form a persuasive authority, but not a binding authority. They are said to be 'by the way' remarks. They are not declared at the time to be principles which other courts must follow, but experience has shown that they are a pretty good guide to what courts should decide in a particular type of case.

activity

INDIVIDUAL WORK 22.5

P4

Visit a civil court, observe a case, and make notes on all mention of precedents. Then, in a format suitable for briefing a new trainee in a legal office, explain, with examples, what precedents are and how they are used in court.

Avoiding judicial precedents

Despite the fact that it is a good thing as a general rule for laws to be consistent and for precedent to determine the outcome of cases, English law is not something that cannot or should not ever change. No two cases are exactly alike; modern life is becoming more complex and unpredictable; and the law has to adapt even though it also has to uphold certain unchanging principles of justice. For these reasons, the law should not always slavishly follow precedents.

In addition, courts can and do make mistakes. Sometimes the mistakes are very serious and keep innocent people locked up for years, while murderers and others go free and unpunished because the wrong person has been found guilty.

Distinguishing previous decisions

Distinguishing a previous decision happens when a judge decides, for a specific reason, not to follow a precedent in a particular case. The usual reason is that, while the case appears to be like the one providing the precedent, there is, in the judge's view, some fundamental underlying difference which means that the precedent should not apply.

Reversing decisions

This happens when a court hears an appeal and changes the original decision, not simply by annulling it, but by replacing it with a decision which has the opposite effect from the first one. This can happen not because the judgment of the first court was legally wrong so much as because its results had not been foreseen. An example from 2002 describes a decision that was reversed because the effects of the first decision were considered undesirable, and the law had been rapidly changed by Parliament as a result. Following this change in the law, it was then possible for the Appeal Court to reverse the previous decision of the High Court.

case study
22.14
A reversed decision

Last year the government brought in regulations under the act to regulate research on embryos, which requires a licence from the Human Fertilisation and Embryology Authority. But Mr Justice Crane's ruling last November [in the High Court] that the act did not cover clones left research on cloned embryos unregulated. In the wake of his ruling, the government rushed through legislation banning the use of cloning to produce a baby. Last week's appeal court judgement means that research on cloned embryos with the aim of growing human tissue for transplant is once again tightly regulated in line with the government's intention.

(Source: www.bmj.com)

activity
GROUP WORK

Had Mr Justice Crane done anything wrong? Analyse the situation and explain your viewpoint.

Overruling previous decisions

This happens when a higher court, after hearing an appeal, decides that the lower court (whose judgment is being appealed against) was indeed wrong in its decision. The previous decision is annulled, and the decision of the higher court stands. This outcome, of course, is what the appellant wants. The difference between overruling and reversing is that overruling simply cancels a previous decision, while reversing produces a new decision which has the opposite effect of the previous one.

Practice statements

Practice statements, sometimes called 'practice directions', are put out in writing by a number of legal bodies, notably the House of Lords and by the Ministry of Justice. Some practice statements are lengthy and detailed; others give simple advice. Although they don't have the legal status of Parliamentary Acts and Regulations, practice statements amount to a code of practice giving advice on legal procedures.

Practice directions put out by the House of Lords give guidance on handling appeals.

The following are examples of practice statements (directions):

- '10.16 In a case involving a child, where delay might affect the facts of the case or the interests of the child, parties should draw this to the attention of the Head of the Judicial Office not later than the day of presentation of the petition of appeal.'

(Source: www.publications.parliament.uk)

- 'I will take as my starting point the existing approach adopted in the case of adults sentenced to a **mandatory** life sentence. In the case of adults the usual length of **tariff**, or punitive term, (which means the amount of time actually to be served by a person convicted of murder in order to meet the requirements of **retribution** and general deterrence) will be a period of 14 years before the possibility of release arises for consideration at all.'

(Source: www.hmcourts-service.gov.uk)

case study 22.15 — Aggravating and mitigating features

In all cases of murder, the sentence may be increased or reduced to allow for aggravating and **mitigating features**. Without seeking to be comprehensive, **aggravating features** will include:

- Evidence of a planned or revenge killing.
- The killing of a child or a very old or otherwise vulnerable victim.
- Evidence of sadism, gratuitous violence, or sexual maltreatment, humiliation or degradation before the killing.
- Killing for gain (in the course of burglary, robbery, blackmail, insurance fraud, etc).
- Multiple killings.
- The killing of a witness or potential witness to defeat the ends of justice.
- The killing of those doing their public duty (police officers, prison officers, postal workers, fire-fighters, Judges, etc)
- Terrorist, or politically motivated, killings.
- The use of firearms or other dangerous weapons, whether carried for defensive or offensive reasons.
- A record of serious violence.
- Attempts to dismember or conceal the body.

Again, without seeking to be comprehensive, the following may normally be regarded as mitigating features:

- Age.
- Sub-normality or mental abnormality.
- Provocation (in a non-technical sense) or an excessive response to a personal threat.
- The absence of an intention to kill.
- Spontaneity and lack of pre-meditation (beyond that necessary to constitute the offence: e.g. a sudden response to family pressure or to prolonged and eventually insupportable stress).
- Mercy killing.
- A plea of guilty.
- Hard evidence of remorse or contrition.

[Source: *Practice Directions [part of] Practice Statement Life Sentences for Murder*. The Lord Chief Justice Of England and Wales, 27 July 2000. www.hmcourts-service.gov.uk]

activity
GROUP WORK

1 Discuss whether you agree with the descriptions of aggravating features.
2 How far do you agree with each of the mitigating features?

How statutory rules are made and interpreted

Statutory rules are different from the rules and practices based on common law outlined in the previous few pages. Unlike common law, which existed before it was ever written down and was not devised by the government, statute law is put together by the government, passed or approved by Parliament and is then part of the law of the land.

Statutory legal rules

The main statutory legal rules are statutory laws. There are two main kinds of statutory law: Acts of Parliament and Statutory Instruments, which are often called Regulations. Acts of Parliament are big general laws which are, to some extent, open to interpretation by the courts or by the people whose actions are controlled by these Acts. Regulations are much smaller and more exact laws which control particular activities in some detail.

Stages in making an Act of Parliament

 Link

See pages 34–37 in Unit 1, where the stages are discussed more fully.

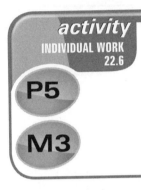

 activity
INDIVIDUAL WORK 22.6

P5

M3

Produce a flow chart, showing how an Act of Parliament is made, and an information sheet outlining and explaining the different rules for statutory interpretation. These should be suitable for distribution at the 'Law' stand at a careers convention for school leavers.

Link

See pages 397–399 for more information on statutory interpretation.

Public and Private Members' Bills

Public Bills are introduced by the government after a longish preparatory period, often involving months of consultation even before the white paper proposing the Bill comes out. Over 90% of Bills that are passed by Parliament and made into Acts (i.e. statute laws) are Public Bills. Because the Bills are Public ones, the government is able to put plenty of pressure on its own MPs to support them, and, because the government has a majority of MPs in the House of Commons, such Bills are likely to be passed.

Private Members' Bills have nothing (officially) to do with the government, as they are proposed by MPs themselves. There are four ways these Bills can be introduced:

- after a ballot held by MPs
- through the '10-minute rule'
- through 'ordinary presentation'
- by peers (members of the House of Lords).

remember

A Bill is a law which has not yet been passed by Parliament. Once passed, it is called an Act.

Parliament's ways of dealing with Private Members' Bills are complicated, but the main point is that most of the Bills suggested never become law because there is not enough time to debate them. Even when there are debates, on the second reading, these can be sabotaged by long, time-wasting speeches by opponents of the Bill. However, not all Private Members' Bills which fail disappear without trace: if the idea seems good, the government is likely to take it up and incorporate it later into one of its own Bills.

See page 37 in Unit 1 for more on how legislation is created.

Doctrine of parliamentary sovereignty

Parliamentary sovereignty is the name given to the fact that Parliament is the most powerful institution in the government. Parliament alone has the power to make or unmake (repeal) laws. The courts, including judges and others who work there, have no power to change laws, only to interpret them. If the original law is worded in a way which is unclear, it might be that the courts act on it in a way that was not intended by Parliament, but, once this is noticed, Parliament can, and usually does, take steps to clarify the situation.

Limitations to parliamentary sovereignty do exist. One is that the judiciary can and sometimes does question the legality of laws passed by Parliament, either because the new laws conflict with other laws or because they seem to be against the public interest or badly thought out. Another is that the EU is now able to make laws that the British Parliament normally has to accept.

See pages 400–403 for more on the EU and legislation.

Primary and delegated legislation

Primary legislation is laws that are debated in Parliament before they are passed. These laws are called Bills, while they are still being considered, and Acts, once they have been passed.

See pages 34–37 in Unit 1, where these are discussed more fully.

Delegated legislation (**secondary legislation**) is law making which is passed on by Parliament to individual government departments, such as the Home Office, the Ministry of Defence, and the Department of Communities and Local Government. The departments make laws which can be attached to Acts which have already been passed by Parliament and which contain provision for small bits of legislation to be added on to them. Those laws that are produced by government departments in this way are generally called Statutory Instruments (SIs) or Regulations.

Statutory Instruments which nobody is likely to disagree with become law without being examined outside the government department which makes them. Others, where there could be disagreement, are 'laid before the House of Commons' so that MPs can look at them. If these draft SIs are 'disapproved', they have to be redrafted (rewritten) or abandoned. Many SIs are also examined by the Joint Committee on Statutory Instruments. This is a committee of MPs and peers who check that the draft SIs are properly worded and that government ministers are not trying to exceed their powers by making laws which are more far reaching than they ought to be.

activity
GROUP WORK
22.7

M2

You work for an organisation which aims to increase the understanding of citizenship among young people. Give a presentation showing how laws were and are made in both the common law and statute law systems, and explaining in some detail the similarities and differences between the various methods.

Fig 22.12 A parliamentary committee – where proposed laws are sorted out in detail

United Kingdom Parliament

www.parliament.uk

See Legislation Series factsheets produced by the House of Commons Information Office

www.parliament.uk

L1: *Parliamentary Stages of a Government Bill* (Revised January 2007)

L2: *Private Members' Bills Procedure* (Revised November 2004)

L7: *Statutory Instruments* (Revised March 2006)

Principles of statutory interpretation

Laws, whether statute law or case law, are written down, and it is the job of judges, magistrates, coroners, etc. to understand these laws and then apply them to the cases they have to hear. The general word for this process of understanding and applying laws is 'interpretation', and it is 'statutory' because it involves laws, or statutes (which are the same thing).

As anyone who works with documents (e.g. assignment briefs or BTEC Specifications) knows, interpretation is not always easy and there are various ways of doing it. Over the years judges and lawyers have developed a number of 'rules' or approaches for getting at the true meaning of the law and applying it in the best possible way to real-life cases.

Literal rule

The **literal** rule simply states that laws should be **interpreted** according to the exact and/or normal meaning of the words in them. This approach means that laws should be followed 'to the letter'.

Advantages of the literal rule

Judges do not take the law into their own hands by twisting the meanings of words in the statute book. If all judges use this approach, the interpretation of the law should be consistent.

Disadvantages of the literal rule

Laws are not always worded precisely, either because Parliament wanted to leave room for interpretation or because the wording was ill thought out in the first place. Giving undue importance to bad or inaccurate wording leads to inaccurate or sloppy interpretation.

Words do not always have definite meanings, and individual judges may interpret them differently even though all judges are well educated.

Concentrating on the meanings of individual words and phrases may mean that judges do not see the wider purpose of the law: in other words, they miss the main point and 'cannot see the wood for the trees'.

The weakness of the literal rule is shown in the case of *London North Eastern Railway* v *Berriman* [1946]. A woman was claiming damages for the death of her husband. The contract said that a wife could claim damages if her husband was killed while 'relaying or repairing the tracks'. However, since the evidence showed that her husband was merely doing 'oiling and routine maintenance', she got no compensation for his death.

The mischief rule

Nowadays 'mischief' means small-scale naughtiness, but in the past it meant more serious wrongdoing. The **mischief rule** in law is used when the judge looks not at the exact wording of the law, but at the wrongdoing it is trying to prevent, and whether the decision that he or she makes in a particular case will prevent that wrongdoing.

Advantages of the mischief rule

The judge is more likely to uphold the spirit of the law, rather than simply the letter of the law. Even if the law has been badly written in Parliament, it can be interpreted in a way which will be just and will benefit society. If the basic duty of the law, as some people claim, is to 'act in the public interest', then applying the mischief rule may be a way of ensuring that some of the absurdities and misused technicalities which cause miscarriages of justice do not actually take place. Applying the mischief rule also allows the judge to act more independently of the government. Where a country is well governed this may not matter, but in some countries (e.g. Zimbabwe) judges play an important role in protecting ordinary people from the unreasonable behaviour of the government.

Disadvantages of the mischief rule

The main disadvantage is that, if the mischief rule was carried too far, it would mean that judges were simply doing what they personally thought was best rather than what the law says that they should do. Judges are public servants; they are not elected (as they are in the US), and their job is to interpret the law, not to try and change it.

The golden rule

This is similar to the literal rule. The basic idea is that the common-sense meanings of the words in the law should normally be followed. However, if the wording of the law is such that this would lead to an absurd or unfair result, common sense should be used to ensure that the judgment in the case is a good one.

Like the literal and mischief rules, the **golden rule** is not one that any judges have to follow. These rules are approaches to dealing with difficult cases, when the wording of the law isn't clear or the case itself is not clear cut. Most judges will apply the rules differently in different circumstances, using one and then the other according to the wording of the law and the nature of the case they are judging.

Integrated and purposive approaches to statutory interpretation

To understand the integrated and purposive approaches to statutory interpretation (understanding and applying laws) it is useful to be aware of all four main approaches: textualist, statutory derogation, integrated and purposive.

The textualist approach

The textualist approach is that no one can know what the intention of the lawmakers (i.e. Parliament) is; all the judge has to go on is the text (the wording) of the law itself. Textualism is a more developed form of the literal rule. Its advantage is that it discourages judges from second-guessing the intentions of Parliament and putting their own personal interpretation on a law. Its disadvantage is that, by approaching the interpretation of law in such a dry and academic way, judges may lose track of the fact that the law is about people and about righting wrongs in society.

Statutory derogation

Statutory derogation is the idea that if a statute law conflicts with common law, common law should be followed. This would mean that, when in doubt about the correct interpretation of a statute law in relation to a particular case, a judge could look up the common law related to the statute law and use that as a guide in making a decision about the case. The strength of this approach is that common law is the 'collective wisdom' of society, and its statements are seen as established fact by many people (e.g. that murder is a very serious crime; that the intention matters in murder, and so on). Statute law, by contrast, is produced by a lot of lawyers arguing in Parliament. The weakness of statutory derogation is that it may be seen as a cop-out from understanding and using the statute law, especially as case law and common law are not exact sciences.

The integrated approach

The integrated approach to statutory interpretation is closer to the purposive approach given below, and indeed it is sometimes considered to be the same. The integrated approach begins by looking at the exact wording of the law (in other words it starts off in a textualist way). It then examines the meanings of the words as they have been interpreted by other legal experts and judges in the past. This is called the 'context' and the integrated approach has sometimes been called a contextualist approach as well. The aim of the integrated approach is to avoid interpreting the law in a narrow and limited way so that cases can be decided sensibly and in a manner which people can understand and support. The integrated approach is integrated because it is in effect a combination of approaches, whose aim is to apply the law in a balanced and reasonable way. The advantages of the integrated approach are that it appeals to common sense and helps courts to understand complex problems. The disadvantages are that it can be time consuming and may lead to varying interpretations of the law.

The purposive approach

The purposive approach to statutory interpretation is rather similar to the mischief rule given above. It says that judges and other people who have to interpret laws should do so according to the purpose behind the law – i.e. what the law sets out to do. The advantage of the purposive approach is that it avoids judgments which are based on 'technicalities' (e.g. the narrow definitions of words taken out of context) rather than on the real rights and wrongs of the case. The disadvantage is that the judge's interpretation may end up being based on personal opinion rather than what the law says. An added disadvantage of the purposive approach is that it is hard to know exactly what the purpose of the lawmakers was, whereas the text of the law is there for all to read.

---

activity

INDIVIDUAL WORK 22.8

D2

You work for a civil liberties pressure group. Write an article for a civil liberties magazine published by your organisation, explaining, criticising and defending (as appropriate) the role of judges, magistrates and tribunal members in making legal rules and in interpreting them.

European Union legal rules

The European Union (EU) started as the European Economic Community in 1957 with the Treaty of Rome, but Britain joined later in 1973. Other treaties which turned the EU into what it is today were the Single European Act 1987, the Treaty of Maastricht 1993, the Treaty of Amsterdam 1999, and the Treaty of Nice in 2003. The EU is not a country but an association of countries, so its organisation, government and law-making methods are different from the British ones. In 2007 it had 27 members and is likely to grow still bigger in the future.

Laws in the EU are made by three main bodies:

- the European Commission, a body of unelected politicians brought together from the member states

- the European Council, made up of government ministers from the member countries

- the European Parliament, made up of MEPs (Members of the European Parliament) elected in each member country.

European Union

www.europa.eu

Legislative process

This is the process by which the EU makes laws. In the EU, the process of primary legislation (the equivalent of Acts of Parliament in Britain) was agreed, developed and is carried out through the treaties mentioned above. These treaties have defined the extent to which the European Parliament and the other parts of the EU government are able to influence the laws within member countries such as Britain. Basically, the EU is able to pass laws, which apply to member states, on most issues but not in matters of foreign policy, security, fighting crime, and justice systems. This is why laws on trade, the environment, human rights, etc. are now very similar throughout the EU, yet the foreign policies of the member countries differ significantly (e.g. in the way that Britain sent forces to support the Americans in Iraq and the French did not). The very areas in which the uniformed public services operate are the ones in which the individual countries have preserved their separate systems. Cooperation in the areas of security and crime-fighting is certainly becoming much closer as time goes on, but even so, in these areas the EU has no power to force Britain to follow its laws.

Eur-Lex – the website provides free access to European Union Law

www.eur-lex.europa.eu

EU regulations, directives and decisions

Secondary legislation (the equivalent of Statutory Instruments or Regulations in Britain) is put out by the EU in a number of forms. These are:

- binding – regulations, directives and decisions

- non-binding – resolutions, recommendations, opinions.

Each of these types of secondary legislation is different. They are outlined below.

Fig 22.13 shows the route (in simplified form) taken by a new law in the EU before it is passed and enters the statute book.

Table 22.4 Types of secondary legislation

Type of legislation	Produced by	Addressed to	Other points
Regulation	Proposed by the European Commission; Council takes decisions on the proposal; EU Parliament proposes changes. The Regulation is approved (a) if the Commission supports it or (b) if the Council and the EU Parliament together support it	Everyone in the EU	Immediately becomes law in each member state without the national parliaments needing to take any action
Directive	As with Regulations	Addressed to the governments of the member states	Must become law in each member state, or citizens can take their own government to court; in UK these are considered by UK Parliament first
Decision	Either (a) the Council or (b) the Council + Parliament or (c) the Commission	Addressed to a member state or to an individual citizen in the EU	An individual measure; the individual affected must be notified individually
Resolution	From the Council, Commission or Parliament	Member states, institutions, citizen(s) of the EU	Not compulsory
Recommendation	From the Council, Commission or Parliament	As above	Not compulsory
Opinion	From the Council, Commission or Parliament	As above	Not compulsory

Fig 22.13 The four main steps towards an EU law

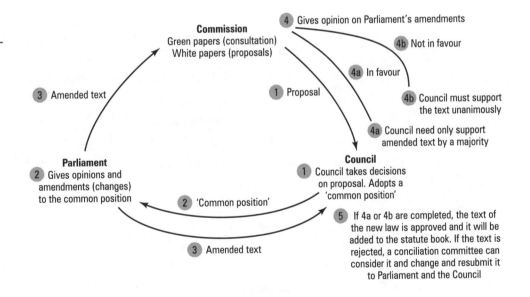

There are three main procedures, distinguishable by the different role that the EU Parliament plays:

- Assent Procedure – EU Parliament has a clear right of **veto** on new laws.

- Co-decision Procedure – EU Parliament has the power to weaken the chances of a law from being passed.

- Cooperation Procedure – EU Parliament can make amendments but the final decision rests with the Council only.

There is also Consultation Procedure, under which the EU Parliament is consulted but cannot stop the Commission and the Council between them from making a law.

Conflicts between EU and domestic legislation

EU legislation covers a wide range of subjects, and under the rules of the EU much of this legislation has to be adopted by the member countries – including Britain. Case study 22.16 shows the areas covered by EU law.

---

case study 22.16

Areas covered by EU law

01. General, financial and institutional matters
02. Customs Union and free movement of goods
03. Agriculture
04. Fisheries
05. Freedom of movement for workers and social policy
06. Right of establishment and freedom to provide services
07. Transport policy
08. Competition policy
09. Taxation
10. Economic and monetary policy and free movement of capital
11. External relations
12. Energy
13. Industrial policy and internal market
14. Regional policy and coordination of structural instruments
15. Environment, consumers and health protection
16. Science, information, education and culture
17. Law relating to undertakings
18. Common foreign and security Policy
19. Area of freedom, security and justice
20. People's Europe

(Source: www.eur-lex.europa.eu)

activity
INDIVIDUAL WORK

Can you find any major areas of law making which are not covered by this list?

Conflicts between EU and domestic legislation are based on the fact that all laws coming from Brussels (the EU seat of government) potentially undermine British sovereignty. Up to joining the EU in 1973, Britain had a completely free hand in making and interpreting its own laws. Now many new laws are made in Europe, and the British Parliament spends a lot of its time incorporating laws that originated in Europe into British law. This upsets people who feel that Britain is less free than it used to be. There is also the fear that these laws may benefit another EU country, such as France, while making Britain suffer. This is the case, for example, with decisions made about fishing quotas, which are perceived in Britain as making British fishing fleets suffer, while those of Spain, France, etc. go round removing huge amounts of fish from British waters. This may not in fact be the case, but, if people feel that it is, it becomes a political issue and an area of conflict.

To reduce such conflicts, various measures have been put into place:

- the European Scrutiny Committee –a parliamentary committee (made up of MPs) which looks carefully at all EU legislation that might affect Britain or which Britain might have to adopt
- the House of Lords Select Committee on the European Union
- the Scrutiny Reserve – the principle that ministers should not agree to new EU legislation before it can be examined by Parliament
- three European Standing Committees, which discuss new European legislative documents in detail
- Parliament itself can debate them.

The main issue often concerns **subsidiarity**. This is the idea that a law should not be made at European level if it would be better made at national or local level. People like laws dealing with local issues to be made locally or at least in their own country and not in Brussels. The House of Lords Select Committee on the European Union tries to avoid these conflicts by flagging up potential problems on subsidiarity with its 'early warning system'.

Another issue is **proportionality**. This is the idea that the law should cause no more restriction than is absolutely necessary in order to achieve its desired effect. Past EU regulations banning export of British farm products on health grounds were sometimes criticised as disproportionate, in that the risk was slight yet the law was heavy handed (and was allegedly intended to favour the farmers of other countries).

There have been conflicts on specific issues. The free movement of people about Europe under the Schengen agreements was not something the British government agreed with, and it took advantage of opt-out arrangements with the EU in 1997 to be stricter than most other EU countries about the entry of foreigners. Britain has also taken a tougher line than many other EU countries over accepting migrant workers from the new accession countries, Bulgaria and Romania, in 2007, because of fears over the way that the British public might respond.

Role of the European Court of Justice

The European Court of Justice has 25 judges and eight advocates-general. The court is not adversarial as the British ones are. The advocates-general explain the cases which the judges have to pass decisions on.

Its fundamental role is to sort out legal disagreements between member states and the EU, or between different EU institutions.

See pages 368 and 369 where the role of the European Court of Justice is described in more detail.

Progress Check

1. List the types of civil court in England and Wales.
2. List the types of criminal court in England and Wales.
3. What are the main differences between magistrates' courts and the Crown Court?
4. Explain the differences between barristers and solicitors.
5. What do legal executives and paralegals do?
6. What are the responsibilities of judges?
7. What is judicial independence and why is it important?
8. Why are lay magistrates not trained in the law?
9. What are the qualifications for jury service?
10. For what reasons can people be exempted from jury service?
11. What are the differences between case law and statute law?
12. What are the literal rule, the golden rule and the mischief rule?
13. What are the differences between primary and delegated legislation?
14. How does law making in the EU differ from law making in the British Parliament?
15. How do EU laws affect British laws?

Glossary

Abseiling
A method of going down cliffs using ropes, a harness and steel clips (also called rappelling).

Absenteeism
Avoidable absence from work.

Accelerated promotion scheme
Any scheme which allows graduates or people with clear managerial ability to be promoted faster than other employees.

Accountability
(a) Any system that makes it clear who does what and who is responsible for what in an organisation; (b) good record-keeping, showing where money comes from and how it is spent; (c) any other form of good record-keeping – e.g. in health and safety, equal opportunities; (d) taking the blame if something goes wrong.

Accountable
(a) Open to inspection, not secret; (b) responsible.

Act
A law which has been passed by Parliament.

Action plan
A document stating what has to be done, by whom, and by what date.

Action points
Skills that a team or individual should work on, to improve performance.

Administrative
To do with organisation and paperwork.

Advanced Expedition Leader
A qualification in expedition skills used by the army.

Adversarial (of courts)
Based on a contest between two opponents (prosecution and defence, or complainant and defendant); this is the English system. The system is quite different in some other countries.

Advocacy
Arguing a legal case.

Aerobic
Describes any activity which 'burns fat' using oxygen – especially jogging, fast walking, long-distance swimming and, of course, aerobics.

Aerobic capacity
The ability of the body to use oxygen (linked to endurance).

Ageism
Age discrimination.

Agencies of social control
The family, the peer group, school, the media: i.e. the people and organisations that train and mould us into social adults; this process is sometimes called 'socialisation'.

Agency
Any organisation or body that carries out actions for the government.

Agenda
A written programme telling people what a meeting is going to be about.

Aggravating features
Factors which make a crime more serious.

Aim
Something an organisation wants to do; a general intention (e.g. 'to reduce crime').

Air pressure
The 'weight' of air on a place, usually measured in millibars; low pressure often means bad weather.

Alienation
A sense of being cut off from society or other people.

Allocation (courts)
The process of deciding on the best court procedure for a given case (e.g. fast track or multi-track in a County Court).

Amending
Making small changes.

Amendment
A small change (in the law).

Anabolic
Body-building.

Anaerobic
Used of ways in which the body can create energy without using oxygen; anaerobic energy is used in weightlifting and other strength-related exercises.

Animist
Of religions which believe in a number of 'spirits'.

Antagonistic (of muscles)
Working against each other.

Appeal
A demand to try a case in a higher court on the grounds that the wrong decision has been made by a lower court.

Appellant
The person appealing against a court decision.

Appraisal
(a) Assessment of strengths, weaknesses, training needs and career aims of a team member by the team leader or a manager; (b) assessment or self-assessment.

Aptitude test
A test of how quickly a person can pick up skills (usually coordination or awareness of shapes).

Arteries
Vessels carrying blood away from the heart.

Articles
Paragraphs in a statement of human rights.

Assertiveness
The ability to deal with other people in a firm, polite, honest and direct manner.

Asylum
Safety (from war and persecution).

Asylum seekers
People fleeing from persecution in one country to find security in another.

AT
Adventurous training in the armed forces.

ATP
A chemical which muscle cells change into energy (adenosine triphosphate).

Attitude
(a) Basic beliefs or emotions; (b) behaviour resulting from these.

Audit
Inspection of paperwork, records and systems (of spending, equal opportunities, etc.).

Audit Commission
A government-funded organisation that inspects public services to see if they are giving value for money.

Audit system
A way of recording and checking money collected and spent.

Authoritarian
A style of leadership where the leader gives orders which should obeyed with little or no question.

Authority
(a) The power and the right to command or enforce obedience; (b) an organisation which has local control over a public service (e.g. a fire and rescue authority).

Backpackers
People who travel a long way carrying their belongings in a rucksack.

Back-up team
People who support or help an expedition but do not go on it.

Bail
Any arrangement to ensure that a defendant will appear in court at the arranged date.

Bar Council
The professional association for barristers.

Barrister
A lawyer specialising in criminal law and trained to plead cases in front of a jury.

Base camp
The camp in an expedition where most of the equipment and food are kept.

Battalion
A battle group of about 650 infantry soldiers.

Battle groups
A general word for divisions, regiments and other large collections of troops.

Bearings
Directions expressed in degrees using three figures.

Benchmarks
Standard information that other information can be compared with (e.g. in 'Crime has gone up by 15% since 2003', the figures for 2003 are being used as a benchmark).

Best Value
A system of target setting, to try to improve the quality of a public service.

Bias
Giving an unbalanced or one-sided view of an issue (e.g. in a newspaper).

Binding authority
A judgment (from a higher court) which must be followed in similar cases in lower courts.

Biometric
Using computerised data based on the unique measurements of each person's body, face, etc.

Bivouacking
Sleeping out in open country without a tent; aka bivvying.

Bivvy bag
A waterproof sack for sleeping out in.

Blasphemy
Insults towards a religion.

Board
A committee; a group of people who make decisions.

Body
A general word for a publicly funded or voluntary organisation.

Body Mass Index (BMI)
A measure of a person's weight in relation to their height.

Body systems
Groups of organs that work together to do a particular job in the body (e.g. respiratory system, which deals with breathing).

Brainstorm
Thinking of ideas quickly and then sorting them out afterwards.

Brainwashing
Changing people's beliefs and behaviour by constant repetition of lies, threats and propaganda.

Brief
(a) Written instructions; (b) to instruct a team on what they are going to do.

Brigade
A battle group of about 5000 soldiers.

Budget
The sum of money available to spend on a particular project.

Bureaucracy
Paperwork, official procedures.

Bureaucratic (of leadership)
Based on rules, systems, procedures, paperwork, office work, etc.

Cabinet
A powerful committee of ministers chaired by the Prime Minister.

Calorie
A measure of heat (and therefore also a measure of energy, e.g. in foods); the heat needed to warm one cubic centimetre of water by one degree centigrade.

Glossary

Camp craft
Camping skills such as pitching tents and cooking outdoors.

Cardiorespiratory
To do with heart and breathing.

Case law
The study of precedent – deciding cases by reference to other cases.

Casework
Work with individual people ('cases'), e.g. in probation, social work, immigration centres, etc.

Census
An official count of all the people living in a country.

Ceremonial
Putting on a show, but not linked to decision-making (like the role of the Queen).

Ceremonial occasions
Parades, displays and public events.

Chain of command
A rank structure (e.g. Major, Captain, Lieutenant).

Challenging
A process of disqualifying jurors because they might be unsuitable for some reason even though they have passed the vetting.

Chaplain
A Christian minister or clergyman who works with the armed forces.

Charisma
The ability to project a sense of power and leadership by force of personality, good looks, body language, etc.

Chastisement
Physical or verbal punishment (e.g. a 'rollocking').

Checks and balances
Systems designed to prevent a government from abusing its power.

Chronometer
A clock designed to be accurate in all weather conditions, used mainly at sea.

Citizen
A member of a political community or state.

Citizenship
(a) Nationality; (b) (the study of) the rights and responsibilities of citizens.

City council
The local government of a city.

Civil
Civilian (non-military).

Civil cases
Cases in civil courts.

Civil courts
Courts that deal with cases about disputes between organisations and/or individuals – on compensation, family problems, personal injury, etc. (e.g. a County Court).

Civilian
(a) Non-military – i.e. not the armed forces; (b) to do with non-uniformed staff, such as 'civilians' who work with the police but are not police officers.

Civil liberties
Human rights or basic freedoms (originally freedom from race discrimination in the USA).

Civil rights
Right to vote, equal treatment, etc.

Civil war
A war between people(s) who live in the same country.

Claustrophobic
Afraid of being shut inside enclosed spaces.

Client group
The people that an organisation serves.

Climate change
Global warming = 'greenhouse effect'.

Coalition
A group of countries acting together for a particular purpose (e.g. invading Iraq).

Code of practice
A set of official instructions on how a job must be done and the procedures that must be followed.

Cohesion
The ability and desire to work together.

Cold front
The advancing boundary of a mass of cold air, bringing rain or snow.

Collective responsibility
When all team members publicly support the majority decision even if, individually, they disagree (e.g. in the Cabinet).

Colonialism
The long-term occupying of foreign countries in the 17th–20th centuries by European countries (especially Britain).

Commission
A body which has been set a task to do by the government (usually to do with investigating facts and producing reports).

Commissioning course
Officer training.

Commitment
Persistence, determination, enthusiasm and self-belief.

Commonwealth
An international organisation of countries that were once British colonies.

Community
(a) A large collection of people who can be identified by where they live, their ethnic background, or any other shared characteristic (e.g. 'the Bangladeshi community in east London'); (b) 'the community' – society in general.

Community-based
Closely linked to ordinary people, or to a particular area (e.g. a suburb or housing estate) or to an ethnic minority group living in a particular district.

Community cohesion
A government name for schemes reducing local conflict or antisocial behaviour.

Community projects
Schemes set up to help a particular group of people in a local area.

Compensation
Money paid to a complainant by the defendant in a civil case.

Competence
Ability to do a job.

Competencies
Specific skills or abilities often listed in objectives or National Occupational Standards.

Complainant
(a) The person who complains in a civil case; (b) any person or organisation making an official complaint.

Compliance
A general word meaning either obedience or conformity – to rules, regulations, people, etc.

Components of fitness
Types of fitness (e.g. skill-related).

Conformity
Doing what other people do without having to be asked.

Consent
Agreement; 'age of consent' – the age at which a person can legally agree to have sex.

Consent form
A form giving consent (e.g. by a parent to let a child go on an expedition).

Constituency
The area represented by an MP.

Constitution
(a) A rule-book (organisations); (b) a collection of laws, rights and responsibilities (for a country).

Consultation
Asking people what they think before deciding.

Consultative (of leadership)
Asking team members' opinions before making a decision.

Contingency
A possible problem or danger in the future.

Conveyancing
To do with buying and/or selling houses, etc.

Coordination
(a) Different teams/individuals working to a complex overall plan; (b) good muscular control.

Copyright
Legal ownership of music, films, TV programmes, published photographs, the exact wording of books, etc.

Corruption
Using a position in public service to gain a dishonest personal benefit (e.g. through bribery or blackmail).

Councillor
A person elected to represent local people in local government.

Counselling
A way of helping people to solve problems by listening to them and using a variety of psychological approaches.

County council
The elected local government of a county.

Course of conduct
In the Protection from Harassment Act 1997, this refers to action, speech or behaviour.

Court martial
A military court which tries soldiers and other military personnel who have been charged with serious offences.

Crime and Disorder Reduction Partnerships
Groups set up under the Crime and Disorder Act 1998 and the Police Reform Act 2002 to tackle crime, disorder and drug misuse; CDRPs include the police, fire and rescue service, primary care trusts and other public, private and voluntary organisations. They are sometimes called Community Safety Partnerships.

Criminal cases
Cases heard in criminal courts.

Criminal courts
Courts where people accused of criminal offences are tried using evidence prepared by the police and the Crown Prosecution Service.

Criminal justice system
The police, probation and prison services, the courts, and any other organisation dealing with offenders.

Criteria
Standards of comparison.

Crown Body
A public service or government-run organisation.

Crown Court
The court where serious criminal cases are heard.

Crown Prosecution Service
The organisation of lawyers which prepares criminal cases, using evidence collected by the police.

CSP
Community Safety Partnership: a local organisation similar to a Crime and Disorder Reduction Partnership.

Culture
(a) The lifestyle and beliefs of a social or ethnic group (the meaning used in this book); (b) the arts.

Current affairs
News and political events going on at the present time.

Data protection
Keeping stored personal or confidential information private.

Debrief(ing)
The process of questioning a team after a task to find out how it went and what can be learned from the task.

Defendant
(a) The person who is complained about in a civil case; (b) the accused person in a criminal case.

Dehydration
Excessive loss of water from the body.

Delegation
The act of passing down leadership tasks to team members (e.g. 'I'll put you in charge of pitching the tents!').

Glossary

Democratic
(a) A system of government where people freely elect their representatives by secret ballot (and have various other non-violent ways of influencing the government); (b) of leadership styles where team members play an active part in decision-making.

Democratic rights
The right to vote in elections, demonstrate peacefully, contact an MP, etc.

Demographic changes
Changes in the total population or in the types of people living in an area or country.

Department
A large section of an organisation (or a group of offices) which specialises in a particular type of work.

Deportation
The compulsory, official removal of individuals from one country to another.

Deterrent
A threat (something which frightens people from committing crimes, or frightens enemies from attacking a country).

Development plan
A written plan for improving your own skills over a period of time.

Devolved
Working at a more local level (than central government).

Diabetes
An illness where the body cannot control the level of sugar in the blood.

Diet
(a)What people eat; (b) 'a diet' – eating foods of a certain type for a reason.

Diplomats
People who work in embassies and are official representatives of their own national government in another country.

Direct discrimination
Discrimination which is openly and obviously based on race or colour (e.g. 'Blacks must sit at the back of the bus').

Directive
A kind of EU law which has to be followed by member states.

Directorate
A government-run team of managers and policy-makers working in a specific area of enforcement (e.g. the Policing Policy and Operations Directorate).

Disability Rights Commission
A government body which looks after the legal rights of disabled people.

Disaffected (of young people)
Not interested in school or work; at risk of turning to crime.

Discharged
Dismissed (from the armed forces).

Disciplinary system
A procedure for dealing with discipline problems within an organisation, or independently if necessary.

Discipline
(a) A system of rules; (b) good conduct and orderly work; (c) control and/or self-control; (d) penalties or punishments for breaking rules.

Disclose
(a) Give out private or secret information; (b) the giving of evidence to the prosecution or defence while a criminal case is being prepared.

Discrimination
Unfair treatment (of minorities etc.) by people in power.

Disproportionate
Too much (or too little).

Distinguishing (a previous decision)
Not following a legal precedent.

District council
A small local government area, part of a county council.

District Judge
Paid senior magistrate.

Diverse (of society etc.)
Containing people of many different ethnic and cultural backgrounds; a mixed society.

Diversity
Differences of lifestyle, culture and ethnicity in a community.

Diversity awareness
Training given to the police and others to make them more effective in working with a diverse society.

Division
A large unit in a public service.

Drill
Marching practice.

Dynamic strength
Strength while in movement.

EC
European Community.

EEA
European Economic Area.

Effectiveness
How well an action achieves its aim.

Efficiency
Getting maximum output from minimum input.

Employment tribunal
A type of court which deals with cases involving unfair treatment at work or wrongful dismissal.

Endurance
The ability to be active for a long time without getting tired.

Energy pathways
Chemical reactions giving energy to muscles.

Equal opportunities
Laws and procedures designed to prevent discrimination in work, job advertising and recruitment.

Equity
The principle of being fair in a legal judgment.

Esprit de corps
Loyalty to the team or service; team spirit.

Established church
The 'official' church of a country (the Church of England in the UK).

Ethic
A series of moral values, such as honesty, integrity and hard work.

Ethnic cleansing
Removing people of a certain ethnic group from an area by terrorising and/or killing them.

Ethnicity
Cultural and social differences linked to national or geographical origins.

Ethos
The values and tradition of an organisation and its character, spirit and attitudes.

EU
European Union.

European Court of Human Rights
A court to which EU residents can appeal if they feel that human rights have been denied them by their own (EU member) country.

Evaluation
(a) Assessing the cost of work in relation to the benefits (or expected benefits), either while the work is going on or when it has finished; (b) judging the success or value of a piece of work.

Excluded groups
People such as ethnic minority groups, the unemployed or the disabled, who do not take part in ordinary social activities or decision-making, and miss out on the benefits of modern society.

Executive
The branch of government which puts decisions into practice (usually the ministers and their departments).

Executive agency
A government-funded body which does specialised work for the government or a public service.

Expedition
(a) A journey with a definite purpose; (b) the people going on the expedition.

Expedition Leader
A qualification in expedition skills used by the army.

Facilitation
In the context of laissez-faire leadership, a technique of making it easier for people to do their work by giving them what they need, but not telling them what to do.

Family-friendly
Suitable for parents with children, single parents, etc.; it usually refers to job-sharing, flexible working hours.

Fast-twitch fibres
The muscle cells used in anaerobic exercise.

Feasibility
Whether something is possible or not (feasible means possible).

Fibres (muscle)
Muscle cells.

First Instance (Court of)
Part of the European Court of Justice, so called because it hears cases for the first time (i.e. not on appeal).

Fiscal
To do with money, charges, tax, etc.

Flexible working contracts
Contracts that enable workers to vary their working hours.

Focus
Concentration on the task.

Focus group
A small group of ordinary people who are questioned in detail about their political views; the government can use the information to help it plan policies.

Food Standards Agency
A government-backed organisation which gives advice on healthy eating.

Force
A battle group of any size.

Formal
(a) Following strict rules of conduct, layout (of letters), speech, dress, etc.; (b) (of rules) written down.

Formative review
Carried out during an activity to shape the process.

Forum
A discussion group that involves the public and gives advice to services such as the police or local government.

Freedom of assembly and association
The democratic right to meet in large groups (e.g. for political or campaign purposes).

Freedoms
Human rights, especially freedom of speech, the right to vote, etc.

Frontline
(a) Of troops – fighting the enemy directly; (b) of civilian public services – dealing directly with the public.

Gender
Sex (i.e. being male or female) seen as a social or political issue; gender issues are about the roles of men and women, their equality (or lack of it), etc.

Gender reassignment
Sex-change.

Gender specific (fitness tests)
Easier for men to do than women.

Generalisations
Exaggerated and wrong ideas; assumptions or stereotypes (e.g. 'all Americans are rich').

Geneva Convention
An agreement drawn up by the UN, laying down rules for the treatment of prisoners of war and asylum seekers; Britain has signed.

Genocide
Actions intended to exterminate an ethnic group or race.

Globalisation
(a) The formation and activities of huge international companies; (b) closer economic, political, social and media ties with other countries all over the world; (c) the increased ease of international transport – the environmental, economic and cultural effects of these.

Glycogen
A substance formed in the body which helps supply energy to the muscles.

Glossary

Golden rule
Using common sense when judging a case.

Good character
Not having a (recent or serious) criminal record.

Good citizen
A person who obeys the law and is considerate towards others.

Green paper
A consultation document put out by the government when it is thinking about making a new law.

Gridlines
The blue horizontal and vertical lines on an OS map.

Grievance
A complaint from inside an organisation (e.g. of unfair treatment by a manager).

Grievance procedure
A system for dealing with complaints by employees.

Gross Domestic Product (GDP)
A measure of how wealthy a country is, based on the value of everything the country produces in a given year.

Guy ropes
Ropes supporting a tent so it won't blow down.

Handrail
A feature such as a path or stream which you can follow without having to look at map or compass.

Harassing
Systematically hurting, insulting, offending or bullying another person or group of people.

Health and Safety Executive
The official organisation of health and safety inspectors.

Health-related fitness
Fitness linked with muscle strength, stamina and flexibility.

Heart rate
The number of times the heart beats in a minute.

Hepatitis
A liver disease.

Hidden curriculum
The norms or values put across in teaching – other than the subject officially being taught. (For example a woodwork lesson is also a lesson in following instructions, so what is being taught in the hidden curriculum is obedience.)

Hierarchy
(a) A rank order, order of importance or influence (e.g. a court hierarchy, where higher courts try bigger cases and can overrule lower courts); (b) any system or structure where there is a structure of ranks or a chain of command.

Holocaust (the)
Extermination of six million Jews during the Second World War.

Home Office rules
Rules and conditions laid down by the Home Office (about the reasons and lengths of time foreign nationals are allowed to stay in Britain).

Horizontal management
A system with fewer different ranks and more operatives; it is said to save money because there are more 'workers' and fewer 'managers'.

Hormones
Chemicals in the blood that affect growth and behaviour.

Humanely
Kindly; without cruelty.

Humanist
A person who believes in humanism (the belief that people understand what they are doing and can be trusted) and/or puts the ideas of humanism into practice.

Humanitarian
To do with relieving suffering and hardship.

Human rights
Aspects of freedom and justice to which everybody is entitled, as listed in the articles of the United Nations Universal Declaration of Human Rights or in the Human Rights Act 1998.

Hyperthermia
Heatstroke; getting too hot during exercise.

Hypothermia
Getting too cold.

Hypothesis
A testable statement that is based on theory.

Ideology
A system of (extreme) political beliefs.

Imam
The leader of a mosque and a spiritual adviser in Islam.

Immigrants
People who arrive in a country with the intention of staying permanently.

Immigrant status
The right to remain in a country while keeping another nationality.

Immunity (judges)
Protection from criticism or disciplinary action after making a wrong (or unpopular) decision in a case; judges are hard to sack.

Impartiality
Being fair minded; not biased one way or the other.

Implementing
Putting into practice (of a law etc.).

In the public interest
What is best for society in the long run.

Inclusive
Allowing people from all backgrounds to participate; non-discriminatory.

Increment
A small yearly increase in pay which comes automatically.

Independence (judges)
They cannot be influenced by government, the police, big business, etc.

Indictable (offence)
Serious and tried in the Crown Court.

Indirect discrimination
Any official action which unfairly treats specific groups without targeting them by name (e.g. some dress codes, or fitness tests which are more difficult for women than for men).

Industrial action
Strikes, go-slows, working to rule, refusal to do certain duties, picketing and marching – usually to protest about pay, conditions of service, or some unpopular management decision.

Industrial Revolution
The period in British history (1750–1850 approx) when large factories and industrial towns were built.

Infantry
Soldiers who traditionally travel and fight on foot.

Inflation
Price rises; increasing costs.

Informal (of rules)
Rules which are not official or written down.

Infrastructure
(a) Roads, water, electricity, communication facilities, etc.; (b) for tourists, – hotels, travel companies, camp sites.

In-service training
Training while working; short courses for which a person is given time off work.

Insolvency
Having no money.

Inspectorate
An official body of inspectors.

Institution
(a) A prison or secure hospital; (b) any large establishment, such as a school or college; (c) official or socially accepted practices, customs or systems.

Institutionalised racism
The tendency for organisations, such as public services, to be racist even when they are not aware of it: the expression was famously used in the Macpherson Report (1999) into the poor police response to the murder of the black teenager Stephen Lawrence in 1993.

Insubordination (in the army)
Refusal to obey orders; defiance.

Insurgents
Rebel fighters (especially in Iraq or Afghanistan).

Integrate
To unify society by encouraging people from ethnic minorities to become part of mainstream British society.

Integrated Personal Development System (IPDS)
A new system of training and staff development in the fire and rescue service, which is more flexible and more suited to individual needs than the old training system.

Integrity (e.g. of a police officer)
Honesty: someone with integrity cannot be bribed or corrupted.

Intellectual property
Copyright or patent.

Intelligence
Military or police knowledge (e.g. about enemy plans, or about crime and criminals).

Intensity
The amount of strength used in an exercise.

Internal (of complaints procedures etc.)
Carried out within the organisation which is being complained about – not independent.

Internment camp
A large centre where refugees or prisoners of war are kept and which they cannot leave.

Interpreted (of laws)
Understood and then applied in real life by the courts.

Interpretive features
Aspects of surroundings or weather which give clues about direction (e.g. the lie of the grass, or the position of the sun).

Intimate search
Searching a person's body orifices – e.g. for weapons/drugs.

IRA
Irish Republican Army (Irish nationalist terror organisation which used to operate in Northern Ireland and, occasionally, on the British mainland).

Islamist
Following an ideology which claims to come from Islam; used of Al-Qaida etc.

Islamophobia
Fear or hatred of Muslims.

Job description
A written outline of what a particular job involves.

Job-related fitness
Ability at physical skills which are needed in a particular job.

Joined-up government
The idea that public services and other organisations should all work closely together so that there are no gaps in services, provision or protection.

Joint service
Includes army, Royal Navy and RAF.

Judge
A highly qualified person in charge of trials at the Crown Court, and other higher courts.

Judiciary
Judges and courts.

Jurisdiction
Legal responsibility.

Jury
Twelve people chosen to hear a case in the Crown Court and to make a decision on whether the defendant is guilty.

Laissez-faire (leadership)
Letting people do what they want.

Lawful discrimination
Discrimination which is allowed by law (e.g. choosing a white actress to play the part of the Queen).

Law Lords
Senior judges attached to the House of Lords (may be obsolete after 2008).

Law Society
The professional association for solicitors.

Glossary

Lay (personnel, law)
People who work in the courts but do not have legal training (e.g. a law degree).

Learning style
The way in which a particular person prefers to learn a new skill or subject (e.g. some people like to learn by solving problems; others by listening to the teacher).

Left-wing
Politically leaning towards socialism or ('extreme left wing') communism.

Legal Adviser (magistrates' court)
The person who advises magistrates on points of law (used to be called 'the Clerk of the Court').

Legal executives
Legal support workers qualified by the Institute of Legal Executives (ILEX).

Legally accountable
Can be taken to court (prosecuted).

Legal Services Board
A regulator of the legal professions, likely to be set up in 2007.

Legal Services Ombudsman
An office dealing independently with complaints against solicitors and law firms.

Legislative
Law-making.

Legislature
The branch of government that makes laws, i.e. Parliament.

Liaison
Communication and working together between teams.

Lifestyle
The way we live, the things we eat and drink, the exercise we get, and any things we do which might harm our health.

Ligaments
Tough bands made of protein; these tie joints and other parts of the body together.

Line manager
A person's immediate boss or superior officer.

Literal
Following the exact, dictionary meaning of words.

Litigation
Taking people to court.

Live exercises (military and disaster planning)
Simulations using the people and equipment that would be used in real life.

Local policing plan
A plan produced by a Police Authority for policing the local area for the coming year; it sets performance targets that the police have to try to meet.

Logistics
Transport and supply.

Lord Chief Justice
The top judge, who is allowed to sack judges if extremely serious complaints have been made about their work.

Magistrate
A person usually without legal training who hears cases at a magistrates' court.

Magistrates' court
A local criminal court trying relatively minor cases, where the sentence cannot be more than 6 months in prison or a £5000 fine.

Mainstream
A word loosely meaning 'typical', 'average' or 'majority'.

Management
Motivating, controlling, directing and organising people.

Managerial
To do with organising, controlling, motivating and directing employees.

Mandatory
Compulsory.

Manslaughter
Deliberate killing, but in circumstances which make it slightly less serious than murder.

Manual handling
Lifting or moving heavy weights by hand (or without machines).

Marginal constituency
A constituency where the sitting MP has a very small majority and which could easily be lost at the next election.

Marrow
A soft substance in the central parts of some bones.

Maternity, paternity, parental leave
Legally allowed time off work for mothers, fathers, parents.

Media (the)
Any or all of the following: radio, TV, films, music, newspapers, advertising, the Internet, books, magazines.

Mentoring
The giving of individual advice and training, on a fairly frequent basis, by an experienced worker to a new recruit; this is a planned part of probationer training in the police and some other services.

Metabolise
Change one chemical in the body into another.

Metabolism
The chemical changes related to the different functions of the body.

Methodologies
Systems, methods.

Metropolitan council
The local government of a large town.

Migrant
A person who leaves one country and goes to live in another for an indefinite period of time, but without taking new citizenship.

Migration
Movement of people from one country to another (e.g. from eastern Europe to Britain).

Milestone
A short-term target, against which an organisation can check if it is likely to meet its main target.

Military offences
Actions such as desertion and insubordination, which are illegal in the armed forces but do not exist in civilian law.

Militia
Unofficial or part-time soldiers, usually acting for an undemocratic government or warlord and often carrying out human rights abuses.

Minister
(a) (government) The head of a government department (ministry) such as the Ministry of Defence; (b) official title of the second-in-command in a government department.

Ministry of Justice
The government department in charge of the court system, prison and probation services; it replaced the Department for Constitutional Affairs in 2007.

Minorities
Ethnic minority groups, lesbian and gay people, the disabled, the old, the young, and any other group that might be discriminated against.

Minutes
A written report of a meeting sent to those present, usually a day or two later.

Miscarriage of justice
A situation where a court has made a wrong decision.

Mischief rule (law)
Making a decision which will tackle the problem that caused a case in the first place (i.e. following the spirit of the law and not just the letter).

Mitigating features
Factors which make a crime less serious.

Mitochondria
Microscopic strings in muscle cells which generate energy.

Monetary
To do with money and the value of money.

Money laundering
Investing money from crime so that it looks legal and respectable.

Monitor
Carry out regular or frequent checks on how well an operation, system, project, task, etc. is going.

Moral
(a) Based on accepted ideas of good and evil; (b) to do with the study and theory of right or wrong actions.

Moral courage
Knowing what is right and not being afraid to do it.

Morale
Confidence and determination.

Motivation
(a) The desire to do something; (b) influencing other people so that they want to do something; (c) generally, building enthusiasm and determination.

MP
Member of Parliament.

Mucus
A protective slime produced in the nose and elsewhere in the body.

Multi-agencies
Partnerships; teams from different organisations or services working together.

Multicultural
To do with diversity and with people from different ethnic and cultural backgrounds living together in harmony, while keeping some of their differences.

Multi-level entry
The idea that a person can enter a uniformed public service at a rank which suits their abilities, rather than having to 'start at the bottom and work up'.

Mutiny
A rebellion by people in the armed forces against their commanders.

National Crime Recording Standard
A system for recording crime which all police forces have to follow, so that figures are reliable and can be compared across the country.

Nationalisation
The taking over of private companies or services by the government.

National Occupational Standards
Objectives stating the essential elements of public service jobs (defined by an organisation called Skills for Justice).

NATO
North Atlantic Treaty Organisation.

Naturalisation
Obtaining citizenship by applying for it.

Navigation
Finding your way (usually using map and compass).

Negotiating
Reaching agreement by discussion, bargaining, persuasion, give and take, etc.

NHS
National Health Service.

Non-departmental public body
A body that advises the government or a public service (but the advice does not have to be taken).

Norms
The shared behaviour, customs, lifestyle, language, etc. of a society or social group.

Notification forms
Forms such as consent forms, doctor's name and phone number; contact addresses for family or next of kin.

Nutritionists
Food experts.

Oath of allegiance
The swearing of loyalty (to the Queen).

Obesity
Being very overweight (defined by the World Health Organization as having a body mass index of 30 or above).

Obiter
'By the way' – a form of persuasive authority.

Objective
(a) (training) A clear statement of a learning outcome (e.g. 'Deal safely and effectively with vehicles which fail to stop' – an objective used in the training of traffic police); an objective describes what must be done and how it must be done, making clear what the context and limitations are; (b) (in a general sense) a limited aim or target; (c) without bias, prejudice or personal opinions.

Ombudsman
An independent person (or office) dealing with complaints about some public services (e.g. the Prisons Ombudsman).

Operative
(a) A name sometimes given to the 'lower' ranks of a uniformed service; (b) a person who carries out manual tasks (works with their hands).

Opinion poll
A questionnaire given to a sample of, say, 1000 people to find out what they think about political and other issues; the findings are then processed to give a picture of what the country as a whole might think on those issues.

Organic compounds
Chemicals which contain carbon (among other things) and combine different elements.

Orientation of map
Setting (turning) the map so that it points north.

OS
Ordnance Survey.

OSCE
Organisation for Security and Cooperation in Europe (against terrorism, illegal immigration and cross-border crime).

Pace
(a) A general word for speed of walking; (b) the action of measuring distances by using steps of 1 yard or 1 metre, or of counting steps while running (as in orienteering).

PACE
Police and Criminal Evidence Act.

Pacifists
People who believe it is always wrong to kill people or go to war.

Panel
A team of experts that gives advice and makes decisions.

Paper-based
Worked out on paper using plans, diagrams, flow charts, lists, written scenarios, etc.

Paralegals
People who work in law offices (or in the legal departments of other companies) but are not solicitors or legal executives.

Paramilitary
Army style (used of groups like the IRA or UDF – Ulster Defence Force).

Parish council
The local government of a small area (e.g. a village).

Parliament
The House of Commons and the House of Lords.

Participant (experiment)
The person (formerly called 'subject') who is being experimented upon and observed by the experimenter; a participant may be a volunteer who is paid a small fee.

Participative leadership
A style of leadership where all team members can take part in leadership decisions.

Partner
A team or organisation which works with another team, group of teams or organisation.

Partnership
A grouping of teams or individuals from different organisations.

Party
(a) A political grouping with members who share roughly the same political ideas (e.g. Labour, Conservative); (b) in civil law – one side in a civil case.

Patents
Certificates of legal ownership of inventions.

Pathfinder
A government scheme to improve living and social conditions in poor neighbourhoods.

Peacekeeping
Maintaining law and order and rebuilding or redeveloping an area or country which has recently been at war.

Peer assessment
Assessment by equals (e.g. colleagues, classmates).

Peer group
The people we see as equals, such as friends, work colleagues, class-mates and team-mates.

People-oriented
The well-being of people (e.g. team members) is what matters most.

Performance indicators
A system for measuring how well a public service does its work.

Personal development plan
A plan, with targets and a timescale, for developing your own skills and abilities in a particular activity (e.g. expeditions).

Personal injury
Physical or mental injury or harm.

Personality
A general word for the way a person behaves and relates to other people.

Personnel
Employees.

Persuasive authorities (case law)
Precedents (previous judgments) which should be followed in similar cases (but it is not compulsory).

Physical competence
Strength and fitness.

Physiological
To do with the body and its needs.

Picket
A demonstration at the gate of a factory, military base, etc.

Plaid Cymru
A Welsh political party, in favour of greater independence for Wales.

Pledge
A serious promise (to be a good citizen).

Policies
(a) Rules; (b) approaches or attitudes towards an issue.

Policy
A planned course of action by a government.

Politically correct (journalists' slang)
Used of words or ideas which are designed not to offend minorities.

Post-traumatic stress disorder (PTSD)
Mental illness caused by experiencing shocking or terrifying events.

Potholes
Vertical caves which need a rope ladder to get down.

Power gap
The difference in power and influence between leader and followers; the power gap is greatest in authoritarian leadership.

Practice statements
Legal advice from a higher court (similar to a code of practice).

Precedent
(a) What has gone before; (b) a legal term, meaning that past cases are used as a guide for judging present cases.

Prejudice
Judging people or ideas before you know anything about them.

Pressure group
An organisation which protests against a specific aspect of government policy.

Prestige
A good reputation.

Primary care
The health care which is given first, by paramedics or GPs (before specialist doctors are brought in).

Private sector
Any business, enterprise, etc. which is run by an individual or company and aims to make a profit.

Privatisation
The selling by the government of public companies, services or utilities (e.g. water, electricity) to private buyers, or getting private companies to do the work of public services.

Probate
The legal process of checking wills.

Probationary period
Probationary periods vary from one service to the next (in the police, it's a recruit's first two years); a 'settling-in' period – it is easier to be dismissed during probation than afterwards.

Procedure
A systematic and regular way of carrying out a job, inspection, process, evaluation, etc.

Proceedings
Actions by lawyers (e.g. suing, or taking someone to court).

Productivity
A measure of the amount and quality of work done, in relation to the time, money and effort put into it.

Professional standards
The expected (high) quality of work; also, honesty and a sense of responsibility.

Proficiency
A qualification in expedition skills used by the army.

Programme (training)
A written plan or timetable outlining how and when you are going to train, and what you hope to achieve.

Progression
Improvement in strength or fitness (as a result of training).

Project
A new scheme or task (usually attempting something that has not been done before).

Proportionality
The idea that the scope of a law should match the scale of the problem (e.g. small problem, small law).

Provisional IRA
Part of the IRA with a Marxist (very left-wing) ideology.

Provisions
The instructions contained (provided) in a law.

Psychological addiction
Needing a drug because it is intensely enjoyable. (When addiction is physiological, the drug is needed because the body has become physically dependent upon it.)

Psychologist
A person who studies how the mind works, usually by carrying out disciplined and organised studies of human behaviour (e.g. through experiments, surveys, etc.).

Psychosomatic
Used to describe illness where the physical symptoms are caused by mental problems (e.g. if asthma is caused by stress).

Public authority
A body such as the police, or a court, which has to obey the Human Rights Act.

Push and pull factors
The problems that make people leave a country (e.g. poor standard of living, lack of work, political persecution) and the potential benefits that attract people to a country (e.g. high standard of living, plenty of work, respect for human rights, etc.).

Quality
An aspect of character or personality (e.g. patience).

Race
Classification of people based on inherited physical characteristics (appearance).

Racism
Hatred or discrimination against people from other ethnic groups.

Radical
Looking for major political change.

Radicalisation
The process of turning people, through teaching and propaganda, into activists or 'extremists'.

Rank
Levels of power, status, pay or seniority in an organisation; each rank usually has a name (e.g. 'sergeant', 'watch manager') and has the authority to give instructions or commands to lower ranks.

Rank and file
Ordinary workers.

Ratio decidendi
The underlying reason behind a binding authority.

Recession
A period of low industrial activity.

Glossary

Redundancy
When a worker loses a job because of a lack of work for them to do (e.g. Father Christmas becomes redundant in January).

Referent Nutrient Index (RNI)
Government-recommended daily allowance (need) of a vitamin or mineral (RNIs are not used for carbohydrates, fats or proteins).

Refugee
A person fleeing war or persecution.

Regiment
A battle group of about 650 soldiers.

Region
A large section of England (e.g. the East Midlands, the South West), consisting of several counties and having its own regional government office.

Register (speech)
Way or manner of speaking.

Regulations
Laws (usually covering carefully defined aspects of work or employment).

Regulator
An independent body which ensures that services to the public are provided honestly and at a professional standard.

Renegotiating
Changing a target etc. by bargaining and agreement, because the target cannot be met.

Representative
A person who communicates (represents) the views of one group of people to another group of people (e.g. MPs are representatives of their constituents in Parliament).

Reps
Repetitions.

Rescheduling
Changing a deadline (e.g. for a target); the target can be met but more time is needed.

Reservists
Volunteer or part time troops.

Residency
Living (in a country).

Resilience
Government systems for dealing with major emergencies and minimising casualties (comes from a general meaning of the word, i.e. flexibility and toughness).

Resources
Money, people, equipment – any or all of these.

Respondent
The party opposing an appeal.

Retainer
Money paid to a part-time firefighter ('retained firefighter').

Retention
Keeping workers in an organisation (encouraging them not to leave).

Retribution
Punishment.

Review
A regular check, usually carried out in meetings, to see how well an organisation is performing against its targets.

Right-wing
Politically leaning towards conservatism or (the 'extreme right wing') fascism/Nazism.

Risk-assessed
Checked out systematically for possible dangers.

Role
Job and the work done.

Role model
A person who sets a good example; someone people want to be like.

Role structure
A new (non-military) name for a rank structure.

Roster
A list of duties.

Route card
A piece of paper giving clear details of the way you intend to follow on a mountain walk.

Rules
Instructions which people are expected to follow but which may not have legal backing (e.g. basketball rules).

Rules of engagement
The rules the armed forces have to follow when they are fighting (e.g. when they are allowed to shoot; whether they are allowed to attack or must simply defend, etc.). Rules of engagement are usually secret and change with each war, conflict or peacekeeping operation.

Safari
Travel (in Africa).

Safe seat
A constituency where voters always (or almost always) vote for the same party.

Sanctions
Punishments, deterrents, withholding of privileges.

Scrutinising (of new laws)
Examining closely, line by line.

Secondary legislation
(a) Minor laws, which are not debated beforehand in Parliament, such as Regulations (Statutory Instruments); (b) EU Laws, such as Regulations, Directives and Decisions, which are not included in the main EU treaties.

Secretariat
A group of people overseeing a planning organisation.

Secretary (capital S)
The head of a government department – a top government minister (e.g. Home Secretary).

Sectarian
To do with conflict between communities with different religious beliefs.

Sectarianism
The splitting of a community into violently opposed groups, often on religious lines.

Section
A small unit in a public service.

Self-appraisal
Systematically and honestly examining your own success and/or failure at a task.

Self-discipline
(a) Self-control; (b) the ability to resist temptation; (c) the ability to work hard without being distracted.

Self-esteem
The way we see ourselves; our opinion of ourselves.

Sensitive
Secret (of information).

Sensitivity (teamwork)
The ability to know and understand what other people are thinking without having to be told – and then to react in a sympathetic or caring manner.

Separation of powers
A principle of democratic government, which states that the legislature (which makes laws) should be separate from the executive (which puts laws into practice) and the judiciary (which administers and interprets laws).

Sextant
An instrument for measuring the angle of stars above the horizon.

Sexual orientation
Refers to whether a person is gay, lesbian or straight.

Sharia law
A system of justice derived from the teachings of the Qur'an.

Shia Muslims
Muslims who believe that the leadership of Islam should have passed to a direct descendent of the Prophet Mohammed.

Simulations
Realistic and large-scale role-plays (e.g. of emergency service responses to a disaster) used in training and planning for real-life situations.

Single pitch
A short rock-climb which can be done without a belay (tying onto a rock for security).

Sinn Fein
A Northern Ireland political party with strong Catholic support.

Skill
An ability which can be learned and practised.

Skill-related fitness
Fitness involving coordination and control of muscles.

Sleeping mat
Aka carry mat: foam oblong to put under a sleeping bag, to insulate the sleeper from the coldness of the ground.

Slow-twitch fibres
The muscle cells used in aerobic exercise.

Small Claims Court
A system for dealing with small civil cases quickly and cheaply in a County Court.

Social class
The idea that people in different occupations, or with different standards of living and educational background, are different from each other in their lifestyle and beliefs.

Social grooming
Chatting, joking, etc. for shared enjoyment; it gives a feeling of friendship and 'belonging' to the group.

Social justice
Giving everybody fair and decent treatment.

Society
People in general; the public.

Socioeconomic
Related to social class and level of wealth.

Solicitor
A lawyer who represents people in both civil and criminal cases, who gives legal advice, and deals with many civil matters; solicitors prepare cases for the police in the Crown Prosecution Service but do not plead before juries.

Solicitors Regulation Authority
A regulatory body that checks that solicitors do their job honestly and properly.

Speaker
The person who controls debates in the House of Commons.

Specialisation
Concentrating on a particular type of work.

Sponsors
People paying for a project such as an expedition.

Staff development
Work training on the job; going on courses to learn new work skills.

Stakeholder
Someone who is actively involved in the success of a project (e.g. sponsors, organisers, local government, local people).

Stare decisis
The Latin name given to a judgment whose guiding principle (basic idea) has to be followed in other similar cases; a 'binding authority'.

Statistics
Figures about organisations or large groups of people which have been processed to show an underlying truth that could not have been found out by any other way.

Status
Rank; a measure of authority – higher ranks have higher status.

Statutory
Set up by law; official.

Statutory Instrument (SI)
A law (Regulation) which does not have to be debated in Parliament; it lays down strict instructions for a specific task or process (e.g. reporting industrial accidents).

Statutory rules
Laws, Regulations or rules which are written down and passed by Parliament or the government (e.g. Acts, Statutory Instruments and official codes of practice).

Stereotyping
Taking an oversimplified or false view (e.g. of what other people are like).

Stimulus
Any action which provokes (stimulates) a reaction or response.

Strategic
Long-term.

Strategy
Long-term plan.

Strike camp
Take the tent(s) down.

Stroke
The effect of a blood clot in the brain; it can lead to death or paralysis.

Structured
Organised, with roles, plans, etc.

Stuff-bag
A bag that goes round a rolled-up sleeping bag.

Style of leadership
Authoritarian, laissez-faire, transformational, etc. (ways of classifying different types of team leadership).

Subordinates
People of lower rank; assistants; people who are expected to obey orders or follow instructions.

Subsidiarity
The idea that laws in the EU should be passed at the most local possible level (e.g. the EU shouldn't pass a law if the same objective could be achieved by individual countries passing the same law).

Summary justice
The punishments carried out by commanding offices in the armed forces for minor offences; in these cases there is no court hearing.

Summative review
Carried out after a project is finished.

Summit meetings
Meetings of heads of state (prime ministers and/or presidents).

Sunni Muslims
Muslims who accept that leadership of Islam passed to Abu Bakr on the Prophet's death.

Supervisory officer
The name sometimes given to a line manager (e.g. in the police).

Supreme Court
A new court which in 2008 will, probably, become 'the highest court in the land', replacing the House of Lords in this role.

Surgeries
Offices where constituents can talk individually to their MP.

Survival bag
A person-sized plastic bag designed for sleeping in (with a sleeping bag) if you get caught out at night on a mountain.

Sustainable
Can keep going successfully, once it is started (of development, forests, communities, etc.).

Symbols
The tiny signs on a map which represent what is really there (e.g. tiny black rectangles are symbols for buildings).

Table-top exercises
Group planning exercises based on a scenario and using simulation but not using all the equipment etc. of a 'live' exercise.

Target
A figure for improved performance in a public service which should be achieved by a certain date (e.g. 'to cut gun crime by 5% by 2008').

Target setting
Fixing the level of success required for key tasks in the coming year (e.g. if 70% of crimes have been solved this year, the target might be 75% for next year).

Tariff
A sentence, seen in relation to the seriousness of the crime.

Task-centred
What matters is the job being done.

Task-oriented
Doing the job is the thing that matters most.

Team
A group of people organised to work together.

Team-centred
What matters is the formation and development of the team, and the well-being of its members.

Team roles
Typical behaviour patterns of individuals in teams.

Team spirit
Enthusiasm and team loyalty (also called 'esprit de corps').

Terms of reference
Duties.

Terrain
Land, land surface or land areas (e.g. rocky terrain).

Terrorism
Violent acts designed to frighten and shock civilians, and to grab media attention.

Tone (of muscle)
The 'quality' or 'fitness' of muscle.

Tort
Civil 'wrong' (negligence or wrong action) which requires compensation.

Toxicity
How poisonous something is.

Trade union
A workers' organisation set up to protect the rights, pay and working conditions of its members (e.g. the Fire Brigades' Union). Many public services (e.g. the police) are not allowed to have trade unions or to go on strike.

Traditions
Customs and lifestyle that have existed for a long time in a society.

Training
Developing fitness through planned exercise and sport.

Trangia
A kind of portable cooking stove which burns methylated spirits (meths).

Transactional (of leadership)
Based on rewards and punishments, or on the promise of them.

Trans fat
A kind of fat found in margarine and fried food which is said to be bad for health.

Transformational (of leadership)
Changing the way people look at themselves, the world, or a task they have to do.

Traumatic
Shocking and upsetting.

Treasurer
The person in a team or organisation who looks after the money.

Trekking
Long-distance walking.

Tribunals
Special civil courts dealing with major cases of injustice and discrimination (usually appeals).

Troubles (the)
Violence and political unrest in Northern Ireland between around 1970 and the 1990s.

Trust
An organisation which funds health (or other) care.

Tsunami
Giant tidal wave caused by an earthquake under the sea.

Under-secretary
Third level of command in a government department.

Values
The shared beliefs of a society, service or a social group.

Veins
Vessels carrying blood to the heart.

Verifiable
Able to be checked.

Veto
To prevent something being done by saying 'No'.

Vetting
(a) Checking if someone might be a security risk; (b) checking jurors for criminal convictions or other factors that might make them ineligible.

Victimisation
Tormenting or abusing someone on a regular basis.

Vigil
A small peaceful, often silent, protest demonstration that lasts a long time.

Violations
Breaking of treaties, ceasefires or of international agreements, human rights abuses, etc.

Visa
Official permission to stay in a country for a fixed period of time, obeying certain conditions; it is usually stamped in a passport.

Vocational
To do with work or careers.

Volatile (of areas)
Unstable, liable to violence.

Voluntary code
An agreement by an industry to control itself.

VOSA
Vehicle Operators and Services Agency (traffic inspectors).

Voscur
A council for voluntary service based in Bristol.

Warm front
The boundary between warm and cool air, with the warm air advancing (light rain).

Water-borne infections
Illnesses such as dysentery and cholera, caused by drinking unclean water.

Wealth
Money and property.

Whistleblowing
Telling the media or someone influential outside an organisation that an organisation is doing something illegal or morally wrong.

White paper
A proposal for a new law giving clear and definite information.

Wild camping
Camping without the landowner's permission.

Windbreak
Something which can protect a tent (or stove) from the wind (e.g. a wall).

Withdrawal
Getting out of a drug habit.

Women's rights
The right to vote, the right to equal pay, the right not to be discriminated against because of being a woman, married, being pregnant, having children, etc.

Work–life balance
Working in a way which leaves you enough leisure time or time with friends and family.

Youth Court
A court linked to a magistrates' court which hears cases where defendants are young people aged 10–17.

Index